Shaping Students of Color
from Preschool to Graduate School

Shaping Students of Color from Preschool to Graduate School

The Impact of Families on Education

NATHAN DURDELLA

Published by State University of New York Press, Albany

© 2025 State University of New York

All rights reserved

Printed in the United States of America

No part of this book may be used or reproduced in any manner whatsoever without written permission. No part of this book may be stored in a retrieval system or transmitted in any form or by any means including electronic, electrostatic, magnetic tape, mechanical, photocopying, recording, or otherwise without the prior permission in writing of the publisher.

Links to third-party websites are provided as a convenience and for informational purposes only. They do not constitute an endorsement or an approval of any of the products, services, or opinions of the organization, companies, or individuals. SUNY Press bears no responsibility for the accuracy, legality, or content of a URL, the external website, or for that of subsequent websites.

EU GPSR Authorised Representative:
Logos Europe, 9 rue Nicolas Poussin, 17000, La Rochelle, France
contact@logoseurope.eu

For information, contact State University of New York Press, Albany, NY
www.sunypress.edu

Library of Congress Cataloging-in-Publication Data

Name: Durdella, Nathan, author.
Title: Shaping students of color from preschool to graduate school : the impact of families on education / Nathan Durdella.
Description: Albany : State University of New York Press, [2025] | Includes bibliographical references and index
Identifiers: LCCN 2025003551 | ISBN 9798855803693 (hardcover : alk. paper) | ISBN 9798855803716 (ebook) | ISBN 9798855803709 (pbk. : alk. paper)
Subjects: LCSH: Children of minorities—Education. | Minority families. | Education—Parent participation.
Classification: LCC LC3715 .D87 2025 | DDC 370.117/5—dc23/eng/20250523
LC record available at https://lccn.loc.gov/2025003551

To Mireille and Paul,
Thank you for your profound love and selfless sacrifices as parents.

Parents can only give good advice or put them on the right paths, but the final forming of a person's character lies in their own hands.

—Anne Frank

Contents

List of Tables — ix

Acknowledgments — xi

Preface — xiii

Introduction — 1

Chapter 1 Parenting Roles, Early Experiences in Families, and Resistance to Gender Norms for Children — 35

Chapter 2 Parental Relationship Quality: Physical and Relational Distance but Emotional Closeness from a Young Age to Adulthood for Children — 75

Chapter 3 Parental Values Extend Far for Children: The Importance of Education, Hard Work, Family Unity, Empathy, and Spirituality — 97

Chapter 4 Honoring Sacrifices that Parents Make to Get Children to College and Beyond: Education, Immigration, and Racial Discrimination — 153

Chapter 5 Familial Contexts and Parenting Shape Self-Reliance, Independence, and Resilience as Students: From Elementary to Postsecondary Education — 181

Chapter 6	Educational Connections in Precollege and College Years: Effects of Parents on College Choice, Transitions to College, and Experiences in College	211
Chapter 7	Parenting Relationships While in Graduate School: Changing Roles, Conflicting Demands, and Remaining Connected Later in Life	255
Chapter 8	Where Parents, Families, and More Fit into Academic Life and Student Outcomes	285
References		321
Index		337

Tables

Table I.1	Participants by Name (Pseudonym), Identities, and Graduate/Undergraduate Degree Programs/Affiliations	26
Table I.2	Sex of Participants	33
Table I.3	Racial/Ethnic Identity of Participants	33
Table I.4	Sexual Orientation of Participants	33
Table I.5	Generational College Student Status of Participants	34
Table I.6	Graduate Degree Program Type of Participants	34

Acknowledgments

I would like to thank the love of my life, Caroline, whose unconditional support, critical insight, and wise vision always enhance my work. Caroline's unbounded intellect and profound beauty shape who I am. Caroline's close and careful review of drafts of this work transformed it. I am very grateful for the immense intelligence and creative brightness of my stepdaughter, Madeleine, and daughter, Emmie—who uniquely shape my life. Madeleine's and Emmie's talent, beauty, and hearts of gold inspire me every day to be the best person and parent I can be. Your lights shine brightly, and you are special beyond what words can describe. I hope that I've given you good advice as you set out on your journeys in life. I share my deepest gratitude to my parents, Diane and Allan, who inspired me to pursue my interests from a very young age and taught me the values of compassion, empathy, and hard work. Diane and Allan put me in the right path in life, and my work reflects how they started me on a course to do good.

I'm indebted to Angela Carpenter, who worked closely with me on this project, serving to search for and annotate sources, process interview data, draft tables, and discuss ideas about the direction of the project. Angela's dedication, care, and work ethic helped the book evolve into what you see here. Tracy Buenavista and Miguel Ceja offered critically constructive feedback and generously shared their expertise, respectively, in this work—and I'm deeply grateful. I owe Tracy a special note of gratitude for offering feedback early in the proposal process; Tracy's suggestions influenced the book's title. Miguel not only shared feedback early in the manuscript development process but also reviewed the full manuscript, demonstrating his selfless support of colleagues and talent to resolve issues that arise in the course of a research project. Pamela Eddy, Don Haviland, and Kyle McJunkin all reviewed and offered critically constructive feedback on the work—their respective comments reflect a deep sense of commitment to the highest standards of research and scholarship and improved what appears in this book today. My deepest gratitude goes to Pam, Don, and Kyle for their time and resources to support this work. John Bond got me to a publisher by helping me to think more critically about my project and focusing the story that I was trying to tell. I express my deepest gratitude to John for his expertise and patience as the work evolved. Leah Fargotstein has been central to my success as an author, and I owe Leah all of my gratitude for her wisdom and kindness. Leah helped me find my way on all of my book projects, including this one.

I am incredibly grateful and thank the staff at SUNY Press with whom I worked on this project. Specifically, the unique and insightful contributions of Richard Carlin to this work have made it what it is today. From the time Richard and I met to the final steps of publication, Richard's keen insight, caring approach, and expertise guided me to a book that is worth reading and makes strong contributions to research and practice. I'm immensely grateful to Richard.

Land Acknowledgment

I recognize and acknowledge that work on this project occurred on the traditional lands of the Sesevitam, the first people of the unceded and ancestral territory of Sesevenga, whose descendants are the citizens of the Fernandeño Tataviam Band of Mission Indians; and the Tongva, whose descendants are citizens of the Gabrieleno San Gabriel Band of Mission Indians and traditional land caretakers of Tovaangar. I encourage you to learn more about the histories and current projects of Indigenous people where you live and work, which helps to continue conversation and action to restore rights and land repatriation for Indigenous people.

Preface

Origins of This Work

Shaping Students of Color from Preschool to Graduate School: The Impact of Families on Education started at the intersection of my own parenting with my kids and my work with doctoral students at California State University, Northridge (CSUN), where I serve as a professor. Like many dimensions of our recent lives, the pandemic touched me in ways that I'm still processing. At the height of pandemic-related public health orders, I worked as CSUN's education doctorate program director. In this capacity, I interacted with and supported students whose lives had been devastated by the rapid spread and deadly and debilitating toll of COVID-19 on their families, especially in communities of color. I responded to an immense call to action and intervention to support them, not just to continue in the doctoral program but to pick up the pieces of lives they had lost in their families and understand more about what family meant to them at a trying time in their lives.

Looking back at the early days of the pandemic, I see how the values that I had learned as a child encouraged me to empathetically approach graduate students of color in the doctoral program. And that got me thinking about how parents impact children at home and in school over the life course—not just during early childhood or adolescence but as emerging adults and beyond. More broadly, what stuck with me was the nagging need to join a growing group of scholars and practitioners who are moving beyond conventional measures of and approaches to student success to support students of color. Before I delve deeper into the empirical basis for this work, I take an inward turn and reflect on my experiential understanding and deeply personal connections to the work in this book.

A key question here is: How had I been shaped by my parents and, in turn, how do I impact my children as a parent today?

As a dad, my work with my kids comes first—by far. Care work trumps paid work every time, and it's not even a close competition for me. In my home, you only need to be around most days of the week and many weekends to see what I mean. The deeply emotional work and tiring physical labor at these hours requires a bizarre mix of disjointed multitasking, acute focus, clairvoyant attentiveness, rote zombie movement, cajoling and persuading, and plain old luck to get things done and people where they need to be. Compare that to teaching, advising, meetings, emails, writing, and doing interviews? No comparison at all, especially when you consider time and resources needed for the respective jobs (a lot more at home), life satisfaction (higher when parenting), and personal well-being (generally good at the end of a long day of care work and housework).

That's not to say that I don't love my day job—it's a calling and incredibly rewarding and fulfilling work. My time in the classroom and office and direct interaction with students in teaching, advising, mentoring, and supervising is my life's vocation. Doing research and writing to reach folks and connect with communities is what keeps me going and helps to make life meaningful. My contributions to the broader good and the human condition, particularly for families of color who have been excluded from the education of their children in college, are essential to who I am. I'm writing this book now from interviews I did and background research in collaboration. I'm highly motivated by engagement with scholars and practitioners alike.

From one graduate student to another, I can relate to some of the experiences, emotions and feelings, and lessons from life connected to parents while being a student in a master's or doctoral program. While I cannot connect to each individual's intersectional identities, complex positionalities, and rich lived experiences who participated in this work in terms of racial and ethnic identity, gender identity and expression, sexual orientation, class, location, and institutional culture and climate in graduate school, sharing some common ground with participants about their experiences with parent relationships, family values, religious affiliations, and much more facilitates a more meaningful contribution of this work to supporting adult children, fathers, mothers, and families along with faculty, staff, and administrators. Where my identities and lived experiences don't overlap with participants', I relied heavily on an ethic of care, use of member checks or follow-up interviews to facilitate first-person accounts, and consultation with colleagues who share identities with participants in a co-interpretive practice. Note that throughout this book, quotations

Preface | xv

are deliberately kept intact to capture the voices of students, even when there are grammatical errors.

In my multiple roles, I serve as an ally who works closely with graduate students of color and am committed to dismantling institutional systems of racism, sexism, homophobia, and xenophobia. To be sure, I've benefited from systems of racial and gender oppression in my life. I am in a privileged position as an academic researcher and writer, but this project conarrates personal stories related, in part, to racial and gender microaggressions and exclusion based on race, ethnicity, gender, sexual orientation, and more, to help us move closer to a more just and equitable society with colleges and universities that are welcoming and validating of students with intersectional identities, particularly women, students of color, and first-gen students who have been historically and are currently excluded from a vast swath of institutional and programmatic opportunities and resources. On a personal level, knowing what it's like to be supported by a parent who gets up before dawn to put food on the table, stays up overnight to offer support when needed, listens to decisions about career, and much more helps me intuitively understand, in small part, what participants in this project experience. To be clear, these are participant stories, and they own what they shared with me—I only conarrate research themes in this work in the hope that we all understand more about who they are and how to support them.

As an adult child who lived at home with parents while in graduate school and is now coraising a stepdaughter who recently graduated from college and a daughter who's in high school, there's a bit of an experiential life-course perspective that helps me to co-interpret what has been shared with me here. Engaging graduate students of color with whom I share values about education and family unity, spiritual beliefs, agency at a young age, and much more offers me some insight for co-storytelling. Whereas my identities and lived experiences do not entirely overlap with those of participants, my life's work with students of color in higher education offers me very limited but still meaningful intuitive insight. Throughout the work, I adopted an ethic of care and collaborated with participants in a co-constructive practice.

Purpose, Audience, and Organization of this Work

Shaping Students of Color from Preschool to Graduate School: The Impact of Families on Education tells the story about why parents and families of color are integral to student success. At a time when graduate school enrollment and degrees are on the rise, women and people of color continue to experience comparatively lower outcomes at undergraduate and graduate levels (Baker, 1998; King, 2008; McCallum, 2016; NCES, 2022b; Perna, 2004). Indeed, with a 9 percent increase in graduate school enrollment (2010–2021) and a 6 percent rise expected by 2030 (NCES, 2022b), there is an urgent need to close the racial and gender equity gaps. While racialized and gendered structures, institutional and program characteristics, student background characteristics, student-faculty and peer-peer interaction, academic performance, mentorship, and more explain educational outcomes—we know far less about how parent relationships and family life shape students of color over the life course. In general, parents affect educational outcomes of children (Gordon, 2017; Wigfield et al., 2015), and families are main drivers for both ethnically diverse undergraduate students (Phinney et al., 2006) and Black graduate students (Louque, 1999) to go to school. Indeed, among Asian American, African American, and Latino first-year undergraduate students, helping the family was one of the top reasons for going to college (Phinney et al., 2006).

In this context, this work asked graduate students of color at the end of the educational journey to reflect on experiences and talk about what their parents and families meant to their education. Through intimate accounts, we come to know compelling patterns that counter dominant discourse about disparities in academic success of graduate students of color and first-generation graduate students. Moving beyond conventional measures, we learn what shapes pathways to graduate degree programs, including resistance to societal gender norms that penetrate family systems, values that promote education and hard work, familial circumstances influencing independence early in life, a need to honor family sacrifices and give back to parents and communities, and the importance of extended family, mentors, and peers. We see how parent relationships and involvement in education support children in their pursuit of advanced studies, even as parents appear to have their unique place among a complex web of factors that explain experiences on the educational pipeline.

Detailing the need for empirical research in this project required me to go further back into the literature, and the dated nature of some studies reflects not only the unique focus on events that stretch over the life course but the limited explorations into how families and parents impact children as students relative to the voluminous body of work on factors that impact educational outcomes. With limited empirical research about students of color navigating the educational pipeline and parents of color shaping children in college (Herndon & Hirt, 2004), there is a pressing need to embrace a more holistic understanding of the strengths that students bring with them to campus. While studies on how families of color shape children in postbaccalaureate degree programs have grown over the last several decades, the legacy of racism in academic research has produced a body of work that is essential but not nearly sufficient or relies on a deficit lens (McCallum, 2016). For generations, US colleges and universities have perpetuated a system of higher education that disconnects students from their families and communities and assumes that the curriculum and campus life—Eurocentric and paternalistic—are sufficient for academic and career development and intellectual growth. For far too long, postsecondary education had sponsored systemic inequities in how students learn, from a hidden curriculum (Gair & Mullins, 2001) that doesn't tend to make degree requirements and curricular content explicit to campus practices that create a cultural climate that does not generally welcome students and their families, particularly students of color and first-generation students.

Using a life course perspective (Roy & Settersten, 2022), family socialization lens (Kalmuss & Seltzer, 1989), and community cultural wealth framework (Yosso, 2006) in forty personal interviews with first-generation graduate students and graduate students of color from universities in the Western and Southern US, this work centers a perspective that uplifts and honors families of color and elevates nuances about how parenting roles, reproducing family values, navigating economic hardship and human migration, and facing adversity and overcoming challenges at home and on campus form foundational experiences that impact academic aspirations and achievement.

Uniquely crossing sectors in elementary, secondary, and postsecondary education, this work advances the idea that families and parents impact graduate students of color and first-generation graduate students on their paths to graduate school. With an asset-based approach that normalizes how children relate to parents throughout life, the narrative in this project highlights the interdependency and agency of graduate students in their life journeys and academic trajectories. Through their stories, you see how parental relations with children wax and wane over time, illustrating both how families are one of many assets that students bring to campus and how families are integral to educational systems with essential support and foundational values for students to achieve academically.

The thematic patterns that emerged during data analysis of personal interviews, coupled with an interpretive lens from the empirical literature and experiential insight from participants, affirm the positive roles of families in the long-term success of first-generation graduate students and graduate students of color. Specifically, *on the educational pipeline of graduate students of color and first-generation graduate students, families—and parents, in particular—use a complex system of cultural knowledge, beliefs, values, and actions to socialize children to both reify and resist gendered norms, challenge racialized structures, internalize family values that promote education and hard work, reproduce family values that center family unity and spirituality, honor familial and ancestral sacrifices, facilitate individual agency and personal autonomy at a young age, manage uneven parent involvement in education, and balance sometimes strained but still close parent-child relationships. Situated in these familial contexts, this group of graduate students carried with them the capital to believe there was something larger in life that they needed to accomplish and that they had the wherewithal to do it, and it drove them to pursue the highest levels of academic training.*

In communities of the scholarly study of higher education and the practice of undergraduate and graduate education, this book appeals to a broad range of readers—from scholars and students with specialized knowledge and interests in higher education to university administrators who lead undergraduate and graduate schools or divisions on campus. This book can be required textbook use, especially in graduate-level courses in sociology, psychology, education, and interdisciplinary fields like family studies. Within social and behavioral science fields, interest from students, instructors, and researchers in a range of specialized disciplinary fields may see applications of this work in multiple contexts. In education, subfields in higher education, higher education/student affairs, and higher education administration/leadership may be interested in this work, while the book may appeal to scholars and researchers in educational sociology. Interdisciplinary fields like gender studies and family studies may find the work useful, especially where the focus is on gender and parenting and effects of parent-child relations on adult children.

My Foundational Connections to this Work as a Parent Involved in Home and School Life

Primary socialization in the family and parent involvement in children's lives at home and school are at the heart of this project. Parents serve in critical roles in kids' lives and uniquely contribute to child, adolescent, and adult development—and families are not just partners but essential members of successful schools and educational communities. My focus in this work can be traced to my own experiences as a dad and stepdad. Along with Caroline, Madeleine and Emmie are the center of my world, and most everyone and everything else lands a distance away from the center. To be fair, I love my work, and my extended family and friends ground me, too—but my career, writing, and more tend to revolve around my family. Ironically, this guiding force is what pushed me to do this book and elevated my work in this project, at times over the last few years, above my responsibilities at home. It all turned out well for the book and my family.

My focus on my kids and identity as a parent came early in my transition to family life, and this central focal point is the force behind this book. We're a blended family. When I was thirty-two, Madeleine and I entered each other's lives in the early 2000s. When she was in kindergarten, Madeleine's influence on me was outsized. More than life-changing, more mesmerizing and spellbinding—and certainly captivating—my life changed dramatically. Over the course of several months, I became a dad. Not overnight, but faster than I could remember and right in front of me, I did a lot of fathering work. I found myself shopping for girls' pajamas and hoodies, making sandwiches for school lunches on Sunday afternoons, braiding pony tails (and failing miserably), assembling backpacks in the morning and making sure everyone was bundled up in the very mild and dry Southern California winters, driving to and from dance practice, staying home from work and taking care of a sick kid, scooping up toys from the floor at home, making quick dinners and microwaving Kraft Mac & Cheese for a snack, and fixing flat tires on bike rides around the block.

Later, Emmie came along, and the whirlwind hastened my work as a dad with family time at warp speed. My experiences with parenting all seemed to be milestones for me as a dad, and each little win allowed me to learn more about raising children, parenting with a partner, and much more. At school pick up, for example, I'd chat with parents who'd been at the school for what seemed like generations—through several kids and more than one principal. Getting to know mothers, fathers, grandmother, grandfathers, and extended family members, I learned a lot about parenting and fathering, too. Personal observations and mental notes helped to socialize me into broad normative expectations about how more mothers than fathers tended to stay at home and serve in and homemaker roles, and fathers went to work as breadwinners in the family. Mothers generally volunteered in classrooms at school, served in leadership positions in the PTA, organized after-school activities and groups like the Girl Scouts, planned school events and field trips, and more. By all accounts, parenting appeared gendered, and I had to adjust to fit into this scheme at school. But why? The question may seem easy to ask, but an answer is a bit elusive and difficult to form. Questions like this, about parent relationships with children and family life at home and school, often lack clarity and tend to present with ambiguity—and they explain some of why I worked on this book.

My Early Life Experiences with Family Socialization and Parent Involvement in Education: Brief Descriptions of How My Parents Shaped Me

The reflections that graduate students with whom I worked in this book inspired me to look back at my childhood, where I see how my parents shaped me as a person—who I am, what I value, and how I contribute to my own family, campus community, and beyond. Looking back at my upbringing, I first experienced what a parent involved in the life of children was like—from daily care to school—from my mom. To be sure, my dad showed a lot of love for my older brother, younger sister, and me—but my mom showered us with the love, nurture, and care. From an early age, I can recall how she expressed her maternal love through touch—hugging us when we came home from school, kissing us on the head when we woke up and came out to the kitchen, and lightly rubbing our upper backs or shoulders when we weren't feeling well or were tired. Later in life, my mom would share how physical contact seemed to be connected to maternal and paternal cultural practices in her family of origin. Indeed, she'd cite the ways her parents greeted her with their hands, arms, and lips. My mom would regale us of stories of her mother, whose Sicilian roots meant close contact with extended family and friends and strong emotional ties between parents and children. With her dad, cultural connections to Slovenia seemed to mean lots of kissing hello and goodbye and hugs at holidays and birthdays.

There was more, far more, to my mom than care through physical contact. She was always there for us—accessible and available all the time—and not just in the routine workaday care. She was always there when we needed her and even when we didn't—she knew the exact formula to ease our pain, comfort our sadness, uplift our spirits, spiritually feed our souls, and offer us deeply wise guidance. She protected us from harm, defended us when we were cornered, held our hand when we were alone and afraid, and pushed us when we resisted, challenged us when we were wrong, taught us to come to the aid of folks who needed it, and work to advance social justice.

For almost a decade while in high school and college—from the late 1980s to the late 1990s—my mom seemed to have superhuman strength to rise early to ferry us to before-dawn practices and stay up superlate on a weekday to plan for the next day at school. In these seemingly exhausting moments and chaotically busy times, I found a space to connect emotionally with my mom and learned a lot about how to foster familial and social links and value relationships with people who crossed paths with us. There were intellectual discussions about social issues, and my mom led us to understand how social justice required us to act to support progressive ideas that resisted structural inequities and institutionalized forms of exclusion. We were called to fight against racism, sexism, xenophobia, and homophobia.

Like many graduate students in this work, I lived at home and experienced family life as an adult child as an undergraduate and graduate student. When I transferred from the community college to University of California, Los Angeles (UCLA), a familiar pattern persisted. While intimidated by the vast footprint and new environment on the Westwood campus—to make no mention of my anxiety over upper-division undergraduate courses in my majors—my parents' hard work and unconditional support meant that I could study there. I commuted from home and generally didn't stay on campus long before or after class, so the collegiate experience tended to elude me—but I was so grateful for the opportunity to be a Bruin. Setting up my success as a student at UCLA, my parents helped with gas money, books, fees, and incidentals. When I had a tough day, they helped me to process my feelings, and when I needed time to study or socialize, they gave me space and allowed me to come into my own.

Fast-forward several years, the start of doctoral work at UCLA in 2002 saw me still at home with my parents. Now in my late twenties, I commuted to campus and worked part-time both on campus and later part- and full-time off campus. Much the same as when I was an undergraduate—only with less time spent at home and more at work, school, and socializing. My parents managed a home that allowed me to focus on my studies and work. While my parents don't have graduate degrees themselves, they didn't need one to know that love, care, concern, and general support helped me to navigate a terminal degree program. They offered me the best chance to complete my doctoral studies and negotiate early career directions—a lot like the graduate students whose stories and lives we come to know in this work.

Life Transitions Guide Involvement in My Kids' Education

Where my life left off with my parents shaping me, it picks up in my role as a parent today. This continuum led me to this book, and a set of reflections about parenthood and life transitions had a particularly forceful hand in the project. A constant in the life course of child transitions to adolescence and into adulthood, parent involvement with kids changes over time. Looking back at life before the pandemic, I can remember a time when my involvement with Madeleine changed with sudden, immediate, and far-reaching effects for me personally. Madeleine got her driver's license when she was seventeen and a half years old. I knew this day would come—when Madeleine would have a way to get to where she needed to go in her young life, but I didn't think it would happen so soon. Well, okay, I didn't think it would happen all of a sudden. But it did. Madeleine could drive herself to school, and she seemed so happy and excited to be on her way. Now she would be going out into the world, doing errands, seeing friends, going to see her dad and stepmom, and so much more. But our routine together changed after she started to drive—for the better, of course, but some changes can be bittersweet.

My time with Emmie has changed at warped speed, too. I think about childhood rituals with Emmie, now fifteen and ready to drive, and I can see how things have evolved. As a toddler, I used to take Emmie to several parks in our Orange County neighborhood. She used to climb out of the car and dash toward the playground, grabbing the closest swing or steps up the gym set. Arms waving in every direction in the air, Emmie would zero in on the tallest slide or longest rope and try to make her way to the top or across, then down or to the end. In between slinging and sliding, she'd find every cigarette butt, wood chip, pebble, grass blade, ant, or leaf and pluck it up, holding it up to me and motioning to put it in my pocket. I'm not sure exactly when regular trips to the park ended—maybe by the third grade. Unlike with Madeleine, there was no one event that I can readily recall as the end of this time with Emmie. Hard to pinpoint, there were more just like it—all seemingly blending into each other and blurring the lines between what we had done and are about to start to do in our lives as father and children. Fast-forward, today I'm lucky if I get to go with Emmie and her friends to get frozen yogurt. All good changes in these moments—we enjoy what we do together now and often don't look back at what we used to do when the girls were younger. As a dad intimately involved in the life of his kids, I felt these changes intensely and asked: What do I do with the reflections on these times? How do I manage changes in family life? This book is part of my effort to manage these changes, reflect on their significance in my life, and help to do the same for you, too.

Of course, Madeleine's status as a licensed driver and Emmie's social life heralded many, many changes over the course of their young lives, and the cycles of rapid change and slowly evolving transitions are both countless and innumerable. Madeleine is twenty-four years old now and well into adulthood. I can look at major life transitions for Madeleine meant changes as a dad for me: high school graduation, first job, college, dating, travel, and more. Same with Emmie: promotion from elementary school and junior high school, driver's education, and exploration of college and career. Far more involved, closer emotionally, and physically more present, I continue to do a lot of the things I've done for years—just in different forms—particularly in the girls' education.

What I tend to do now with the girls focuses on more frequent, even if distant, touchpoints and check-ins about school or work and the details of their days—from experiences in the classroom and relationships with friends to interests in specific topics and areas of improvement. More detailed questions, longer conversations (even if I have to mask them through intermittent engagement in conversation). I tend to spend less time on homework help for Emmie and more time on emotional and logistical support and, with both Madeleine and Emmie, intellectual discussions. These changes in relationships with my kids and involvement in their education tend to be a microcosm of what I learned in this project and follow the paths of many graduate students with whom I spoke. At the same time, what I learned from graduate students who shared their stories about parents, families, and school in this project helps me to embrace this time together, before these moments fleetingly fade, and hopefully it does the same for you, too.

Introduction

Broad Context of Graduate School Experiences and Outcomes for Students of Color

Higher levels of education tend to be associated with better life outcomes, including lower unemployment rates and higher median weekly earnings for master's, professional doctoral, and research doctoral degree holders than all other groups (NCES, 2021). Over the last two decades, US colleges and universities have experienced enrollment and degree increases in undergraduate and graduate programs—and enrollment growth is expected to continue over the next decade (NCES, 2022a; NCES, 2022b). While undergraduate enrollment has recently dipped, largely during the COVID-19 pandemic, total undergraduate enrollment is expected to increase by 9 percent between 2021 and 2031. Looking back to 2010 through 2021, undergraduate enrollment of Latinx, Asian, and multiracial students increased (NCES, 2022a). At the graduate level, graduate school enrollment increased by 9 percent—going from 2.9 million to 3.2 million students (NCES 2022b). From 2020 to 2030, the number of students enrolled in master's and doctoral programs, including law and medicine, will increase from 3.2 to 3.4 million students, a 6 percent uptick (NCES, 2022b). What's more, between 2009 and 2020, graduate and professional school enrollment of women, Black, Latinx, Asian/Pacific Islander students increased. During roughly the same period, graduate and professional degree awards rose by 21 percent, and in 2019 to 1920 women earned 61 percent of postbaccalaureate degrees compared to 39 percent for men (NCES, 2022a). Overall, the number of degrees and certificates award at all levels of postsecondary education—from associate and baccalaureate degrees to master's and doctoral degrees—increased between 10 percent and 20 percent during the same general period (NCES, 2022b).

But the news isn't all good, and graduate students of color have experienced the most pressing disparities in educational outcomes and experiences. In fact, racial equity gaps exist for Black students in doctoral degree program enrollment and completion (McCallum, 2016). Even though Black graduate enrollment has increased, Black students still graduate at lower rates (Love, 2017). Among Black graduate students, Black men earn fewer graduate degrees than Black women (Schwartz et al., 2003). What's more, American Indian/Alaska Native postbaccalaureate enrollment dramatically decreased by 25 percent from 2009 to 2020, and the enrollment growth of women in graduate education is projected to increase at a lower rate than men from 2020 to 2030 (NCES, 2022b). Equally discouraging, 61 percent of degrees awarded in computer and information science fields and 51 percent in business still went to men in the most recent period, continuing a gendered pattern of graduate school outcomes. Further, students who identify as white or two or more races were awarded more degrees in STEM fields than students who identify as Black, Latinx, Asian/Pacific Islander, and American Indian/Alaska Native. In joint MD-PhD programs, for example, racially/ethnically underrepresented students appear to be more likely to withdraw or face dismissal (Jeffe et al., 2014). For first-generation students, a smaller proportion matriculate into doctoral or professional degree programs compared to continuing generation students (Cataldi et al., 2018).

Behind these numbers, a broad range of factors shape educational enrollment and outcomes on campus, including structural racialized and gendered oppression, institutional location, type and control, school or campus climate, peer-peer interaction, student-faculty interaction, and more. In historical and current contexts, institutionalized systems of gender and racial discrimination explain gaps in enrollment and academic outcomes for women and people of color in education, and this pattern extends to master's and doctoral programs (NCES, 2022b; King, 2008; Baker, 1998). Indeed, Zarate (2023) argues that an opaque process directs campus officials to decide who gets in and who does not in undergraduate and graduate admissions.

For graduate students of color, the net result of generations of racialized and gendered institutional and program structures shape experiences and outcomes today. Latino/a and Black doctoral students have faced dehumanizing cultural experiences in the academy (Gildersleeve et al., 2011). For generations, historical patterns of racism and sexism have shaped Black graduate student feelings of isolation, exclusion, and disconnectedness (Johnson-Bailey et al., 2008; Johnson-Bailey et al., 2009). Latino/a graduate students experience isolation, alienation, challenges in transitioning to graduate school, and a host of racist, sexist, and classist microaggressions (Ramirez, 2014). Black doctoral students share experiences of racial socialization and racism at the departmental level (Barker, 2016). Further, Black graduate students experience imposter syndrome, stereotype threat (Patterson-Stephens et al., 2017), and a lack of support—leading to a pattern of self-reliance (Jason et al., 2023).

In disciplinary contexts, graduate students of color and women graduate students experience structural racism and sexism. In engineering graduate programs, Black men confront racialized structures in admissions and racialized and gendered interactions (Burt et al., 2018) and, specifically, racial microaggressions in advising relationships (Burt et al., 2020). When fields expand to both engineering and computer science, Black graduate students experience racialized stress, which leads to stress and shapes how self-perceptions of qualifications (McGee et al., 2019). In STEM fields, this structural racism and sexism lead to Black male graduate student experiences with imposter syndrome (Burt et al., 2017). Black women graduate students face racial and gender oppression (Robinson, 2013; Walkington, 2017). Latina engineering graduate students report having to prove themselves to peers who identify as male in the program (Aguirre-Covarrubias et al., 2015).

For students of color on campus, racial microaggressions and racial hostility in the broader campus climate take a heavy toll on their mental and physical well-being. Facing racial, gender, and class injustices, Chicano/a and Latino/a graduate students tend to use a range of strategies of resistance (Ramirez, 2014). Mexican American and African American college students differentially feel negative effects of racial battle fatigue (Franklin, 2019). For Latino/a college students, racial battle fatigue leads to psychological stress (Franklin et al, 2014), while Black students acutely feel the negative cumulative effects (Owens et al. 2019). Black student affairs educators, in particular, report physical effects of racial battle fatigue (Quaye et al., 2020). For racial justice activists of color at predominantly white institutions, racial battle fatigue tends to hasten burnout (Gorski, 2018).

Beyond race and gender, several factors account for outcomes in postbaccalaureate programs in US colleges and universities, including historically developed measures like graduate grade point average (GPA) and Graduate Record Examination (GRE) scores. But less conventional factors seem to play a role in graduate student success, too, including early graduate-level academic and research experiences, disciplinary affiliation, institutional and program culture, academic employment, financial support, and mentorship.

Even more personal experiences related to parent involvement in education and family influences have also been connected to outcomes. Looking more closely at some of these personal experiences, mentoring, socializing, and feeling a sense of belongingness support Black graduate students (Felder, 2010; Marshall et al., 2023). Historically, the academy has not adequately supported mentoring graduate students of color (Brunsma et al., 2016), and race and gender shape dissonance in faculty career decisions for graduate students of color (Levin et al., 2013). Black graduate students often rely on support from Black professors and peers (Johnson-Bailey et al., 2008). For Black women graduate students, mentors (Davis, 2007), study groups, family members, and friends serve as support systems (Alexander & Bodenhorn, 2015; Borum & Walker, 2012).

For both Black and Latinx graduate students, mentoring intersects with more personal spaces in their lives, including family and friends. And when mentoring creates a sense of familial connection, the effects on graduate students tend to be enhanced. For example, African American women graduate students report that African American women mentors have unique effects, creating familial connections between mentors and mentees (Patton, 2009). Black men cite family, spirituality, and mentoring as undergraduate students as sources of support for persistence in engineering graduate programs (Burt et al., 2018), and Latino/a undergraduate students describe family support, peer communities, role models (Martinez, 2018), and student-faculty interactions (Cuellar & Gonzalez, 2019) as important factors in doctoral program aspirations and applications. Similarly, institutional support and undergraduate research support Latino/a student graduate school access and application (Ramirez, 2011), and Latino/a graduate students identify mentors who understand and can relate to first-generation college students as central to their success (Mireles-Rios & Garcia, 2018). For Latina engineering graduate students, interactions with faculty have been reported as positive. Latina engineering master's students, in particular, cite families as important sources of support for self-confidence (Aguirre-Covarrubias et al., 2015; García & Henderson, 2014). Further, when mentors understand the importance of family, a critical connection can be made for Latina graduate students (García & Henderson, 2014).

While we know that peers, faculty, program and institutional environments, and much more contribute to graduate student outcomes and recognize the central importance of families in impacting educational outcomes, we know far less about how parents of color shape students who complete postbaccalaureate degree programs. Given institutional hierarchies that have privileged white men and Eurocentric values in higher education, we do not empirically understand as much as we need to about how parents of students of color and first-generation students shape children's educational journeys. To help close the gap in what we know, the following question guided this study: From the perspective of graduate students of color, how have parent relationships and parent involvement in education shaped educational paths over the life course?

With the weight of historical and current structures that reproduce racial and gender hierarchies and impact parenting and family outcomes for people of color, there is an urgency to undo the intractable and insidious effects of racism and sexism in the academy. At a time when the devastating trauma and damaging effects of generations of systemic exclusion and hate have been investigated and interrogated across institutions of higher education, there is a need to make way for love, care, concern and hope in welcoming spaces in graduate programs and beyond. Focusing on students and families of color supports the primary goal of this work: to build on the body of scholarly inquiry that advances strength-based perspectives and centers the familial capital of students of color. My hope is that this work helps us understand holistically more about the experiences to best support parents and their children in graduate education and disrupts the detrimental impact of racialized and gendered forces on mothers, fathers, and parental figures and resists the structural inequalities that result from these systems and shape, in part, families whose children are navigating programs of advanced study.

Understanding the Central Importance of Parent Relationships and Family Socialization to Children's Development over the Life Course

Parents are central to children's development (Chen & Kaplan, 2001; Putney & Bengston, 2002). Over the life course, parents shape who children are, including values, beliefs, and personalities. Socialization is a complex bidirectional process that involves parents guiding or assisting children in learning moral values and cultural expectations for social norms (Grusec, 2011). Parental modeling of values and parental affirmations are important influences on adolescent children (Putney & Bengston, 2002), and parenting in early adolescence shapes how children parent later in life (Chen & Kaplan, 2001). Parental value transmission tends to happen in early childhood and remains stable well into adulthood, especially for religious beliefs (Min et al., 2012). Across the unique parental contributions to values formation in families, we know that when maternal involvement accompanies maternal reproduction of collectivist values, prosocial behaviors like acts that benefit others and cooperation with others emerge among recently immigrated Latino/a adolescents (Davis et al., 2018).

Love and affection between parents and children impact children's development. Parental rejection, for example, negatively affects children's social and psychological well-being, while parental acceptance tends to be related to psychological well-being, academic achievement, and much more (Rohner & Veneziano, 2021). Moreover, parental acceptance has been inversely associated with health-risk behaviors among emerging adults (Schwartz et al., 2009). Emotional bonds between parents and children shape self-esteem, and the bonds between mothers and children tend to have the strongest effect (Putney & Bengston, 2022)—with mother-child relationship quality remaining stable through adolescence (Bornstein & Putnick, 2023).

Parental relationships with children have been shaped by socio-structural forces, including gender, race, class, education, and more. Rooted in the Victorian-era ideas of separate spheres, where men and women operate in unique and discrete social worlds (Adams & Coltrane, 2005), gendered patterns of behavior in the home and society still dictate what mothers and fathers do in the family and how they relate to their children—even as these changing norms inform role convergence today. In this gendered system, men frequently detach from the family in paid work and function as laborers in the public sphere and women generally do care work and labor domestically in the private sphere. Consequently, differences have been observed in how parents relate to their kids—including findings from Lamb (1977) that showed mothers and fathers engage in differential interactions with kids.

With complex contextual factors that shape what parents do, differences can be seen in familial roles for mothers and fathers and parental relationships with children. Mothers tend to connect their identities to their children's well-being. Among Mexican-origin mothers, self-perception as mothers—including being protective, communicative, accessible and balancing roles—can be linked to children's well-being (Bermúdez et al.,

2014). Working outside the home generally focuses mothers on what they perceive as their responsibility to ensure children's well-being. Even as they delegate mothering duties—due to work responsibilities—to other women, including nannies, childcare center staff, and family members, mothers feel their responsibility to serve as caregivers (Christopher, 2012). More broadly, mothers center maternal roles on a range of beliefs about parenting, including prioritizing children, finding fulfillment in parenting, and believing that females are better at parenting than males (Forbes et al., 2020).

Profound Effects of Maternal Relationships on Children

Given their roles as parents and relationships with children, mothers tend to relate closely with children. Indeed, mothers generally spend more time in tasks associated with care-taking and child-rearing (McBride & Mills, 1993). In childhood, strong bonds between mothers and children tend to be maintained through a number of strategies, including open communication and communication of pride in qualities like respect, commitment, and dependability (Jacobs, 2023). Further, as secure attachment to a mother increases, the more positively a child sees themself on a range of measures, including happiness and physical shape (Özyürek & Çetin, 2022). In African American families, a mother's educational level and satisfaction with parenting among mothers have been associated positively with key child development outcomes (Black et al., 1999). When little or no secure attachment between mothers and children exist, the effects can be devastating on children. This is especially consequential for boys, where insecurely attached boys have been observed as aggressive, less competent, and more problematic behaviorally (Cohn, 1990). When children perceive the relationship with their mother as secure, they tend to report less loneliness overall, experience more peer acceptance and reciprocal friendships in general, and see themselves as less critical and more responsive in same-gender friendship pairs (Kerns et al., 1996).

Even as adolescence marks a time of change for teenagers, mother-child relationship quality tends to be stable (Bornstein & Putnick, 2023), and this is critical to children's development. For example, maternal mental health, education, income, and life satisfaction predict adolescent children's symptoms with anxiety and depression (Coles & Cage, 2022). Early attachment security to mothers—and neighborhood social cohesion—has been associated with adolescent social skills (Hong et al., 2023). When adolescents share close relationships with their mothers and report strong resiliency, they tend to report subjective well-being (Qu et al., 2021). Later, in college, parental acceptance by mothers has been associated inversely with few health-risk behaviors in emerging-adult children (Schwartz et al., 2009).

Mothers' influence on child development can be seen in outcomes like emotional regulation and friendship quality in childhood. More specifically, maternal emotional socialization strategies that encourage children to accept, validate, and process negative emotions and address source issues of problems leading to negative emotions at age 5 have been related to better emotion regulation and positive friendship quality between ages 7 and 10 (Blair et al., 2014). Over time, when mothers show supportive responses to children's negative emotions at age five, children have better emotion regulation at age ten and more social competence in adolescence at age fifteen (Perry et al., 2020).

When mothers explain emotions to children, children tend to demonstrate emotion situation knowledge, rather than relational aggression, and more prosocial behavior like cooperation (Garner et al. 2008). Prosocial behavior in adolescents can be shaped in relational warmth between mothers and maternal self-efficacy. This effect seems to emerge as mothers believe they can act in an agentic way. They may encourage their own affectionate expressions toward children and create an environment where children see mothers as models and act in a similar way (Luengo Kanacri et al. [2021]).Maternal acceptance of children tends to positively impact the regulation of sadness in adolescence, underscoring the importance of mother-child relationships (Vergara-Lopez et al., 2024). When mothers offer coping resources for early pubertal maturation to daughters, there tends to be more help-seeking, managing negative emotions, and resolving stressors for girls (Ye & Rudolph, 2023).

Maternal responses to negative emotion expressions seem to be mediated by race. Indeed, African American mothers tend to differ in beliefs and practices related to negative emotion regulation from white mothers in a way that protects children from discrimination (Nelson et al., 2012). Cultural differences can shape maternal perceptions and practices, too. For example, white mothers tend to view anger in children as a lack of self-control whereas Puerto Rican mothers see it as a lack of proper demeanor (Harwood et al., 1996).

Parenting has been reshaped, in part, by broad social and economic forces—with particularly acute COVID-19 pandemic effects on the changing nature of parenthood. During the pandemic, fathers confronted new realities of family life (Hsu, 2020). In fact, when compared to a year earlier, 50 percent more fathers with school-age children were not actively working in the middle of the pandemic—in fall 2020 (Hsu). For example, with changes in work and home life brought on by stay-at-home orders and shutdowns, many fathers had more opportunities to be more involved in their kids' lives—from schoolwork to household duties. Between the more mundane homework help and dinner duty, fathers could be seen helping kids adjust to life at home. For example, Torrence Burson, a dad in Memphis, Tennessee, did what a lot of parents did when birthdays, anniversaries, graduations, and more could not be celebrated in the usual ways during lockdown: He arranged for socially distanced graduation ceremony for his daughter, Gabrielle Pierce, in the driveway of their home ("Dad Arranges for Special Graduation," 2020). In another example, a dad in Ohio fastened an orange-painted shipping tube to the handrail on the front porch to make a candy chute for kids to trick or treat in a socially distanced way ("Ohio Dad Figures Out," 2020). Kids put bags on one end of the chute and called out "Trick or treat." By contrast, for essential worker fathers, the pandemic forced some of them to bring their kids to work, as Kramer (2020) chronicled in a story about Paul Montanaro and his daughter, Francesca, eleven, who labored together at the family restaurant, Katonah Pizza & Pasta in the Bronx.

UNIQUE INFLUENCES OF FATHERS ON CHILDREN

When we look at familial roles for fathers and explore how fathers engage children in families, we see historical and contemporary patterns driven by gender. Fathers have averaged 44 percent of mothers' time involved with their kids and 66 percent of time mothers were accessible to their kids (Pleck, 1997). Today, men report doing more care work than they have in the past and view care work as positive (Barker, 2023), and this pattern can be seen globally (van der Gaag, 2023). In the US, fathers are spending more time with kids—triple the amount of time in childcare (eight hours per week) spent in 1965 (Livingston & Parker, 2019). But this time still does not seem like enough, as almost two-thirds of fathers say they spend too little time with their kids (Livingston & Parker). And while a majority of fathers say that parenting is extremely important to their identity, just over half report that balancing work and family is very or somewhat difficult (Livingston & Parker). At the same time, over three quarters of fathers feel a lot of pressure to support their family financially (Livingston & Parker).

Historically, fathers have spent more time being available to their kids than interacting with them and being responsible for their care (McBride & Mills, 1993; Nock & Kingston, 1988; Pleck, 1997). While a concern, this pattern now seems to be changing. If we consider what responsibility means for care of a child, we see how awareness or attentiveness to a range of their needs—emotional, physical, social, and cognitive development—is critical (Cabrera et al., & Lamb, 2000; Lamb et al., 1985; Palkovitz, 1997). When fathers participate in identifying and addressing the needs of children, they tend to feel more competent as a parent (Baruch & Barnett, 1986; McBride & Mills).

Relationship quality between children and fathers in early age and more frequent father involvement in adolescent ages tend to be related to parental relationships quality in emerging adulthood (Tefteller, 2014). During the adolescent years, fathers tend to lag in a key measure that matters a lot to teenagers—peer interaction. Indeed, fathers are reported to be less knowledgeable about adolescent peer relationships and less involved in peer-oriented activities of their kids than mothers (Updegraff et al., 2001). Overall, involved father effects are positive for children's development and attainment. With adolescent children, fathers who are more involved tend to be more accepting of their kids (Almeida & Galambos, 1991). The good news is that more time spent involved and the earlier the involvement, the stronger the effect of this approach (Schwartz & Finley, 2006).

Fathers shape child and adolescent development (Schwartz & Finley, 2006), and fathers tend to respond to the needs of children, starting as infants (Lamb & Lewis, 2010). In general, father involvement can be linked to a host of outcomes of children, including academic and professional achievement, social and life skills, healthy body image and sexual behavior, gender identity, sense of security and independence, empathetic and moral responses, self-acceptance, self-esteem, and self-control (Lamb & Lewis, 2012; Leidy, Schofield, & Parke, 2012). What's more, when fathers are involved in children's lives, consistently positive outcomes can be seen, including greater internal locus of control, more empathy, fewer sex stereotypes (Pruett, 1985; Radin, 1994), greater gender flexibility, resilient self-confidence, and advanced development (Pruett, 1985).

Nurturant fathering—where emotional availability, love, care, comfort, support, and concern mark what fathers do (Rohner, 1998)—is a special kind of way that fathering men relate to and approach their children. The benefits of involved fathers extend to adolescent youth who have social or fictive fathers in their lives, including more frequent attendance at religious worship service and more engagement in constructive extracurricular activities (Zagame, 2022). Later, adolescents tend to form committed relationships with romantic partners (Zagame). Here, a social father refers to an adult male who serves in a fathering role and is not connected romantically to a child's mother, including grandfather, uncle, cousin, coach, teacher, pastor, and so on. When we consider engagement—or interaction—there are a lot of benefits to fathers interacting with kids, including development of self-control and self-esteem (Amato, 1987). For fathers, being more available or accessible also seems to shape who they are—positively! For fathers with adolescent children, dads reported being more accepting of their kids when they were more available to them (Almeida & Galambos, 1991).

Among Black fathers, parental satisfaction tends to support cognitive development (Jayakody & Kalil, 2002) and behavioral development in their preschool-aged children (Black et al., 1999). Beyond the reproduction of normative gender roles, racialized structures in society generally reify what parenting is like for men of color. Black men, who have long faced the destructive effects of anti-Black hatred and been shaped by the complex web of structural racism, have been portrayed as absent fathers. In a June 2022 interview with Christina Caron of the *The New York Times* (2022), Michael Hannon, associate professor of counseling at Montclair State University in Montclair, New Jersey, notes that Black men have a "much more nuanced, rich and complex set of experiences" as fathers, including cultural pressure to protect and provide for their families.

While race, gender, and more have shaped parenting roles, what seems to be paramount for child development is an adult care-taker with consistent relational and emotional connections to raise them (Silverstein & Auerbach, 1999). Indeed, emotional stability and relational predictability are key to positive adjustment in children (Silverstein & Auerbach. 1999). From these findings, the message is that parents are important, but parenting as caregiving can be done by an adult of intersecting gender and racial identities, gender expression, and sexual orientation regardless of biological connection to children.

Parent Involvement in Education and Children's Experiences as Students: Moving from Conventional Measures to a More Complete Explanation of Paths to/in Graduate School

Parental effects extend far in children's lives, including educational attainment (Gordon, 2017; Wigfield et al., 2015). Overall, parent involvement in education has been associated with children's success (Kapaona & Ono, 2026), motivation, academic adjustment, and social and emotional adjustment (Barger et al., 2019). In fact, parents who encourage academic success see children with higher academic achievement (Milne & Plourde, 2006), intrinsic motivation (Ginsburg & Bronstein, 1998), autonomy and positive beliefs about potential (Pomerantz et al., 2007), and social and emotional capital (Jacobs, 2023). Further, parents shape student perceptions about English and math (Frome & Eccles, 1998). In college, strong parental social support predicts academic performance as measured by GPA (Cutrona et al., 1994), and parental support is central to outcomes for first-generation college students (LeBouef & Dworkin, 2021; Ricks & Warren, 2021) and first-generation college students of color (Adams & McBrayer, 2020). For Black college students, family values encourage children to go to school and families offer financial, moral, and social support, all of which shapes motivation to achieve (Herndon & Hirt, 2004). Among Mexican-origin adolescents, stronger agreement with positive parenting of mothers tends to be associated with better academic performance (Wen et al., 2022). For Latina mothers, advancing educational equity and being involved in their children's lives as students in school centers their work to challenge traditional gender roles and reify values that elevate education (Velazquez, 2017).

Parental involvement in education happens in many contexts but can broadly be conceptualized as dedicating resources to children's scholastic and academic efforts (Grolnick & Slowiaczek, 1994). These contexts span school- and home-based parental involvement and tend to manifest in diverse forms, including involvement as academic socialization for children. School-based participation may be measured on multiple dimensions, including participating in school meetings or events, communicating with a teacher or counselor, visiting a school classroom, or volunteering in a school organization or event. When parents participate at school, children's academic adjustment increases, although this effect tends to wane over time and decreases through high school (Barger et al., 2019). In the home—where expectations, communication, and support tend to be reproduced—parental participation may range from inquiries or conversations about schoolwork, homework, and projects to class selection, program planning, and extracurricular activities. Further, parent participation in school at home may include direct involvement in homework and academic endeavors, including reading with them and taking trips to the library. Home-based involvement in the form of communication with children seems to be more important, in some contexts, as communication with the school (Jacobs, 2023).

HISTORICAL MEASURES AND CONVENTIONAL PREDICTORS OF GRADUATE STUDENT OUTCOMES

Fast-forward to graduate school, we know that several factors account for outcomes in postbaccalaureate programs, including more standard measures like undergraduate GPA, graduate GPA, graduate record examination (GRE) scores, and gateway and core graduate course completion. Less conventional factors seem to play a role in patterns of graduate student success, including prior and early academic and research experiences at the graduate level, affiliation with specific disciplines, institutional and program culture, experiences with mentors, peer environment and interaction, academic employment, and financial support. Even more personal experiences related to parent relationships and family socialization have been connected to student outcomes. But there have been few opportunities to understand connections between the role of parents and families on children who navigate the educational pipeline to graduate school. Indeed, an obsessive focus on academic measures like GPA and standardized test scores has demanded attention of both scholars and practitioners alike, and program factors have also been given a lot of attention by institutional officers, frontline faculty, and researchers.

From what we understand at the moment, the relationship between undergraduate GPA and GRE scores and graduate program outcomes seems to be mixed. Overall, undergraduate GPA and GRE scores tend to be associated with general success in graduate school. For example, undergraduate GPA predicts biochemistry and biophysics PhD program completion (Mendoza-Sanchez et al., 2022) but does not appear to broadly predict PhD program completion (Lovitts & Nelson, 2000). But undergraduate GPA's effect on graduate student outcomes seems to be mitigated by an intervening variable. In fact, undergraduate GPA tends to be used by programs/institutions to set the levels/amount of funding (which we know affects doctoral program completion and more) to incoming graduate students and, as such, seems to have more of an indirect effect on outcomes in graduate school—specifically, persistence (Attiyeh, 1999). While undergraduate GPA has been connected to outcomes of graduate study, findings that point to no effect (Lunneborg & Lunneborg, 1973) across a diverse range of social, behavioral, and applied science fields (Zwick & Braun, 1988) confound what we know.

Generally speaking, graduate and professional school admission standardized test scores predict academic performance. The test with content connected to the discipline most strongly predicts success, including first-year and cumulative graduate GPA, comprehensive or qualifying exam scores, research productivity and citation counts, and more (Kuncel & Hezlett, 2007). As an illustration, GRE quantitative scores relate to doctoral social work program completion (Johnson-Motoyama et al., 2014). In addition, GRE verbal scores and undergraduate GPA have been correlated to graduate GPA in doctoral social work programs (Johnson-Motoyama et al.). While GRE scores have been associated with graduate school outcomes, they have been found to have little to no effect on doctoral program completion (Lunneborg & Lunneborg, 1973; Mendoza-Sanchez et al., 2022; Zwick & Braun, 1988). When GRE scores may be related to outcomes, specific GRE tests may have differential effects on students. For instance, GRE verbal—but not GRE quantitative—predicts mathematic and mechanical engineering PhD persistence (Attiyeh, 1999). More generally, GRE quantitative scores relate to time to degree in PhD programs (Wao & Onwuegbuzie, 2011).

Graduate GPA, by contrast, can be seen as a factor that predicts timely and actual graduate degree program completion (Johnson-Motoyama et al., 2014; Lunneborg & Lunneborg, 1973; Malone et al., 2004; Sheridan & Pyke, 1994). For instance, first-year graduate academic performance predicts later success in psychology PhD programs (Lunneborg & Lunneborg). Prior and early academic experiences in graduate programs—for example, master's degree program completion, completion of a master's thesis, gateway and core program course completion—tend to be related to doctoral completion in computer science (Cox et al., 2009) and educational administration (Malone et al., 2004). Graduate GPA has also been associated with time to degree completion—specifically, reductions in delays to time to degree are related to higher graduate GPA for master's students (Sheridan & Pyke, 1994; Wao & Onwuegbuzie, 2011).

In addition to undergraduate and graduate academic performance and standardized test scores for graduate admission, additional factors have been found to reduce time to complete a degree in graduate school: funding support, being in a humanities field (master's degree), being in a natural science field (doctoral degree) (Sheridan & Pyke, 1994), work and social contacts (for women), conference attendance and early dissertation research conceptualization (van de Schoot et al., 2013). When considering a different but related metric—timely dissertation submission in PhD programs—being in a science field, receiving research funding support, younger age at entry, and holding an honors undergraduate degree all appear to help (Wright & Cochrane, 2000). Several measures related to dissertations and faculty supervision in the dissertation research process shape time to degree completion, including an earlier start and consistent topic to dissertation research in the course of a program, frequent meetings with a supervisor or chair, and collaborating with a supervisor or chair on conference papers (Seagram et al., 1998) Similarly, a plan to focus on a research career at the start of a joint MD-PhD program is associated with a lower likelihood of attrition. In addition to research funding support, PhD program withdrawal seems to be associated with receiving no financial support (Lovitts & Nelson, 2000).

A range of more nuanced programmatic factors shape doctoral program completion, including institutional and/or program culture and quality (Lovitts & Nelson, 2000) and specific fields—for example, being in the sciences predicts program completion (Wright & Cochrane, 2000) or having experienced mentors and academic employment have been found to be factors that predict successful biomedical PhD program completion (Benzon et al., 2020). Proximity to peers—quite literally, sharing an office with students—seems to be associated with PhD program completion (Lovitts & Nelson, 2000). More generally, both institutional or program and individual factors—including department size, proportion of female students, dissertation advising structure, student academic preparation, and student enrollment status—appear to affect time to degree (Wao & Onwuegbuzie, 2011).

Racialized and Gendered Structures Shape Graduate Student Experiences and Outcomes

Beyond conventional measures cited as important to graduate schools lie intersecting stories of what matters to student experiences and outcomes in graduate education, particularly for students of color who have been historically excluded from these degree programs. In US institutions of higher education, racialized and gendered institutional structures explain gaps in enrollment and academic outcomes for women and people of color in education, and this pattern extends to master's and doctoral programs.

For example, women students and historically underrepresented students in STEM PhD programs at University of California, Berkeley were less frequently encouraged to publish research work (Mendoza-Denton et al., 2017). Still at Berkeley, in math, physical science, electrical engineering, and computer science, women and historically underrepresented students reported lower rates of collaboration with supervisors for manuscript preparation (Seagram et al., 1998) and manuscript submission (Mendoza-Denton et al.). These collaborative activities represent opportunities for faculty mentoring, which contribute to aspirational goals and preparatory development for the PhD (DeAngelo, 2010) and are key measures of scholarly productivity and early career faculty success. In fact, Black female graduate students report that mentoring from Black female professors supports navigating graduate-level work (Williams et al., 2005).

For women in PhD programs, delays in time to complete degrees have been associated with a change in marital status and opportunities to establish international contacts from their research supervisor (van de Schoot et al., 2013). Consequently, even though some research indicates gender is not associated with PhD program completion (Sheridan & Pyke, 1994; Wright & Cochrane, 2000) and MD-only (in a MD-PhD program) program completion (Jeffe et al., 2014), women tend to have lower PhD program completion rates across disciplines (King, 2008) and complete fewer PhD programs in natural sciences and engineering than men (Baker, 1998). In the natural sciences, social science, and humanities, women tend to report lower rates of overall and quality of supervision satisfaction and perceptions of gender affecting degree progress than men in doctoral programs (Seagram et al., 1998). Historically, women who are mothers have been offered less financial support in their first year in psychology compared to men (Lunneborg & Lunneborg, 1973). Knowing that women benefit from social networks and resources in first professional-degree programs (Perna, 2004), patterns that point to less financial support and lower supervision satisfaction among women are particularly distressing.

When we consider the breadth and depth of these conventional measures of graduate student experiences and outcomes, we see a context that lacks any real consideration for what happens outside the confines of the program and campus. Indeed, very few traditional metrics of what shapes graduate students can be connected to who they are in the contexts of their personal lives or backgrounds, including their parents and families. Once in graduate school, more personal experiences have been connected to graduate student outcomes. While parents tend to be less involved in the lives of their adult children, many still tend to be involved in the lives of children who are in graduate school. For first-generation college students, parents generally offer forms of material, financial, and emotional support, including encouragement and visits to campus—and all of this support has been central to their success (Capannola & Johnson, 2020).

Among Black students, nurturant fathering has been associated with higher levels of graduate school adjustment (Davis, 2012), and father involvement of Black woman shaped their interest in doctoral studies and careers in mathematics (Borum & Walker, 2011). For Black doctoral students, extended and fictive family members—communities of caregivers—tend to form networks of support (McCallum, 2016). Among Black female PhD students, family support—including encouragement, financial help, meal preparation, and childcare—tend to be important to academic success, among other factors such as involvement with community service (Loque, 1999). More broadly, for graduate students of color and first-generation graduate students, families function as connective and supportive forces (Walsh et al., 2023) that extend over time and include material and mental health support among a range of forms of support. Further, women of color graduate students use familial capital to call on values promoting education, connect graduate school aspirations to historical obligations with family, and frame hope for future generations as a reason to go to school (McCoy & Winkle-Wagner, 2022). For Latinx students, in particular, family involvement in undergraduate education experiences facilitates the graduate school application process in the biomedical sciences (Monarrez et al., 2022).

Focusing on Parents and Families in the Path to Graduate School for Students of Color

Taken together, the deeply personal stories and rich life histories that graduate students of color and first-generation graduate students shared in this project allow us to see what contributed to who they are today, and this picture helps us understand what's important to student success. We learn that families and parents play a central role in how children navigate educational institutions to complete advanced degree programs. The specific familial and parental effects on children who earn graduate degrees tie into cultural knowledge, beliefs, and values and penetrate multiple dimensions of their lives, including personal identities, professional interests, and community service and campus involvement. As students moved through secondary and postsecondary education, peers, mentors, and faculty played an increasingly critical role, but what we see is that parental involvement in education, parental relationships with children, and familial connections tended to persist over time and continue to be meaningful for the promotion to graduate school.

Affirming the role of families in education and normalizing relationships that children have with their parents over the life course, this work found that family socialization and parent involvement in education impact children on their paths to graduate school. Specifically, what this project found helps us understand that families and parents shape children on the educational pipeline to postbaccalaureate study through an intricate system to internalize values focused on education and hard work and a set of beliefs that connected children to broader forces in the family, at school, and in society. Indeed, families tended to reproduce values that center family unity and spirituality, recognize and honor familial and ancestral sacrifices, and facilitate individual agency and personal autonomy at a young age. Driven to contribute to larger commitments in life and influence social change, these beliefs in keeping family members together and helping each other, understanding family as generational, and being guided by spirituality strengthened skills to manage uneven parent involvement in education and balanced sometimes strained but still close parent-child relationships that accompanied graduate student work in education. In most cases, graduate students felt that they had the resources to accomplish what they had set out to do in education and life.

The specific mechanisms at work in the context of these families leverage generational cultural knowledge, beliefs, values, and actions that support children who journey from preschool to graduate school. In the immediate and extended family unit, parents tend to lead socialization—through a mix of direct messaging, modeling, and encouraging—into a system that both reifies and resists gendered roles and challenges racialized structures; reproduces values that promote education, hard work, family unity, and spirituality; supports personal autonomy in early life; recognizes sacrifices of parents and family members; and encourages emotionally close but generally physically distant parent-child relationships later in life.

Primarily by home-based involvement in education, parents generally engaged in a support role for children's education. From elementary school to high school, many parents of graduate students offered emotional and material support to children in the forms of homework and assignment help, regular check-ins and consistent encouragement, and affirmations of academic self-image and identity as a student. For a small group, school-based parent involvement in parent-teacher conferences, participation in school events, and volunteering in the classroom supported children in their precollege educational journey. For some, anti-immigrant positions at school, institutional barriers to language accommodations, and little consideration for working-class job schedules that prevented daytime participation in school events meant that parents could not directly participate in school and children had to go it alone—shaping more independence and agency. Later, as undergraduate and graduate students, most parents supported students through encouragement and praise.

These stories are infinitely important on their own, but institutionally what we learn from this work can continue to build on the unique experiences and strengths to enhance connections between personal and familial backgrounds of students of color and first-generation students. As efforts to enhance undergraduate and graduate student success and completion continue to evolve, learning about the family lives of first-generation students and students of color may help shift institutional and program approaches with students. Indeed, the findings from this work can be used to more closely integrate parents, families, and lived experiences of students into the curriculum, culminating projects, and programming. At the very least, understanding what led students to graduate school can include curricular and co-curricular programs that honor their familial experiences, parental relationships, and cultural values. Ultimately, building program cultures around who students are and what they bring to campus advances inclusive and equitable contexts where students from diverse backgrounds can thrive in the constellation of campuses whose mission includes training scholars, researchers, thinkers, and leaders in a broad range of professions.

Approach to Learning from Graduate Students about Parental Relationships and Family Ties in Their Lives

Centering families, parents, and children in a project that asks students of color and first-generation students in graduate school to reflect on what has shaped their educational experiences since early childhood requires a unique approach. First, a recognition of primary socialization in the family in early life elevates the roles of parents in child development. Granted, peers, teachers, media figures, and others impact child, adolescent and emerging adult development—but this approach situates families at the center (Kalmuss & Seltzer, 1989). Second, given that the educational pipeline spans the course of multiple development stages, life transitions need to be accounted for—and a life course perspective (Roy & Settersten, 2022) helps to focus on these moments and their significance for students of color and first-generation students. Finally, using a community cultural wealth framework (Yosso, 2006) directs us away from deficit-driven explanations of student experiences and outcomes and toward cultural strengths of students of color and their families. With a specific focus on familial capital, community cultural wealth allows us to reframe what students learn from their upbringing as assets that they take with them into graduate school.

The work in this book is intended to support graduate students and those who serve in caretaking roles for them—whether at home or on campus. Knowing what it's like to be supported by a parent who stands behind their children during graduate school—getting up before dawn to put food on the table, staying up overnight to offer support when needed, helping to make decisions about career, and offering advice about friendships and social networks—I'm so happy to bring all of this with me into this project. And at a time of change in both families and graduate education in US colleges and universities, exploring parent relationship effects on adult children who are students in postbaccalaureate programs is timely. Given how central families are to child development, more personal and intimate stories related to parental and familial influences on children who grow up to become graduate students will help us form a more complete understanding of how best to offer student support in advanced and terminal degree programs. As program and institutional efforts to support students from diverse backgrounds who navigate academic institutions continue to evolve, learning from personal stories about family and fathering offers a more holistic approach in an ever-changing sector in American higher education.

Listening to graduate students of color discuss their experiences in families and schools redirects institutional and program discourse on what shapes student success and presents counterperspectives for faculty, staff, and administrators whose work tends to only peripherally intersect with families. And that's what this work is all about—spotlighting familial and parental experiences of students of color and supporting students of color and those who serve in roles that guide their growth at home and on campus. At a time of immense need to advance outcomes for students of color in graduate education in US colleges and universities, exploring how families affect children as students moves beyond conventional measures by adding new perspectives to the complexity of educational outcomes. Given how central parents are to educational development in children, how empirical research has tended to frame educational involvement of families as peripheral, *and* how students of color have historically received less attention in the empirical literature, more personal and intimate accounts about how parents constructively and complexly impact children illuminates the goodness in these stories, counters historical images and narratives imposed with a deficit perspective (McCallum, 2016), and offers opportunities for institutional and program transformation through an asset-based lens.

A Fluid Methodological Lens: Applying a Grounded Theory Design in the Context of the Project

My approach to the project that informs this book is methodologically qualitative, using a grounded theory research tradition. As a research tradition, grounded theory aligns well with the purpose of this study, which explores how parents and families shape graduate students over the life course. As grounded theory explores relationships between factors and a set of experiences, outcomes, and so on, the lens focuses work in the project on patterns in familial relationships and parental contributions to children's education. Indeed, grounded theory offers a specific way to hone in on the interrelated parts of broader actions or systems. In a grounded theory approach, however, methodological flexibility tends to be common and allows for more discretion in directions of data collection and analysis (Charmaz, 2006). With grounded theory, I worked recursively to interview-analyze-reinterview-analyze/reanalyze—all of which aided in molding an explanation of multiple intersecting and moving parts of a model to understand how families impact children who grow up and go on to complete graduate degree programs. This iterative series of research methods followed a grounded theory approach to concurrent data collection and analysis (Birks & Mills, 2011) to support an emerging interpretation of what's happening in the patterns noted during interviews and observed in early thematic analysis.

Grounded theory offers a broad framework to understand patterns that shape graduate students over the life course while allowing me to explore nuanced details of relationships in families. From the start, I intuitively felt a need to connect directly with participants whose lives are complex and whose experiences are unique and worth cotelling in deep and profound ways. With grounded theory, an open-ended approach to interviewing is a means to learn from participants about relational patterns in families and intimately understand how parents influence children from an early age through early adulthood. The subtle intricacies of graduate student work and family life require a sensitive and empathetic approach—something that social interaction and a live (even if virtual) human connection helps to build. What is helpful, too, is a fluid methodology that relies on a qualitative research approach to dive into the depths of human experiences in the social worlds of education and family in settings as diverse as virtual and physical spaces in academic institutions and family homes. Exploring how parents and their adult children communicate, relate, and live together in often vastly different social and professional spheres begs for a framework that is flexible, dynamic, and connective.

Data Sources and Research Sample: A Mixed Sampling Strategy for Participant Recruitment and Selection

Using a reflexive research practice, I situated myself in the context of design and implementation of the study with intentionality and humility. This approach is both practical—a matter of self-awareness and social awareness—and strategic—helping me to make sense of, or co-interpret and co-narrate, what participants shared with me. Using a grounded theory design, I employed a mixed purposeful sampling strategy to invite graduate students to participate in a single interview. With criterion, convenience, and snowball sampling, I used a combination of professional contacts and LinkedIn to recruit participants. Between March and June 2023, I interviewed thirty-four graduate students from a diverse range of institutions and programs. With a subset of six graduate students who participated in an interview, I followed up and invited them to a second interview. In total, I completed forty interviews with the thirty-four graduate students.

Following the first half of interviews, I updated my mixed sampling strategy to include theoretical sampling, which grounded theory tends to employ to follow patterns emerging in early data collection and analysis and narrow the criteria used to recruit and select participants. While the first interviews focused on a range of topics, including backgrounds, family relationships, parenting involvement in education, and more, the second interviews explored patterns that emerged in initial data analysis and went into more depth in subthematic categories from analytical work. With the focus of this second half of interviews and second/follow-up interviews, both theoretical and snowball sampling directed me to respond to email message referrals from current participants and LinkedIn recruitment.

In what follows, you can see the identities and institutional and program affiliations of students with whom I connected. In all cases, participant names and names of colleges, universities, and programs have been concealed by pseudonyms to protect participant confidentiality. Broader descriptions of regional locations where participants lived and/or went to school have been included to widen the protective circle of confidentiality. Further, academic disciplines, undergraduate majors, and graduate degree programs have been broadened to the highest level or overarching/umbrella fields to limit personally identifiable information about participants. Personal identities, including racial and/or ethnic identity, gender identity and expression, sexual orientation, immigration experience, college generation, family and marital status, and more have been reported as participants shared them with me.

As a group, the majority of graduate students who participated in interviews are first-generation and women students of color from universities in the Western and Southeastern US. A plurality of participants identified as cisgender heterosexual Latinx or Black women. A smaller group identified as Latinx or white cisgender or questioning or gay women, and a still smaller group identified as white cisgender or gay men. Most participants identified master's programs (56 percent) as their degree type, while just under half of participants (44 percent) affiliated with a doctoral-degree program. In general, participants identified graduate programs in public institutions, with a mix of public master's-granting Hispanic-serving institutions (HSIs) and public doctoral-granting, high-research activity universities. In the case of one participant, the institutional affiliation included a private not-for-profit high-research activity doctoral-granting historically Black college and university (HBCU). The vast majority of participants identified biological parents in their lives, including their mother and/or father, while several included extended family members as parenting figures. Overall, mothers and fathers referred to biological parents, and in several cases grandparents, aunts or uncles, older sisters or brothers, and mentors served in fathering roles. While most participants reported not having children themselves, a few shared their parenting roles and stories about their kids. Tables I.1–I.6, which follow, present more detailed numeric figures about participants.

DATA COLLECTION AND ANALYSIS: INTERVIEWING FOLLOWED BY CONSTANT-COMPARATIVE THEMATIC PATTERNING

With grounded theory, interviewing facilitated in-depth, semistructured conversations with graduate students around patterns that the empirical literature review identified as meaningful to graduate student development and family involvement in education. Engaging in candid discussions in the span of an hour-or-so-long interview done virtually on Zoom, we covered a variety of topics with guiding questions that can be categorized as follows:

- Personal identities, including racial and ethnic identity, gender identity, gender expression, sexual orientation, first-generation college student experience, immigrant experience, native language, and more

- Family background, family life, and relationships, including parental figures and family structure; care work and family processes; family philosophies, beliefs, and values; and cultural rituals and family celebrations; and racialized and gendered norms and structures in the family, community, and campus

- Dimensions of parent involvement in life, including relationship quality, closeness, care, love, and warmth; role identities and social awareness; and involvement, time, and change

- Parent involvement in education, including elementary and secondary school involvement—general impressions, parental educational experience; academic involvement and extracurricular involvement in school; college access and college going—undergraduate and graduate student transitions; academic potential and academic attachment; peer attachment and peer-peer interaction; student-faculty interaction; and cultural validation

After the first half of interviews had been completed, I engaged in an initial phase of the analytical process, which focused on processing Zoom auto-transcribed files and setting up a list of codes from early segments of block quotes. Using ATLAS.ti, a qualitative data analysis software program, I segmented and coded chunked text and clustered initial themes from code families.

While early data analysis with the first half of interviews generated segmented and coded patterns, the second half of interview and follow-up/second interviews moved me in a direction consistent with grounded theory's constant-comparative method (Glaser & Strauss, 1967). In this latter analytical phase, I focused on the conceptual literature related to primary socialization, life course perspective, and community cultural wealth to guide coding and pattern finding across transcribed data files. Blending concepts from the following sources, I cogenerated and applied codes meaningfully connected to what we know from current research, the lives of grad students with whom I spoke, and my own life as a grad student and dad. The sources included

- Participant experiential knowledge
- Empirical literature in parent involvement in education and educational outcomes of undergraduate and graduate students
- Researcher observations (via jottings)
- Analytical memos
- Participant feedback (via second interviews)

In ATLAS.ti, code families and early thematic categories from data analysis with the first set of interviews guided the next set of interviews—which included first interviews of the second half of participants and follow-up/second interviews with a subset of participants. Specifically, updated interview questions and follow-up questions focused conversations on emerging patterns in the data, which built on existing literature that drove questions in the first set of interviews and informed code development. In the final phase of data analysis that revolved around Zoom auto-transcribed data files from this second half of participants, work centered on synthesizing ideas across codes in transcribed interview data files, applying theory to code families and themes, and moving themes into an explanatory model. Here, I formed code groups and thematically organized categories—forming the plot to the story conarrated by participants and me in this book.

Table I.1. Participants by Name (Pseudonym), Identities, and Graduate/Undergraduate Degree Programs/Affiliations

Name	Identities	Graduate Program/Institutional Affiliation	Undergraduate Degree/Institutional Affiliation
1 Ping	First-generation straight Chinese man	Doctoral program in applied humanities at a public doctoral-granting, high-research activity university in the Southeastern US	Baccalaureate degree from a university in China
2 Josefina	First-generation straight Chicana woman with children	Doctoral program in applied humanities at a public master's-granting HSI in the Western US	Baccalaureate degree from a public master's-granting HSI in the Western US
3 Brianna	First-generation African American woman	Doctoral program in applied humanities from a private not-for-profit high-research activity doctoral-granting HBCU in the Mid-Atlantic region of the US	Baccalaureate degree from a private not-for-profit HBCU baccalaureate college in the Southeast
4 Zelma	First-generation cis-hetero Indigenous Palestinian and Lebanese woman who is married with children	Doctoral program in applied humanities at a public master's-granting HSI in the Western US	Baccalaureate degree from a public master's-granting HSI in the Western US
5 Zeke	First-generation married cisgender gay white male	Master's degree program in the applied sciences at a public masters-granting HSI in the Western US	Baccalaureate degree in applied sciences from a public master's-granting HSI in the Western US

Name	Identities	Graduate Program/Institutional Affiliation	Undergraduate Degree/Institutional Affiliation
6 Stella	First-generation African American who identifies ethnically as Nigerian, Ghanaian, and Caribbean, uses gender pronouns she/her/hers, and is straight but exploring her sexual orientation	Master's degree program in the applied sciences at a public master's-granting HSI in the Western US	Baccalaureate degree in applied sciences from a public master's-granting HSI in the Western US
7 Jenna	First-generation Filipina heterosexual female	Master's degree program in the applied sciences from a public master's-granting HSI in the Western US	Baccalaureate degree in applied sciences from a public master's-granting HSI in the Western US
8 Leonardo	First-generation straight Mexican American male who is married with a child	Doctoral program in applied humanities from a public master's-granting HSI in the Western US	Baccalaureate degree in the social sciences from a public master's-granting HSI in the Western US
9 Angela	First-generation African American female who identifies ethnically as Nigerian	Master's degree program in applied humanities at a public doctoral-granting, high-research activity university in the Southeastern US	Baccalaureate degree in the behavioral sciences from a public master's-granting university in the Northeastern US
10 Kayla	First-generation cisgender African American female who is married with two children	Doctoral program in an applied humanities field at a private not-for-profit master's-granting HSI in the Northeast US	Baccalaureate degree from a public, high-research activity, doctoral-granting university in the Northeast US

continued on next page

Table I.1. Continued.

Name	Identities	Graduate Program/Institutional Affiliation	Undergraduate Degree/Institutional Affiliation
11 Eugenio	First-generation heterosexual married Latinx male who identifies as Oaxacan from an Indigenous Mexican background	Master's degree in applied humanities from a private, not-for-profit, doctoral-granting, high-research activity, HSI in the West	Baccalaureate degree a public master's-granting HSI in the West
12 Sasha	Pansexual white woman	Doctoral program in a liberal arts field at a public, very high-research activity, doctoral-granting university in the Western US	Baccalaureate degree in a liberal art field from a private, not-for-profit, very high-research activity, doctoral-granting university in the Southern US
13 Hector	Cisgender heterosexual married male who identifies as a person of color with multiracial and multiethnic identities of Mexican, Filipino, Italian, and Native American	Doctoral program in applied humanities from a public master's-granting HSI in the Western US	Master's degree in social sciences from a private, not-for-profit, very high-research activity, doctoral-granting university in the Western US; and a baccalaureate degree in the social sciences from a public master's-granting HSI in the Western US
14 Sharon	First-generation heterosexual female who is married with children	Doctoral program in applied humanities from a public master's-granting HSI in the Western US	Baccalaureate degree in the social sciences from a public, very high-research activity, doctoral-granting university in the Western US

Name	Identities	Graduate Program/Institutional Affiliation	Undergraduate Degree/Institutional Affiliation
15 Andres	First-generation able-bodied cis-hetero male who identifies as Mexican, specifically Mexicah and Tepehuani	Doctoral program in applied humanities from a public master's-granting HSI in the Western US	Baccalaureate degree in liberal studies from a public master's-granting HSI in the Western US
16 Jeremy	First-generation straight white and Italian cisgender male	Master's degree in applied humanities from a public doctoral-granting, high-research activity university in the Southeast	Baccalaureate degree in social sciences from a public doctoral-granting, high-research activity university in the Southeast
17 Holly	Cisgender heterosexual white woman who identifies ethnically as Russian and is married with a daughter	Doctoral program in applied humanities from a public master's-granting HSI in the Western US	Baccalaureate degree in applied humanities from a university in Russia
18 Eileen	Heterosexual married white female	Master's degree in applied humanities from a public doctoral-granting, high-research activity university in the Southeast	Baccalaureate degree in behavioral sciences from a public doctoral-granting, high-research activity university in the Southeast
19 Tanya	First-generation heterosexual African American woman	Master's degree in applied humanities from a public doctoral-granting, high-research activity university in the Southeast	Baccalaureate degree in social sciences from a public doctoral-granting, high-research activity university in the Southeast

continued on next page

Table I.1. Continued.

Name	Identities	Graduate Program/Institutional Affiliation	Undergraduate Degree/Institutional Affiliation
20 Karina	Heterosexual Latina woman who identifies as half Guatemalan and half Mexican	Master's program at a public master's-granting HSI in the Western US	Baccalaureate degree in liberal studies from a public master's-granting HSI in the Western US
21 Maria	First-generation LGBTQ-identified Armenian woman (whose family legally identifies as white) who immigrated from Iran and identifies culturally as Middle Eastern and Armenian	Master's program in applied humanities from a public master's-granting HSI in the Western US	Baccalaureate degree in art from a public master's-granting HSI in the Western US
22 Juan	Man whose dad was from Mexico	Master's program from a public master's-granting HSI in the Western US	Baccalaureate degree from a public master's-granting HSI in the Western US
23 Susan	White and Latina cis-heterosexual female who identifies as Jewish and is married with children	Doctoral program in applied humanities from a public doctoral-granting, very high-research activity HSI in the Southwest US	Baccalaureate degree in liberal arts and social sciences from a private, not-for-profit doctoral-granting, high-research activity university in the Southwest US
24 Winona	First-generation bisexual Asian American who uses she/her gender pronouns and identifies as Chinese and Vietnamese	Master's program in applied sciences from a public master's-granting HSI in the Western US	Baccalaureate degree in applied sciences from a public master's-granting HSI in the Western US

Name	Identities	Graduate Program/Institutional Affiliation	Undergraduate Degree/Institutional Affiliation
25 Hua	Chinese female	Doctoral program in applied sciences from a public very high-research activity, doctoral granting university in the Southeast	Baccalaureate degree in applied sciences from a public very high-research activity, doctoral granting university in the Southeast
26 Edith	First-generation Korean female who uses she/her gender pronouns and is married with a child	Master's program in applied humanities from a public master's-granting HSI in the Western US	Baccalaureate degree in liberal arts and social sciences from a public master's-granting HSI in the Western US
27 Jasmine	First-generation heterosexual Hispanic female	Master's program in applied humanities at a private, not-for-profit, doctoral-granting, high-research activity, HSI university in the Western US	Baccalaureate degree in applied humanities from a public master's-granting Hispanic-serving institution (HSI) university in the Western US
28 Jaime	First-generation Vietnamese American female	Master's program in applied sciences from a public master's-granting HSI in the Western US	Baccalaureate degree in applied sciences from a public master's-granting HSI in the Western US
29 Gail	First-generation straight white female	Master's program in applied sciences from a public master's-granting HSI in the Western US	Baccalaureate degree in applied sciences from a public master's-granting HSI in the Western US
30 Natasha	Straight white female	Master's program in applied sciences from a public master's-granting HSI in the Western US	Baccalaureate degree in applied sciences from a public master's-granting HSI in the Western US

continued on next page

Table I.1. Continued.

Name	Identities	Graduate Program/Institutional Affiliation	Undergraduate Degree/Institutional Affiliation
31 Beatrice	Heterosexual female who identifies as white and Mexican	Doctoral program in applied sciences from a public, very high-research activity, doctoral-granting university in the Mountain West	Baccalaureate degree in applied sciences from a public, very-high research activity doctoral-granting university in the Mountain West
32 Jessica	White female	Master's program in applied sciences from a public master's-granting HSI in the Western US	Baccalaureate degree in applied sciences from a public master's-granting HSI in the Western US
33 Kaitlyn	First-generation cisgender straight Latina	Master's program in applied sciences from a public master's-granting HSI university in the Western US	Baccalaureate degree in applied sciences from a public master's-granting HSI in the Western US
34 Liza	Cisgender bisexual Latina woman	Doctoral program in applied humanities from a public master's-granting HSI in the Western US	Baccalaureate degree in applied sciences from a public master's-granting HSI in the Western US

Table I.2. Sex of Participants

	n	%
Female	23	6867.65
Male	8	23.5324
Unsure	1	2.943
Unknown	2	5.886

Table I.3. Racial/Ethnic Identity of Participants

	n	%
African American/African American and Nigerian/American of African Descent	5	14.71
Asian American/Chinese/Filipina/Korean/Vietnamese American	6	17.65
Armenian	1	2.94
Chicana/Hispanic/Latina/Latinx/Mexican American	8	23.53
Indigenous Palestinian	1	2.94
Multi-Ethnic	3	8.82
White	8	23.53
Unknown	2	5.88

Table I.4. Sexual Orientation of Participants

	n	%
Straight/Heterosexual	23	67.65
Bisexual	2	5.88
Pansexual	1	2.94
Gay	1	2.94
LBGTQ	1	2.94
Unsure	1	2.94
Unknown	5	14.71

Table I.5. Generational College Student Status of Participants

	n	%
First generation	20	58.82
Continuing generation	13	38.24
Unknown	1	2.94

Table I.6. Graduate Degree Program Type of Participants

	n	%
Master's degree program	19	55.88
Doctoral degree program	15	44.12

Chapter 1

Parenting Roles, Early Experiences in Families, and Resistance to Gender Norms for Children

While traditional parenting gender roles persist today, both mothers and fathers share a lot more of the responsibilities at work and home that each did not take on beforehand. Mothers work outside the home and contribute to household income, while fathers spend more time with kids, are far more involved, and center more of their identity on parenting than in decades past. However, parents tend to feel a lot more stress as they balance demands of families and jobs—56 percent of mothers who work and half of fathers who work say they feel stressed with these responsibilities (Pew Research Center, 2013). Driven by a trend toward role convergence, a greater percentage of mothers focus on work and fathers report feeling pressure to bring in money. The result, in part, seems to be that many parents feel squeezed between roles in their careers and with children. The COVID-19 pandemic, changes in the workplace, and evolving social expectations for gender and parenting all contribute to parental experiences.

For most graduate students, parental roles centered on what Liza, who identifies as a cisgender bisexual Latina woman, described when she shared her definition of parents: "[A] parent, I think is just a, a figure who shapes and guides someone through life." Liza clarified that parents range from biological to chosen as she elaborated: "From a biological perspective you have parents, but then you also have figures who are parent-like, you know, who step into roles to, to guide you and to impose their, their wisdom onto you." She concluded by arguing that parents shape the essence of who you are—"They're just figures in your life that, that shape you." For Liza and many graduate students, these observations about parental contributions to their lives seemed to form foundational relational connections that persisted over the life course, reinforced family values, facilitated identities tied to families, and underscored strong needs to honor and give back to parents later in life. Indeed, parents seemed to be at the center of the reproduction of cultural knowledge, beliefs, and values that penetrated deep in to the development of graduate students and undergirded their paths on the educational pipeline.

Even as Liza focused on the general shape of a parent as a figure who shapes children, many graduate students described how gender permeated parenting and family life. Entangled in work, home, and school, gender regulated who parents and children were and how they behaved in the family. For mothers, fathers, and extended family members who served as parental figures, gender norms tended to regulate behavior, dress, and more from a very young age. Often intended to privilege fathers and enforced by both parents, these normative expectations directed what children should know, say, and do. For several graduate students, mothers mediated the effects of gender on women in the family with messages that thwarted efforts to reify gender hierarchies: independence from men and postponement or delay in marriage until later in adulthood and completion of education. These lessons grounded early and ongoing efforts by graduate students to resist gender norms. Indeed, resistance to gender norms followed many women graduate students, in particular, in their relationships and work on campus.

Overwhelmingly, graduate students tended to relate fathers with providing, revealing the gendered structures in families reflective of broader patterns in society. What is more, gender norms and gendered expectations in the family generally regulated fathering relationships with children. Even in cases where parental educational levels were lower, father figures still assumed a role of financial supporter, education promoter, motivational speaker, and guarantor of social mobility through education with either peripheral or indirect involvement in children's education—including grad school in some cases. For some, fathers and grandfathers were "pillars of strength" in the family, serving as a central, if gendered, figure in family life. When reflecting on relationship quality with fathers, gender seems to define time, availability, and accessibility for kids. Over the years, most graduate students shared how closeness tended to be elusive and time together limited or circumscribed by mutual interests or family rituals. Their pillar stature was more than just perceived strength from performative gender behavior; there was substance to what father figures did, according to what many shared with me: they provided materially, including breadwinning, kept extended families together across distance and time, and some served in a supporting care-taker role for kids and spouses or partners.

Understanding Parental Roles as Gendered Scripts in Families for Graduate Students

Citing cultural expectations, in part, Andres referred to his dad as the breadwinner and his mom as the homemaker in their family. He listed his parents' respective roles at home: "Dad, the breadwinner, Dad, the income maker, and all of that. And then mom, like the nurturer, the stay-at-home." Andres recalled the rigid expectations for gendered work at home: "The man is responsible for going to work, and bringing home the food, and, you know. So it's, it's like this, like this, you know this, kind of like this historical tradition of the man, the man goes off to provide and the woman stays home to be a, a, a wife, you know, a mom." These structures shaped what his mom did in life, as Andres remembered how his dad asked his mom to stay home after his middle brother was born. Here's more from Andres.

> So after my brother [middle brother] was born in 1978, my dad told my mom that she, she didn't have to work anymore. Because my dad went from working at a foundry factory. I, I'm not sure if you know what a foundry is, but it, but it's where they like melt, and like mold, and shape metal, right. So it's, it's probably one of the tough, toughest jobs you could imagine, right, is like melting metal and molding it, and eight, ten hours a day. So he left that job because he picked up a new job at the [factory] plant in [another city].

For his mom's part, Andres recalled how privileged he felt with homemade meals, "warm food on the stove," and more. In fact, as the family grew, Andres recalled his dad insisted his mom stay home and take care of the children.

Andres, a first-generation able-bodied cis-hetero male who identifies as Mexican, specifically Mexicah and Tepehuani, described this moment: "[O]nce my third sibling was born, then that's when my dad said, you know what, I think you should stay home and take care of the kids and I'll work more." Later, they moved to a new home, and his dad repeated what he had said earlier, as Andres narrates: "[W]hen they moved in 1978 to the house my dad told her that she needed to stop working so she could take care of the kids, because it, an extra expense was having a sitter watch the kids while they were both at work." Reflecting on his mom's role in the family, Andres spoke to how she did everything to ensure everyone had what they needed. In his words, Andres describe him mom lovingly: "So that's, that's how I knew my mom my entire life, you know, is being at home, and just whatever was needed, you know, that was related to that role as the mom, the wife, the homemaker, the caretaker."

Like Andres, Maria, a first-generation LGBTQ-identified Armenian woman who immigrated from Iran and identifies culturally as Middle Eastern and Armenian, connected her parents' roles in the home to cultural reproduction of values about gendered behavior. She detailed how the general pattern is that a person works, earns income, puts food on the table, and pays rent. Maria framed this sequence as survival: "I was raised in an Armenian household it was more of like the, the person who works and brings money to the table in order to, you know, survive when it comes to paying rent and buying food. And so yeah, just being the provider." Maria then offered a glimpse into how this pattern unfolded in her family, linking her dad to the provider. She said: "[Y]eah, so in my, in my household it was mainly like the male doing the, the work while the woman of the house, my, my mom in this case would stay home um and just do house, household, you know . . . work, and cleaning, and cooking, and taking care of the kids." Motherhood meant that Maria's mom was present in her life at home and school—where she volunteered in Maria's classroom. By contrast, for her dad's part, Maria concluded: "I think for me it means um, fatherhood means more of like the provider um, caretaker. Um, but yeah, that's how it is. It's like the men need to work, work, work pretty much."

Edith also referenced cultural norms for her parents' roles at home. Edith, a first-generation Korean female who uses she/her gender pronouns and is married with a child, elaborated on why her mom served as the caretaker and her dad the breadwinner and what it meant for her as a child.

So you know the, the norm, you know, and . . . it's that it's established through like culture, right? And so he, he was the breadwinner, and so the expectation was he . . . worked long hours. He brought in the most, the more money. So like if we needed anything, we would go to my dad like, hey? Could I have this? Can I get that? So like that was the not just gender norm, my, my mom was, you know, the caretaker, the, the one who fixed the meals. And so, so then, because I identified as, you know, female and the female role I took on the, okay, I, I have to be a caretaker. I have to like, I'll put that, help out with the meals, with the house chores.

Though their respective gender-regulated parenting roles, Edith observed how both her mom and dad worked to meet Edith's needs—she never lacked "security, love, you know, stability, everything that a child would need."

Similar to Edith, Eileen and Kaitlyn described their parents, respectively, in more traditional gender roles, too. Of her mom—the caretaker—and her dad—more the disciplinarian—Eileen said: "I think growing up . . . my mom took on more, more traditional, like . . . a woman's role in the household." Eileen, who identified as a heterosexual married white female, admitted that there was no explicit expectation for her mom to do more domestic work in the family, and her parents tended to be more progressive in their relational roles. Still, she admitted that her dad tended to be stereotypically overprotective and regulated some of her behavior. She said more: "I'd be spending time with, and where I was going, and what time I was gonna be home at night. And when I started um dating [my husband], just, you know lots of worries and questions about that. So I think in that sense that was kind of your typical like dad, dad norm role. Um, and, and he, I'd say he was more of the discipliner, too, uh, growing up."

As with Eileen, Kaitlyn knew her parents as traditional in their roles in the family. "I think uh because my, both, both my parents are very traditional," Kaitlyn, who identifies as a first-generation cisgender straight Latina, said. Details about how gender played out in Kaitlyn's home can be seen in what girls and boys did: "[G]irls would obviously clean the house, and the guys would kind of just be outside working." But Kaitlyn learned to work outdoors, too, given the need to pitch in and clean up a big front yard. Still, her dad was the breadwinner and provided. Kaitlyn described her dad this way.

> I think he grew up, his ideal I think kind of similar to what I described is really, you know that breadwinner or like providing type of role. Um really the only thing that he kind of I guess brings is really, you know loving me obviously, you know unconditionally, but providing is what I think he would describe himself as. And I think we kind of see that um, but we know you know that's our dad, and, and um yeah.

Kaitlyn remembered how her dad furnished birthday gifts when she was younger, and when she first got her driver's license, gave her his car. She knew that he'd eventually help her with a down payment on a house—here's what she said about it: "[H]e's that person of like, I will, I'll help you like put some money down for house." In the end, Kaitlyn linked her dad's provider role to his "really close support for you and . . . you know your success and development."

Like Kaitlyn and Eileen, Susan saw her parents in traditional roles. Growing up, she recalled how gender tended to segment what they did in the family. "You know my dad was like the provider, my mom was, um, stay at home and took care of us," Susan, a white and Latina cis-heterosexual female who identifies as Jewish and is married with children, revealed. Domestically, she said her dad did a lot around the house but mostly outside—"I mean my, he really didn't do much in the household, at least inside the house," Susan said. "Like he was always outside fixing stuff, um, you know, working on our yard, like landscaping, stuff like that," she concluded.

Ping, a first-generation student, detailed more traditional gender roles for his parents, too, with his father a migrant construction worker and his mother a caretaker for him, his three older sisters, and Ping's grandparents in their rural village in China. Even though Ping's father had retired from construction, he did not have a social safety net payment or pension, so his breadwinner role continued to allow him to bring in money. Ping explained: "So like he's living with my mother in my village, so he has to find some more short-term job opportunity, like a work for tiny houses to help people construct their home." When Ping experienced adversity as a secondary school student and undergraduate student, he seemed to rely on his father's strength to get through a period where he experienced suicidal ideations (which he no longer experiences). He intimately shared how he felt as a high school student.

Parenting Roles, Early Experiences in Families | 41

> [L]ast year of junior high school, you know, I want to commit a suicide. I, I feel things suck. I, I, I, my brain and neck are painful and I cannot focus on my study and the, the qualifying examination, uh, college entrance examination for me and for many other poor students. It's the most important, uh, examination in their life, you know. If they cannot go to a good college, their life sucks. They will lose a lot of opportunity.

Ping described how he connected with his father in these moments: "So I, I was depressed, and I, uh, talked with, I wanted to commit suicide. But when I, um, think of my father and mother, it's measured in my father, I think, he's very strong. I learned and it's related to my father. He, he himself is very strong." In a similar way, Josefina encapsulated the idea of her father as a "pillar of strength" when she described how he'd been so resilient: "I can stay here telling all the stories of his struggles and journeys that, and how he's persisted in many ways. I just think like, wow!" Josefina, who identifies as a first-generation straight Chicana woman with children, juxtaposed his strength throughout life to her struggles as a student, which seemed to put it all in perspective: "I think that's harder sometimes even than just an education. [H]e's just been that pillar of moral support, emotional support, um, and a role model." Like Ping, Josefina described her father as a "pillar of moral support, emotional support, um and a role model. A role model of, of persistence."

For Jeremy, who identifies as a first-generation straight white and Italian cisgender male, subtle but clear parenting roles that reinforced gender norms could be seen at home when he was growing up. He mentioned how, when it came to discipline, his dad enforced rules with his brother and him. His mom filled in the disciplinarian role when his dad wasn't around, and his mom was more involved at home and school. He detailed more: "I think like, that lead, that lead to like my mom taking my brother and I [to] school more. Um, or my mom like being the one who cooked most of the meals, um, because, as a result like, [my dad] was always the one that got home later, and my mom had to pick us up." The result, according to Jeremy: a closer relationship between his mom and the two boys.

TRADITIONAL GENDER ROLES SHAPE MOTHERS AS CARE-TAKERS AND HOMEMAKERS

Maternal roles generally focused on care-taking and domestic responsibilities, for most graduate students. For example, Josefina's mother served in a traditional gender role for women, at which Josefina hinted when she shared: "[T]here was one thing, my mom was a fabulous cook and baker. She can bake and she can cook very good." Similarly, Brianna's mom prepared food for her dad—and Brianna remembers playing part of this role, too: "I would give him this big thing of water 'cause I would always take a sip of it and then give it to my dad." Her mom modeled this role for her, as Brianna—who identifies as a first-generation African American woman—recalled about how women had always been in the kitchen and her mom always wanted to be a mom: "[S]he's always wanted to be a mother. You know, when I could be younger, like, hey, you should go back to school, she's like, that's not what I want to do. You know, I want to grow up and be a mom. That's always what she wanted to do." Stella, a first-generation African American who uses the gender pronouns she/her/hers and is exploring her sexual orientation, described how her parents "were more traditional," where "the woman is the stay-at-home mom. Basically, just takes care of the kids, cook[s], clean[s], do[es] all the household things. And then the, the men are the ones that go out, work, um, are the providers."

In a similar way to Josefina, Brianna, and Stella, Hector described his mom's primary role in traditional terms—a homemaker. Hector, a cisgender heterosexual married male who identifies as a person of color with multiracial and multiethnic identities of Mexican, Filipino, Italian, and Native American, focused on the pride his mom took in her work at home.

> I would say that, I think, even, even though there were some, you know, like traditional gender norms, as far as like, you know, maybe women viewed as being like homemakers or working in the house, my mom took a lot of pride in doing that. She did also work. She took a lot of pride in, in, in raising us and being a mom at home. And I, I kind of, the way I kind of looked at that, 'cause I think sometimes it can be viewed as like, you know, maybe viewed, viewed as like disempowering or upholding the status quo, but I, I think like the, at least from my perspective, like the, the pride that she, she took in that.

Hector reinforced this point when he concluded that his mom felt the job that she did at home was really important.

Extended family also served in traditional gender roles as parental figures at home. Brianna's grandfather was a pillar in her life after her father passed away, and Liza's grandmother raised them when she was younger so her parents could both work. Living at home with the family, her grandmother helped Liza to feel safe and protected—and fortunate to have so many figures in her life at the time. Liza described how her grandmother as enforcing rigid gender norms at home, even as her parents resisted them. Liza elaborated: "[S]he would be the one that said, or would say like, oh, that's not how girls should sit, or act. I was told that a lot, but I always felt like, that's just who I am. I always felt that internally. Like don't tell me how to act, you know." The result, for Liza, was traditional gender work for women at home: "And yeah, that's kind of, if I think back on that yeah, she would make me do some of those, housework."

Even as structural gender roles shaped the scope of maternal work in families, mothers were everywhere and seemingly always present in children's lives—and they appeared to singularly shape children's development. With Jeremy, his mother's role was to do almost everything with them—school drop off and pick up, meal prep, and more. Jeremy was close to his mom, and he seemed to connect their relational closeness to her involvement in his life. He described it in this way—"My mom was more present"—and elaborated.

> I think like, that lead, that lead to like my mom taking my brother and I school more. Um, or my mom like being the one who cooked most of the meals, um, because, as a result like, he was always the one that got home later, and my mom had to pick us up. So, I think that was what, what has led to both my brother and I having a closer relationship with my mom then my dad.

Jeremy's mom worked and juggled family and professional responsibilities with a focus on the two boys. Jeremy revealed more: "[M]y mom had, was fortunate enough to like, be able to do stuff remotely with her office. So like she'd be the one that'd pick us up after school and, and take us home. [I]f I needed something I could, and then my mom was the one that was there."

Like Jeremy's mom, Sharon recalled her mother as a figure who did it all. With her mother and father each bringing three children of their own into their second marriage, they welcomed Sharon in birth into the blended family. Her mom cared for everyone, including her own three children who lived at home with Sharon and her dad. "[T]he house was always busy," Sharon quipped. Sharon's mother managed the books for her father's business and did the housework and much more. Nesting, as Sharon put it, while she detailed what it was like: "But she, so always taking care of the home. Just always kind of nesting, you know, taking care of the house, taking care of the dishes, taking care of this and that." Even though she didn't cook more than what a can or container could provide, she would go gourmet on Sundays. "[O]n Sundays she would cook a nice meal," Sharon recalled. She continued: "[S]he would do like a roast, and roasted carrots and potatoes, and things like that, or something."

A consistent presence in her life, Sasha was with her mom all day as her mom didn't work outside the house, so Sasha's mom's life revolved around care-taking. Like Sasha, Leonardo connected his mom to home life. Leonardo, a first-generation straight Mexican American male who is married with a child, reported that his mom stopped working when he was younger to care for the family. He elaborated: "She had to focus her time on . . . raising us. And so, you know, um, we, you know we cared for each other. We loved each other. I was the second oldest, and so, um, there were younger siblings that I, you know, kind of helped raise."

As the family matriarch, Kayla's mom raised Kayla and her siblings plus Kayla's cousins. Kayla referred to her cousins as siblings—that's how close they were growing up. Kayla elaborated: "So my mom played a role in helping to raise them. So you know, my cousins were like . . . you know, brothers and . . . siblings, extended siblings. So, so a lot of cousins all the time, either in the house or when we went to visit in [the Southeast]." The fact that both her parents were the eldest among their siblings seemed to shape her mom's role as a collective care-taker, as Kayla described: "[B]oth of them being like at the top of their sibling groups uh in each family, yeah, being a you know, being in that space of watching leadership, and care-taking."

Stella's mom had to do most of the work to raise her. Stella talked about how her mom had to care for the kids, given that her dad would not participate in parenting. Stella elaborated: "[L]ike doing like fatherly things like it, it's just like pulling a, nail out of like someone's foot. Like it, it takes a lot for him to actually do something. Which would cause a lot of conflict, right? With my mom and my dad, 'cause like my mom would have to make him do stuff to like, take care of his kids." Stella concluded: "And there was times where he would just like, would leave for weeks at a time, um, cheating on my mom and doing things that he's not supposed to."

Gender Norms Direct Fathers to Be Breadwinners and Providers

Broad normative gender expectation seemed to define what fathers did in families, just as with mothers. At a foundational level, child-rearing centered paternal roles at home. Tanya, Jeremy, Winona, and Hua associated fathers with child rearing. For Tanya, who identifies as a first-generation heterosexual African American woman, this figure helps you "on the journey of just like growing." Tanya clarified that this is "a male figure that could be biological or not related." Jeremy's description included a "person who helps you grow up to be the person you become." Jeremy went on: "So it's the figure in your life, whether or not it's your, um, biological, the biological person who has helped uh birth you I guess you could say, um, like it's more so just the person in your household who um raises you to become like who you are." Similarly, Winona, a bisexual Asian American woman who identifies as Chinese and Vietnamese, said a father "is the person who raised you as you were growing up." Hua, who identifies as a Chinese female, connected fathering to partnering to "work together with the mom, and always show up when you grew up, and always be supportive, no matter what."

Beyond childhood, there appeared to be a common feeling that a father cares and "wants you to do better, and is always there," according to Jessica, who identifies as a white female, who illustrated this point: "Um, who like shows up to your dance recitals, or your baseball games, or something." In similar terms, fathers "would always, you know, have your back," Kaitlyn described. Kaitlyn connected fathers to an unconditional loving guide in life. Fathers, she said, "you know, obviously, you know, love you endlessly, unconditionally." They "[g]ive you guidance if you need it." Kaitlyn described fathers as caretakers in the extreme—as someone who would give the "shirt off their back to, you know, to provide for you." Winona did the same—saying that a father is "someone who is supportive, um, and can be someone that you can reach out to, to talk with."

For many parents, structural gender inequality and gender patriarchy tend to inform a polarized system of parenting roles. Fathers who want to be involved in their children's lives confront a conventionally circumscribed mothering job of care work in a domestic context. For many graduate students, gender norms seemed to circumscribe a paternal provider role. Josefina, a first-generation straight Chicana woman with children, identified this role immediately: "I think he always saw himself as, as a provider. Like he needed to make sure that he provided. And that he wasn't gonna allow . . . anything to get in the way of making sure he provided for all his kids." Even as over half her siblings were in Mexico at the time, Josefina's father provided across vast distances. Given his childhood experiences of financial instability back home in Mexico, Josefina surmised that her father would never allow his children to "go without eating or having shelter." A similar pattern of provider role appeared to be a part of fathering in the early lives of graduate students. Brianna shared that they never went without, connecting her dad to their financial security and stability at home: "But I knew that my dad, I knew he loved me. I knew, he had this heart, you know, interior, but we never went without. You know, we had a place . . . to live. Um, we stayed, I stayed there of course until I was eighteen, until I moved out and went to school. [H]e was like the provider and gave you like the main things, if that makes sense."

Providing and breadwinning seemed to be go hand in hand for many graduate students who recalled early life with fathers at home. When asked about gender and parenting roles, Gail, who identifies as a first-generation straight white female, felt like her dad "is more like the breadwinner of the house." She knew right away "[t]hat's kind of a gender norm." Eugenio, a first-generation heterosexual married Latinx male who identifies as Oaxacan from an Indigenous Mexican background, said something similar about his dad when he described him in the following way: "I remember my dad was just providing the always, just working, working, working." Andres shared a similar image of a provider role with his dad. He talked about how his dad always worked and supported the family "with authority"—raising his voice to a response of "Yes, sir," according to Andres. Andres went on to describe his roles as "our protector, our, our breadwinner." Andres had special memories about family vacations that he connected to his dad's roles: "[M]y dad would always tell us that he would work Thanksgiving, he would work Christmas, so that he can afford those vacations. I remember every year around summer break going on vacations, and that's what I associated my dad with." Andres connected his dad to the figure that kept them in the house and ensured they had food on the table.

Describing her dad as "the strong family figure," Karina, a heterosexual Latina woman who identifies as half Guatemalan and half Mexican, said he stood up for the family when needed. Buttressed by images and messages about gender in their Christian religious beliefs, Karina mentioned how her dad did everything he had been expected to do based on gender. She said,

> And so, you know, in our religion the man is the head of the household, he's the one who needs to do all that. And that's also what my family believes, so he was the one, pretty much did everything for us. But, um, just in our family in general, that's how he was raised as well. Like my grandma never held a job, she never finished, uh, middle school, so, um, my grandpa was always seen as the very, uh, big family figure in our lives, and so. Um, but in our culture that's how it always is, like the men are the ones that work and things like that.

In much the same way as Karina, Sharon, a first-generation heterosexual female who is married with children, noted how her dad was the breadwinner, "so he wanted to know the cost" of Sharon's high school tuition, etcetera. He had more questions and wanted to know details about how he could provide for Sharon's life as a student: "How much is this going to cost? Um, you know, what, you know, where is the school? How are we gonna get you there?"

More than a provider, fathers tended to be cast in protector and leader roles, too, further evidencing reproduction of gender patriarchy in families. Kayla, who identifies as a first-generation cisgender African American female, married with two children, framed her father as "[p]rotector, provider, uh, leader." Kayla explained how he seemed to project masculine behavioral characteristics: "I know even at [his age now] I could, if I needed something I could, he would be there . . . without, without question." Kayla surmised that "I think you know men do that. I think that just from my experience of what I've seen in the men that I've, you know, my uncles was, are like that, too, or have been like that. My father's brothers and my mother's brothers as well. Just like, not a whole lot of conversation about it, but you know, yeah, if this is what you need, this is gonna help you be a good person and achieve your goals, I'm gonna help support you, right."

Leonardo, identifying his father as "the provider" in the family, tied the role to "being Mexican there's machismo, right. I'll take care of, you know, I'll work hard," he recalled his father saying when he was younger. As a provider, Leonardo felt his dad did so much for his family: "So just making sure that, you know we had, you know breakfast, lunch, dinner, we had food on the table. He, you know, making sure we had clothes." Leonardo shared a general impression of his father as a provider: "[H]e's someone who was always, you know, pushing us in a, in his own way, you know. He, he worked hard. He showed us what, what it was to, to be that father. To, you know, care for your kids and provide the, the provider right?"

Leonardo witnessed dominant masculine characteristics complementary to his father's gendered role. He described how his father was the disciplinarian and seeming CEO of the family. Leonardo described how his father would admonish his siblings and him and call family meetings when needed.

> You know whenever, you know, 'cause kids fight, kids argue. And my mom, she, you know, she, she tried her best to try to, you know, tear us apart or whatever, but my dad would always come home and say, well, you know you shouldn't be treating your sister like that. You shouldn't, you know, and so we always knew that because Dad was gonna come home we had to, you know, behave, right. He would call family meetings. He would, you know, let us all know he, you know, this is going on, this is, you know, I'm dealing with this. Or, um, you know, we need to do better at this. And so he would always just kind of bring us in the loop and make us feel part of it.

Leonardo aspired to be like his father in his own family—but not in every gendered way his father was. To this point, he disclosed that family was most important in his life. He tied this value to his dad: "That's what he taught us. And, and so he wanted us to, to do the same, right?"

But Leonardo admitted that he wanted to avoid the dominant male figurehead and gender patriarchy in his life. He intimately shared how he had to go in a different direction than his dad: "I kind of saw something that I wanted differently. I didn't want someone to necessarily be at home and raise the kids. I wanted someone who was gonna, you know, also be a provider, but also build a, build a family with, build a life with. And so, um, not that I, you know, told my dad he was wrong, but I didn't feel like that was necessary, you know." "[B]eing in a relationship," Leonardo shared, means "having someone who, you know you're, you're building a

Parenting Roles, Early Experiences in Families | 49

home with, it, it's important to have communication. It's important to be a team, and not just, you know, like a, a dictatorship."

Sasha, a pansexual white woman, noted how her father was around but not involved in her life. She shared more: "I guess in some ways he, he wasn't around 'cause I, I mean no, he was. Like I always know like, like this is my dad. You know, like I knew he was always like, for the most part like gonna be like a part of our family unit. I know some people like don't have that sort of like feeling about the, either of their parents."

Behavioral Expectations from Parents to Children: Gender Policing, Monitoring Sexuality, and Regulating Emotional Expression

Just as with the general shape of parental roles, gender regulated how parents tended to impose expectations for gender expression, gender identity, sexuality, and much more. For several graduate students who identified as women, these behavioral norms set conditions in the family for what to wear and how to interact. Through cultural reproduction in the family, parents tended to be clear in their support for traditional norms for gender expression, identity, and behavior—especially with what fathers communicated to daughters. As restrictive as these norms could be, they seemed to lay the groundwork for resistance to such structures and later questioning of sexual orientation and gender identity. What's more, within gender structures in families, some mothers told counterstories about delaying marriage, finishing school, and relying on yourself for financial support—effectively undermining efforts to shape children in the same mold as had been generally taught.

FATHERS AS AGENTS AND FAMILY SYSTEMS AS STRUCTURES TO ENFORCE GENDER NORMS ON BEHAVIOR, DRESS, AND MORE

In general, fathers and grandfathers tended to control sexuality and enforce gender expectations for romantic relationships with some women graduate students. With outward signs of gender in clothing and personal style, parents, grandparents, and extended family often enforced normative dress codes for women to conform to feminine ideals at home and in the community. To this point, Jenna, who identifies as a first-generation Filipina heterosexual female, recalls resisting calls to conform to gender norms in what she wore: "I want to challenge the, the gender, the female, I mean, how do I say it? The, the conformity. There you go. And so I would not, I would want to wear something blue. I'd want to wear baggy pants. I'd wanna like, oh, I'm not going to sit dainty like in a dress. I will cross my leg, like I'll do whatever I want." But Jenna's father and grandfather pushed back, as she shared more, detailing how they would both instruct her how to behave and what to wear.

> And my dad would be very, you know, um, the way he grew up as well, you know he came from a military background, a military family. You know his, my grandfather was part of the, the war, so he, um, he grew up with that you know, girls are this way, boys are this way, you know? And so he instilled that in, in us growing up, um, where it's okay, when you're in a dress you have to sit like a proper way. But in terms of expression through clothing, he would actually support me and say, hey, I don't want this shirt anymore. Do you want to wear it?

Both Jenna's parents struggled with the idea of independence in teenagers exhibited with American cultural norms versus cultural standards reproduced in the Philippines. She spoke to this point here: "But then around high school or undergraduate, there's been this conflict with both parents where, I don't know if it's generational or cultural from Philippines, but you know the, a little bit of that independence in American culture." Jenna's mom had something to say when it came to dressing not "for boys," with an admonishment: "don't wear it." Later, the dynamic intensified with her mom, but her dad allowed her to present a more "tomboyish" look: "[M]y dad would say, yeah, take my shirt. Style it however you want." Jaime had a similar experience to Jenna, where her father asked her sister to "wear more dresses because she, she didn't like dresses." However, Jaime admitted that her father never "really imposed . . . traditional female norms" on her and never explicitly directed her "to be hyperfeminine."

In addition to dress, Beatrice, a heterosexual female who identifies as white and Mexican, connected interior decor and bedroom furnishings to gendered norms in her family when she was a child. Her brother's room, she reported, had a sports theme, while her room had been covered in shades of pink and fairies. She described it in more depth.

> Yeah, um, it's kind of funny if you, I don't have pictures of it, but my baby bedroom compared to my brother's baby, or like toddler bedroom, like his, my brothers was all sports. And we always make fun of this all the time. Like his like, he literally, the, the lamp ends were like little footballs, and they had like sports stuff everywhere, and jerseys and stuff. And then mine was all like pink, and fairies, and stuffed animals.

The result, Beatrice reflected, was that she reproduced the same normative gender patterns. She noted: "And, like I was into that stuff when I was a kid." Beatrice found it ironic, in spite of these early reproductions of gender norms at home, that she resisted them and focused on softball as her dad became her coach.

Beyond dress, behavior and movement tended to be monitored in a small group of families—generally by fathers. Josefina readily recalls how her father monitored her comings and goings when she was younger and knew why her father watched her so closely. Thinking more about it, she recalled: "A very old school way. I mean my father was born in the thirties. So you know, small-town Mexico. So that's his way of thinking in terms of gender. So he didn't want any guys around the house." At the time, this approach extended to Josefina's future husband, as she recalled with a smile: "Not even my husband. You know we got engaged, even after being engaged he was like, no." She concluded: "I was never allowed to bring a boyfriend home."

Reflecting on her dad's strictness, Zelma, a first-generation cis-hetero Indigenous Palestinian and Lebanese woman who is married with children, shared: "I would, you know, I think my . . . dad in particular, because my mom was a little more gentle, my dad was very, very strict. Very Middle Eastern, very stern." Zelma called it what it was: "patriarchal structures and toxic masculinity." So when Zelma tried wearing her heart on her sleeve, to so speak, she learned it was not acceptable.

Gender regulated more than just forms of emotions constructed as masculine and feminine in Zelma's family. In fact, her grandmother reproduced cultural norms that monitored whom Zelma could date romantically. Here, Zelma recalled: "You know, like I grew up in a place where, if one of my aunts saw a family member dating somebody who was not Arab, oh, our girls don't do that. Like those were, that was the messaging." She observed a kind of gender policing: "And it had a lot to do with, with morals, and ethics, and religion, and shame, or haram. Like these things can't happen, you know? Because we have to remain pure." Zelma went further.

> [W]e didn't have arranged marriages, but we did, you know, we weren't allowed to date before marriage. We had to be engaged, you know. Like the woman's virtue and her purity, right? It's like, okay, you have to be up here. And so um, that's how religion played a role. And I, I think, um, even at sixteen I had men in their thirties proposing marriage so that I can date them 'cause their families were interested in my hand in, in marriage.

As she grew older, Zelma became increasingly critical of how gender controlled who she was and how she was expected to act, and stress of gender-based role strain wore on Zelma, as can be seen more broadly in family roles of graduate students of color (Walsh et al., 2023). But her mom resisted traditional gender roles and messaged that Zelma had to move away from the idea that women are "one husband away from poverty." Instead, her mom insisted that Zelma stand on her own two feet. Zelma shared her mom's backstory that led to this position: "My mom was eighteen when she got married. She didn't know any better. She went from one abusive home, which was with my, my grandfather was abusive. He, there was physical abuse. And so, moving on to, again, a domineering male. And so my mom was silenced." But the message that her mom instilled in her, where "you need to be able to stand on your own two feet," led Zelma to focus on education, as her mom insisted that she do, and take care of herself.

What emerged from gendered experiences in the family and messages that resisted gender roles from her mom was a critical skepticism that prompted Zelma to scrutinize dimensions of who she was. Referencing her strong critical thinking skills, Zelma observed the following:

> [S]eeing the way my dad would treat my mom. I would say, this is not what I want out of my life. Like, this can't be. And when I realized, you know, again, being around all of that, and how, seeing how, seeing how Arabic women or Arab women were treated I was like, it's because of gender. Like I knew from a young age that I'm being treated like this because I'm

a woman. And the way I saw that play out was, you know, our male cousins, we didn't have brothers, but I saw how males who are our age were treated as opposed to how we were treated.

Later in life, Zelma soured on religious beliefs that reproduced gender norms, remarking how "growing up, because I was also critical of gender, I was also very critical of religion."

Stella described behavioral expectations similar to Zelma. For Stella, normative gender beliefs about a woman led to an emerging adulthood where she wondered how her family would not approve of who she was. She described in more detail.

> [O]bviously me being the woman that I am today, and being one, not only someone that takes care of themselves but also as a provider, and how I'm very independent, and how I work like, that was something that you know, is a shock to a lot of, you know my family members. And, you know they, like I said, they would think that I was gonna get pregnant, or you know find a man that was gonna take care of me.

But Stella resisted these ideas: "[F]or me that's not what I want. I want to build my own career, my own life."

Circumscribing roles at home characterized gendered experiences for several graduate students who identified as women. Brianna recalled a moment when her grandfather, who served in a fathering role, questioned where she should be in the house. "My grandfather was in the living room, and they were watching football. It was just him. And so he said, do you think you should be in there, in the, in the kitchen? And I said no. And it made me so upset. I can still remember that." She connected this time to who she was as an undergraduate student and who she is now: "And so I'll never get my freshman year a woman saying, well did you ever think about how those women, your family members, love those men? And that's why they wanted to serve them? You know. That was a real eye opening, um, but it's irritating, too. You know what I'm saying? I think I kind of felt like, I'm not gonna let people run over me, even though that may not have been the case. Um, yeah. Yeah." Brianna concluded: "I remember going to college, and, um, maybe that's why I'm single now."

As a child in her home in Russia, Holly recalled how cultural expectations likely "rubbed off" on her dad's "traditional ideas about, um, generally the family roles, and you know, things like, like what the girl should do, should be." But her dad's academic training and advanced education seemed to undercut his ideas about conventional roles for women and, consequently, Holly remembered a more complex duality to what he expected her to do. On the one hand, she mentioned, she had to be feminine in the traditional sense in Russia at the time and, on the other hand, needed to pursue higher education and a career where she could contribute to society. In her analysis, Holly—who identifies as a cisgender heterosexual white woman and ethnically as Russian, felt she had no gender boundaries to hold her back. She reflected: "I never felt there were limits for me, because he, um, he always encouraged me, and always, always pushed me. And, um, so, so yeah. So I would say he probably was, in terms of who I am today, he probably was my biggest influence." More specifically, Holly posited that it was her dad's intellectualism that shaped who she was. To this point, she remarked: "I just feel like I always had this like philosophical, uh, like they were not philosophical, but I was like, you know, really very pensive. And, and part of it was that, I think my father found in me, maybe, maybe he just like sort of, um, molded me in that."

GENDERED EXPECTATIONS FOR EMOTIONAL EXPRESSION IN FAMILIES

Even as changing norms opened opportunities to complicate parent-child interactions and enhance forms of connection between mothers, fathers, and children, gender still seemed to penetrate emotional expression. In many ways, emotions tended to be exhibited in traditional ways—with mothers more expressive and more closely bonded to children and fathers more distant and less connected relationally with children. While several graduate students reported closeness with fathers, too, the normative patterns in relationship quality tended to be experienced between parents and children. For example, Eugenio admitted that he was very close with his mom, comparatively describing it this way: "[M]y mom was more loving caring. She hugs us and she gives us a kiss. But at the same time I guess her mentality was to always kind of provide, have a better future, always get something like for themselves, but at the same time that would benefit us in the future." Jaime recalled a similar closeness with her mom. Even though her mom had been less involved in her young life, Jaime felt a closeness with her. When Jaime, who identifies as a first-generation Vietnamese American female, was in elementary school, she recalled experiencing her mom's affection. She qualified her mother as the more affectionate parent, even though she was not as present. Jaime explained: "Um, so I, I really gravitated to her more than my dad, who of course was like almost always punishing me for my little homework mistakes at night. Um, he, he gets the hard end of the stick."

Some graduate students shared memories about how it wasn't always easy for fathers to share how they felt or disclose details about personal experiences. Hector remembered how his dad was more "clean cut" and had a harder time with sharing "something a little more delicate . . . or intimate." It was definitely more difficult for his dad, but he did try and pushed for expressing how he felt. At times, though, his dad was more reserved, as Hector cited the complex transnational and generational contexts in which his dad grew up. Hector mentioned cultural norms and religious practices—particularly with witnessing his dad's parents process trauma experienced during World War II in the Philippines. About these forces shaping his dad, Hector said succinctly: "[T]he way he grew up, and the way that he was taught masculinity, or taught how to be male, um, or to be cisgender male." But between sports, music, and humor, his dad expressed himself and processed emotions more publicly. Hector detailed more.

> but a lot of it I feel like came through humor . . . and being able to joke about certain things. [O]r using music I think was a way to like, you know, express how you're feeling. And then of course sports. [E]specially my uncle with his brother, and my aunt and . . . sister, you know big, big sports fans. So you know, the expression of the emotion is very public in that way, you know in that space because it, because it could be because sports allowed you to have this kind of otherworld to share a whole range of emotion.

Hector reflected further on what situational contexts and masculine gender norms meant for men. He said: "I hear about people say like, oh, men don't really show their feelings, I'm like yeah, it, it depends on the setting. [I]f it's an awkward one, you can hear all sorts of emotion. You sit us in front of a basketball game or wrestling match or, something that is kind of like masculine focus, or like, you'll see a lot. You'll see a lot of touching, and it's all sanctioned. It's all okay to hug, and cry, and, and grab each other, everything."

More than just sports, graduate students described a range of activities acceptable for fathers to express themselves in more masculine forms. Sharon described her dad's interest in firearms, including handguns and rifles. Her dad taught Sharon how to shoot at the cabin, where "he would stack beer bottles or beer cans on a picnic table" and trained Sharon how to shoot them. Back at home, the firearms locked in a safe, Sharon remembered how powerful her experiences at the cabin were: practicing firing a gun, hunting deer, and more.

But even as behavioral gender norms tended to regulate emotions, some fathers manifest more intimate moments with children. For example, Josefina recalled when all the siblings would ask for simple things like treats from an ice cream truck passing by the house, her father provided for them. She shared: "You know, so we would run out, and he would always just have so much joy, you know, from seeing us, [g]iving us treats like that." Another time Josefina remembered her father in this role: "And he would bring in the summers always a big watermelon. And he would, he would say, 'Go get a knife from inside the kitchen.' And then we'd go get the knife, and we sit in the front lawn of the house and cut the watermelon and eat watermelon." Tanya mentioned how her daddy had a "kind of old-school mind-set," where he provided and went to work—but he also participated in the family, cooked, etcetera. Granted, Tanya's mom was more involved with child-rearing—more hands on—and her daddy "paid all the bills" so her mom would not have to work. Beyond these more conventional roles, Tanya's dad planned vacations, went to amusement parks, cooked meals, and more, centering his involvement in their lives at home.

For some, closeness had been experienced by both parents, and this experience defied gender-regulating norms. In Juan's early life, he recalled how his parents had a loving relationship—until late high school, when their relationship deteriorated. Even as his parents exhibited less affection toward each other, they showed a lot of love and affection toward Juan and his brothers throughout their lives. He shared how he felt: "[I]n my eyes that was between them, um, and you know their love towards myself and my brothers individually, and even though . . . their love toward each other now, it's just different. Um, you know they, they don't have romantic love towards each other now but they definitely still get along. Um, and we're able to share, you know family moments. We're able to still meet up for Christmas and birthdays."

Changing Parental Roles: Navigating Complex Contexts in Families and Role Convergence as Resistance to Gender Norms

While gender prescribed parental roles in traditional terms, many graduate students told stories about how parents split domestic responsibilities, created opportunities for more equitable roles in the family, and shared duties at home. In this way, parents communicated an updated perspective that challenged traditional gender norms and hastened changing sets of expectations for parents to relate to children and meaningfully share in child-rearing. To illustrate, in some cases, mothers led households and served as the providers. Liza's parents balanced the family workload and evenly split labor at home, where her mom managed the bills and her dad went grocery shopping. There's an ironic twist to the story, from Liza's perspective, because her dad worked in banking even as her mom did the family finances. "And even though my dad worked at a bank at the time, you know, like it's kind of funny. So he was like the bank guy but my mom handled all the finances, so it's kind of funny." Liza went on to talk about how her mom made many decisions at home—"she was pretty much the decision maker and all that." This meant Liza had to ask her mom for permission even if she initially approached her dad. "So Mom was always the one that had the final say with everything," Liza said. What's more, Liza never really felt gender as a regulating norm with her parents, even as her grandmother imposed expectations for housework and more on her as a girl growing up. Liza recalled how her parents seemed to resist gender for norming behavior: "But in terms of the gender roles and how it affected, affected me, I don't think I noticed it as much with my brother. And I think if you asked him, I don't think . . . it was necessarily, but the amount of attention that was placed on me because I was playing soccer, playing field hockey, and I was doing fairly well in those sports at the time."

Sharon's parents worked as a team—in the family and the family business. At home, Sharon recalled how they made decisions together and, to Sharon's chagrin, tended to be unified in their response. Sharon detailed more.

> And one thing that I learned early on is that if one of them said no, and I went to the other one, they would say, what did the other one say? So I would, you know, if I, if I asked

Mom, I would probably ask Mom first for permission to do, you know, whatever it was going to be, and if she said no, if I went to my dad, he would say, what did your mother say? So they, they were aligned. They were a team.

As a testament to how Sharon's parents shared responsibilities in their work and home lives, Sharon's mom maintained the books in the business and, when she was working at home, you knew not to disturb her. Sharon shared: "You know, little, little carve out where she could manage the books, and pay the bills for the business, and all of that. So there were times when, you know, that, that door would be closed, and it's just like, she's working. You leave her alone."

As changing gender norms encourage rethinking parenting forms and evolving connections between parents and children, some graduate students described more nuanced parental roles in the family.

For fathers, roles as providers, caretakers, and more seemed to come to the fore, for Maria framed fathering in more complex terms: as both traditional (provider) and resistant (care-taker) gender roles. So did Beatrice. In her case, fathers are "there to guide you as you grow up." Beatrice personalized how fathering meant to her: "And a lot of things, tough lessons that he's learned in his life he's able to share with me and just kind of help me prepare myself until college." Susan, a white and Latina cis-heterosexual female who identifies as Jewish, linked fathering to both guiding and providing. She mentioned that a father is a "type of parental figure who helps guide you throughout life, supports you. I mean I would say normally financially." Susan's image of a father seemed to be related to her dad's role as more than just the typical gendered parental figure. Even though her parents operated within traditional gender boundaries at home—her dad was the provider and her mom the care-taker—she explained how, as a small business owner, he had flexibility in his schedule and did school drop off and pick up.

In the end, Maria, Beatrice, Susan, Edith, and Jaime connected fathering to providing and care-taking in a more complex picture of gendered parenting roles. What Maria shared reflects gendered norms that shape parenting. "I think for me it means, um, fatherhood means more of like the provider, um, caretaker." Similarly, Edith talked about her father as "the male parent," who is "the breadwinner of the family." Edith's childhood memories of her father formed her perception of fathers, whom she described in fond detail: "He worked. He's six days a week to in income to, to, you know, make sure his three children were fed, and, and clothed, and housed, and all that." But Edith's experiences included her father as "very nurturing," too. She elaborated: "He, he worked hard and long hours, but always made time and room to allow us to just share and, and share our day and be with him in that way. And just like, yeah. The fault, my father, you know, was, or did, did contribute in, in that, you know, in, in some important decision of, of making." Jaime focused on the social construction of fathering as more "probably someone who I would see, um, kind of like presenting in a masculine role. Whoever plays that kind of social, socially masculine role."

Expansive Parental Roles for Mothers with Gender Barrier-Breaking and Shifting Norms

Just as fathers tended to be framed in a more traditional masculine provider role, mothers seemed to be seen as care-takers—but similar to fathers, maternal roles evolved into more complex functions in families. To this point, Kayla recalled her mother "taking care of inside of the house, and taking care of the kids," including making sure there were "three meals a day" and ensuring that her dad "ate dinner, um, every night you know." She raised children and did so much every day to get them what they needed to succeed. Kayla recalled: "She would get us ready in the mornings, to go to school. She would give us breakfast, which was cereal and eggs, you know, like nothing out of the ordinary. She would make sure that everything, we're ready to go. She would walk us to the bus stop, or, like before we started going to public school we went in private school." Similarly, Zelma described how her mom cooked, cleaned, and shopped for groceries, serving in a more traditional domestic role. She said: "My mom would do all the cooking and the cleaning."

Karina talked about a similar role as Kayla and Zelma, but she felt her mother's work in the home challenged gender norms, too. Over time, Karina, said, her mother assumed more head-of-household duties and decision-making authority for the family. Karina shared more about this pattern: "But as I grew older, I started to recognize that my mother also did a lot. So, um, so it's kind of transitioned like, from like the, the societal norm that he's the one who does everything that, then it transitioned to my mom also does really great work with our family." Karina connected

60 | Shaping Students of Color from Preschool to Graduate School

the traditional gender roles in her parents to cultural norms that had been reproduced in the home. She elaborated: "[I]n my race, like Mexican and Guatemalan, there's machismo culture, and so the men are always being served food, the women are always cleaning, you know. Um, and so my father has kind of been like that, but, um, he also recognizes the hard work that my mom does, so he, he also cooks, he'll clean."

In this way, maternal roles were more complex and not simply a direct reflection of broader images of gender for women. In many families, mothers were homemakers, care-takers, *and* providers—either working part- or full-time outside the home and/or ensuring that children had food, clothes, school supplies, and much more. This complexity could be seen in what Josefina, who identifies as a first-generation straight Chicana woman with children, said about her mother as a provider—beyond her roles as a cook and baker. Yes, there was always "fresh, homemade food," but her mother worked full-time in a sewing factory. Still, Josefina's mother ensured that there "has to be fresh food on the table every day. Our meals, making sure there was clean clothing. You know it's, it's you know she was just that kind of person who was just loving and giving." Josefina reflected more

Figure 1.1. Parental roles shift as families of graduate students navigate changes over the life course. *Source:* By mynameisharsha, CC BY-SA 2.0.

on these multiple roles, including her mother's provider role: "I feel like my mother was one who she really tried to make sure that there's, there was always food on the table. Because she come from a very traditional upbringing in Mexico. Really played the role of, the mother role where the, the women, you know they, they cook, they you, you don't, you don't pop anything for the microwave." While Josefina described her mom in a primary role as care-taker, she transcended traditional terms for what she did in the family. She raised children and provided materially—all to ensure everyone had what they needed. Josefina put it this way: "Our meals, making sure there was clean clothing. You know it's, it's you know she was just that kind of person who was just loving and giving."

Like Josefina, Hector argued that his mom had agency in the family and challenged gender norms at home. Hector witnessed his mom promote the idea that women were not passive and subservient, offering a counternarrative to dominant messages about gender roles. Hector reflected on this pattern.

> I think in a lot of ways like our home became like a little hub, you know, for . . . I would say like that, that to me kind of challenged like the, the traditional norms of like, you know that, that women are passive. That they're not allowed to do anything. Like, that she had agency, she had voice. She could speak to things. She, you know, and, and at the exact same time, you know, held some, some views about, you know women, women's rights. You know that like, that women need to be at the lead, women could and needed to be at the lead of different movements, you know. Like a lack of women in those movements.

Hector connected his mom's activism to her mom, mentioning that his mom's mom was the youngest of eighteen children and got a lot from what she saw growing up.

The idea that moms served only in traditionally subservient roles ran counter to the descriptions of many graduate students who framed them in family leadership roles. Indeed, while Kayla talked about her mom as a care-taker, she also was seen as the family matriarch, a leadership role that thrust her into decision-making at home. Kayla described how her mom was the older of three siblings in her family and served in this matriarchal position early in life. "I think that kind of set the tone of how she was as a, as my mom, just being so much of a leader, in a leadership figure," according to Kayla. This translated into her mom pushing Kayla to lead, too. She elaborated: "Okay, you have to do better, you have to, you know take the lead, you have to. If you, if you know as far as leadership, okay, if, you know you have to." Similarly, Brianna recalled her mom as a leader. To this point, she said simply: "[M]y mom, definitely, really, leader within our family." Zelma talked about her mom in leadership terms, too, when she described her as a matriarch who's been the cornerstone of the family. "And she's, she's a tough little cookie," Zelma remarked about her mom's character.

Even as mothers served in a caretaking role in the family, many worked outside the home, too, and managed multiple roles for the family, including breadwinner and income contributor. And while mothers generally fulfilled roles of care-taker, homemaker, comforter, tutor, liaison between families and schools, and more, some served in strong leadership roles—modeling independence as an imperative for daughters—even as they navigated oppressive systems of gender patriarchy. These often competing, conflicting responsibilities—care-taking, providing, and leading—tended to complicate how graduate students remembered them as challenging structural gender hierarchy at home and work.

Angela remembered well how her mom served as the breadwinner and achieved educationally to provide for Angela's family. First as a nurse and later in health-care administration, Angela's mom worked in sectors that required strong care-taker roles—so her professional life carried over into her family life raising children. Angela, a first-generation African American female who identifies ethnically as Nigerian, talked about the gender and cultural contexts that shaped her mom's decisions for work and family. She detailed: "I've noticed within like the African mother community, a lot of them start off as nurses, or go to nursing school and end up, of course, becoming a nurse. And then that was kind of the story for my mom. She went to get her associates degree, then eventually did like her bachelor's degree online. And then, of course, eventually became a registered nurse and was working as a registered nurse." When Angela was in high school, she recalled her mom going to graduate school to earn an MA in health-care management, which supported her promotion into a nursing director role. Her mom sacrificed, working in a stressful director-level position, to provide for the family.

Early in life, her mom's breadwinner and provider roles confused Angela, as she had few friends whose moms did the same, She revealed what this was like.

> I think growing up, um, for context, my dad currently he's been driving taxis and Ubers ever since he got to this country, and my mom has been the one who's pursued higher education. And I think growing up that kind of like . . . it kind of skewed like what I viewed success as or . . . what the, I don't know. It's just very backwards 'cause I think growing up and looking at other people's families I would see like the father being the breadwinner of the household. Whereas in my household, like my mom was the one in school. My mom was the one studying. My mom was the one, right now she's a director of a nursing home in [the Southeast] right now, and like she brings home, I'm, I'm transparent, she brings home six-figures to the household, whereas my dad not so much.

At times, Angela felt like extended family and friends questioned her mom's provider role in the family and pursuit of postsecondary education. Describing her mom's friend's husband, she elaborated: "One of her friend's husbands would get so annoyed that her, his wife was going to school, and he would blame my mom like, why are you doing this?" This seemed to be part of a broader pattern that Angela aptly described: "I saw a lot of people whose parents were like stay-at-home mothers where their mom stayed at home, and they didn't have a job, and that was kind of confusing to me at first. I thought the dad was supposed to be making more."

Angela reflected on how she felt "different" in relation to her friends, whose parents exhibited more traditional gender roles. And this difference led Angela to stand by her mom's advice about school, as she revealed here: "I think I stood more towards hearing advice about schooling for my mother 'cause she went through it. She has her master's degree." Angela shared more about how her mom wanted her to have more choice and be less shaped by gender roles. She said: "She never had choices to dictate what type of lunch she had, what type of food she had, all these different things. So now when she raised us, like we have a whole full menu. We get to choose what we want to eat. And it's something so simple, cause other people would come to my house and be like, your mom lets you guys pick whatever? I'm just like, yeah. It's not a big deal." Angela talked more about this pattern, searching for a reason why her mom insisted they have more choices. She noted: "[G]rowing up she didn't have choice so now she wants us to have choice. [S]he also vowed to like . . . not let other people raise us. So she's very big on just like being at home, supporting us, 'cause again in her childhood, she moved out of her house when she was six years old."

In their village, while Ping's mother served as care-taker, she also contributed to household income by working with domestic animals on their family farm. Managing daily feed and care requirements for livestock left little time for Ping's mother to rest and enjoy time for herself. Ping, a first-generation straight Chinese man, soberly observed how she could not watch TV, and so on. More broadly, Ping revealed his parents' "need to earn money, and the most of, a lot of Chinese people, the . . . couple, they have to separate like my parents." Similarly, Juan described his parents as both providers, sharing how his mom earned a higher salary than his dad—which shaped his perception of the provider role in the family. About his dad, Juan said: "[W]ell firstly his, his sort of role in the family was, was actually not much as the sole provider." Citing his mom's income contribution to the family, Juan noted: "[M]y mom actually earned, um, just as much as him, and eventually a bit more. Um, and I'm, I'm actually not sure how to answer the question of how gender norms, uh, influenced any of that because I'm not, I'm not sure it did at all."

While both Hua's mom and dad tended to be involved in her life, each parent occupied a unique place for her twin sister and her. In fact, Hua recalls how she and her sister would each go to one parent or the other at the same time. Despite their closeness, Hua's mother was "always a powerful one," and Hua cited regional Chinese cultural norms for mothers leading households where she grew up. Hua described what these cultural norms meant for her family—from the perspective of her dad: "So three times like my dad is like I had, he said, I had to battle with three girls in my family to how cause me my sister and my mom, so we are a crew. I don't, I don't have much power to say no to this family. If they three decide I follow what they have." Hua's parents shared a close relationship—but Hua remarked how her mom said "everything" in family processes and decision-making. She elaborated: "But then my mom is like the one always want to handling everything, and he, she want to like involve every moments of our life, like it's always age and mom thing, and my dad is always show up in the I think importance points of your life."

Like Ping and Juan, Stella shared how her mother worked to put food on the table and a roof over her head, even if the mothering relationship with Stella was not healthy. Why? Stella cited gender norms that seemed to limit what her mom could do for her. She explained further.

I know she did the best that she could for her kids. She didn't get support due to the stigmas of our culture, and how they treated kids. Of course, it makes sense of how she treated us. But I know at the end of the day, uh, she just wants her kids to succeed. Um, she makes sure that she had food on our tables, a roof over our head. And if she didn't have food, she'll find a way.

Stella concluded that her mother did more than put food on the table, she taught her children how to do the same—ensuring that they could provide for themselves as they got older. To this point, Stella said: "[S]he will teach us on how to find a way to have food on our table."

Like Stella's mom, Jessica's mom did more than put food on the table, too. Jessica's mom worked in a male-dominated field and modeled how to dress, act, and achieve everything what you wanted in spite of gender norms. Jessica talked about how her mom had to navigate "gender stereotypes" in the computer science field. When she first started her career, her mom had to break patriarchal structures. Relying on lessons she learned as a child, she seemed to use her "tomboy" experiences in the family to overcome barriers. Jessica spoke more to this pattern in her mom's young life: "[S]he's more of like a, I guess a tomboy would be the quote when she was growing up. Um, but her dad, this is what she told me, I don't know cause I wasn't born, or he's not alive now, but he said that she was more of a son." What this meant for Jessica is a life without conventional gender norms in the home. She illustrated: "I definitely did like the, like I picked what I wanted to wear and what colors were my favorite. Like at one point green was my favorite color. Technically that would be like a boy color, but, um, so I was able to choose like what I wanted to wear, and how I wanted to dress and be." Speaking about her mom's influence, Jessica said: "I don't think she really had to like reinforce like, that I was, that I am biologically female or anything when I was a kid."

A MOTHER'S WARNING TO DELAY MARRIAGE OR LIMIT LONG-TERM RELATIONSHIPS TO FOCUS ON STUDIES

While graduate students generally framed their mother's work as caretaking, several offered clear examples of how their mothers advised against doing the same and promoted independence from/in romantic relationships and a push for education in emerging adulthood and beyond. Here, Kayla remembered her mother's example. After returning to school and starting a part-time job at school, her mother "didn't teach me how to cook. She didn't teach me how to clean, like she didn't force that on me." In stark contrast, her mother "was very much encouraging . . . all of our, all of us, the, the girls to work, and, you know get a education to work and things like that. So I don't think she really wanted us to have that, um, more traditional female house focused role." Later in life, Kayla took the advice to heart, reflecting on how her mother continued to be a force in her life: "You know even when I got married, you know and I was trying, I was, you know part of me, you know I did stay home for a while and she's like, well why would you stay home? Like you can, you can have something for yourself. You know get a job, you know. So I got that message very loud and clear from her." Similarly, Brianna argued adamantly that she would not take care of a man in her life: "But I'm not supporting a man. My grandfather had a job. My dad had a job. You know, I would not be, that would be beneath me."

Like Kayla, Stella mentioned how her mom warned her that interpersonal or romantic relationships could hold her back—and sometimes "not relying on people" seemed to be the best position to take. Stella vividly recalled her mom's advice: "Always having your own things . . . developing your own career, your own life. Build your own self up and not relying on other people, especially men." Stella's mom's experiences with her dad informed her messages about living independently to Stella. When her mom relied on her dad and built a life around him, her "dad took that all away from her where he left her with nothing. And basically she had to start off from scratch and had two kids on her own pretty much." Stella promised herself she would not do the same: "I'm not gonna, again wait around for a man. Like I'm gonna do my own thing, and I'm, I'm gonna build a life for myself." She concluded that she has seen herself as a provider and role model.

Similar to Stella and Kayla, Josefina remembered what her mother taught her about being strong and resisting traditional gender roles. She detailed more about this message.

> But there's one thing that I think the positive side of it is that she's taught me to you know, to be strong. That women are also smart and capable of doing the things that maybe typical men would do. For example, going to school. You know,

> having positions or roles in a, in a career that typically would be males, but doesn't mean that you a, a woman can't do it. So she taught me that perseverance. She taught me just, you know, when you love something, give it your heart, and keep pushing through and persevere, and don't allow anything to come in your way, and I think I've been able to see that her as a, as a woman who, you know, you know, have nine kids and migrated to this country and you know she has her, she has her story of herself, which is her journey, her struggles.

Josefina reflected on what her mom's journey meant for her: "I think to me has shown me that no matter if you're a woman, you can still persevere, especially when, if you're challenged in spaces where it's male dominated."

EVOLVING GENDER EXPECTATIONS RESHAPE PARENTING ROLES FOR FATHERS WITH MORE INVOLVEMENT AND GREATER ADVOCACY

For a small group of graduate students, fathers countered behavioral gender norms and advocated for their daughters, in particular, to be as independent as possible and resist traditional roles. In Tanya's case, her dad reproduced the normative expectation that she be self-reliant and provide for herself, moving away from the notion that she be dependent on a male partner as the breadwinner. She spoke to this pattern here.

> I always knew that my daddy had me, but he also wanted to make sure that like I was self-sufficient and didn't depend on a man. Now that doesn't mean that like I was, I'm hyperindependent, or I don't want to be married, or things like that, but he just was very big on like, no, like I want you to be able to take care of yourself no matter what happens. Um, and then very big on like autonomy, and just, um, just being a, a fully functional adult.

Tanya summed up what her dad wanted for her: "Like he was, my dad was just, is very big on making sure [I] knew how to take care of myself." What Jaime's father messaged to her seemed to have a similar effect on her expectation to not be shaped by patriarchal gender norms. "[M]y father also never really pushed on like, oh, you have to do it because I'm a man," Jaime commented, "and it was like because I'm your dad." She summarized: "Yeah, he never said anything like that. Never went back to like his gender."

Karina had a different experience than Tanya or Jaime, but the effect on Karina seemed to be similar in that she felt she could do more in life than her dad had cautioned her about. What seemed to be a life lesson for her turned into a challenge to overcome barriers to where she needed to go. As an undergraduate student, Karina shared how her dad warned her about gendered structures in society: "And so my dad, uh, like going into my education, especially college, he, he did, you know, warn me. He's like, you know because you're a woman, it might be harder for you to, to get opportunities, but that's just, that's just life." Referring to her dad seemingly resigning her to operate within gender norms at work, she continued: "And that's my dad's motto—That's life. Um, and so, and that's always just, it's just been ingrained in him because you know that's how he saw his mother as they grew up, you know. She was always the one cooking, cleaning, taking care of the kids. Um, so that was kind of like the warnings he did." But her dad seemed to advocate for her to challenge what she encountered in the workplace: "Um . . . he's like, you know, just so that you know, it's gonna be harder, but that means you just have to work harder."

While Kaitlyn and Beatrice had much different childhood experiences, they both seemed to challenge normative gender expectations—and their parents, respectively, shaped how they "broke out of those traditional roles," as Kaitlyn put it. As a kid, Kaitlyn loved being outdoors. Even though she learned to cook and clean, as she shared, she hated doing those things. Her parents helped her to hate them, too, as they "were really good not really enforcing them." Kaitlyn detailed more of this dynamic growing up: "Like obviously my mom would, you know dress me with, you know girl clothes and things like that, but I always hated dresses. Um, but again my parents were, fortunately they were really good at not enforcing gender roles or things like that in our house." In childhood, Kaitlyn connected this critical consciousness of not being limited by gender norms to her interest and motivation to persist in advanced studies in graduate school. She reflected: "I think one big thing is, is the fact that I'd be part of like the very, like less than ten percent of Latinas who, Latina women specifically who have a master's degree. That is something that's really pushing me, um, because I feel like we need to, again, add to that diversity in, in every field."

At a young age, like Kaitlyn, Beatrice similarly broke free of the diminishing and restrictive effects of gender norms. She spoke about how her involvement in athletics—with an intense focus on softball—accompanied her dad's involvement in her life and his encouragement and support to do whatever she wanted to do. She explained further.

> Um, because I was definitely the . . . like stereotypically athletic one. I was still into music and a bunch of other stuff, too, but that was a predominant part of my upbringing, as, was sports. Um, and with my brother, he was not like that. And I know that my dad definitely like tried playing basketball with my brother, or tried teaching him baseball. Like he, I've learned softball through my dad. Like we would play catch and stuff, and then I did tee-ball as a kid and I started liking it. And so that's how I was like, hey, can you take me out hitting? Like can you give me some pointers and stuff?

"And so it was all my own volition," Beatrice concluded, linking these experiences to her sense of independence and self-image that she could achieve in life.

Figure 1.2. Many graduate students learn moral values and cultural expectations for social norms from their parents. *Source:* By Danny Mualim, CC BY-NC-ND 2.0. https://www.flickr.com/photos/55130103@N08/7248971716.

Diverse Family Structures and Early Life Experiences with Parenting Roles

Families today are diverse in size, shape, and dynamics. Family structure or the presence or absence of two parents, adoptive parents, and stepparents matter less than family processes—parent relationships, satisfaction, and disagreements; child-family relationships and disagreements; and family life related to family cohesion and parent time with children—in terms of parent and child well-being and the quality of family relationships (Lansford et al., 2001). Indeed, in diverse family structures, family processes shape outcomes for single fathers and gay fathers who experience microaggressions when they don't conform to social norms for traditional gender roles and parenting. Carone (2021) found when these men ruminated over microaggressions, they had lower sensitivity levels in interactions with their kids. Finally, social stigma associated with negative stereotypes of stay-at-home fathers seems to impact relationships with kids and family members (Holmes et al., 2021).

In some cases, graduate students shared how changing gender roles in their families seemed to reproduce an ethic of care and imprinted a more equitable approach to caregiving—including fathers who shared or led primary care-taking. When her family immigrated to the US and her mother returned to school, Jenna's father would step into a lead care-taker role, but Jenna recalled parenting roles occupied by Jenna's grandparents as a young child. In adolescence, Jenna remembered her dad as their primary caregiver.

> [W]hen we went back to the Philippines, and then moved back to the US it was, I think the early beginning stages my dad was out of the house because he was working different jobs, odd jobs. And then eventually my mom became a, an international student. And then so my dad stayed at home more. And that was just, um, how, I think since then it's been up to this point usually my dad at home. My mom will be out of the house.

Jenna went on to describe how her father managed his care-taker role in the family: "He, basically he did everything in, I think most things. [H]e would do the cooking, and cleaning, and basically all the driving because my mom doesn't drive. So he also drove my sister, me, and my mom around. And so that was his duties. And then, um, let's see, I can't think of anything more. I think he also handled taxes, so a lot more of the money management and domestic stuff." As Jenna transitioned to college, her dad did less domestic work, with "more of a shared thing amongst the family."

In more diverse family structures, adoptive fathers and adoptive stepfathers demonstrate high levels of involvement and nurturant fathering, when viewed from the perspective of their stepchildren (Schwartz & Finley, 2006). However, stepfamilies tend to experience more variable quality in parents-child relationships—and developing close and connected relationships in stepfamilies can challenge both parents and children (Bray et al., 2005). For example, a mother's remarriage may mean more tenuous relationships between mother and child (Cavanagh et al., 2006). On the flipside, mothers who are happy in their remarriage tend to support closer connection between stepfathers and children (Marsiglio, 2005). In Zeke's case, several destructive or traumatic experiences characterized his stories about home life at an early age. For example, Zeke—who identifies as a first-generation married cisgender gay white male—described how his mom and stepdad partied and drank: "[M]y mom and my stepdad were, they were heavy partiers, drinkers. There was drug use. Um, you know, parties on the weekends and, and that kind of stuff. Not even just weekends. But that, that was kind of what I saw. That was my, my normalcy at home." Eventually, Zeke left home and was on the streets before he moved in with his biological dad.

For nonresident biological fathers, divorce tends to strain relationships with kids (Amato, 2010), and less access to children may impact feelings of obligation on the part of stepfathers. With nonresident fathers, payment of child support, feelings of closeness, and authoritative parenting tend to be positively associated with children's academic success and, by contrast, not positively associated with externalizing and internalizing problems with kids (Amato & Gilbreth, 1999). In Zeke's case, he realized when he started high school that he needed to leave home, where he lived with his mom and stepdad, and move in with his biological dad: "I was staying with some friends just trying to like get to school. I was a freshman in high school. And when I made the decision to live with my dad it was, I was fifteen, you know they straight out said like, you're not going to make it. Like you're not going to succeed in life if you move in with him. Like you're, you're gonna be nothing if you move there, you know." But Zeke shared how his dad was both spiritual and compassionate with him, offering his support at that time in his life.

Stella shared how her dad had to be removed from the home when she was younger, after he had experienced drug abuse and conflict with her mom. These events started a period where Stella could not see her dad without a third-party monitor and led to years of strain between them. She shared more: "Due to all the stuff that was happening in my childhood, and the government got involved." Stella focused on the outcome of this episode: "[M]y mom had a restraining order against him, that's where the disconnection between me and him happened. And honestly, he wasn't really a very stable father to begin with, which caused me and him to not communicate as often."

Diverse family structures included kinship care, where grandparents, aunts and uncles, and older siblings cared for them in parenting roles in their young lives. For some graduate students, grandparents cared for them while parents worked. Early in life, when Jenna's family lived in the Philippines, her grandparents raised her due to her parents' work schedules. She described it this way: "[B]asically my life in the Philippines it was my grandparents who raised me. My parents would work opposite shifts, and they were tired when they came home." Similarly, Brianna's grandparents participated in parenting and, specifically, her grandfather was a central fathering figure in her life. Brianna, who identifies as a first-generation African American woman, talked about who her grandfather was to her and what he did for her: "[M]y grandparents to come pick us up. [Grandmother], Grandfather, they're right there. Pick up the kids, you know, for elementary education. Highly much involved for [middle school]. And then, of course, um, we were right, we were like maybe ten minutes away from our high school."

Brianna's grandfather was so involved in her life that her friends at school knew him well. She illustrated his presence in her life, referring to her twin brother and her in this story: "[P]eople knew, they knew [Grandfather], you know. Come up to the school, hey [grandfather], you know. Okay, you bring, you're getting twins? Yep, they're right here, you know?" Brianna had more stories about her grandfather, including this one where she described what happened when her twin brother cut school.

> I remember one time [my brother] had cut school. Um [my brother], my brother, like didn't do like high, high, high grades, but he, he was still a good kid, you know. Like, but it was one day that he cut school, and you know everyone was all on his neck, especially Grandfather, you know. So Grandfather would just tell him, okay, you're not gonna drive the car for a whole week. You know, or, you know what I'm saying?

Brianna concluded: "So it's very highly, highly involved. Highly, Grandfather, oh, my gosh. You know. It was huge. That was such a great time."

Winona talked about how her uncles raised her until she was five years old, then her dad joined the family as he emigrated from Vietnam to the US. Her uncles never substituted for her dad, as she described, but they were "the men in the family type of vibe." When her dad arrived in the mid-2000s, he immediately assumed a care-taking role as he stayed at home and cooked, cleaned, and dropped off and picked up Winona from school, and served supportively in the family. While he regulated her dress in some ways—nothing too revealing or in violation of dress codes at school—he never really reproduced gender norms in Winona's life. She narrated more of the story.

> Um, he never discouraged me from like oh, soccer is for boys. Like he never said that. He was always like, you're doing bad, do it again type of aspect. Yeah, like so he never just, he never discouraged me of like oh, football's for boys. Or this and that for boys. Like, or that's for girls. Like he never really said like oh, like wear this. I've, like I said, like since he was in a sense conservative, um, didn't really influence my clothing style as much, but I personally chose not to wear revealing clothes or things like that. Um, color was never a factor of being like oh, like red is for boys. Like he never did that. He was like, oh, just wear it, it looks nice, and stuff like that.

Winona's dad's own childhood experiences seemed to shape his view of gendered norms for dress, behavior, and more. Winona described how he had been teased by classmates after having to wear his sister's shirt to school because his family lived in impoverished conditions and didn't have resources to purchase additional clothing. She reflected on these experiences for her dad: "But he, he was able to grow strong out of it. In the sense of like he was able to identify, even though this woman's shirt has, you know the, a certain sewing pattern, he was able to like, oh, this is how you sew a women's shirt versus a men's shirt." Winona concluded, referring to her dad's perspective: "[C]lothes is just clothes. It just looks good or not."

For Jasmine, who identifies as a first-generation heterosexual Hispanic female, the divorce of her parents and distant relationship with her dad—there was no contact between them for a time when she was younger—led to her uncles stepping in and providing "some love," by

Jasmine's word. She described how they helped her at a time in her life when she really needed loving parenting relationships. She said,

> I think my uncles just kind of gave me like, like some love I guess. And like support. Like, I distinctly remember like one uncle, I just had this feeling like always like, when I would see him at my family parties, he would always like see me and he'd open his arms like to give me a hug. And like I, as a kid like I really liked that. Like I would like try to find him to give him a hug. I thought it was really fun.

As an adult, Jasmine shared how she told this uncle how he was a father to her. Here's how she put it: "And I told him that one day when we were older, like over a beer I just said like, you know, I always saw you, like that felt like that's what a dad feels like." For a time in her life, Jasmine's older brother also served in a fathering role. She explained what he meant to her: "I have an older brother. I guess he would be more like a father figure to me. He's about twelve years older than me. Not going to high school or college, her older brother was always home and around her life when she was younger." At first a "meanie older brother," he later assumed a parental role. With twelve years on Jasmine, he had a strong personality and seemed to be a constant presence in her life.

Jessica's parents also divorced when she was young—in the first grade. Growing up, Jessica talked about how her mom served as a primary care-taker and breadwinner, raised her to resist gender norms, and modeled a successful career for Jessica. Later, Jessica described how her fiancé's father and grandfather served in fathering roles for her. Recalling her college graduation, she illustrated: "[W]hen I graduated last May, uh, my family left early, which is fine, but like his family, like his parents stayed and waited until, um, I was able to walk out, and we took pictures together. So, um, I really do feel like his, so my father-in-law is more of the father figure than any of the two that I've had in my life." Speaking to her fiancé's grandfather's special place in her life, Jessica recalled how his wisdom and, more recently, interest in her graduate school experiences, meant a lot to her. While he had been hospitalized recently, her fiancé's grandfather was "just like in a like, like in awe," when Jessica shared news of her TAship. "[L]ike he didn't, 'cause he grew up in like the fifties and stuff like that so he didn't really think of like, like he didn't go to school and stuff," Jessica revealed, so he had expressed amazement with her news.

Chapter 2

Parental Relationship Quality
Physical and Relational Distance but Emotional Closeness from a Young Age to Adulthood for Children

As a function of traditional gender roles in parenting, fathers generally worked outside the home and provided, while mothers tended to be more involved and do more at home, spend more time with children, and be foundational to child development. In clear and compelling terms, many graduate students described mothers as central to their childhood. They were more available, more accessible, and had more profound impacts on what children recall from early childhood and adolescence. As gender regulated interactions between women graduate students, in particular, and fathers, relationship quality tended to be lower but, in many instances, recovered to be a bit closer in emerging adulthood, with expressions of love, offers of support, and regular communication via text and video. However, for a small group, father-child relationships tended to be just as strong, or stronger, than with mothers. These seemed to involve special bonds formed at a young age that persisted into adulthood. With mothers, closeness tended to permeate mother-child bonds and strengthen relationship quality, for most but not all graduate students. For a small group, more distance could be felt between mothers and children, where work or competing demands came between them. Still, from many stories shared with me, mothers seemed to be everywhere at once in families—all while balancing either paid work outside the home and domestic duties with immediate and extended family.

As young children, most graduate students recalled parents who loved them and family life that promoted love, care, and concern for well-being. Childhood memories of time spent together and parents involved at home focused on special moments and routine activities that facilitated close ties to parents and tight-knit family units. By and large, mothers, fathers, parental figures, and extended family members filled unique roles with constructive contributions to children's lives. But this was not the case universally, and reports about tense interactions and more complex connections with parents emerged in conversations with some graduate students. From gender norms to experiences with family migration, as familial contexts and conditions outside the home shaped families, parent-child relationships evolved to the point where challenges emerged and changed the dynamics—resulting in a waxing and waning effect of more distance and closeness between parents and children. These patterns appeared to continue into adulthood, where many graduate students described emotional closeness but physical and relational distance. Later, as undergraduate and graduate students, these close emotional ties to parents made all the difference as part of efforts to persist in their studies and complete degree programs.

Whether closer or more distant relationships evolved over the life course, what appeared to be true for many graduate students is that ties to parents or parental figures at a young age enhanced communication and opened opportunities to transmit cultural and familial values and teach children about cultural knowledge and beliefs. For most, early memories of love, affection, and care permeated home life, even as a small group experienced trauma in the family. In the latter cases, relationships with parents could be tenuous, especially where regulated by gender norms, but may have healed a bit over time. Where forces outside the home—like migration and family separation—negatively influenced relationship quality, children seemed eager to learn from their parents and continue family traditions and more.

Parental Contributions to Early Life Development of Graduate Students

The youngest of six, Andres felt there was a lot of love in his family. Both this mom and dad created a home where the three girls and three boys could grow up around each other as a supportive unit. For Andres, a first-generation able-bodied cis-hetero male who identifies as Mexican, specifically Mexicah and Tepehuani, there was a lot of fun and excitement as a child, especially when his dad came home from work and they'd spend time together or play in the street—riding bikes or playing baseball or football—until it got late and the streetlights turned on. Like Andres, Eileen recalled spending time with her parents as a child, and her dad had a flexible work schedule—so he would be available for her. Eileen spoke to this time in her life: "[S]ometimes we'd eat in front of the TV, but we would always like weave in conversation around there, too. Um, but with my parents very like present and active in my, my childhood, um, yeah, always, you know, around, and um, going to like sporting events, and after school things, and chaperoning field trips, and things like that." For her dad's part, he "would chaperone field trips, and things like that, very present."

Love and affection abound in many families. Josefina shared how she grew up in a very loving home with parents who nurtured and supported her. She said: "I can honestly say that . . . I've been very blessed in . . . that . . . both of my parents were very caring, and they express their love and their affection for us." Josefina, a first-generation straight Chicana woman with children, emphasized how her parents expressed a lot of love and affection at home—with her mother demonstrating how selflessly giving she was. Josefina talked about how her mother's "very unconditional love" made for "a healthy relationship" with her. She reflected: "I always felt like I could lean on her, reach out to her, talk to her. So yeah, I don't know if that answers my question." And her mother modeled unconditional love everywhere she went. At the laundromat, Josefina illustrated how her mom helped her to understand how to extend unconditional love to people in your life, even if strangers you've just met: "Better in the sense of respecting and caring for others. She's someone who taught about giving back, you know, to less fortunate folks. If you have something, give back, you know, whether it's your time, or is it something that you have, if you don't need anymore, pass it on to someone that could really use it."

Graduate Student Reflections on Early Relationships with Fathers Focus on Special Moments and Time Together

For his part, Josefina's dad uniquely showed his love for her through storytelling, and special treats like watermelon, donuts, and ice cream. Josefina remembered these sweet treats well, recalling the following:

> [H]e would bring in the summers always a big watermelon. And he would, he would say, "Go get a knife from inside the kitchen." And then we'd go get the knife, and we sit in the front lawn of the house and cut the watermelon and eat watermelon. And he was always the kind of father that, doesn't matter what time of the . . . year, you know, when you would hear the ice cream truck. And so every time we heard the sound of the truck, and my father would be like, Oh! I think he . . . would get joy just from seeing his kids asking "Dad, can you buy me an ice cream?" He goes, "Oh, well go, go stop it! Go stop it." But we're like, "Dad the donut truck is passing by." "Well just, just go stop it." You know, so we would run out, and he would always just have so much joy, you know, from seeing us. Giving us treats like that.

He hugged a lot, too, which Josefina remembered well. She shared: "[H]is joy was always being with his kids." These recollections seemed to prompt Josefina to share how her dad played an outsized role in her life.

Josefina's stories illustrate how nurturant fathering supports positive young adult outcomes for daughters. Indeed, Petersen (2007) found that father involvement and nurturant fathering related positively to young adult daughter self-esteem and life satisfaction. With more nurturant fathering, children's social, emotional, cognitive, and linguistic outcomes tend to be positive (Lamb 2010; Connor, 1997; Easterbrooks, 1984; Shannon, 2002; De Woolf, 1997). For graduate students who related fathers, in particular, with nurturance, unique experiences with love and care at home emerged from their stories. For example, Jenna, a first-generation Filipina heterosexual female, described her closeness with her dad, who did everything for her, and she recalled being close to him as he stayed home and served in the care-taker role while her mom returned to school and finished college when Jenna was younger.

As a child, Edith was also close with her dad and described how he would start his day later in order to help her get going in the morning. "He was, he and I were very close growing up. And we still are. I remember, like he, he would start his day later," she recalled. Edith, a first-generation Korean female who uses she/her gender pronouns, revealed more about how her dad connected with and cared for her: "Like my dad can understand and empathize a bit more. So I would go to him about my first crush, or I would go to him about friendships." She continued: "[H]e would be

Figure 2.1. Love and affection characterize families of many graduate students. *Source:* By Photos by Danny B., CC BY-NC 2.0. https://www.flickr.com/photos/16916814@N02/30440966173.

very empathetic. But then, also, you know, basically say to me like, you know, think about the other person and what they might be thinking or feeling, too, when . . . there were like problems with like friendships." So close was her dad to Edith that her Korean American girlfriends would comment on how unusual it was. Edith related his approach to his character—very open and supportive.

Hector, a cisgender heterosexual married male who identifies as a person of color with multiracial and multiethnic identities of Mexican, Filipino, Italian, and Native American, remembered how his dad would drive him and his teammates to practices and games. "You know we had this like, an old VW Bug," Hector remembered. He continued: "And we would pick up all these guys who, he basically picked up half the team to get to the game, or get to practice. Um and yeah, that was . . . a really big part of, you know like, uh, you know like the educational experience like, like you, you want to do well 'cause you want to be on these teams." Hector later realized how special this closeness with his dad was. He was close with his mom, too, and talked about her in similarly loving terms. When recalling his time at home when he was younger, he talked about his mom as "very, very supportive. Always, always encouraging you to, um, do your best." Hector elaborated, revealing how close he was to his mom: "[T]he relationship I had with my mom, or have with my mom, you know she has been incredibly loving and supportive. You know, a huge, the, maybe the biggest cheerleader that, that you, you could have in your corner, you know, from a young age." Hector described in detail how his mom had been there for him in school and at home. He spoke to his mom's presence in his life at the time.

> [A] big part of it was like, you know early on, like, you know, kindergarten, first grade, you know, I know there was helping me, you know, complete homework assignments. But also being enthusiastic and, and excited about school. I think I always had a good feeling about going to school, and it felt like a, a safe place. Felt like a good place to learn. Felt like a place to be, that, like, like, like I had a, I felt like I had a purpose there, at the school, was, was to, to learn

Hector concluded: "I feel like my mom helped me with that, like, you knew your role."

While Zelma remembered her dad as very strict at home, she recalled him as the life of the party—and at social events and family gatherings he would show his more nurturing side.

She summarized the seemingly contradictory sides of his personality and parenting: "At home he was very strict, but when he would go out places he's the life of the party. My dad was a big jokester. You know it was like, you know, people would say, oh, your dad is so funny. I'm like, yeah, okay, you wait till he gets home."

For Black teenagers, father involvement shapes behavioral, psychosocial, and educational outcomes. Black adolescent boys who spend more time with their fathers tend to report lower levels of depression and anxiety, while father nurturance in the form of emotional support increases self-esteem and life satisfaction (Zimmerman et al., 1995). With African American adolescent girls, close contact with their fathers tends to lower depressive symptoms (Coley, 2003). After the transition to adulthood, Black children report feelings of closeness with their fathers, and Black adult children share stronger emotional connections with nonresident fathers than white children with nonresident fathers (Thomas et al., 2008). Kayla shared how her father, to this day, is "not very affectionate" but very involved in the family and at home. Kayla cited gender-regulating behavior, in part, for her father's less affectionate approach: "You know just taking care of, you know the things outside of the house. 'Cause I, I saw that a lot. He did everything in the yard, and you know, the cars and all that stuff. So that was kind of what the role that he, he played."

For some, extended family contributed to the love and affection felt at home. Brianna, a first-generation African American woman, lost her dad early in life, when he passed away after an illness. But she had her grandfather, who shared a father role in her life. As a child, Brianna remembered her dad as a character, engaging in banter between Brianna and her twin brother. She remembered him this way: "[Y]ou could get to him. He tried to do a silent treatment, and then we gave him a whole present. Why y'all do this, you know." She continued: "[H]e'd be mad for a few days but he, he still had a heart, you know what I'm saying?" Her dad worked long hours and, when Brianna was a little bit older, he got sick. After his passing, Brianna remembered his absence and how much he loved her. Speaking of him, she shared more: "I knew he loved me. I knew, he had this heart, you know, interior, I know I wouldn't be where I'm at if it wasn't for him." After her dad passed away, Brianna's grandfather stepped in, becoming "heavily, heavily involved." Briana remembered how he would do the things that fathers tended to do at the time in her life as a teenager, including teaching Brianna and her brother how to drive. He described how they would go practice driving. Where'd they go? To the cemetery, given her grandfather's professional association with his role as a funeral home director. Why there? "[Y]ou can't kill anyone here," her grandfather quipped. Remembering both her father and grandfather, Brianna remarked how "their legacy is just strong."

Tanya grew up in a middle-class "Black American experience . . . home." She talked about how they had a wonderful time with vacations, weekend outings, and more. "Very close family as well," Tanya said. She illustrated the closeness she felt in her family, saying: "I was raised, my first cousins are like my siblings, and my kind of second cousins are like my first cousins. So extremely, extremely close family." In this closeness, Tanya identified her grandpa's love and affection to her early years. "Even though . . . my daddy was in my life, when we talk about like affection, emotion, like what a father is, it was my [grandpa]," she said. Her grandpa passed away when she was young—seven years old—but he gave "the love of a lifetime, you know to know what a father could truly be." Tanya was quick to point out that her dad was very involved in her life—just not as emotionally as she needed. She shared that her dad worked a lot and couldn't be there as much as she needed. "Not saying my daddy wasn't a good daddy, it's just like that emotional intelligence was off with him," Tanya revealed. But her grandpa emotionally connected with her at a young age and created a sense of safety for her, and she recalled going to the park and feeding ducks or going to the country and sitting in his blue truck. This was the personal, intimate and "one-on-on time" that Tanya needed.

Both Kayla and Susan described close connections with their fathers, respectively. Kayla, who identifies as a first-generation cisgender African American female married with two children, shared how her dad and her were more similar than her mom and her. "Both him and I, because he loves sports I ended up loving sports because of that reason," Kayla remarked." She continued,

> And so we kind of bonded over that a lot. And I enjoyed it. It's not that I felt like I was forced to enjoy it to have a relationship with him. I generally enjoyed watching sports and getting into it. And I remember like when the [local team] went on to [win], all of us were watching TV, you know like really intensely, you know. So the, a, a good relationship with my dad. After I moved out and stuff, that was a little bit different.

Susan described her relationship with her dad as "superclose." As a mother now, she talked about how she can reflect on how her parents raised her from the perspective of a parent. She spoke to how her parents had to overcome their own childhood experiences with parents who were not so involved. They valued their involvement in Susan's life and seemed to model love and care in the home. Susan, a white and Latina cis-heterosexual female who identifies as Jewish, elaborated: "I think they did really well with, you know where they were coming from in life. Um, they both had not so great parents I would say that weren't superinvolved. Um, so, so they really valued being parents and really tried, um, hard." While Susan's dad didn't serve as the primary care-taker for her brother and her, he would always play with them and share time together at home. No bathing Susan, getting Susan dressed, or preparing food for Susan and her brother—but she did recall him being there to help her with homework. As an immigrant from Argentina, Susan's dad spoke

Spanish fluently and insisted on helping her with her Spanish homework in middle school and high school.

Love and Care Accompany Graduate Student Relationships with Mothers in Early Life

Just as stories about closeness with fathers emerged in conversations about relationship quality, so too did accounts about mothers. Overall, a recurring theme in descriptions of relationships with mothers focused on love and care—almost an existential presence in the lives of graduate students—even as a range of relational characteristics, from nurturant to distant, had been referenced. Brianna talked about how close her mother and her are—to the point where she worried a lot about her mom, who lived in a different state in the Southeast. For her part, her mom worried about Brianna, too, and tended to use nurturant terms with Brianna. As an ordained minister, Brianna's mom prayed for her, which comforted Brianna and helped her get through tough times in graduate school—keeping her in the program when she wanted to leave. "So I think our relationship has gotten better as we've gotten older," Brianna remarked, sharing how she often updates her mom: "[H]ey, this is what's going on." Similarly, Zelma referred to a close relationship with her mom, whom she doesn't see every week now but who remains close at heart. "[W]e at least talk two or three times a week," Zelma remarked, "I visit them . . . they're in [a different city] now from [my city], so yeah, close relationship still."

So many stories dotted descriptions about close connections between mothers and children. Holly summed up her close relationship with her mom and listed the reasons why. She said: "I generally have been very close with my mom, always. She has been my biggest supporter always. She adored my daughter, you know. And so that was, you know her, like the sun and the moon for her." At the time of our conversation, Holly had lost her mom seven years ago, but it felt like just yesterday that she had gone. Holly reflected on her pain: "So, you know, the pain subside[s], like I was told it takes five years." She continued: "[B]ecause after five years, like the pain subsided a little bit, but it's still, I, I, I think I'm still in denial and disbelief that, that she is gone." What especially hurt for Holly was her mom's optimistic, positive outlook that seemed to balance Holly's more pessimistic viewpoint. "She was always the sunshine," Holly remarked, "like when you have such an optimist next to you, you don't have to be an optimist, because you can just go to your mom and cry in

Figure 2.2. Many graduate students recall closeness to their mothers. *Source:* By francisco_osorio, CC BY 2.0. https://www.flickr.com/photos/30330906@N04/6837004331.

her shoulder, and she would be the one who will tell you everything will be okay, and it will work out."

Josefina, Angela, Sharon, and Andres all shared similar stories of closeness to their mothers, respectively. For her part, Josefina described her mother as giving, and this is—in part—what connected them. "Very loving, very unconditional love," Josefina said, "I was a healthy relationship with my mother. I always felt like I could lean on her, reach out to her, talk to her. So yeah, I don't know if that answers my question."

Angela, a first-generation African American female who identifies ethnically as Nigerian, also referenced closeness with her mom, citing their shared interests: "I think we're definitely close. I'm much closer to my mom than my dad. I think maybe it's just a girl thing . . . we have similar interests and everything like that. But yeah, we're definitely really, really close." Sharon recalled always having a good relationship with her mom, talking about how her mom lived with her for the last fifteen years of her mom's life. Her mom passing away a year before speaking with me,

Sharon recounted how they spent time shopping together—one of her mom's favorite activities. "So our shopping became catalog shopping at the end," Sharon—who identifies as a first-generation heterosexual female married with children, recalled, "[b]ut she was still, she would still say, can we do some shopping today? Pull up the computers, I'd grab the laptop, and I'd sit, sit with her next to her in the bed, and we would, you know, shop through a couple of stores, and, and she just loved having something new." With Andres, his mom's nurturance made all the difference in the loving relationship that they shared. He remembered his mom as gentle but, at the same time, "stern." Andres recalled it this way: "We knew my mom was gentle, and my dad was like strict. Like, as soon as, like if we did something wrong my mom would be like, watch when your dad gets home. And we're like, that's about three thirty. You know, that's about four o'clock so get ready." Andres's mom's nurturance could be felt in so many ways, including the more mundane details of life like when Andres listed who would get them what they needed every day: "who would put on our socks in the morning, who would make us our breakfast, you know. Comb our hair, make sure we look nice, you know."

Figure 2.3. Parental love and care accompany many graduate students from childhood into adulthood, even as more complex relationships emerge later in life. *Source:* By Ryan Smith Photography, CC BY-NC-ND 2.0. https://www.flickr.com/photos/77138929@N00/31431624956.

While most stories about mothers centered on closeness and nurturance—like Andres's descriptions—a few focused on more distant relationships with mothers. For example, Liza referenced how her grandmother raised her brother and her as their parents both worked outside the home. This seemed to put space between the relationship with her mom, where Liza recalled her mother more as a "spectator" in her life. She recalled: "[M]y mom was more of just the spectator and my dad was more of like, he involved himself in the coaching aspect." Similarly, Kayla described her relationship with her mom as not very physically nurturing, but her mom always supported her. "Yeah, she wasn't like very affectionate," Kayla recounted, but she always felt supported. To this point, Kayla said: "So I always felt like supported, but the, like the affection and love and . . . like the, the softer part of nurturing, I didn't really feel from her growing up." As a result, Kayla was closer to her dad, "only because my mom was hard to open up to her about things because she was very reactive." Over the years, her mom has changed, having grown and matured, as Kayla observed, so they enjoy a closer relationship today.

Even as Closeness Characterized Relationships, More Complex Experiences with Parents Emerged in Childhood

Just as there were memories of nurturant parenting, close connections between children and parents didn't always seem to characterize relational connections. Stella, for example, shared how she identified as a daddy's girl, and here's what she remembered about him: "Like my, me and my dad were very close. If anything, comparing to the relationship I have with my mom, like I was way more closer to my dad. Me and my dad were very like similar. So that's why I would always go to him more." However, past a very young age, she recalled an absent father when she needed him most. Stella, a first-generation African American who uses the gender pronouns she/her/hers and is exploring her sexual orientation, painted a more complex picture of him, saying how he was present emotionally for her but had to be forced to be more involved in her life. She shared more: "[L]ike to be an actual, like real father, like doing like fatherly things like it, it's just like pulling a, a nail out of like someone's foot. Like it, it takes a lot for him to actually do something." This pattern caused conflict at home between her parents, and Stella felt it. Stella retells more here: "With my mom and my dad, cause like my mom would have to make him do stuff to like, take care of his kids. And there was times where he would just like, would leave for weeks at a time." Overall, this dynamic led to what Stella described as very unstable family, where "values were broken." And, Stella said, "Boundaries were broken." Similar to Stella, Sasha described her father as a great guy, and his relationship with her was important to her, but they did "not have that good of a relationship, and there was just a lot of like, like emotional instability going on really at all times." Sasha, who identifies as a pansexual white woman, concluded that he never knew quite how to act and seemed to be more private—where you never really knew how he was going to respond or what he was going to say.

When Angela talked about her childhood, she recalled her parents being a part of her life. Even as her dad was not as involved in her life, she recalls memories of going to the amusement park, traveling on family vacations, and food with him. She shared more about his love of food: "Other moments of joy? My dad is a big food person, and he likes to cook. So I think having him cook, um, in the house, or like getting us food is also a moment of joy that I can think of." Angela surmised that her dad may not have been as involved in her life because he didn't seem to have a father figure in his life. She spoke to this point here: "I think his lack of exposure to what a father looks like . . . in his childhood, growing up, my dad was born in like the sixties, um, so I think having, and he grew up in Nigeria so that looks like totally different from what it looks like in America." Angela reflected: "I think that lack thereof definitely plays a part into just like how he parents, and how he views money, how you views success, all those different things."

Sharon remembered her father struggled, at times, to be close with her, likely for reasons related to the relationship with his own dad, whom he did not know as a parent. In fact, Sharon's dad's first connection with his dad was at his dad's funeral. Consequently, Sharon described how her father didn't express a lot of physical affection with her. Beyond the occasional pat on the back, Sharon said: "You know nothing, I wasn't like sitting in his lap reading books. You know . . . not, there was like no cuddling. But, um, he was never that kind of hands-on love, it was more at a distance." Still, Sharon recalled how she felt loved and supported at home. She could always go to her father for whatever she needed, including help with schoolwork. What's more, Sharon witnessed a lot of love between her parents. She detailed more.

He adored her just through and through. And I know that, that was one of the things that have, you know each of them divorced and got married together because it was just love at first sight, and there was no way he was going to live without her. So her, that relationship was everything to him. He would do anything he could for her. I think that was his motivation to work hard, to, you know, be able to buy her nice clothes, put her in a nice home, you know he, he just really wanted to take care of her. She worked for the family business, too, as a bookkeeper.

Sharon concluded: "[H]e just always loved her."

In Karina's case, there was closeness with her father at a young age, but then they seemed to grow apart as she aged. She recalled how their relationship evolved over the years: "Yeah, so, um, when I was very young, like elementary school, that's probably like the most time that we would spend together. Like he was very present in my life, which I'm very grateful for." She continued: "I think that as we got older though, it's kind of different. Like, um, we can still talk and have great conversations, but, um, you know there's, we're both trying to avoid conversations that we don't want to argue about." When she was younger, Karina recalled how her dad's connection to "machismo culture" limited his ability to express a range of emotions and affection with her brother and her. Even though he shares more affectionate feelings with Karina, he failed to do so with her brother. Karina, a heterosexual Latina woman who identifies as half Guatemalan and half Mexican, further described her relationship with her father: "[W]e always say I love you every time we leave, or even through text." But Karina noted how he didn't display a lot of emotions: "You know he never really shows that emotion. Like he never really says I love you to my brother because, you know it's another male so it's very different.

Beatrice's father was always involved in her life but was "sometimes harsh," "hard," and "strict," all of which caused friction in the relationship. Beatrice, a heterosexual female who identifies as white and Mexican, described how her dad would get mad at her brother and her and—in those instances—her mother had to be the "voice of reason" and "would just kind of like reel him back in." Fortunately, Beatrice's father mellowed as Beatrice aged. As her softball coach, her father spent a lot of time with her on the field of practice and play. "I appreciate it 'cause he's a really good player, and he, he was a phenomenal coach," Beatrice remarked. This all meant a lot of Beatrice, but he was hard on her, too, and seemed to single her out for being the coach's daughter. She remembered him this way: "But he was always way tougher on me to make a point to the, all the other parents and all the other kids, like, hey, there's no favorites. But in doing so it was, you know reverse." Still, Beatrice knew he was always there for her, and he moved on to be involved or interested in what her brother and her were doing as they matured—be it pickleball, jazz music, or anything else. "He's loves, you know, learning about things that we were passionate about," Beatrice commented.

Juan, a man whose dad immigrated from Mexico, had all the support he needed when he was growing up, even if his dad did not develop close bonds with him. Always a bit distant, Juan's dad worked with his mom to express love and give to the family. With both parents, Juan felt his family was into "showing love" for each other. When he spoke about his dad, Juan recalled how he did things that he knew could help him connect with Juan. Here's how Juan remembered his dad's involvement in his life: "He helped me rearrange my bedroom. So things like that is sort of the only way that we would sort of bond and show love to each other, like I want to be spending this time with you. Um, and, I mean working on cars is another thing. Even though I, I'm extremely disinterested I would try to seem interested and learn, um, so that he could feel like I wanted to, you know, do that with him." Beyond mechanic work on cars and work around the house, Juan fondly recalled his father's role in making birthday celebrations as special as could be. In addition, Christmas was big for Juan's family, and his father went all out for brother and him, making them "as happy as [they] could be during those days," according to Juan.

Jaime's parents divorced when she was young, and she didn't seem to be particularly close with them. Jaime, a first-generation Vietnamese American female, observed about how her notion of close family and parenting relationships changed over time. "I lived with my aunt, and I have three aunts, and I lived with two of them, um, at different stages," Jaime described as she discussed her closeness to her aunts. She observed: "[W]hoever was living in that house suddenly became my, uh, nuclear family." Jessica, a white female, described a similar family structure—only later in life. Discussing her parents-in-law and her fiancé's family, she talked about how love and affection could be seen in their home. In stark contrast to her in-laws, her parents seemed to model a "tough love type of family," from what Jessica shared. "Like we don't show our affection," she said. She elaborated: "We like, we help you out by like services, like we'll help you like mow your lawn or something type of dynamic. Um, but with my in-laws and their family, they're very, um, more showy in affection than my family."

Relationship Closeness as Tenuous with Parents Where Family Immigration Shaped Children's Experiences

In some cases, graduate students described relationships where closeness could not be attained due to migratory movement or long work hours, days or months away from home. For Ping's father, who was a worker in the city rather than in their rural village in China, he rarely spent time at home with Ping and his three older sisters. Ping, a first-generation student, remarked about this reality: "I seldom have the opportunity to like live with him, or talk with him. And may probably, in the traditional Chinese New Year, . . . my father will go back, and we will have time, like one or two week[s]." With only annual visits home, Ping generally connected with his father over the phone, when they spoke twice a week. Still, when they did see each other in person, Ping recalled how he would follow his father everywhere for a week or two during Chinese New Year visits together at home. When he went to visit relatives, Ping would go—and when we went to play poker, Ping would tag along. Ping spoke to this pattern: "I think that when I was young . . . whatever my father do I will follow, follow him. I . . . was very eager to see my father." In his father's absence, Ping grew closer to his mother, with whom he lived until he moved to a larger urban center for junior high school.

Josefina remembered how her dad worked multiple jobs and spent a lot of time outside the home. She detailed her dad's work schedule, saying: "[M]y dad always had two jobs. He had his full-time job, and then he had his 6 to 3 p.m. job, 6 a.m. to 3 p.m. And then go do landscape work 'til like, sometimes 5." This schedule meant he missed school events and extracurricular activities for Josefina, typically when these events happened after school.

Zelma knew both her mom and dad had been shaped by their experiences with their own families of origin and, later, with immigration to the US. She shared what their general approach had been from a very early age at home: "They just wanted to make sure that we survived, and, um, love was very transactional," where you didn't get a lot of positive feedback. Zelma asked rhetorically: "It was always the negative right?"

And if you misbehaved? "If you did something wrong it was like," Zelma said, "we got yelled at. We got scolded." Her dad yelled a lot, and Zelma shared how her dad had been subjected to physical abuse at home when he was a child—and maybe this is why he yelled at Zelma and her siblings.

Cultural value conflicts shaped relationship closeness for some graduate students who shared immigrant experiences with families. In particular, a tension between cultural values and practices tended to shape Zelma's identity as a first-generation cis-hetero Indigenous Palestinian and Lebanese woman, which in turn may have driven a wedge between her father and her. She spoke to this point: "I'm trying to figure out my identity. I'm trying to figure out who I am in this space of straddling two cultures. And still being demanded to do things a certain way. You know, um, it was, it was rough." She shared that there was "a lot of sneaking around." She admitted more: "There was a lot of, I'm dating but no one's gonna know, you know. Late night phone calls where we'd have the phones, you know the corded phones, that kind of thing."

Like Zelma, Maria's dad's immigrant experiences seemed to shape how he interacted with her. Maria, a first-generation LGBTQ-identified Armenian woman who immigrated from Iran and identifies culturally as Middle Eastern and Armenian, shared how her dad worked long hours in Armenia and in the US. Before he emigrated and joined Maria and her mom and brother in the western US, he took on two jobs—which disconnected him from Maria. As she aged, things hadn't improved much, she said. With two jobs and not much time at home, Maria said their relationship is even worse. Beyond work, Maria shared, there seemed to be cultural and familial divides between her parents and her. For example, Maria talked about how her parents never seemed to be able to express themselves well to her. She elaborated further.

> So, um, unfortunately I'm not that close just because he himself as well grew up not being as expressive, and when I try to, it gets very much awkward. Um, they tend to not know how to like communicate um in a healthy way. But I would say, compared to my mom he's, he tends to be more to himself, and like quiet. So that kind of makes me feel disconnected because I like to um express more now, or, or I guess the need of wanting to express because I've realized how important it is to let out feelings to the loved ones, especially parents, but he's not used to seeing that, so it tends to be a bit awkward.

Later, when Maria came out to her parents, it seemed to drive them even further apart. She reflected more on this time in her life.

> I think also another thing that plays a big, uh, role is that when I came out to them, my relationship got very distanced because they're very traditional. So, um, you know that really played a big role, and I, for both of them I didn't feel connected whatsoever because, you know, like I wasn't getting that respect anymore. Even though I knew deep down they, they care about me, it's just their views was different, which I understand, but again it still hurts not having that family support.

Even with the strain of disconnectedness from her dad and tension from her coming out to her parents, there seemed to have been many moments when Maria remembered time together with them. Growing up, she recalled fondly, her parents would take her brother and her to the park and events. Her dad would teach them how to play musical instruments and—to her astonishment and surprise—bring pets home for them. There were family get-togethers, too, where her parents, brother, and her would all be together. For birthdays, her dad would leverage his creativity and "would design all like the artwork on the walls, um, like happy birthday, and, um, or like the birthday hats."

A lot like Maria, Winona's dad remained in Vietnam and lived apart from the family when she was young and immigrated to the US when Winona was in kindergarten. With her mom working outside the house, her uncles served as a father figure presence in her life before her dad arrived when she was five years old. She recalled fond moments with her uncles, gaming on PCs, taking her to water parks, amusement parks, and more. They joked around, too, and played tag around the house—all fun for Winona. "So yeah, so they, they were present," Winona remembered. Speaking to all of her memories with her uncles, she said: "Things like that were, were around for everyone, too." One of her uncles, in particular—who passed away in 2012—introduced Winona to cartoons. He would rent DVDs with Disney Channel cartoon series from the 1990s, and they would watch them endlessly. She detailed what this time meant for her: "So he was the one that always was bringing home things for us to watch. And, um, us as in like his, his, his daughter and then myself, so, cause we were living in the same house. So we would be watching those cartoons, or anything new. Um, *Dora Explorer* was very popular.

Go Diego, Go was very popular. Um, anything in that realm of cartoons was, it was always." Winona remembered how, once her dad arrived, they all watched together. Later, she realized how unique this time was for her uncles, dad, and her. She said: "As well as in regards for my dad, he and I connected with *Tom and Jerry*, because Tom and Jerry didn't need audio. They just needed visuals. And he and I were able to relate, because for him, like he didn't get cartoons as a child. So it's kind of like a way for him to reconnect with his childhood, and for me to just be there with him just watching these cartoons as well, too."

Gender as a Regulating Factor in Relationships with Fathers: Quality and Time with Children Shaped by Normative Expectations

As patterns reproduced structural inequality in gender roles and a gender hierarchy, normative expectations tend to push men to the outer boundaries of the family, alienating fathers from children and undermining relationships in the family (Adams & Coltrane). Overall, love and care exhibited in relationships between fathers and graduate students, especially earlier in life, generally followed conventional norms for masculine forms or displays of affection and relational closeness—more words, fewer hugs and kisses, some embraces. In these cases, closeness may have been elusive where gendered behavioral patterns persisted in fathers. To illustrate, Zelma associated her dad with a "generation of men where I just want to provide for my family. Um, and that would have been enough, right?" The result, said Zelma: "[M]y dad was not very affectionate, right? Very stern, even with three girls, you know. He grew up in a male-dominated environment." Gail recalled her dad as stricter, too, like Zelma, and described her dad this way: "I think he was probably more strict of the two parents, and like less emotional. Um, like less physically caring at least like in my later childhood, teenage years." She connected her dad's role as the "rock of the family" with more controlled emotional expressions. She observed: "I've only seen my dad cry like a handful of times, so I think he's very like, wants to be sturdy for us, you know."

With his father serving as a gender-regulated traditional provider role for the family and his mom doing most of the care work and house chores at home, Leonardo recalls fewer but meaningful moments with his father. Traditionally associated with masculinity and gender expectations for men to socialize, sports seemed to bring his dad and him closer and facilitated bonding between them. Soccer was big for his dad, and Leonardo remembers watching countless matches together—"right there with him watching." His dad was there for him for special events, too. Gail had a lot of good memories from her dad's time with her and what they did together. "I remember going on trips with my dad, like going hiking, or we'd go to Mexico sometimes." She continued: "I remember having fun with like him and his family. He has a really big family, so it was fun when we did stuff with that side of the family." But Gail also talked about how her dad seemed stoic about his feelings and never really allowed her to express a range of emotions. Instead, he tended to be more punitive if she showed emotional responses that included crying. She seemed to resist his gender-regulating behavioral expectations, which caused friction between them and a "rocky" relationship when she was younger.

Even when fathers exhibited limited emotional closeness, they tended to message love and care for kids. Maria said her dad was never very nurturing. But compared to "you know how the stereotypical, masculine thing that people say, like he's not like that," Maria conceded. "He tends, he tends to show more of that nurturing side, but not often, if that makes sense," she concluded, referring to her dad's infrequent but meaningful expressions of love. Like Maria, Eugenio, a first-generation heterosexual married Latinx male who identifies as Oaxacan from an Indigenous background from Mexico, shared how his dad tended to lack emotional expressions of love to him, but Eugenio knew his dad loved him. Never hugging, kissing, or the like, his dad didn't grow up with a parental figure who modeled how to develop close bonds with a loved one. Eugenio mentioned that his father's father was absent, and maybe this was a reason why he couldn't form meaningfully affectionate closeness with men in his life. Beyond lack of father in his dad's life, gender may have played a role in his dad's inability to get close to him. Eugenio surmised that maybe his dad thought such physically expressive gestures between men was discouraged. He shared briefly: "I don't know if it's because he's a male and I'm a male, I'm not sure exactly." Fortunately for Eugenio, his mom was nurturing and caring with him—so he felt emotionally cared for and strong bonds to her. And even though he recalled his dad as more distant and mom as closer relationally, both parents spent time together in the family and made many memories with Eugenio and his cousins. He described more: "I really remember we would always spend time together. So that's the, the best time of like the year, especially Christmas, I mean those are times, um Thanksgiving. That's a time where we all meet together. My cousins will join and stuff. Um, that I spent time with them exactly just like, unless we were at the end like at midnight when we open gifts, of course that's the time we were just us."

Chapter 3

Parental Values Extend Far for Children

The Importance of Education, Hard Work, Family Unity, Empathy, and Spirituality

There's something special about what I learned from speaking with this group of graduate students who looked back at their lives and reflected on foundational values that have driven them. Individually, they lead vastly different lives in all corners of the country, but together there are several clear beliefs important to who they are. Across their unique stories, they respectively seemed to center on a collective set of ideals that rise above their immediate situations, transcending the machinations that surround daily decisions and larger directions in life for most of us. That's not to say they didn't share beliefs that tend to guide us—doing what's right, getting the job done, striving for better, getting ahead, taking care of our families, and so on—they demonstrated all of them. But they prioritized values that tended to be other-directed and advanced a sense of selflessness. They generally believe that there was something bigger than themselves to work toward and give to. Whether related to advancing educationally, caring for family, honoring elders, and contributing to solutions to community problems, most graduate students linked their lives to others from a young age. These values tended to swirl around their ambitions for academic aspirations in the educational pipeline and grounded their paths toward advanced study in graduate school.

Central to early childhood development for most graduate students seemed to be a set of family values—reproduced primarily by parents but also siblings and extended family members—that promote cultural knowledge about school as important to life outcomes, education as key to success in life, and academic achievement and aspirations to go to college as critical. In fact, talk of how parents pushed the idea of educational advancement formed the very earliest memories and most recent recollections for most graduate students. For some, there was an anthem of "go to school, go to school," messaging how important education was to get ahead and build on the gains families made by immigrating to the US and/or working for social mobility from marginalized communities. Often in our conversations, stories tended to center family value systems that reified the importance of education, hard work, family support and unity, compassion and care for each other, and spirituality. Even when values didn't seem directly connected to education—like family unity and spirituality—they seemed to be part of a system of core beliefs and daily rituals that reinforced why academic journeys led to graduate school and why careers and lives centered on getting ahead, giving back, and making an impact. Among both first-generation and continuing-generation students, above all values, education permeated dinner table discussions about homework, volunteering in school activities—especially by mothers—and plans for college and beyond.

"Go to School, Go to School": Education as a Central Family Value

As one of the most important values that parents reproduced in families, students frequently recounted stories about education as a means to get ahead in life and be upwardly mobile, particularly for children of color whose parents immigrated to the US. Describing their earliest memories in life, this central orientation to education defined childhoods. Hua, who identifies as a Chinese female, remarked how "universal" education seemed to be a value at home. "Education is always the most important in my family, and they work getting higher education," Hua shared. She continued: "I think first thing is for my parents, and like they agree that education is most important in this family." Similarly, in Hector's family, there was an expectation to go to college "to move, advance. And not just, not just economically, but . . . to engage, to help communities, and to make a difference. And, um, and also to, to expand your thinking." Hector remembered how going to college was not an option in his family—it was an imperative. From a very young age, he recalled how college "wasn't like an option, it was like a thing that was going to happen." For generations, Hector's family achieved academically at and earned degrees from institutions of higher education, including his great-grandfather, who "immigrated from the Philippines [to] here, and then got his doctorate, he got his bachelor's, and then he got a doctorate here." Hector recalled how both parents emphasized academic achievement—"doing well in school, working hard to get good grades, and taking education seriously."

Cultural Values Center the Importance of Education

Several graduate student stories about their earliest memories of parents promoting education connected their cultural identities and experiences with family value systems. Black college students report that familial and parental values about the importance of education instilled at a young age frame college as mandatory and a college degree as the best chance for upward mobility (McCallum, 2016). For Black women, in particular, family involvement is critical to academic and career interests in mathematics fields (Borum & Walker, 2011) and beyond (Pearson & Bieschke, 2001). In professional careers, Black women share stories of family values that focus on education as central to both academic achievement and career success (Pearson & Bieschke). As a child, Brianna, a first-generation African American woman, described how her grandparents redirected her to a career that required a college degree when she announced that she would be going to beautician school. Here's what Brianna recalled: "[B]oth of them, they said you'll be a beautician at night. You can be a doctor, lawyer, or whatever you want by day. But you won't be a beautician. Choose another. So, it was kind of like they were shaping."

Later, Brianna talked about how she was bullied in junior high school. Down and hurt, she recalled how her grandfather would put it all into context and—at the same time—promoted academic achievement and educational advancement as critical to Brianna's rising above these experiences. She shared: "But he would always say like, twenty years from now, doesn't matter what these people think. You know. It's all gonna be about your grades. It's all gonna be about your grades and like, what you do with your grades, you know. So, I think it was good." With Brianna, her parents reproduced "education as liberation" in her family as a way to resist, challenge, and overcome racist structures in society. And Brianna's mom lived these values as she was "huge" into PTA and much more at school. Similar to Brianna's story, Kayla recalled how her father's family moved him from the South to the Northeast out of the family's fear for his safety following a racist interaction, in which he questioned white supremacist and racial hierarchical effects on the family. Kayla, a first-generation cisgender African American female, connected these experiences to her parents' insistence that education was a way out of a racialized system of anti-Black oppression. Kayla elaborated.

> I remember that, being told that story and having an understanding of the dynamics of that, and why, you know my parents work so hard, make sure all . . . like we had. Like, going to college wasn't even an option for me. It was like, I'm the youngest of three girls, so we all went to college. It's kinda like, you know, because we had the opportunity. Like my dad, as hard as he worked, he didn't necessarily have that opportunity where he [grew up], you know, so. And it was almost honestly his, even his high school education was almost taken away from that experience. So education is very much . . . encouraged in our household. And that's one of the, one of the reasons why.

Kayla understood how her father, in particular, never had the same chance to go to school as a function of a racially segregated system of education and exclusion in the South. For Kayla, she knew he wanted her to be educated and get away from what he had experienced.

For Tanya, a first-generation heterosexual African American woman, education was a central value in her family, and she recalled two messages her dad and grandpa communicated to her: "I was pretty and I was smart." For her dad, in particular, "education was a huge value." When she was younger, Tanya received "ten dollars for every A," and A's came easy for her—so she took her dad's money and made a small fortune. Tanya remembered how it felt like she didn't have a choice but to go to college. She described it this way: "[E]even though my parents did not pressure me to go to college, it was just kind of like an unspoken rule." This expectation aligned well with what Tanya felt as a connection to education or, as she put it, "a natural gravitation to education." She liked learning and knew she wanted to go far in her educational journey. She engaged academically, the stronger the expectations seemed to be that she'd go to college. She repeated this unspoken rule, connecting it to her studies: "[It] was understood, like unspoken rule, Tanya was going to college. Tanya was gonna do good in school, because I've just always done good in school."

With Kayla, her father completed high school and vocational studies, which helped Kayla understand how important education was. She commented: "[T]he education piece, 'cause as I mentioned, you know education was very important in our, in the family, you know." Kayla shared how her going to college was an expectation—it was implied from early in life in what her parents discussed with her. Indeed, Kayla recalled how she had to go to college, no question about it.

> Oh, I remember being in high school, and you know, going to college like, it was kind of like okay, I'll go 'cause that's what I'm like, that's what I'm supposed to do, but it really wasn't like, it really wasn't what I wanted to do. But I felt like if I didn't I would disappoint like, my fam, my, my father and my mother. I felt, I felt a, a sense of obligation to go to college, and I did. And you know it did, being there and, you know being in that space, I understand why they encouraged that, but you know, uh, it took me a while to get to this place where I kind of like, okay, this is what I was supposed, this is the path I was supposed to follow.

How did her parents set this expectation? Kayla explained: "[It] was like maybe a question, okay, you graduated high school was, what are you doing? Or did you apply for, are you going, are you going to college?" Kayla really felt obligated to go to college, after her father who—never "made more than like $50,000 a year"—promised to pay for her siblings and her to school. That pushed Kayla toward academic excellence, as she put it, and always being oriented toward achieving.

For Angela, a first-generation African American female who identifies ethnically as Nigerian, going to college "was . . . always a thing." Angela linked her cultural values and immigrant experiences to parental expectations about education. She said that "education was always at the forefront." Moreover, you were "always expected that you have to go to school. You have to make good grades. You have to go to college. There was just no ifs, ands, or buts about it." Angela mentioned how she encountered this message at home, school, and more: "[G]rowing up, and even the schools that I attended like elementary, middle school, like they all, like [there was] messaging of going to college." Similar to Angela's focus on cultural values and immigrant experiences that promoted education, Jaime and Edith—respectively—described how education as a family value was elevated and centered in the home.

For Jaime, her dad wanted her sister and her to be educated. Conceding that it's a complex question to answer, Jaime went into detail about why her dad focused on education.

> Um, the first thing that came to my mind was that culturally, culturally education is so important, um, in both my mom and my dad's households. Uh, it's a, it's like a status. It, it shows a higher status. Um, but also my dad, because he's an immigrant, he really, um, what's the word? He, I think he thinks that all of the success that he's had in life is due to his education, by the end of his college education. And because his life, it felt so bad, like oh, the divorce, and then the death of his mother, right, he needs to take care of me and my sister. He is a single dad, freshly single dad, and he has two little girls. He needs to take care of them. What's the best thing he can do? Education.

Edith talked about immigration as a driver for her parents and their focus on education. "I think a lot of immigrant children would identify with my answer of, you know, they, my parents came here for a better opportunity," Edith shared," and they were, they were saying education is going to, is the ticket to that opportunity."

First-Generation Graduate Students Recall Consistent Parental Messaging about Education

For many first-gen students, there was a clear connection between what parents messaged about the importance of education and their home- and school-based participation in children's education. In Jeremy's case, both parents had been involved in his life as a student—each in their unique way consistent with their respective roles in the family. Jeremy spoke to this point: "I think they were both, up until about sixth grade they were both very involved, like academically, with like, hey, show me your homework, make sure you do this, do that, and if I needed help, they would help me." In the sixth grade, he started to do more homework and school projects on his own—with his parents doing more check-ins

Figure 3.1. Graduate student families reproduce college-going cultural norms from an early age. *Source:* By Seattle Municipal Archives, CC BY 2.0. https://www.flickr.com/photos/24256351@N04/13429022673.

and school-based participation. Jeremy elaborated on changing forms of parental support as a student: "They always made sure like that was the first thing that got done, um, at least up until high school. I think high school was like the first time when like they stopped checking up on me. And, but they still asked. They'd be like, hey, do you have homework this weekend? Hey, are you doing homework? Do you need us to get this, get that for you, like with projects, especially since I couldn't drive yet." Jeremy concluded: "[T]hey were very much present in the aspect of like, if I needed support, they were there."

Like others, Josefina, a first-generation straight Chicana woman with children, remembered how her parents elevated education to "the forefront" as a child. Despite only completing formal education to the fourth grade for her mother and her father never having gone to school, they both messaged that education was the best option for a better life. She emphasized this idea when she shared how her parents, and her mom specifically, reinforced how education would offer them an opportunity to provide for their family and lifestyle. To this point, Josefina said: "You know now, after you know, going on to college, and you know, and you know she, both of my parents always pushed the importance of an education. And their, their message was always so that you can have a better lifestyle than ours, so that you don't have to worry about what are you gonna provide to your family." For his part, Josefina's father "always said, you gotta go to college. You gotta go to school." Josefina, a first-generation straight Chicana woman with children, shared how her father connected education to opportunity as an immigrant to the US: "[H]is story of that was always shared to say, hey, you know you're born in the US. You should be able to get a, an education, and I hope that you do." Josefina emphasized how her father reminded them about education as inaccessible to him as a child. She said: "It was just conversations, and, and using him as an example of, you know, not being able to go to school." Josefina said she felt her father's support. She offered: "I think it was again the . . . moral support, the verbal support, the words of you know, of encouragement. You know, keep trying. Keep going. Don't give up. And, and check in, how did school go today?"

When parents could only participate peripherally in their children's learning at school—due to long work hours, institutional barriers for second language speakers, and more—parents promoted education as critically important. To this point, speaking about her father, Josefina shared: "Well, I mean in terms of helping me prepare, he never helped me prepare. Um, I think mostly his, his way of preparing was to encourage the importance, or just speak highly of what an education can do if you go to school." Josefina vividly recalled how her dad would check in about school every day. As a young child in elementary school, here's what Josefina said about those moments: "[H]e would sit us down at the dining table whenever he'd come home from work. [W]e're eating together, and he would always say, how, how was your day today? [H]e would then say, oh, how was school? You know. And he always talked about school like, okay, make sure you focus. Make sure you respect your teachers. Make sure you don't goof around. Don't, don't cause any problems at school. You know, be respectful." Josefina noted how her dad often prioritized education at these dinner table conversations, which helped the family focus on education as a central part of their lives.

Leonardo's father promoted education by sharing his own experiences in learning English after emigrating from Mexico to the US decades ago. "[H]e was very proud of the fact that he was fluent in English," Leonardo shared. He continued: "You know even, even though he was born in Mexico, even though his primary language was Spanish, he went to school. He went to school when he came over . . . to take English classes, and he worked hard at it." Leonardo beamed when he described his dad's fluency in English: "And so, um, you know no one would know that he didn't, you know that he didn't speak English when he was, you know, first learning the language because he was so fluent." As an immigrant, Leonardo's dad tied education to opportunity in the US, as you can see in how Leonardo summed up his dad's approach: "And, and so for him that kinda, he showed us, look, you know yes, I, I'm, I'm fluent in English, but I, there was only so much I could do by the time I came, you know, from Mexico here, but you guys have that opportunity."

For Leonardo, a first-generation straight Mexican American male, his dad pushed a focus on education. Education would make the kids in the family better, as Leonardo explained.

> You know . . . through education we would, you know, be better. We would have a better life. We would have a better job. You know, we would have more opportunities. And so this is something that he wanted us to understand. Even though you know, he, whatever we chose to do he was okay with. You know, every single one of my siblings, you know, went to college, and we all, you know, have, you know, pretty decent jobs because of it. And so he, you know he always focused on that. He always focused on, again, being better than he was, you know. Uh, you know he, he was like a manager at a warehouse, but he wanted more for his kids. And you know he never put us down and said, oh, that job isn't good enough for you, but he would tell us. You know, you, you have great opportunities here, and you should, you should take advantage of those opportunities.

Leonardo's father emphasized education as a way to be better and get to more "decent" jobs and careers that interested his kids. Leonardo remembers how his father "was always, you know, pushing us in a, in his own way, you know. He, he worked hard. He showed us what, what it was to, to be that father."

Even when parents didn't participate directly in children's schooling, what they said seemed to make a difference in how children identified strongly with school. For example, Kayla recalled a chat with her dad after she decided to skip school to rest up for her part-time job at the mall. This resulted in her dad not only admonishing her but also helping her recognize education as the highest priority in her life at the time. Kayla set up the story this way: "When I started working, I think I was fourteen, and you know working, I think I had like a retail job. I had a . . . part-time job after school . . . at the mall. Back then you could do more hours than you can now as a kid. I was doing those hours . . . trying to make extra money . . . I got all these things I wanted." After her father found out she didn't go to school to work longer hours, here's what happened: "[M]y father really never got like, mad, but he got so upset. Like he was so, like he would, like if we got in trouble a lot of times it was communicated through my mother, but if he said something, if my father said something, it was like, he was really, like it was really bad, right." What Kayla learned is that "going to school was like, you go to school. Like there's no reason, why do you, if unless you're like, I don't know, you have to be really, really sick not to go to school, right."

For some first-gen students, what parents said sometimes fell short of what children needed at the time. For example, Zelma's father would share his pride at special events like graduations but not really in between these milestones. Zelma, a first-generation cis-hetero Indigenous Palestinian and Lebanese woman who is married with children, revealed more: "I think the few times that he would say he was proud of us was when we, you know, graduated high school, graduated college. So there was never that positive reinforcement and feedback growing up. Um, probably because he didn't know what the hell that meant." Where her dad remained silent and distant in her life as a student, Zelma's mom centered her life in the kids' education, participating in back-to-school nights, parent-teacher conferences, and more. Zelma reflected on how supported at school she felt by her mom.

> [M]y mom was the one who would sit with us late nights. In math particularly. My mom, you know, was the one who would sit with us and test us on our spelling. You know, we would get rote, we did a lot of rote memorization. Um, now I remember that like at first we went to a public school that was like second through third grade for me, first, second, third. But in elementary school she, we would be there, sitting there 'til sometimes 9, ten o'clock. We're like, I don't want to do my homework! No, you're gonna sit here and you're gonna do your homework. Whether it meant we got spanked or not.

Beyond school- and home-based participation, Zelma's mom messaged the need to get an education as a means to independence from men. Zelma admitted her mom had few options in life with the expectation that she marry young and start a family, but her mom never wanted that life for her kids. She insisted that they all finish school and get a degree to expand their opportunities in life.

Promoting education and tying it to getting ahead in life can be seen in what Ping—who identifies as a first-generation straight Chinese man—said about his dad. "But my father said," Ping shared, "uh, you study for yourself. You study hard you will get a bright future." But Ping didn't hear this message a lot, as his father lived apart from the family for work and only traveled home once a year. Still, even at infrequent intervals, Ping revealed how his dad communicated his pride in his son and their future to his.

Continuing-Generation Graduate Students Remember Parents Promoting Education in the Family

Like first-gen students, continuing-generation students remembered how education had been a part of their lives from a very young age. Sasha described how her parents sent mixed messages about college. While they both seemed to focus on education beyond high school, her dad framed postsecondary education less as bachelor's degree completion and more as technical skills development. Sasha explained that his family's lower-income status, coupled with his vocational training during his military service, seemed to inform messaging to her. She further elaborates, as follows:

> I think that . . . not that my dad hasn't been supportive of like getting more education, but I think in general like for him I think, 'cause my, my dad had tried to do like the normal college thing, but he like didn't have the money, and like, you know, ended up like getting a degree through the military. But like he never, but it was like you know people coming on base and teaching, it wasn't like this like, like real like . . . typical college experience.

Despite his bachelor's degree, Sasha's dad saw more meaning in vocational training and immediate employment in a technical field—and this is what he reproduced with her. Sasha seemed to feel that his Protestant belief system shaped a focus on hard work and education as an investment.

She reflected: "I think for him he's always [tried] to like instill the value of . . . learning technical skills and finding like a real job." By contrast, Sasha's mom messaged Sasha's path to a baccalaureate degree and repeatedly reminded her about it. Sasha recalled the roadmap in detail: "Well yeah. Like I even remember my mom telling me that like when we were like, like living on the farm. Like okay, first you're gonna go to college and get a degree, and then you're gonna get a job. And then you're gonna settle down and get married, and then you're gonna have kids. Like it goes like that." Like Sasha's dad, Holly's dad had a college degree and family friends tended to be educated, too, so Holly grew up in an intellectual environment, which immersed her in a world of politics, society, and creativity. In fact, Holly, a cisgender heterosexual white woman who identifies ethnically as Russian and who is married with a daughter, recalled well how one of her dad's colleagues impressed on her that she could do a lot more in life if she explored new educational opportunities. Her educational journey took a turn when this colleague, who taught at an English school in Holly's native Russia, suggested she apply for admissions. It was these moments that Holly understood as her dad's influence on her and what his focus on education meant for her. Her dad personified this importance when he returned to school in his fifties to learn a new language so that he could accept a job in Northern Europe. Holly reflected on her dad's expectation for her to go to college: "I mean that was the only expectation for me. [T]here was not even a consideration that I would not . . . go to college." She shared what he used to say to her: "[I]t's never too late to learn. You know anything, you just, you, you started doing something, you just need to, you need to finish it and, and give it all."

Holly's father's value on education could be seen in how he took her and her friends to museums, on architectural tours, and more on the weekends in her native Russia. By the time she graduated from high school, Holly shared that she had been in every museum in the area multiple times. Beyond visits to museums and trips to cultural institutions, Holly recalls how her father welcomed his friends and colleagues to the house, which created an intellectual environment where Holly felt surrounded by people who valued education, scholarly debates, and discussions of social and political issues. She recalled this atmosphere: "[T]here was something else. [T]he level of the elite surroundings, intellectual surroundings, like they were not, we never had any material wealth, um, but the level of, um, just the people who surrounded me through my father's friendship was like off the charts. And, uh, you know the conversations, the memories, the, they all spoke several languages, and, uh, highly intellectual, always, always up the latest, whatever the books, you know what whatever there was. Very philosophical."

Holly reflected on how this influence helped her understand how important—how essential—education was to her life and career. Like Holly, Eileen shared how, as a professor and department head, her dad had emphasized education from the earliest age in her life. Eileen, who identifies as a heterosexual married white female, remembered her parents would talk with her about school at the dinner table or eating in front of the TV. Spending a lot of time around her parents' friends and her dad's colleagues, she recalled how growing up around adults seemed to make her home a bit more "serious." Between social celebration for the publication of a colleague's book and department parties, Eileen's environment at home immersed her in a world of education. She shared more.

> [W]e would host the department parties, and other, like if someone had a book published or something like that my parents would usually host a get together. And then, you know, friends coming over. I guess that was kind of a big part of growing, there would always be, a lot of times, be someone over, and it was always like another professor, and so my mom and I would always make fun of, you know, kind of joke about the weird conversations they would have, or the weird questions they would ask me. You know, really like kind of philosophical, like big picture questions that my mom and I are just much more practical and, and hands on.

In adolescence, Eileen preferred to spend time with friends in her room than with her dad's colleagues and parents' friends during social gatherings—but she remembers how interested in her education the family's circle of friends would be. She elaborated: "I'd say very invested in like my life and what was going on with, with me, too, in a very, um, a very nice way. Um, but the conversations were always a little, very school focused, very like, what's next? What are you? You know I, when I like started dating my now husband, not, not a kind of interest in like, um, romantic relationships or things like that, it was a lot of very like, career, education-centered questions." Even if some questions seemed condescending or off-putting, as Eileen described, they tended to reflect a care and support for her educational pathway.

The mechanics of a value system that elevated education seemed to vary widely—from monetary awards and rigid expectations to family lore and pragmatic considerations. In practical terms, getting kids to and from school conveyed a sense of commitment to education—like how Zeke's mom would drive him to school every day. Daily logistics aside, family educational values set expectations to achieve academically, and parents tended to reinforce this system through a rewards structure, complete with verbal praise or monetary cash payments for "A" grades and more punitive measures ranging from gentle reminders to achieve scholastically to communicating deep disappointment with academic performance when it came time for reports cards to go home. Leonardo recalled his dad's pride when schools sent home report cards: "And you know, growing up, and you know when I would bring home report cards, just being proud of the grades that I was earning and, and telling me that, you know these are big accomplishments and letting me know that, that this is something that, that he, he was proud of." Similarly, Zelma recalled how her dad monetized report cards: "So, um, you know, growing up, I think, for us, you know, just the report card. When the report would come in it was always a stressful time. You know, and my dad, you know, he would give us money every time we had an A on that card, you know. So again very, it, it was literally transactional."

Beyond report cards and commutes to school, parents advocated for the educational services and opportunities for their children. In Stella's case, her mom pushed education in the family. Stella detailed how her mom focused on what her brother and she needed to succeed in school—tutoring, academic programs, and more. Whatever Stella needed as a student, her mom ensured she and her brother had. Stella explained: "[M]ainly when it came to stuff, like my mom would try to help with homework where she can, more with the math, science, and stuff like that." Stella's mom connected them to resources at school, too, inquiring about support and enrichment programs whenever periods of challenges arose in her elementary and secondary school experiences.

According to family lore, Sharon's dad "went to high school for a couple of days and jumped out the window and never went back." That was what she heard growing up, and she learned he just wanted to get out into the world and start working. "He . . . just didn't have the patience to sit in the classroom, and he wanted to be out in the world," according to the stories retold in Sharon's family. But later, Sharon, a first-generation heterosexual female who is married with children, found her father's photo in a senior yearbook from the era—so she questioned the veracity of the story. Even though he may not have liked school, Sharon's dad always supported her life as a student. In Sharon's case, there was no cash payment or monetary rewards for academic achievement, but there were clear financial implications for academic performance.

Preparing to transition to high school, Sharon recalled how close peers planned to go to a local Catholic high school—and Sharon wanted to go, too. She talked about how supportive her parents seemed to be, but the conversation about going to school there focused on finances. She explained more: "[T]hey wanted to know the details, you know. How much is this going to cost? [W]here is the school? How are we gonna get you there?" Logistics aside, Sharon's dad pressed to hold her accountable for the financial investment.

Referencing gendered roles in parenting, she continued: "But I remember both my parents, and as, and especially dad, because you know, dad, dad was the bread winner, so he wanted to know the cost. And I remember him saying something like, um, if we do this, you know, we'll, it was kind of in the . . . tone of, we'll only do this as long as you're going

Figure 3.2. Education is a central family value for graduate students. *Source:* By Tim Evanson, CC BY-SA 2.0. https://www.flickr.com/photos/23165290@N00/36540772461.

to be successful." But Sharon didn't seem to need much from her parents to be into school. In fact, she related her academic engagement in high school and beyond to a love of education. She recalled how she used to be into reading independently, go to the library by herself . . . as a way to learn more about the world and herself.

Between Sharon and Andres, parents made every effort to ensure children had the best education possible—and these actions demonstrated their value on education. With Sharon, her parents agreed that it was better for her to go to a Catholic high school than her local public high school. Andres's parents emphasized education in the family, and they showed how important education was to them by enrolling Andres and his siblings in a public school miles away from the house, where Andres boarded each day a bus to get to school. Andres, a first-generation able-bodied cis-hetero male who identifies as Mexican, specifically Mexicah and Tepehuani, recalled it this way: "I remember my parents always emphasizing education, 'cause we're always like, why do we have to go to this school? It's so far. And they're like, it's better. They're like, it's a better school, it's a better school, you know. So that kept being emphasized." That his parents sent him to a school so far from home was all the more powerful an act for Andres that demonstrated their value of education, given that the family lived "literally . . . like 500 feet away from an elementary school." Andres knew: "So that emphasis of education was always present in our home."

For Karina and her brother, college had been framed as the best option in their lives. Karina, a heterosexual Latina woman who identifies as half Guatemalan and half Mexican, recalled how it was always just the way it was going to be for her brother and her. Their dad had encouraged them to think about college at a young age, and both parents focused on the two kids getting their college degrees. Focused on her dad, Karina discussed how he used many strategies—drilling it into them, comparing their cousins who didn't go to college, to them, and more—to communicate the need to get a college degree. Here's what she said.

> So my father was like, you need to go to college. Like, um, you need to get your degree, to both my . . . brother and I. Um, and he, he would also compare us to our cousins as well. He's like, you know, they are, they don't have an education, you know. So he would, um, kind of, uh, you know, talk down about, about them. Um, so he's like, you don't wanna be like your

cousins. You don't want to, you know, live off your parents all the time. You want to . . . get your education, do something that you're gonna be paid really well for. So, there's a lot of comparisons there, and still is.

Another strategy that Karina recalled—this one used by her mother—involved illustrating what a college degree can mean for a career. Here, Karina talked about how her mom, referring to her own career, identified limited options to achieve her dreams for career.

Um, and then my mother, she only completed high school, but she has also noticed that, um, in her, in her, um, career, she's actually kind of like an administrative assistant for brokers, and so, um, she's noticed throughout her time that individuals with college degrees were always being promoted instead of her, even though she had a lot of experience. And so she always told us like, you know, you need to get your degree, and just a degree is gonna help you out. And so, um, it was always like wanting to make her and my father proud. Um, so she always wanted what, what she wanted she wanted for us, um, because she did start college, she went to a couple of classes, but she, it just wasn't for her.

More than just talk about cousins or career, Karina's parents participated directly in her education—through both home- and school-based participation, starting with attending school awards assemblies and special events. Karina shared more: "Um, yeah, so ever since I was very young, um, my parents have always been very supportive of me. And they also like, they would come to all of my recognition ceremonies, like when they give out those little certificates and things." She knew what this support meant for her: "And so because they were always supportive of me since I was little, you know, I've always managed to make them proud since then."

Beyond awards ceremonies, though, Karina's parents set expectation for strong academic achievement. As a student in elementary school, Karina remembered having to get good grades—but she struggled as she transitioned to middle school and started to resist parental aspirations for her. Still her parents always supported her as a student, as she recalled: "So my parents have always played a big role in my education all throughout. Um, so I, you know, I always had to be good, getting good grades."

Academic work intensified, she started to lose interest, and focused less on school. Marked by lower grades and a strained relationship with her dad, Karina talked about this time in her life: "I remember my father's and my, my relationship was not the best as well, because we weren't very connected. . . . Like the, the grades thing was also very hard for us both because I wasn't, he wanted me to do much better. So, um, there was a lot of tension there." Later, in high school, Karina mentioned that it got easier at school and she matured a bit more, so things got better.

Doing experiments with her, Gail felt like her dad's work as an amateur chemist helped her see the transformative power of education and the excitement in exploring her world. Gail, a first-generation straight white female, recalled this time in her life: "I feel like, so my dad is like an amateur chemist, so like he would like to do experiments with me. . . . Um, like he made like a fire tornado with like a waste basket on like one of those spinny things, so it would like make this fire tornado. So he was always doing experiments, so that was more educational I'd say."

Because her dad was a math faculty member at a community college in the Mountain West, Beatrice, a heterosexual woman who identifies as white and Mexican, felt like she had a built-in mentor in her dad. She reflected on how he never forced unrealistic expectations about academic performance on her—unlike a lot of her friends' parents. Instead, Beatrice and her dad engaged in conversations that seemed supportive at the time and helped her appreciate learning. She shared more.

> I really appreciate the way that they went about things, because I have a lot of friends that had extreme pressure on them to do well. And I was, like, I did good in high school. I got good grades. Like I actually got all A's, but not once did they ever ask like, oh, what are your grades? Or, um, what's your grade on this exam? Like I would talk with them and, and share stuff if I, you know, oh, hey, I got a good grade, but I never felt pressure from them to do good. Or oh, you gotta B, like here's a punishment. Like it was never, um, I never associated grades with, you know, harsh um criticism from my parents. It never happened, which I appreciate.

She talked about how he focused on broadening interest in a range of academic disciplines through his love of math. She said more: "He definitely made me appreciate math, because he has the philosophy that a lot of people that hate math just haven't taken the time to understand it, or appreciate it, too. Like if you have a closed mind-set when you're younger, you're definitely not gonna like it when you're older. . . ." She concluded: "I feel like all he did in helping me with my path was just making me realize that."

Framing Family Members as "Trailblazers" Who Model Educational Values

In families where parents had college degrees or older siblings went to college and served as "trailblazers," higher education was never a choice but an expectation, reinforcing an idea of academic aspiration. In Susan's family, her dad preceded her in going to college. As an undergraduate student at the time Susan was still young, her dad's college education meant a lot to her. Susan, a white and Latina cis-heterosexual female who identifies as Jewish, talked about how she saw her dad as a model college student. When she was younger, seeing her dad go to school seemed to motivate Susan to want to do the same. She spoke to this dynamic here: "I feel like seeing him go through his education, um, was a big, important part of me wanting to get a graduate degree, get my college degree. I wanted to be like my dad, and that meant going to school. I mean I don't know if I wouldn't have seen him go to school, um, it would have sparked as much interest in me." In very real ways, Susan experienced college life as a child with her dad. He took her to campus with him, and she observed him at his commencement ceremony—all of which meant a lot to her.

For first-gen students, being around older siblings in college connected younger siblings to campuses, modeled student life, and helped them navigate college decision-making and transitions to college. An early experience with his oldest brother and college revolved around a letter in Andres's family. By chance, Andres shared, his father found a letter in the trash discarded by his older brother. Andres told the story this way.

> [B]eing the vigilant parent that my dad is, he opened up the letter, and he saw that my brother was being offered an opportunity to spend the summer at a public master's-granting HSI university in the West as a high school student, as a senior. So I remember my dad telling my brother, like, you know, like what's this, you know? And my brother's like, holy shit,

where'd you find that, you know? So he's like, like why did you throw it away? He's like, oh, I don't want to go, you know. I don't want to spend my summer in college, and this and that. And I remember, being as young as I was, I remember them arguing about it. But my dad said, there's no question. Like I'm not asking you. You're going.

When summer arrived, Andres said, his parents drove his older brother to campus. His brother cried on the way there because he didn't want to go, but he complied and went. Andres remembers these moments—the letter in the trash, the car ride to campus—for the unique and routine ways his dad supported them as students and promoted education.

In so many ways, Andres experienced his older brother's time in college viscerally—with a rush of emotions and almost total immersion. While his mom completed education beyond high school in Mexico—she went to a technical school for a secretarial program—Andres looked to his older brother for cues about college when he was young. With his oldest brother already in college when Andres was still in elementary school, there was a lot to emulate. For as long as Andres could remember—during impressionable years while Andres was in elementary school and junior high school—his brother was in college, earning baccalaureate and master's degrees from a public masters-granting HSI close to their home in the western US. This all had a profound impact on Andres, and he absorbed as much as he could about college going. With his older brother in a fraternity—actually a founding father of the first fraternity of its kind on campus—Andres recalled going to fraternity parties with his middle brother because they would be hired as DJs for the parties. There, he would witness a peer environment that had him hooked, and he knew what he wanted to do: "I want to go to college one day, but it wasn't because I wanted a degree, or I wanted to be a professional. I want to be in parties like this."

At nine years old, Andres remembered running up and down the hallways in buildings where his oldest brother had classes, and the campus was his playground. From a young age, Andres recalled wanting to be like his oldest brother, who not only was the cofounder of a fraternity but also president of another student organization. "He was just superactive, super active. He was always on honor roll, dean's list," remembered Andres. Later, in high school, as his interest in fraternity partying faded, what was left for Andres was a strong desire to go to college. When it came time for

Andres to start looking at colleges, his oldest brother had a major impact in his college decision-making, which focused him on going to the same public master's-granting HSI university, because that was all he knew.

Older siblings modeled academic achievement and student involvement for Kaitlyn. Kaitlyn, a first-generation cisgender straight Latina, remembered how her older sister always supported her. When Kaitlyn was younger, her older sister helped her with schoolwork. She had a similar role model in her older brother, who was more into sports in high school and Susan witnessed how her interest in sports grew stronger with his presence in her life. Taken together, the effect of both older siblings on Susan can be seen in what she said about them: "I think with my brother and I, we just kind of always internalized that and really always wanted to, to kind of go after what they wanted." Juan, a man whose dad immigrated from Mexico, had a similar experience with an older brother who played sports. When Juan was in high school, he felt his brother's involvement in playing football supported his own interest and participation in football. Over the years, they grew closer as siblings. Here's how Juan put it: "I started playing football at [our high school], and he played football [at our high school] as well. So he would, you know ask me how practice went, picking me up from . . . he was genuinely excited to, to see me develop and to go to the games, and, um, and he just got a lot more involved."

Older siblings' effects on college going could be seen in Kayla's experiences, too. Kayla mentioned how her older sisters went to college and, when it came time for her to think about it, she had no choice but to do the same. Between her parents and older sisters, she was college bound from a very young age. Kayla confirmed: "I knew then in that space, after seeing my sisters go, go to college that if I said no, then it's kind of like, all right so, what are you gonna do?" Similar to Kayla, Karina linked her brother to her college decision-making, connecting his status as an undergraduate student to her interest in going to the same campus. She elaborated, as follows.

> Yeah, so, um, I knew I was going to . . . go to college right after high school, but I wasn't sure what I wanted to do, um, like what my career was, and that's why I just went with whatever my mom said I'd be good at. Um, and so I, I remember, I remember I only applied to two colleges, um, because I was secretly hoping I wouldn't get in and I could just go to community college so that I could figure out what I wanted to do,

and also save money at the same time. And so I only applied to two universities, and I, I actually got into both. Um, and I decided to go to [the public master's-granting HSI university in the West], and that was because my brother was also a student there at that time, and so I was like what, it'd be just very convenient for me to carpool with him.

Karina concluded: "That was the main reason why I picked [the public master's-granting HSI university in the West]."

Ping had three older sisters for him to follow when he was in elementary school. As high school students, his sisters had access to a broad range of textbooks, and these texts offered Ping plenty of opportunities to read deep into topics at a very young age. Instead of playing games and socializing, he recalled delving into their books.

> I don't have a lot of books to read or toys to play. I'm a poor kid and my family are poor. So I, I don't have things to, for entertainment; but three sisters when I was like a ten years old I can read and write. My sisters, my . . . older sister is six years older than me. So when I was elementary school student she is [a] high school student, so she has a lot of old textbooks and reading materials from the school. Then I . . . read all the books. Even though I'm a elementary school student I read, uh, books from all junior high and the high school.

Ping leaned into his introverted personality and recalled being a bookworm while his three sisters were in junior high and high school. Ping noted how this helped him "build the interest about the reading and study" and cited access to textbooks from his sisters, who were in high school at the time, with his interest in a broad range of topics as a child.

With nearly two decades between Josefina and her older brother, the family had a child in college when she was born. She noted how her father would hold up her older brother as an example of how to get to college and the advice that would follow. To this point, Josefina shared: "The first brother goes to college. I always saw my brother who went on to med school as an example. And so my dad would use him also as an example for us who were younger. Well, look at your brothers doing it. You can do it, too. You just gotta work hard. Don't lose focus."

Not only did older siblings model what is was like to go to college but extended family members did the same. For example, Brianna, a first-generation African American woman, listed aunts and uncles who all had college degrees and/or successful professional careers, witnessing how important education was to the family. Here's what she said: "[M]y uncle's a doctor. My aunt is a nurse. My mom, she didn't go to college, but she is a minister, um, and so she's an ordained minister. Then I have a aunt who is, she's, she has her EdD, and, um, she's in k–12 education. We've seen our aunts on my mom's side go to college, and you know, just see how access was just so important." In a similar way, Gail's cousin played an important role in her decision to go to a public, Hispanic-serving community college in the western US, when she first started in college. Gail's cousin went there, and Gail wanted to be close to her. "She's been like a sister to me growing up," Gail remarked, and she needed her to navigate the transition from high school to college.

In some first-gen families, while older children shaped how parents viewed higher education and facilitated a model for parents to reference for younger children, sometimes parents clung to beliefs about how to behave and what to expect from children as college students. For example, Josefina mentioned how her father expected her to be home after a day on campus. She shared: "[H]e understood but at the same time he didn't understand; because, although my sister came to [campus]. [Y]ou know this Mexican old school mentality is like, why do you need to be in school all day? Like, you go to your classes . . . you're there from eight to three." While not exactly the same, Ping's experiences with his older sister had a similar effect as Josefina's father. Ping explained that his older sister didn't outright support his study abroad in the US, or she indirectly undermined his efforts go to graduate school. Here, he described siblings who were on a career path that didn't include college or actively undercut their pursuit of undergraduate or graduate studies.

As older siblings in first-gen families, sometimes it was harder for students. As the older sibling herself, Stella felt like her immediate and extended family didn't seem to care about her path to college. Referring to her family members, Stella, a first-generation African American who's exploring her sexual orientation, commented on this pattern: "I tell them I'm not here to show off. I'm doing this for myself. and I hope that from you seeing what I'm doing, I just hope it motivates you. That's the only thing. I tell my brother, I tell my cousins, I tell my mom, I tell my auntie, like and my dad like, I hope that you see me as an example to motivate yourselves to achieve anything you want."

Like Stella, Leonardo was the older sibling in his family, and he had to blaze a path for his younger siblings, even if it meant a lot of pressure on him. Speaking to this role, he reflected: "And that's what I tried to give to my siblings as well like, it's important. We're going to college. We're all going to college. And, and so I wanted to let them know that it was possible, you know." Angela and Hector had similar experiences as Leonardo, having respectively felt pressure to lead younger siblings to college. In Angela's case, expectations from extended family and church family all seemed to converge on her. She shared what it was like.

> Um, but yeah, and then like I said, I have two younger sisters so being like the oldest, I feel like there's this like, pressure. And even sometimes messaging from our parents of just, or even like, um, elders, or cousins, or aunts, or like, I'm also a Christian so I have a big church family, too. And like again, there wasn't no one around me who didn't go to school or who didn't get an education. Um, so I think there was just also, just this pressure to lead by example. You're the oldest daughter, you have to lead, you know all these different things.

While Hector didn't explicitly say he felt pressure, he recognized that his parents saw his ability to model life for his siblings. He revealed more. And his parents witnessed his work as an older sibling modeling college going. To this point, he said: "And I think they, they saw that I was capable of doing that, you know, because they saw me with my siblings and how I was with them, always encouraging and supporting them."

Similar to Hector, Angela, Stella, and Leonardo, Jeremy's the older sibling and led the way for his younger brother, who was still in middle school when Jeremy was applying to and transitioning to college. Jeremy walked through what it was like for him to serve in this role in his family.

> [L]ike both of them still call me all the time and ask the exact same questions. Like, the stuff that like I have discussed with them for over four years, like it's still things that they ask questions about. And a lot of times like, I think like my mom at this point has now so become the person who's like,

hey, you should talk to your brother about this. And then my dad's more so the point person who comes to me and he's like, hey, we're looking to do these things for your brother, your brothers looking to do these things, I have questions about this, especially sort of thing.

Jeremy, who identifies as a first-generation straight white and Italian cisgender male, responded regularly to both his mom and dad, and he was the go-to person for a range of questions about college from his family, including ones about meal plans, housing forms, and more for his brother. Jeremy listed the questions he answered when he visited for spring break: "[D]o we have to submit this for housing? Where do we submit this? Who do we contact about this? Where do we submit these forms to?"

Figure 3.3. Parents and older siblings modeled college-going for children and younger siblings in some families of graduate students of color and first-generation graduate students. *Source:* By ivanx, CC BY 2.0. https://www.flickr.com/photos/20605823@N00/2131726729.

Show Up, Work Hard, Get Ahead, and "Hustle" in What You Do in Life

Education tended to be bound up in hard work as an ethical imperative to do the best you can and achieve goals you set for yourself and your family. Reflecting on childhood, many graduate students looked back at how hard life was for their parents: the hustle to make ends meet, daily grind of getting children through school, and the balancing act of managing a household and taking care of aging parents. The hustle—that's what several mentioned in describing how hard parents work. Along the way, lessons in how to put in the effort to get things done were learned: laboring long hours, sacrificing for what you're called to do, and doing the best you can. Angela's mom embodied this ethic—Angela described her mom as a "go-getter," who earned undergraduate and graduate degrees while promoting in the health-care management sector. She always achieved, Angela noted, and inspired the same in her children. Later, when it was Angela's turn to transition to career from her graduate program, her mom seemed to push her to consider promotion and salary in her decisions about job opportunities. Angela reflected on how this focus sometimes challenged her. Referring to her mom, she shared: "So she's accepted that I've done student affairs, like she supports it. And you know, I told her my goals are just like rising to the ranks of like being a senior-level administrator in higher ed, maybe a VPSA [vice president of Student Affairs], we'll see. And I think a lot of the conversation surrounding that had to back it up with numbers. I'm like, okay, if you wanna know their salaries, this is what they make." For Angela, this seemed to assuage her mom and her support for Angela. "I feel like that kind of helped my case up a little bit, so I think that's kind of what's helping her," Angela concluded. Like Angela's mom, Kayla recalled how achievement tended to be central to her mother's message to the children. Growing up, Kayla remembered what her mother used to say about setting and achieving goals and doing your best in all you do. The idea stayed with Kayla—"just doing my best," she summed up. "Working really hard . . . since I set the goal, to achieve that goal," Kayla shared.

Embedded in their gendered roles as providers, fathers often messaged how hard work requires commitment and effort. Frequently apart from kids and sometimes employed at two or three jobs, fathers lived and worked the idea that your labor is what distinguishes you from peers and pays off. Leonardo reflected on how his dad returned to school later in life—prompted by job requirements, in part.

I do know that he like, you know, part of working for a major company, or you know he, he did take some trainings and stuff, and it was like [college-level] classes, uh, but never, never finished a college degree. [F]or me, it was about not only working, you know, going to school and studying, but also working hard and knowing why you were, you were going to school, right. And so, um, that's, that's something that, you know, and he always encouraged both, you know.

Leonardo connected hard work with education, "working hard" to get through school and go where you want to in your career. His dad always seemed to be pushing Leonardo and his siblings to work hard.

Hard work and job responsibilities often meant long hours away from kids and home. To this point, Zelma remarked: "My dad worked really, really hard. He would work twelve-, sometimes fifteen-hour days. He would be gone to work before we would wake up." When he was younger, Ping remembered brief biweekly phone calls "with my father to talk about daily issues . . . because my father is very busy." Ping learned about how both his parents "are very diligent" from these calls. Similarly, Sharon rarely saw her dad when she was younger. She remembered how hard he worked in a family business and described how "[h]e would put in very, very long days. He had a little . . . gas station auto repair shop. And then, and, but that started to do really well, and then he launched into . . . a tire store," which did very well, too. Being all about work, Sharon emphasized her dad's long hours away from home, which resulted in "very rarely seeing him during the week, because he was up early and out of the house by, you know, 6:30, 7 o'clock, and he wouldn't be back home until after 8. And typically, you know as a little kid, we were already getting into bed and closing down for the night." Similar to Zelma's and Sharon's fathers, respectively, Andres recalls his dad working seven days a week, including Saturdays, Sundays, and "whenever there was over time he would take it, holidays they paid him double time." Andres remembers his dad would start the 7:00 a.m. shift and would finish for the day at 3:30 pm—but he'd frequently stay later for overtime work.

Within gendered systems of organizing work at home and in the office, mothers reproduced values that promoted hard work and hustle. Indeed, many graduate students recalled how mothers managed it all—balancing family and career responsibilities, meeting the demands of children and colleagues, and leading a majority of school-based participation activities. Stella spoke to this pattern when she talked about her mom raising her to work hard. Stella reflected on how her mom modeled his mantra in their family: "[M]y mom always made sure that I had that hustle mentality." Similarly, Jenna, who identifies as a first-generation Filipina heterosexual female, talked about how she is "very career focused" and tends to have "a lot on my plate throughout the week," working to overcome obstacles in what she does at school.

Hard work required personal sacrifices as central to what mothers did in families. Angela spoke to this when she mentioned how her mom has been burdened by being the sole breadwinner. While her mom has a well-paying job, she has had to carry a lot of responsibility for her family's financial health. Angela remarked, "I've seen like the hard work and the burden that's been put on my mom." Growing up, her dad drove taxis and Uber, while her mom went to college and was promoted to management in health care, so Angela witnessed the imbalance in contributions to family income with her parents, and this did not sit right with her. She spoke to this point: "I just didn't like the amount of pressure that was put on my mom to like get the bills rolling, and everything like that."

Another form of personal sacrifices that many connected to what their mothers said and did was the idea of prioritizing commitments while delaying personal gratification. Jeremy spoke to this point when he remarked how his mother had consistently messaged this mantra: "And there's certain things that he says, like are always sticking in my head. It's always like, do what you have to do before you do what you want to do." Long before Andres's mom served a primary care-taker and raised children, she worked as a seamstress and a secretary. Between physically demanding work in the factory and office, and later in the home, his mom put the needs of the family before her own.

Hard Work Masked a Subtext of Family Survival for Many Graduate Students

For many graduate students, a message of survival could be readily recalled in stories from parents about hard work. Karina knew this message from an early age, as she described how her father said you can never get anything in life for free. Explaining how this idea was likely tied to her father's childhood spent in poverty, Karina shared more: "[M]y dad has always like said that we have to work hard, we have to do things on our own. We can't, you know, get things for free." Working over a lifetime provided proof to Josefina that her father worked hard and described how her father "worked in the [redacted] for about twenty-five years. And that's what he retired from. And I, and then after work, he still went home to do more work. He used to do landscape work on his own."

Survival seemed to manifest in a constant mantra of work, work, work—from an early age to late in life—particularly as graduate students recalled fathers. For example, Maria, a first-generation LGBTQ-identified Armenian woman who immigrated from Iran and identifies culturally as Middle Eastern and Armenian, said simply of her dad that he "would just work, so he's been pretty much working his entire life." Like Maria, Kaitlyn saw both parents as work-oriented, but she focused on her dad as being work-driven, working hard, and never complaining. She revealed how he planned his career and then achieved what he had set out to do. She revealed more, "Um, he always sets out, um, his own plan of what to do and he always executes it. And, um, I, I really admire that about him, how he, he just, he works, and he, um, he just kind of, not unhealthy like works, but he, he always works." Kaitlyn shared how her dad tried to balance work with rest and leisure time with family, going to baseball games, and so on.

Another message about working hard centered on showing up and rarely missing work. In the case of Jeremy's father, who worked as an outdoor service technician for a large communications company in the southeast, the more he worked the more likely he would be eligible for overtime. And Jeremy's mother reinforced this idea when she shared how Jeremy needed to follow a simple rule: Do what you have to do first, then what you want to do. Kayla, a first-generation cisgender African American female, recalled her father's "work ethic, you know, showing up, being, doing what, you know, doing a good job, and just being, you know, and not just in the workplace, but in family, too. Like showing, showing up is important." She remarked how "[t]here was never really like, you know no complaining. You don't. complain about it, you just do it, right." For Kayla's family, showing up and doing your best gave you a sense of pride in your work.

Jaime's family centered an ethic of doing your best, too. She remembered how her father would say that you have to do the best you can or "it's not really worth it." Jaime internalized this idea and used it to guide her academic work—from a very young age. "[W]hat motivated me to do my work," she said, "it was kind of like self-worth." Over time, education was bound up in her sense of self. To this point, she said: "I put education in my self-worth, and it's like, oh, if I can, and multiple other skills, um, because that, because he told me, he's like, oh, you have to be the best or else people won't want you, won't, will not want you in like the workplace." Edith shared a similar story about her parents—"do your best"—but her father would message moderation, too: "[D]on't overwork yourself." The moderating influence emerged from her family's experiences with her mother's terminal cancer. Edith elaborated: "I lost my mom to pancreatic cancer years ago. And the way I remember my mother was, you know what, with the skills that I have and the opportunities that I have. I'm just gonna, we use it. Work it, exploited to the, to the utmost, and sacrificing my own health. So be it, like that's what was communicated through her behavior."

Hard Work as Manual Labor, Service, and Sacrifice on the Part of Parents

Working hard tended to be associated with physical or manual labor on the part of parents. Sasha recalled how her family messaged "hard work, but then hard work, you know like, hard work is more like physical labor type things. I guess like know the value of like going out and like working outside." This seemed to be connected to their Protestant religious beliefs—especially with her father. Sasha remembered: "[I]t's probably like a Protestant thing you know, of like hard work being really tied to, um, you know like, you know, God, and you know." But this notion of hard work had a tinge of distaste to it, as when Sasha shared: "[I]t's like this idea that like you are not working unless you're like completely like miserable. Like you're not doing hard work unless like, you're unhappy about it." As gendered patterns in the workforce and labor market tended to push men to work in the industrial sector, this idea of manual labor could be seen. Evident in memories of parents, and fathers specifically, from jobs in industrial plants or manufacturing facilities and work in more physically demanding roles in commercial sectors. Brianna referenced this experience: "So, um, my dad . . . he worked in a factory. And, um, so every day he would go to work from eleven to seven. And, um, so he did that for nineteen years working in the factory. And, um . . . his favorite quote—nothing in life is free. So we, we knew that it was really about hard work." Her dad summed up his approach to hustling in the following way, according to Brianna: "I'm not gonna let people run over me."

Not just Brianna's father but her grandfather centered his life on work as service, which can lead to something bigger than yourself—yes, career achievements but also community well-being and civic contributions. He tied his work ethic to education, according to Brianna: "I don't know how to explain it. But my grandfather, it also was about hard work. He, um, when we would be in school, um, he would have us, crazy, he would have us type. We, he bought a new computer, and I'm like, let's just use the new computer. No one's gonna use the typewriter. I want you to use the typewriter. Type up the death certificate for one of my clients." Brianna's grandmother "worked for thirty-plus years as a janitor," and both grandparents "knew how to live and how to carry themselves if that makes sense. I don't know how to explain it." Back to her grandfather—a father to Brianna—was a central figure in the community. As a funeral director, her grandfather dressed in suits, kept a strict schedule, and managed business affairs adeptly. This is the strong work ethic that he passed on to Brianna and her family, as she recalled.

In the end, hard work paid off, and multiple forms of achievement could be seen in what parents communicated to children. "Earning your successes was a big thing," Beatrice said, "because both my parents worked hard to go to college." Beatrice remembered how her mom told her that she had to do everything on her own to apply and transition to college. Beatrice marveled at how her parents had complete college on their own. "They just did it on their own volition, both of them. Um, so they, yeah, they're very hard workers." She concluded: "That was a value, uh, that they instilled in me, too, was just earn your successes and, and work hard for things." Similarly, Eugenio, a first-generation heterosexual Latinx male who identifies as Oaxacan from an indigenous Mexican background, recalled how his dad always told him to put the work in now and see results later. Eugenio connected his dad's messages of perseverance and persistence with accomplishments. Here's what he said: "[Y]ou have to be determined. You have to go for what you want. You have to persevere." He summarized: "I remember my dad he said, I completely remember he's like, you have to persevere in life because it, it, it's difficult, but at the same time it could be accomplished." Juan's dad advised him to find something he loved doing and do it knowing that it would pay off—"there's also that, that value of, uh, you know work hard to, to be comfortable financially," Juan commented.

Unity and Support for Family Members as Vitally Important to Parents

Beyond a focal value on education and hard work, family unity and support could be seen as important ideas in what most graduate students shared. While graduate students almost universally described values that elevated education in their families, many shared values that didn't seem directly related to education—like family unity and care. However, the set of beliefs that surrounded family unity appeared to translate into a practice of supporting each other—including in school—and seemed to serve as a support system in pursuit of educational goals. In the end, these beliefs buttressed academic success and impactful careers and reinforced the ethic of giving back to family members and the community.

For many graduate students, parental figures centered families in the lives of their children or grandchildren, reproducing an ethic of care for immediate and extended family members. We stick together and help each other out was often reported as a message heard while growing up. In turn, graduate students offered their own take on caring for and maintaining a closeness between family members. This pattern followed many of them throughout their lives—no matter the physical or emotional distance today—and supported a sense of relationality and mutuality. Indeed, there was a feeling that parents, grandparents, and siblings are available to support you, and together everyone counts more as a family unit than alone. Intensely present as adults, knowing that family members had their backs seemed to help through moves to campus as undergraduates, challenges with programs in graduate school, and questions about careers and more. In fact, many shared how their parents were there when they needed them most and how they paid back to parents and forward to extended family and friends.

Family unity formed foundations in value systems. Family values, as many reported, reproduced beliefs about how family orients everyone connected by blood, marriage, or agreement. Beatrice and Susan recalled how family get-togethers reified messages of connectedness and closeness. From her recollection, Beatrice knew how "family is a big value, too," especially exhibited on holidays. She described more: "Like we always take time on holidays to visit everyone, and see everyone, and, and call everyone. And we always do letters in the mail, and, and cards and stuff. So, they're very connected with all of their family." Beatrice focused on her paternal side of the family, reflecting on how last Christmas, they "spent an entire week just hopping around in [the West] saying hi to everyone, so yeah." Susan's parents stressed family, too, and Susan associated the importance of family unity with immigrant experiences. She reflected: "I think that does go back to the immigrant status of my dad, because that's all they had to rely on when they moved to the US." As a kid, almost every weekend passed with aunts, uncles, cousins, and grandparents. "Like, that was basically what we did," Susan mentioned, "like we saw them all the time, so family values. It was always this expectation that family is very important."

In practice, close relationships with immediate and extended family members connected grandparents, aunts, uncles, and cousins to children. Keeping the family together—whether across town or national borders in cases where migration split spouses, partners, parents, and kids—was paramount. In the most direct terms, Josefina's father used to say, "family unity is what matters." Sasha referenced her immediate family as "being like the most important like, societal unit." Holly heard a similar message, where her dad pressed her to love and center family in her life. So did Maria, who recalls, growing up, how there would be "a lot of families around."

Not just words alone, parents often expected, insisted, or demanded that family members spent time together. Through birthday parties, holiday celebrations and cultural rituals, religious observations, and weekday dinners around the table, many grad students remembered how close bonds between their members of the family shifted priorities to focus on each

Figure 3.4. Many graduate students of color connect family unity to their system of values. *Source:* By @yakobusan Jakob Montrasio, CC BY 2.0. https://www.flickr.com/photos/37803129@N00/399329025.

other in times of need. Eugenio connected cultural values to his family's value on unity, illustrating how everyone expected him to be present at parties. He said "And within my extended family also, like very like traditional Hispanic values. Like, you know . . . if we're having a party, you can't really say you're not going." Similarly, Jasmine, who identifies as a first-generation heterosexual Hispanic female, described how you had to go to get-togethers. She elaborated briefly: "Say you're not going, you're gonna, like people gonna be mad. So like, very like, you know, it is what it is kind of, and you should do it 'cause of family."

Family Gatherings Reproduce Values of Closeness and Celebrate Togetherness

Social gatherings and special holiday or birthday celebrations tended to reproduce values oriented toward family unity. For Josefina, frequent family get-togethers brought everyone home. Josefina remembered her father messaging his love through celebrations: "But know that love is here. And family unity is what matters. [T]hat's kind of what I grew up with my father in terms of celebrations. It was, that was it. Family, family unity and gathering. That was his joy." Tanya recalled a very close-knit family unit and big family reunions manifest in a lot of time together at home. She described what this all meant: "And we, my family's also big on like family reunions, and so people from all across, you know um the country, you know that are my family members, we come to this and we take it very seriously, um, our family reunions." She counted on special surprises—like a printer as a gift when her family celebrated her college graduation.

Liza recalled how family on both her mom's and dad's sides got together. With her dad's mom, they saw each other "almost every weekend." Liza narrated what this looked like for them when she was younger: "We'd go, that was a for sure thing. Like, so we'd always go with him, would spend time over there at grandma's house." Beyond their tight-knit immediate family, Liza's extended family on her dad's side seemed to be scattered all over and "did their own thing with their own." On her mom's side of the family, extended family saw each other often. Here's how Liza remembered these times.

> And so we, that would be the family that we got together for birthdays and holidays. [W]hen I was growing up we were the

house that everybody would come to, right. And the house was fairly small, and you know we were thinking back at the room that we had. I don't know how we fit that many people in there with all these chairs and tables. Well, you know, we made it work. But yeah, we do the Thanksgiving, and the Christmas, and the New Year

All these get-togethers tended to be a lot for Liza's mom and seemed to be a source of stress, as Liza recalled: "I can only imagine how stressed my mom was during that time of the year, you know. Hosting three consecutive holidays back to back with that many people."

In between family festivities, Leonardo understood his family's focus on a sense of connectedness to each other. He continued to share how his dad came from a big family and wanted to create the same feeling of closeness in his family. Leonardo, a first-generation straight Mexican American male, continued: "With family, making sure that, you know spending time, you know, calling, you know, talking, checking in, all that stuff was important. He . . . made, when we were with him, he made us feel like we were important." Doing what he loved most, Leonardo's father was there for the most important life events to connect with his kids and be a part of their lives. In a similar way, Eileen remembered how her parents emphasized "spending time together as a family, like a nuclear family." While her family unit was smaller, they still did what Eileen described as time together with each other.

With Kayla, time together "was always [an] . . . intentional time being planned for those occasions." As the family grew, she remarked, parties and birthdays required larger venues to get together. Kayla recalled how "during the summertime, family cookouts were always a thing at our house. And I know, you know my, my dad is just, he just took pride in having his family together." Kayla connected her parent's care-taking to parenting roles with their own siblings.

> [F]ather being the oldest and, you know just really being a father-figure to his sibling, our, our house was the center of a lot of different activity. Parties, you know celebrations. Um, but yeah, just a, just remembering the sense of, um, us in our house being like the center of our family for a lot of things. Yeah, extended family, close family, um, you know, even with my mom, my mom, as I mentioned being the oldest of three,

her sibling, my, my uncles lived in [the Southeast], but every year they would come to [the Northeast] for some period of time, you know. So bringing their families. And then my mom is, in her family she has an extended, she was also a matriarch in a sense, too, because her, my grandmother's sister, I guess my great aunt, she had twelve kids.

Like Kayla, Hector described family get-togethers as a constant in his life as a child. Hector is the oldest of four children—with a younger brother and two younger sisters. Hector recalled his upbringing as "very family oriented," with frequent opportunities to see extended family, including cousins, aunts, uncles, grandparents, and great grandparents. Between holidays, parties, and regular weekly visits, Hector recalled Sunday night dinners at his grandparent's home on his dad's side and—when he was older—Friday evenings with his mom's parents. These Friday night dinners would mean seeing lots of cousins, as Hector remembered, with her mom and her six siblings and all of their children—plus family friends. Hector detailed more about parties on his mom's side of the family: "Portion size of food, everything is big, and . . . a lot of people, and so you know . . . it was a lot of parties . . . a lot of gatherings. [Y]ou didn't always need a reason, you know to, to get together with people, you know we, we did. And those were really fun experiences." Hector reflected: "Good, good moments in my life, being with my cousins, and, or being with my brother and my sister's in the, in the atmosphere was always fun." He contemplated these moments more, sharing how a mix of humor, jokes, fun and storytelling combined to form memories of appreciation, respect, and care.

Family Care Accompanies Family Unity as Values for Graduate Students

The idea of a tight-knit unit meant that everyone relied on and supported one another whenever needed. As graduate students looked back, many saw how they could always count on their parents, grandparents, and siblings—but also aunts and uncles—to get them through college. As adults, they used the same approach and took care of family members, especially aging parents and younger siblings. Even if it was just the thought that they were accessible, if needed, they felt comforted by the relational approach in the family. Karina talked about family support when she said: "And then another value in itself was family. Um, that we always had to be by each other's side, we have to support one another. Um, and so yeah, that's been a, a big value in my life." Winona heard something similar in her family. When she shared that family orientation meant being there for each other. Here's how she put it: "But family orientation in the sense of like, if we do anything we stick together. Like we're not, it's not gonna be you on this, you know car alone, or just us two, it's always just three or none."

In Leonardo's case, extended family members who immigrated to the US from Mexico needed support, and Leonardo described how members of his family took care of each other.

> It was, it was all about family. It was all about, not, not just our immediate family, but it was, you know, my mom's side, my dad's side, we were just always together. We were, you know, we were always just with the cousins, and you know, knowing who was doing what and just being, you know, it was, it was never like we're gonna be home by ourselves. We, we had so many, you know, relatives, so many cousins, a lot of people who had come over after my dad from Mexico.

With his own siblings and parents, his father labored to bring everyone together, as Leonardo shared here: "And so he also took care of his siblings, and he also made sure that he, if he was able to help, he did. He always did. And so it was very family involved, you know, with, with grandparents too, you know." His dad would "[b]ring them in and, you know, taking care of them and making sure they had everything they needed. So it was, it was just, that was the importance was family, taking care of each other."

Within families, some graduate students themselves lived the family mantra of taking care of each other, especially with siblings. For Black women who shared stories in this project, family support centered their family lives and grounded them in a strong system of care. Angela exemplified this ethic of care, sharing how she ensured she'd not financially burden her parents with school loans or asking them for financial support for college so that they could support her younger siblings: "I have younger siblings. So like, if they can't pay for me, the least they're gonna do is probably pay for my younger siblings. So I'm like, I have to make a way." Kayla cited her parents "being like at the top of their sibling groups, uh, in each family, yeah, being a you know, being in that space of watching leadership as a primary reason behind their care-taking role with extended family. Brianna mentioned how she planned to take care of her twin brother, who didn't want to go to college: "And I think also, when I think about my future me, you know, hands down, you know it's not even a question of, am I gonna be supporting, you know I help my brother, 'cause he's different. It's my brother."

Similarly, Kayla recalled how her parents helped to raise her cousins: "So you know, my cousins were like . . . you know, brothers and . . . siblings, extended siblings. So, so a lot of cousins all the time, either in the house or when we went to visit." After finishing dissertation research, Brianna described how she wanted to spend more time with family. Why more time? Her grandfather used to make them write letters to maintain close bond between family members, as Brianna explained: "My grandfather would be, oh, my, he would make us write letters to my dad's, my dad's mother. We were like, we can send an email. No. You're gonna sit here, you're gonna get this piece of paper, and you're gonna write a letter to your grandmother." She continued: "I have to get this PhD so hopefully there'll be more opportunities so I can take care of myself. I can help take care of my brother, kids. Not saying like just take care of them but, I want to do more."

FAMILY SUPPORT MANIFEST IN AN ORIENTATION TOWARD EMPATHY, COMPASSION, AND CARE

Amid conversations about family unity and support, the idea of empathy, compassion, respect for each other and a working toward collective well-being seemed to be related to a need to hold up members of the family and community. Hua illustrated this value in what she recalled as a child: "You should love your family members, no matter what be [supportive]." Reflecting on how her dad instilled an empathic orientation to others in her, Stella said: "I would say the empathy I get from my dad." Even the little things in life seemed to invite an empathetic approach to family and friends. Kayla illustrated this point when she remembered how her father behaved at a gathering: "I just remember, you know being, sitting at a party and backyard, and my mother-in-law came, and we didn't have any Diet Coke for her, or like anything sugar free. So I had to go to the store and get her, like stop, you know like kind of just leave the party, go to the store. Like he was the one that always made sure that everyone was comfortable and had what they needed, regardless of who they were." Kayla summarized: "So, you know those, those type of gatherings, you know, the care that was taken to make sure everyone was comfortable and had what they needed."

Family support shaped a deep respect for each other and, in particular, elder members of the family. In Leonardo's case, his father messaged how they were expected to "love each other, and we have to be respectful. And, and we have to make sure that, you know, when we talk to mom we're respectful, and because, we knew that because of, of how Dad talked to us, right." Similarly, Angela recounted how her family's collective immigrant experiences and cultural values honored elders, including her parents. She spoke about how these expectations mean not "necessarily repaying, but almost taking care of your elders when they get to a certain point."

Angela talked specifically about what her mom said with respect to caring for her mom as she aged. She elaborated: "Like my mom, my mom currently works in a nursing home, and she's like anti-nursing home. She's like, do not put me in a nursing home. You guys are gonna take care of me. You guys are gonna provide for me. [I]f you want us to do that, I need money to make that happen. I think it's that messaging . . . I mean again, they didn't explicitly say this all the time, but it's just like, it's kind of implied." Winona recalled similar values of respect and care for elders. "I mean family orientation," she said at the start of our conversation. Winona, a first-gen bisexual Asian American who uses identifies as Chinese and Vietnamese, illustrated what family orientation looked like when she was growing up—linking it to being social at parties and revering elders. She elaborated.

> Like doing stuff, well, in a sense of like being respectable to your elders was a factor for sure. Because, like it was a thing when you go to a party, at least for myself was that you had to go to say hi to every single individual, and then when you leave you also have to say bye to every single individual. But it wasn't just a wave, it's like you gotta cross your hands and bow type of hi and bye.

Winona concluded: "So, um, it was a sense of like, you have to establish like kind of being respectable to your elders, as well as like making it known."

Not only with elders and not just limited to family, Hector shared stories about his family, where he described an ethic of looking out for one another and showing care, kindness, and respect in what you do with others. Hector's family modeled this ethic, including his grandparents.

Grounded in Catholic social teachings "around service, around, you know, connection to a community," Hector talked about the care and love shown to each other as an example of living a meaningful life where you are not the center of everything. He shared more.

> [W]e grew up with that . . . kind of mentality and that kind of ethic cause, you know, looking out for, for other people besides you, so you're not like the, like the center of everything. You know there's other people out here who need support, who need help. Uh, and you could be part of that. Um, you know I think that . . . I think just being kind, showing respect. You know, treating people with dignity, treating people with um care, um, and respect.

Hector shared how he connected to care and compassion around Native issues with his family. Hector's dad "had done a lot of work in the seventies . . . within American Indian population . . . with a lot of youth," and this work had inspired and connected Hector with Indigenous people on campus where he served.

For Hector, compassion and care extended beyond family, and his dad introduced him to what it meant to care for others as part of a calling in life. Working in sports recreation for the Veterans Administration at a location in the western US, Hector recalled how his dad brought his brother and him to work, where Hector was taken under the wings of several veteran service members. He explained more: "They all took care of us. [T]hey always looked out for us. I feel like they had a sense of like, you know, kind of like care-taking, like responsibility to, to be a good model for these young guys, me and my brother who were there, you know trying to learn how to like flip hamburgers, and, or be on a softball team, or whatever we were doing they could help, you know." At the same time, Hector talked about how he learned how to listen to and connect with people—and where to find community and family in spaces outside of the home.

More broadly, his dad grounded Hector's other-directedness toward "looking to ensure that, you know that the, the voices and experiences of people on, on the margins could be, you know . . . to the center, and, or highlighted, you know." Hector connected his social justice framework in early and ongoing life conversations and experiences with his dad. He referenced discussions with his dad after "Supreme Court decisions, or police brutality, you know anything like that. When . . . in 2020 yeah, um, when it was those, you know massive protests you know, after the murder of George Floyd, you know we, we had a lot of conversations about that" in 2020. Hector also reflected on how, when he was younger, he engaged in protest movements. On this point, he recalled a conversation with his dad:

> But I remember talking to my dad about it one night. [H]e's like, you know and he had this very reassuring thing, he was like . . . one, you know, this isn't, this isn't new. This has happened before. Two, what do you expect when people have been, you know, dismissed and marginalized? People are, people are gonna be angry. People are, you know, they got a right, um, to be upset. And it was just like, the way he was talking about it, it just, it, it's just all things that I knew, but just reassuring. And I think talking to him and other people in his generation, you know to, it was, it was just, it was really helpful.

Hector shared this final thought about his dad that focused on his open and caring relationship with him.

Similar to Hector, the effect of Jessica's family's values on other-directedness led her to find a career in service to patients in the healthcare field. Jessica explained how she wanted to go into physical therapy to help people: "I've always wanted to help people and be involved in having them get better in either like a, like a hospital like postsurgery hospital setting or, um, like a rehabilitation, like if they're like poststroke, or some sort of like um illness or disability that they overcame," she explained. She repeated: "So I've always wanted to help people."

Like Hector's mom and dad, Andres's mom messaged a push to care for others framed as kindness to people you meet in life. Andres explained more: "with my mom it was, you know, that, again, that nurturing role, like, you know, be kind to people 'cause you don't know what they're going through. Be nice to people, you know. And my mom was always that person that, if they, anyone needed anything she would drop what she's doing and she'd go do it." Josefina's mother did the same, modeling how dignity and respect for others came in everyday acts—like sewing a garment that needed repair. Josefina illustrated: "[S]he knew how to sew, so people would ask for her help. Can you, you know, fix the, my pants, or can you tailor this? And you know, again they would want to say, oh, let me pay you, and my mom would say, no, no, it's okay. You don't have to. So I think her giving and her acts, I think her acts of giving, and her kindness is what I think of her as a giving person." From a young age, Holly learned the value of respect. For Holly's dad, the idea of respecting others meant "integrity, um, and empathy," where you would "fight for the underdog." Holly stressed how her dad felt an intense sense of fairness and justice for others.

Similar to Hector and Andres, Liza immediately identified how her parents instilled a sense of "just being good to people and good will come back" in the kids. Liza framed this principle as old-school—"you know, you know, treat others the way you'd like to be treated." Liza's parents applied this principle to a range of social situations, even prickly interactions and encounters with bullies at school. Liza connected us to the backstory here: "[L]ike those type of you know things when it came to, you know, people being mean at school, you know, you always have to just treat them with compassion, and as much as you didn't want to, you know. Because at that point they understood, you know, maybe those kids were going through some more difficult family lives, you know, and they understood that." Bottom line for her parents, Liza said: "And so just treat them with compassion, because they probably don't get that a lot of the time."

For some, mothers emphasized a call to care for others, respond to the needs of others, and treat others as you would want to be treated. While this pattern may have been linked to their gendered roles as care-takers in the family, these principles seemed to transcend maternal roles and socially reproduced gender norms for women. Describing her mom as "always was one that always gave advice," her mom sought opportunities to help people in everyday places and routine activities. Josefina elaborated as follows:

> You know, if we went to the laundromat to do laundry she always took that moment to just always give words of wisdom and to teach and to become someone better. Better in the sense of respecting and caring for others. She's someone who taught about giving back, you know to less fortunate folks. If you have something, give back, you know whether it's your time, or is it something that you have, if you don't need it any more, pass it on to someone that could really use it.

When someone needed help, her mom never hesitated to be there. Josefina, a first-generation straight Chicana woman with children, illustrated this is her mom: "[S]he knew how to sew, so people would ask for her help. Can you, you know, fix the, my pants, or can you tailor this? And you know, again they would want to say, oh, let me pay you, and my mom would say, no, no, it's okay. You don't have to." In the end, her mom's acts of kindness showed Josefina what a giving person did in life.

Focusing on social justice, Edith talked about advocacy for issues in the community. Both her parents seemed to message a sense of justice, but Edith's father had a special role in messaging how important it was to do the right thing and stand up for someone in need. Edith elaborated, referencing her father's role in what she learned about social justice as a child: "And it was like he was always about what was the right thing to do, even if they, it, it was unpopular. It was, if it meant that you would be in the out group, it's about being the right thing, and, and standing up for people who need somebody to be in their corner."

Growing up, many graduate students framed care as community—in neighborhoods, church groups, school communities, and more, where a commitment to well-being of the group tended to be practiced. Eugenio linked strength and support to communities where his mom and sister connected with their disabilities, respectively. His parents committed the family to the greater good in the community. "One thing for sure," Eugenio said, "my . . . dad and mom always say community. In community you're stronger, and with community you can do so many things. [I]t was very like we need to help each other." Kaitlyn described how, as a child, her mom and dad welcomed neighbors into their home. Recalling messages of "always being a good person," Kaitlyn framed community as neighbors that her parents welcomed into the home. She detailed what this was like as a child: "I grew up in [the West] and everyone that I looked [at] around me, every single classmate was Latino. So we all understood each other's experiences. And with that, my parents were always, you know, humble, and they provided not just for our family, but you know for other people. They allowed other people into our family." After a childhood with this community of care, Kaitlyn felt compelled to do the same in her life, saying, "we, um, again we modeled after that." Susan talked about being a good person, too. She spoke to this point when she said: "[M]y parents um, they really stressed being a good person." She connected this value to her parents' belief in God, even as the family was not religious. Spirituality grounded Eugenio's family's values of love and compassion. As an undergraduate student, when he started getting involved at church, he returned to what he felt was community. Susan, too, feels like doing good work and helping others is what matters in life and is important to her career. Comparing career interests and directions of her friends to hers, she talked about how higher education is where she feels she can make a difference. She elaborated: "I don't think I could just ever work at like a company that's just, you know, profiting. I have so many friends in tech and in startups and I don't think I could ever do that 'cause I'm not passionate about the mission. Um, so higher ed's just a really good fit."

In Sharon's family, her father framed treating others with respect in terms of borrowing and lending. Sharon understood this as a call to care for others, whether their property or their humanity. She illustrated: [T]here were other things that he would say like . . . if you borrow something from somebody, return it in better condition then, then you got it. You know if you borrow a car, you return it with a full tank of gas, and, and you clean it, you know, that kind of thing." While not focused on borrowing or lending things, Jeremy's parents frequently reminded him that understanding people is central to learning to maintain relationships in your family, community, and beyond. Over the long term, this idea meant that you never burn bridges, for Jeremy's parents, and consistently manage relationships as you never knew what you may need in the future.

Family Focus on Spirituality as a Foundation for Navigating Life

Related to family unity, care, and compassion, spirituality bonded families—with either mothers or both parents engaging children in a range of spiritual beliefs, religious practices, and faith-based rituals. Similar to valuing family unity, when graduate students discussed their spiritual faith, there seemed to be a connection to support for academic and career success. Many graduate students shared how they grew up in a church, generally a Christian denomination or in the Catholic Church, and often experienced early life connections to a belief system. For some, these experiences had been profound and shaped who they are today, defining their core identities and undergirding a value system focused on hard work, community connectedness, and care for others. For example, when talking about what she recalled about her family's faith, Karina said: "[O]ur main thing was our religion, um, our belief in God, and we went to church almost three times a week when I was younger. [I]t's still a very big thing in our family." For some, while religious observations from childhood had not continued in adulthood, spiritual practices seemed to persist in one form or another. Even where little religious or spiritual practices continued in their lives, a few graduate students explored new spiritual ideas and belief systems. In a small number of cases, little or no spiritual practice or beliefs persisted to present day.

Religious Holidays and Holy Days Center Spirituality in the Family

A focus on religious holidays, high holy days, or Sabbath rituals tended to dominate recollections about family faith practices. For example, Zelma described her family's affiliation with a subset of Christianity and talked about church service, when she recounted family religious rituals: "Um, so we would commute whenever we could, particularly on high holidays. Whether it was Easter, Christmas, you know Good Friday, Holy Saturday. Um, and we would commute to [the Church] on those Sundays. We didn't have a local church." Similarly, Maria talked about how, as Christians, Easter and food defined childhood memories. She elaborated: "I think food as well is a big thing for us. That's how we can connect, through traditional food. So when there is like holidays, and like, um, Easter, and so because they're also like Christian, um, they tend to really connect as a family with food." In Kaitlyn's family, Christmas was huge—in part due to their Catholic faith. She explained more: "I think Christmas in our family is a huge thing, um, because we, we did grow up like Catholic so we, we have those like nine days that we pray I guess, and growing up that we were more like religious in that sense." Kaitlyn detailed what Christmas meant to her family, revealing how holiday get-togethers and gift-giving created lasting memories: "Um, so we would always go to like every aunt's or uncle's house to do that, um, and . . . my parents would obviously participate, we were always there. Um, Christmas we'd always spend together. My mom would always try her best to give everyone a gift, at least one or two. Um, with my dad, he'd just provide the money to, to go by those gifts."

For those who identified a strong Catholic faith in childhood, religious practices and identities tied to the Church framed their shared experiences at home. Jenna offered a glimpse into her family's Catholic religious faith, walking us through a journey from regular religious practice earlier in life to closer connections to her faith community as an adult.

> And so growing up, you know um, we'd go to church every Sunday. And then as . . . when we were younger, my sister and I, you know we didn't want to go to church, and my dad would be the one to say, okay, let's not go to church this week. We can just skip this weekend. And so my sister and I had that [growing] up. And then, um, we even took some CCD classes when we were young. And this is all like elementary school. But then as we got older, my sister and I just, we really, uh, liked the, the faith behind, the faith behind Catholicism, and like the people, the communities that we grew up with. And so we stuck with the faith. And up to this point, you know, uh, we're all Catholic and we attend Mass regularly every week,

Jenna tied the family's religious identities to their Filipino cultural norms and her close ties to her parents. Similarly, Leonardo explained how, as Catholics, they "were definitely going to church every Sunday." Reflecting on religious rituals at home, Leonardo continued: "And, you know, we knew what each holiday, you know, as far as the religious holidays, we knew why. You know, we knew, um, you know, it was always about, you know, what the church, you know wanted us to, to, you know, do." While his mother "was the one that was like dragging" Leonardo and his siblings to church, the family prayed and went to Mass together.

Like Jenna and Leonardo, Hector recalled his family's ties to the Catholic Church well, retelling how they went to church every Sunday. As an elementary student at a Catholic school, Hector shared how he was really into being an altar server, a volunteer role where he helped the presiding priest with duties at Mass: "So, um, my fourth grade to eighth grade I was a very committed alter server." "[H]aving like this deep reverence for the Church" on both side of the family, Hector remembered "this sense like, like for me [growing] up with like a sense of coolness to be . . . on the altar, being in service. You know being . . . close proximity to it, to you know this, this priest and this whole ceremony, and this ritual. It was, it was very special, and to get put on this like, this uniform is Catholic, and all this kind of stuff."

Similar to Jenna, Leonardo, and Hector, Eugenio focused on his Catholic faith and grounded his identity in his faith. "I'm also . . . Catholic," he said, "I'm really, that's really, that's one of my identities I identify myself with so much." He talked about his parents and how they go to

Mass three days for the weekend and participated in spiritual encounters in the Church. When Eugenio was older, he recalled how his Catholic faith helped him resist a pull to spend more time on the "streets" and supported his call to a spiritual life. His dad has been central in Eugenio's movement toward his faith. Referring to how his dad had modeled a life of Christian service, Eugenio spoke about his need to serve in God's name: "Of course he's always there, he's always trying to serve, and that's one thing for sure I look forward to doing myself in the future, um, 'cause I think it's giving back . . . spirituality and part of connecting to God is really important." In the end, Eugenio linked his Oaxacan cultural, indigenous Mexican, and religious identities with his faith and ability to overcome obstacles. He said: "Like I said in my culture, my Indigenous background, my religion, as in like a little bit I connect on my spirituality the way I have overcame certain obstacles in life, or how that impacts my life, too, as well."

Mothers Lead Spiritual Practices in the Family

For many, mothers tended to form family religious practices that led children in their faith formation. For example, Brianna's family is Christian, and she described how the family worshiped at the same church, her grandmother still belongs to the same church where they went as a family, while her mother participates in another church. With her mother an ordained minister, faith was huge. With her mother's central role, Brianna, who identifies as a first-generation African American woman, described what faith meant to her: "So she's been really a leader in making sure that we not only believe in God, but really have our own relationship with Christ. And that's been really huge." While her mother served the faith community, often going to church on Sundays, Tuesdays, and Saturdays, Brianna's father tended to feign illness and didn't go as much as her mother, brother, and extended family. "Still," she remarked, "my dad loved Christ." Even as her mom led the family's spiritual development and churchgoing, Brianna recalled how her grandparents used to be central figures in the family's participation in Sunday church service. She shared more: "[W]e would have like, Sunday dinners. We'd go to church. Get picked up at eight. Go to Sunday, Sunday Bible at nine, then church would start at eleven. But then we'd take a break and go home to my grandmother, she'd make this big, big dinner." Looking back, Brianna recalled her mother's Christian faith's influence on her.

> I would not be here had it . . . been for my mom and our faith. You know, I think that's, when I wanna quit, or when I'm just done with this, you know, it's my mom who's like, nope, let's pray for you. You know we're, we're gonna get through this. You're gonna get through this. I'm just, I'm really thankful because she's allowed, she taught Christ, you know. She put Christ in me, made sure that that was a value, so that when one day, a hundred years from now, when she leaves this earth, you know, I still have that through hard times.

Brianna emphasized what this foundational faith translated to in her life: "And without prayer, you know, I mean, if it wasn't for prayer, if it wasn't for her support, I wouldn't be where I am now, you know. So I really wouldn't be able to do it without my mother." Brianna thanked her mother: "So, I love my mom. I love my mom."

For many graduate students, when it came to faith in the family, mothers and fathers did a lot, even as mothers led faith formation in some families. For Brianna, Stella, Angela, Kayla, and Tanya, spiritual support tends to be important for success as Black college students (Herndon & Hirt, 2004). In Stella's case, her mom shaped a Christian faith formation in Stella's life. Stella, a first-generation African American who's exploring her sexual orientation, admitted that she "came from a very religious household." Referencing her upbringing in Christianity, Stella talked about how she was "that kid where my mom got me involved in Sunday service." Stella continued: "[M]y mom made sure we'd go to church every Sunday." By contrast, Stella's dad "is not really religious." Whereas her dad was Catholic, her "my mom was superreligious. She is Christian and she made sure that her kids were at church every Sunday."

Describing her Nigerian Pentecostal faith, Angela shared how her "mom is like woo! She is serious. She is on it. She is serving in the church. She is, she does it all." On the other hand, her dad is "like nope. It's like, it's there. I acknowledge it, but I don't take it seriously at all." Angela took to her mom's faith and described her spiritual foundation: "I take my faith very seriously, too, and we're very big on like, I think like in Christianity the, the consensus is like, you know marry someone who's equally on the same page as you." Angela always felt her mom's faith supported her—particularly in prayer. Her mom's praying for Angela and committing Angela to God helped carry Angela through a lot in life. Without this faith, Angela felt she wouldn't have had many opportunities in life. Here's what her mom used to say to her: "I hope that favor will find you, that things that are so hard for other people would be made easy for you. Like those type of words and declarations that she speaks over me I think are so important."

Kayla shared similar experiences when she described her dad's experiences with faith: "I never really heard my father, you know express, you know, any like spiritual, um, I don't know, um, guidance. I don't . . . I don't know. He never really spoke like, or he was, he's not the type of person, he's not quoting from the Bible, or you know, repeating any type of Christian values that, you know that, or dogma, or anything like that, that for, to anyone, including us, like I never got that from him." Still, Kayla conceded that her dad lives by Christian values, including "being a good person, being respectful, you know things that you would find in the Bible."

In Tanya's family, spiritual practices tended to be a mix of private and public—but generally did not involve an organized religious service. For her dad's part, a spiritual faith tended to be private—playing a sermon, watching a televangelist, and keeping a Bible in the car—and prayer happened in larger family gatherings. Tanya remembered more: "[W]e always pray when we get together. I know one year we had Thanksgiving over at my house, and all of my family came. I mean like, phew, all of my family came, you know. We prayed, prayed over the food, we always kind of pray over our food when we have a whole bunch of people around. Or you know, pray for things that need, that need to have prayer on." From these spiritual experiences in the family, Tanya concluded: "[W]e know about God."

Josefina's mother exemplified a spiritual life integral to her maternal role—serving as a catechism teacher and volunteering at the annual festival in their Catholic parish, where she helped to fundraise for the community. In fact, her mother started a tradition of making churros for the festival—a culinary delight not yet offered at the event. Beyond festivals and religious formation programs, Josefina's mother taught her siblings and her about the power of prayer and faith to get you through challenging times. Josefina spoke to how her mother centered a prayerful life for the family: "[M]y mother taught us about just prayer was so important, going to Mass every Sunday, always making prayer a priority and attending Mass on Sundays, no matter what was gonna happen. And if we were gonna travel, go somewhere on Sunday and it's gonna interfere with going to church she always said, okay, well, there's Saturday Mass.

We're all gonna go to Saturday, so there's always that." Prayer was for tough times, too, according to Josefina's mother. "Pray 'cause this is the way we find strength within those moments," Josefina said. In the end, Josefina's mother helped her see how a moral compass could guide you on your journey in life: She elaborated: "I would say that she has been, she was someone that really was, was really a lot of guidance in my life, more in terms of the, I guess, trying to find the words, more of being that moral support, but also my mother was very spiritual. So there's a lot of spiritual, how can I say, a lot of spiritual guidance." Josefina illustrated what her mom used to say about faith and life: "[M]y mom would say, very short words she would say, she said, you know what? There's nothing impossible. Put your, put your project in God's hands, and this is where the spirituality would come in, she would say, put your project in God's hands. That it's meant for you to, to do this, it's gonna, you're gonna finish it. If it's not God's plan, then it's not gonna happen. You know have faith and, and do what you can do. You're capable and we're here to support you, whatever we can do to help you, we're here." Josefina's mom did more than impress on the family the importance of prayer, she lived it in the home and community. At their church, growing up, Josefina recalled her mom being involved in the church community—from making churros to supporting ministries. This helped Josefina to see what her mom's faith was all about and what it meant to her mom.

Jaime felt like she knew God, too, and connected her upbringing in the Catholic Church to what she believes as a moral arc in life. Jaime talked about going to Sunday school, learning about the Bible, and going to Mass. As a student in parochial school, Jaime discovered how her teachers "would talk about, uh, good and bad, and you know, really introduce the dichotomy of like the God and the devil. And oh, what do you do? You pray! You pray your way out of it." She summed up what she learned: "God will send you a boat but you got to get in, is the attitude." Edith had similar deeply religious experiences and strong identity in Christianity as a child—like Jaime. Edith described how her family practiced their Protestant faith: "We went to church every week, sometimes twice a week, maybe three times a week, because church was not just church." Korean cultural connections and social networks among Korean immigrants supported their faith. To this point, Edith remarked: [I]t was a community of like people, Korean immigrants who like can, can come together and, and be a community for each other, and be a network onto each other, too. Yeah. But it was yeah, it was their social circle."

Forms of Spirituality in Adulthood: Prayer, Belief in a Higher Power, and More Personal Practices

Later in life, most still remained connected to some form of regular practice, generally prayer, and talked about how belief in a higher power comforted them and helped them get through more stressful events in life. For some, continuing to embrace their faith linked them to their parents and formed a part of their support system. When recalling a conversation with her grandfather, Brianna shared that she connected her call for financial support for her undergraduate education with the central importance of faith and, specifically, prayer: "But coming back [home] I had, uh, money issues. And I remember I was trying to find money. And, um, right before he passed away, like the day before he had passed away, um, he said, ask God. You know. Ask God for the money." Angela reflected on how her faith today supports her career trajectory and provider role in her family. "I'm not just gonna be stagnant and stay in the same job for twenty years like my dad did, but in fact I'm gonna use the resources and knowledges around me to advance in my career, and to hopefully provide for my family, give a better life, because I believe that's what the Lord has called me to do."

Today, Tanya shared how her spirituality has grown immensely. As in her childhood, she generally mixes both private prayer with public conversations in community of her graduate program peers who share spiritual faith. She detailed her spiritual journey: "I've gotten very big into like spirituality, and just calling on . . . God, because this year was . . . a huge transition going in to grad school. And so, call on my God, but also . . . my family . . . and . . . my newfound community here [on campus]." For the latter, Tanya shared how she connected with peers to have conversations about what they're going through.

For some, early religious practices in the family had not continued in adulthood—even as more personal spiritual faith systems developed. Stella described how she moved out at the age of sixteen, due to instability at home, and hadn't returned to the church from her childhood. Stella's unstable family dynamics seemed to extend to church, where expectations to socially engage led to everyone being in her "business" and perpetuated a "toxic and dramatic environment." Stella just needed a less stressful spiritual experience. As an adult, Stella enjoyed Sundays for her, as when she described what they meant to her: "I cherished my Sundays to sleep in or catch up on work and life." She concluded" "I'd rather sleep in on a Sunday than wake up at seven in the morning to get ready for an 8 a.m. service." Instead, Stella described a spirituality that connected her to nature that moves away from Christian religious practices connected to her Nigerian cultural identity:

> I feel like as I became older I became less religious and more spiritualist. You know I tapped into more of my spirituality. I, you know, manifest more than do natural prayers, and I feel like, you know, and there's different types of Christianity too that kind of embodies different people's cultures, and how they utilize that. So in the Nigerian culture I don't really feel comfortable on how they take . . . to religion and Christianity, and which is why I do my own type of things to make me feel like I'm still in touch with my spirituality and, and religion in my own ways.

Stella finished: "I still tap into the Bible at any time I, I need to, but definitely I'm more spiritual, I manifest. And obviously that's not something my mom or my family is into."

Jessica shared a story similar to Stella. Jessica talked about how she identified as a Christian and, as a youngster, went to church with her family, including her cousins. But Jessica's Christian identity seemed to wane as she transitioned into adulthood. She commented: "I feel like when I was a kid I was a lot more religious than I am now. Um, which I still identify as a Christian." Jessica went on to explain how her grandparents-in-law had been very religious, and she learned a lot about being a "better person overall" from them. Jessica elaborated on what she learned: "Um, caring, and giving, and things like that. Like you don't steal, you don't cheat. You don't, like the normal things, you don't do that." For Jessica, "religion kind of like helped back that up," even if she revealed that she did not participate in Sunday service.

Even when their parents continued to participate in more traditional religious practices, children sometimes turned to a less religious but still spiritual way of life. Zelma illustrated this pattern, describing how her humanist interspiritualist identity emerged in her life. She shared more: "Like I don't have a very specific like, religious belief. Um, but I do believe that we're all spiritual human beings, and I believe in viewing people as humans and using a humanistic approach in treating people." While Sharon's parents had never really been religious—even with close ties to the Mormon Church—she grew up around Catholics when she went to a parochial high school. But her faith today focuses on an agnostic spiritual practice. She explained: "I never adopted . . . a formal faith, [T]here weren't those kind of values in the home. I don't know what my parents experience was with faith. I suspect it wasn't positive, because you know they . . . never attended . . . [church]." Beatrice admitted that her family is not religious, but she started to explore the peripheral connections to Christianity that she remembered from her grandmother. As a college student, she described what she did: "I picked it up again in college, but I just started going to a Bible study. Um, so I . . . didn't start going to church, but I just went to a Bible study just to learn more and I appreciated learning different things and just discussing things with people, and just, there was many different layers of, um, people's understanding or appreciation of it."

Where religious affiliation in more than one denomination marked childhood for a small number of graduate students, a mix of religious identities and practices tended to persist today in ways that created unique meaning and centering in their lives today. In Susan's family, her mom was Christian and her dad Jewish, and they celebrated major religious holidays in both denominations. Susan described how her parents didn't identify closely with either religion and believed more in God as their spiritual focus. She explained more: "Um, in terms of holidays he was always around for those as well. So, um, in my family we celebrate, so he was actually Jewish so we'd do, um, Jewish holidays, and then also like Christmas, um, cause my mom was Christian. [T]hey both believed in God but we weren't religious. Didn't, um, belong to like any sort of church, or . . . place of worship." Referring to how her parents wanted her to explore her own religious identity, Susan mentioned that they encouraged her "to be educated about different religions;" Today, Susan identifies more closely with her Jewish faith and has traveled twice to Israel.

Similar to Susan, Winona grew up in an interfaith family—her mother a practicing Buddhist and her father a Catholic. She recalls always having to balance both Catholic and Buddhist religious practices—so her family went to church and cleaned the altar for vegan days dictated by Buddhist teachings. She shared more about these practices: "[T]here was always, um, cleaning the altar for any of the vegan days. So with Buddhist religion was that on, vegan days are the full moons and the new moons. But in addition, if I clean the Buddhist, I, I also have to clean the, the Catholic side, too." Winona's dad helped her reconcile differences in the belief systems, which seemed to facilitate Winona meaningfully embracing teachings and rituals in both faiths. She described his perspective.

> So, um, my dad did play a factor in the sense of trying to create that balance, because understandably Catholicism doesn't allow the belief of other gods, so my dad himself as a Catholic man was like, well, I do still believe in God and I don't betray you, but Buddha is my teacher. So, because of that he was able to explain to me like, hey, this is what I think, um, and I would encourage you if we can to create this balance of like, if we pray to God we also pray for our well-being with Buddha, and stuff like that, too.

Referring to her dad's work to support the family's approach to religious practices, Winona concluded: "So he was the one that created that balance between the religion, which is why currently right now we still practice both of them, and we are able to."

Hua talked about both Buddhism and Christianity in her life, too—in some ways similar to Winona. Hua had been raised all her life to follow Buddhism, and she connected her family's faith and religious practices to "like a more like the Chinese culture." Later, Hua's family's Buddhist traditions intersected with Christianity when her grandparents started to identify with and practice Christian rituals. It all seemed to center on her maternal grandmother's nursing school studies, according to Hua. There, her grandmother went to church and learned about the Bible. Later, in graduate school, Hua enjoyed "the atmosphere, all the things there, and the feel[ing] of [being] welcomed" at churches in the southeast US. Now, both her parents accept that she's a practicing Christian. Here's what they said to her: "I think . . . if [this is what] you I want to be a, a Christian, they support it."

Even when religious identities or practices tended to not be central to families, graduate students reported a range of spiritual connections or religious affiliations. In this way, Zeke, a first-generation married cisgender gay white male, reported that "[t]here was no religion at home at all. Like there was no, there was none of that." But Zeke went to Catholic school, even as his mom didn't require him to go to church. With divorced parents, Zeke experienced a more spiritual presence at home with his father. Zeke shared that, at a time when he had struggled when he was younger, his dad brought a candle in his room and inquired about what was going on with Zeke. Similarly, faith wasn't an early part of Liza's family. While she recalled growing up Catholic, in some ways, "religion didn't play that much of a fact" in her life. Gail recalled how her parents weren't very religious. She explained that her dad was raised Catholic, but her parents never really encouraged her "to go to church or anything like that, like cause they didn't go to church." For Juan, who was raised Catholic, there never seemed to be deep connections to religious practice in his family. Later in life, Juan drifted away from his Catholic faith, saying: "I, uh, reached maybe high school I didn't really follow the religion much anymore, uh, but it was never really a huge topic or a huge issue for my family, and I think that's probably very rare also." Today, he doesn't follow Catholicism, and his family seems to be fine with his decision.

Chapter 4

Honoring Sacrifices that Parents Make to Get Children to College and Beyond

Education, Immigration, and Racial Discrimination

For many graduate students, seemingly equally important to reproducing family values was a need to honor parents' hard work and sacrifices. In fact, most graduate students frequently framed their intense focus on academic achievement, strong interest in high-status and/or high-paying fields, and resilient commitment to completing undergraduate and graduate degree programs to their persistent resolve to honor what their parents, grandparents, and ancestors had built, particularly as immigrants of color and people of color in educational and commercial environments where racist and anti-immigrant patterns persist in the US. This drive to achieve academically and persist on their educational paths—all the way to graduate school—reflected a deep dedication to the family unit and cultural values that not only promoted education but also encouraged an ethic of care between family members and a recognition that family is central to identities, beliefs, and experiences in life.

To let down families and, focally, parents who worked so hard to provide and spent far too much time away from home doing so, would be difficult. So strong was this force for some grad students that they closely tied their success to the success of their parents and the need to provide for their parents today or someday in the future. Not only their success but their behavior and dress—even if contested as teenagers—tended to be ways to honor parents, as a fear of forgetting "where you're from" worried some parents who migrated to the US. For a small group whose parents earned degrees while their children were young, achieving what a mother or father did in college drove them to persist in their studies. Over the life course, honoring familial and ancestral gains, losses, pain, and healing all seemed to encourage a need to set goals, keep going, and accomplish what you set out to do.

Leaving Home and School: Appreciating What Family Immigration Means for "A Better Life for Us" in Education, Work, and Much More

Across regions of the US, where many graduate students live and go to school, immigrant experiences shaped shared identities in their families, common experiences among siblings, and a deep respect for how their parents uprooted and moved so far from home at young ages. What Zelma, who identifies as a first-generation cis-hetero Indigenous Palestinian and Lebanese woman, shared seemed to embody this appreciation, admiration, and respect for her parents. With a lead role in a decision to immigrate—generally tied to the traditional gender roles her parents reproduced in the family—Zelma reflected on her dad's sacrifices and what she was most grateful for. She shared: "[A]s an adult and reflecting back I'm like, you know, thanks, Dad. You did sacrifice a lot. You did. You know, you're here. I acknowledge everything that you've done to get us here, right?" Now speaking to both her mom and dad, Zelma further reflected: "[T]he fact that they brought us here, you know . . . I'd be remiss in [not] acknowledging that, you know, America is the country you go to . . . have freedom, right?"

Later in life, Zelma revealed that, as a child in an immigrant family, there's a sense of obligation—or guilt—to not let your parents down as you navigate life and make major decisions about career, work, school and more. She paused and thought about this common experience: "I think you carry this with you . . . immigrant child guilt, like I don't wanna let my parents down. And so we didn't give up. You know, we were just, I guess the resiliency, and the, I, you know my parents, knowing what my parents went through just to get here. And for me not to continue, like even, at the very least I was like, I just want to get my bachelor's degree." To this day, Zelma viscerally felt respect for what her parents did to come to the US. After she received her doctorate in applied humanities, Zelma tied her appreciation to the pride her parents felt with a doctor in the family. Speaking about a conversation she had with her dad, Zelma shared: "[W]e had a conversation not long ago about like, you know, what he had hoped. And he was like, you know I had dreamed that all of you guys would have doctor in your name." She continued, relaying what her dad said to her: "I've always wanted, you know, part, you know, to bring you guys here so that you could have those, you know, degrees. You have those, um, initials behind your name." Zelma understood what a doctorate meant for her career and life, but she also revealed that she still wanted to make her dad proud.

Following a business lead with her father and his siblings, Zelma described her family's early decision to travel to and remain in the US: "I remember landing at [the city], in [the airport], and it was just really kind of jarring. And I, you know what we thought was going to be a vacation, um, ended up being a business proposition for my dad." Zelma continued the story: "I had two uncles that lived here, um, who both owned a business. It's like, okay. Um, they own, and one of my uncles wanted, you know, out. And so my dad decided to buy him out." By her dad's own account, Zelma recalled a drive to look for a better life in the US. She described how her dad "barely got through high school" and her mom "barely got through the eighth grade," before they embarked on a search for a better life for the family. For her dad, a better life focused on education, and a college education equated to stability in her life and redemption for parental sacrifices made in leaving home at a young age. To this point, Zelma remembered how her dad insisted that she go to college. She said: "[L]ike educational attainment you know, there was no 'if' or, or 'but.' It was like, you're going to get an education. You know we came here, you're going to college. You are going to become a college-educated person."

Recognizing racism, sexism, and many more forms of structural exclusion in the US, Zelma still felt that this was the place her parents knew to go to in order to give their family a better life. She said: "[E]ven though there's certain issues, you know, even to this day, but it . . . was, it's the land of opportunity till this day. And it's still the land of opportunity for a lot of immigrants and a lot of people who want opportunities, even in some of it's, you know, structural and systemic, um, issues that are happening." Zelma ended by repeating her parents' profound sacrifices: "And that, that's not, um, that's not a small sacrifice. Giving up your citizenship, you know. There's, there's a, a ton of stories that have happened through my family based on just who they are, their refugee status, all of that."

Even later in life, Zelma still felt that this was the right decision for her family, and she contended that she's better off for it—allowing her to raise her own family and journey to where she planned to go in her career.

Both Maria's and Kaitlyn's parents, respectively, were "big on education," as Maria put it. In Maria's family, her parents "literally moved here for education." Maria connected her parents' move to the US to cultural values on education and, as she said, "to study all those higher-paying jobs that are like, you know doctor, law, and all these positions." But Maria, a first-generation LGBTQ-identified Armenian woman who immigrated from Iran and identifies culturally as Middle Eastern and Armenian, reported that her parents remained open to her studying a range of majors in college. For her father, though, questions about major course of study dogged Maria as an undergraduate—and now his focus on her graduate studies seemed to center on pay. "So money, money, money, because he struggled, you know, like, you know working and stuff, so he wants me to be successful," Maria shared. Maria resisted this exclusive focus on salary and tended to pursue a career as a higher-education professional, about which she was passionate. She elaborated: "I don't look at my career as just making money, I'm looking at it as a passion. So even if it's low pay like, it's okay. Like I'll work my . . . way up, but I'm doing it not because of the money reasons."

In the end, Maria shared how her parents were "very much happy" that she finished her program. Her parents' happiness about her educational journey seemed to be critical to their interest in remaining in the US and continuing to work hard to support her. Maria understood her role here: "So, they always remember like, they always remember what, like they use me as like a motivation of being able to just keep, keep working hard so I can be able to, um, finish my education and get the opportunities." She concluded: "So it really gives them the hope and motivation to keep going, and keep going, and you know, provide for me as much as they can."

Similar to Maria, Kaitlyn's parents understood the importance of education but were not as familiar with how the educational system operated in the US. She reflected briefly on her observation: "I think that was really like one of the only things I think with my parents, like they understood the importance of education, but I think where they lacked was really understanding what it meant. Because you always, they always knew like, oh, yeah, you have to get an education, especially in this country." Kaitlyn, a first-generation cisgender straight Latina, intimately detailed how her family had to share a house with multiple families, relaying the sacrifices her parents made to ensure that she and her five siblings achieved their educational goals.

> [W]e lived in a house, I think it was maybe three or four bedrooms. Um, but in that house there was actually like multiple families living there at once. Um, and then, because I think that was really the house that a lot of my uncles lived in, and, you know, were starting to get, you know, jobs that would support not just the family in general, but their specific, you know immediate family. Um, but after, I think for the first twelve years of my life there were two families living in one house with, and then within two bedrooms. So my cousins, uh, there's three cousins and an aunt and uncle who lived in two of those bedrooms. They had their own like makeshift kitchen and living room. And then with my family it was my parents, and then us six siblings in the other two rooms, our kitchen, and then another small living room.

Kaitlyn conveyed a sense of privacy they had, and there would always be parents working outside the house with older siblings caring for younger ones, among the sacrifices that they all made as a family.

Similar to Maria and Kaitlyn, Eugenio focused on how his parents wanted a better life for him in the US. He shared more: "I remember they would mention that they want, they want, they came here for a future, for best for us. They wanted that for us. They always mentioned doctor, lawyer, you know, they always mentioned the, and that's why I guess what I remember." He heard his parents' mantra in their communication with him: "We want you to succeed. We want you to go have a career." Eugenio, a first-generation heterosexual Latinx male who identifies as Oaxacan from an Indigenous background from Mexico, journeyed into a career in higher education. He detailed how hard his parents worked when he was younger. In fact, his parents rarely saw each other and alternated childcare duties and care-taking at home.

> My mom and dad always worked. So what actually happened was, we were little, um, my mom was there, she was taking care of us. And then when she started working they were both, and this is what I also was told when they were like with, for elementary school they, they both of them would work. My

mom would, uh, work in the, the daytime, my mom, my dad would work at night time. So like, that's where, they don't even see each other, and we will be with my mom, and then my dad will be at night, and then it's like vice versa.

Eugenio had a lot of pride for what his parents accomplished—they had three properties in Mexico—and they did all of it for their kids. And now is the time that Eugenio feels he needs to give back to them. He spoke to this point: "But now that I know that, I understand that, I'm trying to give back to him. Letting him know like, hey, we have a . . . pool . . . dad. Let's go swim. Let's have a good time."

Even as parents had limited educational opportunities beyond elementary or secondary school, children knew how much education meant to them. Josefina—who identifies as a first-generation straight Chicana woman with children—exemplified how, even when "not being able to go to school," her dad "was going to do everything he could to provide a roof over us." Indeed, Josefina recalled how her dad said he would earn enough "money to buy a couple of cows and to buy beds, and you know, and . . . invest a little bit with cows, and hopefully, you know, milk cows, sell the milk" to raise revenue the family. Josefina explained that what she called her dad's "very dysfunctional" childhood in Mexico prompted him to come the US. in his late teens. Saving all the money he earned at this time, Josefina shared that he would send remittances to his mom.

While neither parent had formal education, Ping, who is a first-generation college student, experienced migration on many levels in his life. In adolescence, he experienced his father leaving home for most of the year to work in construction in regions around China, his mother leaving home for long stretches during the day to care for family sheep, and rural-urban migratory movement in China for his secondary schooling and college. Describing his father's schedule, Ping said that he "worked from like 6 a.m. to like 10 p.m. Then he, we have you, yeah, takes shower and sleep," and Ping realized how hard his parents worked for him. Across the vastness between China and the Midwest and southeastern US, Ping realized how much his father did for his family when he shared that his dad never really wanted to leave home. He said simply: "I'm sure he [didn't] want to walk away from [his] hometown, [but] he cannot earn a lot of money." Even when he earned a high salary from construction work, Ping confessed that his dad was subjected to wage theft and the vagaries of a pay system that issued payroll warrants annually. He explained: "[H] e cannot earn a lot of money, a lot of money since sometimes [they] do not pay him at all for a whole year. When . . . he plan[s] to go home like at the end of the year, the boss will steal money."

Like many others, Andres revealed that his parents had secondary and less-than-secondary school experiences, and they left their native Mexico for the US so that Andres had his siblings could achieve higher levels of education. With only an elementary school education, Andres's dad left to meet to agricultural demands in his youth, including tending cows, working the fields of corn and amaranth. His mom completed high school and started technical school for secretarial work, but both his parents left for the US.

Understanding Decisions to Migrate: How Fathers Shape Family Moves for "the American Dream"

In many cases, economic opportunity, financial security, job prospects, education, and more seemed to ground decisions to migrate to the US. And these reasons that drove moves to leave their homes, families, and lives seemed to be associated primarily with fathers. Likely, in part, related to their socially reified gender roles as providers, graduate students tended to relate stories about a better life for their families to what fathers shared with them as young children and throughout their lives.

Leonardo, a first-generation straight Mexican American male, recalled a family trip to Guadalajara, Mexico, that helped him "appreciate what, what we had. That you don't just have to go to school because your parents wake you up in the morning, it's something that you're able to do because you're lucky." How did Leonardo come to appreciate how lucky he was? He shared a story from his family's ranch in Guadalajara about a picture he saw from his dad's sixth grade class: "And, and what he told us was like, well, you know *mijo* [my son], like, when, at that point it was, school really wasn't a priority. It was about, you know, working. You know, working and, and providing for the family, right. You're, you're part of the family, you work. You work, you don't really, school isn't, you know, a priority. And high school, that's not something that, you know, everyone does." For Leonardo, learning about this dad's departure from elementary school to work for the family helped him understand how fortunate he was to have an opportunity to go to school and prepare for a career with which he identifies and allows him to support his family.

But that wasn't all for Leonardo in his appreciation for his father's sacrifices. In fact, Leonardo recalled how his father told stories about US immigration and border patrol. In a system that frequently degrades human experiences and overlooks basic human needs, Leonardo's father faced horrifically dehumanizing treatment. Leonardo explained further.

> So when my dad came over he wasn't documented, and so there was several stories of him . . . escaping from [immigration enforcement]. [H]e would always talk about, you know, the one time that they tried to trap him on a bus, and so he had to jump out the window from the bathroom while the bus was moving, things like that. [H]e talked about how hard it was at first, you know, trying to get established. You know, knowing that you can be deported at any time.

Later in life, Leonardo recalled how his dad said to him in the simplest terms that he wanted a better life for Leonardo and his siblings than what he had growing up. Leonardo recalled: "[H]e wanted us to be better than, than he was, right? He wanted us to have a better life, which is why he came to this country."

Like Leonardo's father, Susan's dad wanted to "make the American, or get the American dream, and, um, you know" as an immigrant to the US "[s]upport yourself, so educate," Susan said, referring to how both parents stressed education. Beyond modeling college-going and facilitating college experiences for Susan, her mom and dad always stressed education. Susan shared how they messaged education as a means to a better life. So much so did her parents want the best education for Susan that they drove her brother and her to a private school an hour or two away from their home. Her parents felt that their public school district didn't have the resources to support them, so they sought it elsewhere and supported Susan and her brother in going to private school. She referenced their support: "Um, so they did all that. And it was a lot, but that's, that's what they felt they had to do, so."

As a young man, Holly's dad followed a migratory path in Europe. Leaving his native Russia at the time, he had a unique experience serving the Soviet Union when he went to Germany in service to his country. Living there, Holly said, he was "exposed to Western values, and actually, before even he met my mom he already served in Germany." She continued: "He spoke German. He was, um, . . . exposed to different country, different cultures. He had friends who were absolutely outstanding, unique, you know, and they actually played a big role in my upbringing as well." Later, when Holly immigrated to the US, she seemed to understand what her dad experienced and could see how his movement for new opportunities helped her in so many ways unknown to her as a youngster. Landing in New York, Holly turned to a best friend who lived there and helped her get to know everything she needed to know to adjust to her new life in the US. But Holly, a cisgender heterosexual white woman who identifies ethnically as Russian, felt like she knew a lot about the world already, given the intellectual and creative home life she had when she was younger and the peer environment at school.

Reflecting on Sacrifices of Mothers to Support Families Who Migrate for Better Opportunities

Like stories about fathers, graduate students recounted how their mothers traveled long distances and left family and home behind to migrate to the US. In some cases, mothers made the trek and settled into a new life alone, while in others they traveled with parents, spouses, and siblings. To this point, Stella, a first-generation African American who is exploring her sexual orientation, spoke directly to her mom as if she were with us in the interview.

> And this is why I thank her every day like, I thank you for all the things you had to go through for me to even be an American citizen, an American-born citizen. To not have to go through the things that DACA [Deferred Action for Childhood Arrivals] students have to go through, undocumented students have to go through. And that I'm able to, you know, achieve that American dream that you're still trying to fight for. And that's what also inspires me to push hard to achieve my goals, because it's like, like my mom didn't do all this for what.

Stella described how she had to achieve so as not to waste all that her mother did for her to be able to go to college and now grad school.

With a similar immigrant story to Stella, Angela tied her Christian faith to her calling in life, based on the fact that her mom made her way to the US. Angela shared the following:

> I can speak for my own experience like, knowing that God has placed me here on the earth for a reason, like I think God is a God of excellence, and He desires for us to walk in our purpose. And I think my mom has an understanding of that. I'm just like okay, like I got to this country. God has blessed me with the opportunity to come here. Like my mom has like ten siblings, and out of all her . . . ten siblings she was the one to be here. So I'm, I'm just like, that says something. So she's like okay, if the Lord has brought me to this country, let me be a good steward of the resources that he has blessed me with.

More than giving back to family, Angela felt that the fact that her mom's immigrant experiences meant something more for herself.

"Taking Care of Your Elders": Immigrant Experiences and the Need to Give Back to Family Members

Tying shared immigrant experiences of parents to a cultural value of caring for elder family members, some graduate students observed how they had been brought up to enact an ethic of care and live to close the circle of support for parents and family members in what they did. Angela shared how she felt a need to give back to them: "[Y]ou know, we brought you guys here for a reason, to make sure that you guys have a better life, better education, so the least you can do is get a good job. The least you can do is do well." Angela further explained how, growing up, she felt pressure to take care of not just herself but others in her family, too. To this point, she revealed: "I've always had this pressure like, I have to do great to the point where like, I can sustain myself and other people. 'Cause let's say my dad wasn't around, like we would be just fine." Ultimately, Angela tied what she felt to family experiences with immigration. Referring to her parents, she elaborated.

> [L]ike you flew like oceans to a whole different continent just to provide for me and my siblings. So I think there's this like pressure to do well. 'Cause I think also in like immigrant culture there is this value of like, not necessarily repaying, but almost taking care of your elders when they get to a certain point. Like my mom, my mom currently works in a nursing

home. She's like, do not put me in a nursing home. You guys are gonna take care of me. You guys are gonna provide for me. So I'm just like, okay, if you want us to do that, I need money to make that happen. I think it's that messaging . . . they didn't explicitly say this all the time, but it's just like, it's kind of implied. Like, you know, we brought you guys here for a reason, to make sure that you guys have a better life, better education, so the least you can do is get a good job.

Angela concluded: "[C]oming from an immigrant household there's this pressure to almost like repay back your parents for their sacrifices when they came here."

In a unique twist on giving back to elder family members and taking care of the most vulnerable relatives, Ping applied this idea to learning environments on campus. He mentioned how he had planned to support his students like they were his own children and sacrifice as their instructor, adviser, mentor, and so on. He explained: "So if I'm become a teacher, should I want to get, uh, something back from my students if I want. I will be a father. Should I unconditionally pardon my children if I like, yeah, that, that, I, I, I want to be, I want to do research and, uh, work related to education because I want to support students like me." Ping reasoned that he benefited from his parents and would like to do the same with his students if he transitions to a faculty role. He said: "I benefit from my parents and my, and my father['s] support, emotional support and the financial support. Uh, the, I want to let other students get a similar thing from our generation."

Like others, Stella embodies unique and touching ways that graduate students talked about giving back to their families for how much parents sacrificed for them. In her case, Stella shared how determined she had been to support her mom when she finished graduate school and entered the workforce. She shared more here: "[I]t's still a big goal of mine is when I have everything that I have and achieve everything that I do have, and have the finances to do something. I plan to support my mom and my family any way that I can."

Supporting family members related to fulfilling dreams that their parents had for them could be seen in what a small group of graduate students described. These dreams tended to focus on getting a college degree, securing a good job, taking care of family, and giving back to the community. All in all, what parents seemed to want most of their kids was a life with fewer sacrifices for families separated by international borders and jobs that required physically exhausting work for pay, according to graduate students.

Leonardo told a story about how he had to reassure his dad that he would have a job that afforded him resources to pay to fix his car. Worried that he'd struggle with income to pay for these expenses, his dad often cajoled him into fixing cars with him in the garage. Leonardo explained how he finally confronted his dad about this concern: "And I'm not gonna have to worry about fixing my own car because I'll be able to pay someone to do it. Like, you know, I won't have to worry about cars breaking down and knowing what to do, because that, that's something that I'll take care of, because I'll have a good job and it won't be necessary."

Jenna, a first-generation Filipina heterosexual female, described her determination to succeed in her graduate degree studies and transition to an early career role. Jenna focused on making a good salary to support herself and her parents, and this was one way she could honor their sacrifices and recognize everything they did for her. She elaborated further.

> I'm so determined to work really hard, um, make enough not just for me but for them. Because you know, they had good positions in the Philippines. They had their friends, their family. And then they move out here, and . . . my grandparents passed away and they couldn't go home because we were here, and if we go back to the Philippines then everything they've been working for . . . would be at stake. So they sacrificed a lot and, um, and I think I really, like I really admire them for it. I remember as a kid seeing them struggle, like not being able to pay for ice cream. And it's just not only seeing it, but also experiencing it, you know, experiencing all of the setbacks they've gone through. Like it really made me want to work harder for them too, you know.

And there's more for Jenna, as when she talked about giving give back to immigrant communities where she lives and works. She said she'd like to work in "helping . . . people like immigrants [and] people from low-income backgrounds. Because my parents really like went from living paycheck to paycheck." Jenna noted that seeing her parents struggle led her to want to work with families who struggle, too.

While Angela recognized that her family life had not been perfect, there was so much she saw in her parents' migration to the US that prompted her to want to make life better for her and the next generation in her family. Taking the long view, Angela shared her gratitude and need to ensure a better future for others: "I am very, very grateful. I know now, it helps me to like, do it better for the next generation. Hopefully, they can do better than me, and better, and better, and better. I think holding on to that [idea] has helped."

Giving back to parents extended to how Karina talked about how pride tended to be a consistent theme in her life. For example, she described her father's pride for her accomplishments as an undergraduate student and now a graduate student. But Karina also wanted to make her parents proud of her. She spoke to all of this in what follows:

> But, um, but even then he was still very supportive of me um to get my degree. And when I did he was very proud of me, and he let me know that. Um, and so it's been really great. Uh, so past my undergrad and now to my grad program, everything's been great. He's very proud that, to say that, you know I'm pursuing my masters. So it wasn't like, college, it was great, um, but I felt like at the time I was doing it for my parents as well, um, because I wanted to make them proud and say.

Karina, a heterosexual Latina woman who identifies as half Guatemalan and half Mexican, connected her need to make her parents proud of her to her dad's family's immigrant experiences. She focused on how her father was the only one of his six siblings to go to college. After her dad's dad migrated to the US, her dad worked hard to earn a college degree, and Karina was well aware of how this hard work paid off for her dad and how she wanted her dad to see how he inspired her and how she was doing the same in her life.

Respecting Parental Concerns for Maintaining Cultural Connections to "Where You're From"

Some graduate students described how parent expectations, family immigrant experiences, and broader peer and social influences challenged them to balance the cultural demands of "two spaces," as Zelma put it. As a dimension of racial socialization, cultural socialization includes messaging about ethnic and cultural pride and heritage (Hughes, 2003), and the reproduction of this cultural pride could be seen in what parents shared with children. As a child growing up in the US, Zelma recalled how her dad reminded her to not forget where she's from as he witnessed her wanting to assimilate and "belong" at school, at the mall, in the homes of her friends, and more. Zelma elaborated when she described how she felt as a teenager "wanting to rebel." She said, "[Y]ou're straddling both, you know, two spaces. And so my parents were very much trying to maintain their original culture, their original identity, their original beliefs[, but] they had this headstrong daughter who wanted to do whatever she wanted to do." Zelma concluded that she'll forever appreciate what her parents did for them in their traveling so far to settle in the US.

Like Zelma, Jenna experienced friction with her dad, particularly during Jenna's high school years. This tension related, in part, to cultural differences between her father and her. As Jenna explained.

> But then around high school or undergraduate, there's been this conflict with both parents where, I don't know if it's generational or cultural from Philippines, but you know the, a little bit of that independence in American culture. There was a lot of fights by the time I was a junior, senior in high school, 'cause I wanted to have that, you know, high school girl experience. I wanted to have a boyfriend. I wanted to go out on dates. I wanted to go to the football games.

Like Jenna, Zelma's dad responded to all of it with an emphatic "no": "[N]o. No. No. You can't do any of that." Zelma knew she was influenced by friends, culture, and society, but her dad insisted: "[Y]ou know, you're an Arab." And Zelma would respond: "But you brought me here to the US. Like come on, you know."

Family immigration enhanced cultural connections to Nigeria in Angela's family. Identifying as a first-generation African American female who is ethnically Nigerian, Angela recalled the Nigerian cultural pride her parents instilled in the children. At the same time, members of her family tended to feel a need to work harder and get ahead to prove who they were and where they came from. Angela explained more: "[W]hen it comes to like being Nigerian I think there is this narrative that like, Nigerians in general like, I feel like we're very prideful." Angela continued: "Like you have to work harder. Like you're Nigerian, like we are the best." Similar to Angela, Hector talked about how he remembered the pride in Native people, Filipino people, and Mexican people—and the need to represent his cultural and ethnic identities and the voices of people of color. Maintaining good relationships is the way Hector learned to do this—human connection and community—particularly from his dad.

Tension emerged in Jaime's young life, too. As a child, Jaime recalled how she had to speak Vietnamese at home. Her father insisted on it, especially when she was in elementary school. Jaime noted: "Um, my first language was Vietnamese, and then when I got into, I believe preschool, they said that I suddenly spoke English. It's like, okay. 'Cause, you know, kids are little sponges. They just catch on to things." As she was promoted through lower elementary grades, her immediate and extended family grew to be concerned that Jaime and her cousins would lose their Vietnamese language skills, "because," as Jaime put it, "around fourth grade I just, I started speaking to them in English." Her parents pushed her to continue speaking Vietnamese at home, even as she resisted. She commented: "[T]hey were like, you know how to speak Vietnamese, and it's like, but I don't want to. And, um, and I didn't mean to not use it as much, but then they started shaming us for not using it."

For Edith, family expectations to preserve cultural and racial connections as Koreans had been messaged to her from a young age. Edith relayed what she heard as a child: "You know when I shared about like things that you gotta do the right thing. Oh, okay. I'll see this, growing up I was told marry within your race, preserve your race. I, I was told that." Reflecting on the familial reproduction of this idea, Edith continued: "Yeah, like there was, there was a, you're Korean. Yeah, they're like you're Korean. You're not American. You're Korean and preserve that."

Beyond maintaining connections to cultural identities, beliefs, and practices, Stella shared how she had to code-switch to navigate family and home environments with school and social settings. Describing how she navigated between her home and school, Stella shared what her life was like as a teenager.

> I grew up in the hood so there wasn't really a lot of Africans, like I grew up around like African Americans. So you know, that culture shock was there as well, because I didn't grow up in the traditional African type of environment. Like yeah, in my household, but once I got out of that household like I had

to kind of code-switch to how my environment is within my neighborhood, my school environment, and like how I would handle myself in those type of different environments.

Stella repeated that it was all a culture shock for her at times.

Racialized Family Experiences and Parents Who Resisted Racist Patterns for Their Children to Have More Opportunities in Life

Just as immigrant experiences shaped graduate student feelings about how parents sacrificed for their families, so too did parental and familial experiences with racist institutions in society and racialized interactions at school and work. For graduate students who identify as Black, Latinx, or Filipina, in particular, a deep respect developed for how parents suffered from racialized norms that degraded their human condition and limited their opportunities in life. More broadly, racial socialization, or race-related messaging about discrimination, tends to include a focus on preparing for bias at greater rates for African Americans (Hughes, 2003), and graduate students retold stories about experiences with parents preparing them for white supremacist and racist norms at school and in society.

Stella, a first-generation African American who's exploring her sexual orientation, recounted how her family suffered from racist and colorist patterns that subjected them to a range of exclusionary experiences. About these experiences, Stella shared: "I am light-skinned and my family, all my family members are brown skin or dark skin. So with that, that came to a lot of segregation as well where a lot of Black, you know darker-skinned people would pick on the light-skinned people, or the light-skinned people would pick on the dark-skinned people." For her personally, Stella shared that she had been referred to as an "eagle, that they would call me and pick on me, like call me a white-skinned lady because I was very fair-skinned." Until she got to college, where she began a journey of self-exploration, Stella "just had a hard time growing up because of the way" she looked, and she felt the effects of these experiences in such profound ways.

Kayla recalled similar racist patterns and their destructive effects on her parents and family. Kayla, a first-generation cisgender African American female, described how her mother experienced racism early in life in the Southern US. Over the course of her own life, Kayla recounted how she had internalized what her mom modeled as socially acceptable public behavior in highly racialized interactions with white people. Kayla elaborated as follows:

> I was modeling what my mother and father may have experienced in the South where you didn't make eye contact with certain, you know, other, you know. So yeah, just like little things like that as a young person and having to, you know you go into, initially, I worked in corporate and just for, you know, you have to like look someone in the eye and shake their hand. It was a whole different, it's like a whole different thing. So just having that experience and understanding, you know how I modeled that, and having an understanding of the history of that. But I knew . . . like, like spending time, you know, in the South, as a young person, you know, family visits, and then seeing the modeling in the community there, and looking at that.

Kayla narrated generational stories of racialized structures where her family worked, lived, and went to school. She shared familiar stories of racial exclusion, segregation, and degradation from her family's ties to the Jim Crow South and revealed that her parents tried to protect her from the brutality of the stories. Even so, she admitted: "I would hear stories like that about you know, race, how race impacted their lives, you know."

Reflecting how powerful these stories had been to Kayla's family, she illustrated how her grandfather and father experienced racism from a defining interaction with a white man.

> [S]o my father in his adolescence, I think he was like fourteen or fifteen, and you know he was very vocal about, so my parents, my both, on both sides my father's family was sharecroppers, working for, you know one of the white landowners, and, and I think one day when my, one of the young, like it was the same age, he was the same age as this young person, the landowner's son, and his son called my grandfather by his first name. And my . . . I don't know, that day my father was like, why can't, why does he get to call you by your first name and we have to call him mister? You know, and they were the same age.

Kayla shared details of the backstory of this interaction, focusing on how racialized norms structured behavioral expectations and her father's resistance to these norms.

> So, you know he got to an age, my dad did where he started to ask questions, and one time he, one of the thing about respect, you know is very much about respect where . . . one of the white landowners . . . he owned the property where they were working, and he would address my grandfather by his first name. But, you know the expectation was that my father would have to call his father by Mr. Such and Such or whatever, I forget. You know, and I think my father, once he . . . it came to a point where he asked the question like why, why do you get to call my father by his name?

As a result of this racist interaction and her father's response, his family sent him from their home in the South to live with family in the Northeast, so he had experienced not only the destructive and dehumanizing effects of racism but also the painful and personal impact of family separation at a young age. Her father's move prompted chain migration to the Northeast, where the family settled and her parents raised Kayla.

While Kayla described her parents as "not like the protesters, marchers, meeting, you know," she learned from them how anti-Black racism impacted her parents because "they grew up in the South." She learned more about how structural racism shaped their lives: "And, you know even as a young family going to the South every year, you know during the eighties, even still, like just not being able to stop certain places, or my parents not feeling comfortable in certain spaces because of their experiences as young people growing up in that, in, in the South."

Like both of Kayla's parents, Andres's mom had experienced racialized systems of oppression early in life. In fact, as she traveled by Greyhound bus from Mexico across the border to the US, Andres remembered how his mom encountered her first racially segregated accommodation at a restroom on an interstate rest stop. Here's how Andres narrated his mom's experiences.

> [Y]ou know, one of the stops once you get into the US. Stop at [the Southwest], take a break, and then keep going. So her, when she got out of the bus, she wanted to use the restroom,

just like mostly everybody else on the bus with her. So they went to the restrooms, and the, the, the restroom said, white and colored. And she was like looking at everybody around there like what, what do, what do we do? You know. And one of the women apparently had more experience crossing over to the states or whatnot, but she said, oh, those are the bathrooms that only certain people could go to. So the ones over here for white people only, the ones over here are for Blacks. And then she's like, well, where does that put us? You know. She said, we're allowed to use the white bathrooms, you know, but the only ones who are not used, allowed to use the white bathrooms are, are Blacks.

Andres imagined how his mom must have felt: "So this was something completely foreign to her, much like the country she was, you know, surrounding herself with now."

Similar to Stella, Leonardo, a first-generation Mexican American male, noted how his father, with darker complexion, endured intense scrutiny from Leonardo's mother's family when his father and mother initially met and started to be romantically linked. "[H]e had to prove himself," Leonardo noted, and continued to share how his father tended to be noted for his darker skin than Leonardo's and his siblings growing up. Leonardo explained how his father shared how with "the lighter skin . . . you know there's always like a favoritism" in cultural beliefs and practices. At the time, his observation to Leonardo is that he would "have a better chance" because of his lighter skin and eyes. Leonardo reflected more on what these racialized patterns mean: "I saw different opportunities because of my skin then, you know, my brother, who has darker skin, didn't necessarily have. I don't think he ever used it as an excuse, you know. But he, he wanted us to just kind of be aware of how the world might see us."

Like Leonardo's mother's family, Hector recalled how his mom faced immense pressure to hide her Mexican ethnic and Spanish linguistic identities in her family and community. Against the backdrop of a highly racialized sociopolitical environment in the 1950s and 1960s in the Western US, Hector's mom had to hide the Mexican dimensions of her identity, because of what Hector described as consistent patterns of discrimination.

You know, she grew up in a time in, she's Mexican and Italian. And those are very defined, each of those is very defined ethnic identity. And, but in the fifties, you know the time when she was growing up in fifties and sixties in [the West], you know, you know, to be openly Mexican, you know, in some ways, because she has like lighter skin, you know it, you know, was, was like, really, very highly discriminated against and stigmatized. And I was saying our, in our family, you know, there was definitely like this explicit, it wasn't even implicit,

The upshot of all this was an explicit "distancing" of "your Mexicaness . . . be it like but not speaking your language, not learning how to speak Spanish, even though her mother was fluent."

Childhood Experiences with Parents and Families Who Experienced Racial Microaggressions

Hector's dad recounted stories about racial microaggressions—only his experiences centered around school. Hector recalled these stories as vivid, candid experiences his dad had to endure as an immigrant from the Philippines. After helping Hector with homework, he would recount his own schooling—almost in a folkloric narration—about when he moved to the US. Hector revealed that as a "dark-skinned kid" his dad faced a lot of racial discrimination in this country. In fact, there was only one other person of color at his school, so he had been targeted racially, including name calling. If not for his athleticism and participation in organized sports on campus, it would've been a lot worse. Hector told a particularly wrenching story about a time when his dad was a student at an all-boys Catholic high school in the Western US. Decades later, the family tends to laugh at parts of the story, but at the time his dad suffered emotional and physical trauma. Hector explained more.

> [H]e was working like on a Saturday on campus and he said he, he cut his finger like near like a, like a vending machine, and, uh, one of these, these brothers saw him and said they thought he was eating some candy on the job, and just came up and slugged him in the stomach. And, and, but you know, and my dad when he'd tell that story, he'd be laughing telling that story, and so you know it's, it's totally messed up, but in your head you're like that's hilarious that this, this guy would do that to you, or hit you.

Hector knew this was abusive, but he focused on how his dad told many more stories about how he worked hard academically and excelled in his studies. In fact, his dad and he would drive by his old high school and more stories about friends, sports, and studies would emerge—which only piqued Hector's interest even more. Later, Hector shared how he attended the same high school as his dad and understood more about how he had to work hard in school, too.

Hector's dad's stories extended beyond his own experiences and inspired his dad to engage in community activism and volunteer to support change and challenge coloniality. Going back generations to his grandparents, Hector recalled his dad's involvement in the civil rights and antiwar movements, which helped Hector to develop a critical consciousness early in life. Hector shared that his dad worked at the Indian Center close to where they lived, and Hector would join him there as he coached in the Indian basketball league. Hector shared what it meant to do this.

> And that was a big, big thing, because, you know our tribe had been terminated in the 1950s, and, um, he fought, he, he fought and also dug up all the paperwork and the stories to make sure that we could be enrolled, that he could be enrolled as a tribal member, and to go to Oregon and talk to the right people, and to talk to family members there, um, because you know that, that was something that was severed.

Hector mentioned that these experiences with his dad informed his understanding of racial dynamics, "you know dismissing Native or not even mentioning Native people ever." He described these connections in more depth.

> Um, so that, that was, and then of course you, being Filipino on that side too, it was this, this sense of, um, you know, what, what the war has done to you, what the war has done to people, what the war has done to your grandfather, grandmother, um, you know what, and then, and then just, just Filipino culture, you know life, and, and how do you, how do you talk about that, think about that. So I think, in, you know I, I credit him and my mom, but I credit him specifically you know in, in those ways for keep, keeping that fire there, keeping that attention

on social and racial justice so that Hector could challenge it in his own in school.

Added to his family experiences with racism, coloniality, and xenophobia, Hector learned a lot about anti-Black racism from his time going to work with his dad at the Veterans Administration (VA), where Hector connected with Black veterans who were experiencing structural exclusion and racial oppression. Later, Hector recognized his own experiences with racialized structures that undermined who he was with "double thinking" and "double guessing" associated with code-switching. He relied on time together with his dad to help him prepare for this time and navigate around these feelings.

Similar to Hector and his dad in how they talked through experiences with racism and interpreted racialized patterns, Jaime, who identifies as a first-generation Vietnamese American female, describes how her father would talk about an experience at work that may have been connected to racist structures. To this point, Jaime remarked: "But when it comes to preparing for, he doesn't really specify racism in general, but if I experience hardships in like the workplace, that's something we kind of talk about."

Tanya, a first-generation heterosexual African American woman, understood generational experiences with anti-Black racism and structural racial exclusion from her family. Born and raised in the Southeast, she knew "all of the history and all the things . . . that Black people just experience within this country, particularly in the South." When her grandpa talked about it, she recalled how her grandmother, as an "extremely light-skinned Black woman" and her great grandmother had been biracial so that they had been shielded, in part, by colorism.

Growing up, Liza recalled her "predominantly white neighborhood," where her parents were the "first Latinos to move into the community." Her parents took note of how they were the only Latino family in the area but seemed to work to assimilate into the fabric of the community. At the time, Liza never felt insecure or unsafe but has since revisited the personal effects of these experiences. Starting with a class she took in college, she revealed how she felt.

> I'll be honest, I had no idea that was affecting me until we took [a college] class. And it wasn't until I reflected back on my life that I realized how much whiteness had affected me and my identity, and how much I was assimilating into white,

whiteness so that I wouldn't be different right, 'cause like in the community I grew up with. And I think in a sense my parents did, too. I think my mom had to.

For her mom's part, Liza shared that she migrated at sixteen years of age and "didn't have the greatest experience in high school." Experiencing family separation from her parents, she started working and going to school and "had to prove her point" in a racialized, gendered, and xenophobic system of employment and society. Liza described what her mom went through: "[Y]ou know and having an accent, you know, being, excuse me, like shorter in stature I think she, and working at the hospital as a respiratory therapist she had to kind of, you know, prove her point, I think, every time."

As immigrants to the US, Jenna's family experienced racialized and xenophobic interactions when Jenna was a child. Jenna remembered broad patterns of structural racism rooted in historical movements of imperialist conquest between the Philippines and the US. In the Philippines, Jenna remarked, there is a cultural sense that "white people will always be better than us who are brown-skinned." Growing up, Jenna recalled how her parents settled in residentially segregated communities. She noted: "[T]he places that we went to, there wasn't, it was more of communities that we were, we were able to kind of mesh with and not feel any type of racism I guess growing up. You know we lived in communities with a lot of Filipinos, a lot of Hispanics. Um, and yeah, there was always, you know, it was easier to get along."

Later, when Jenna was in middle school, her family moved to a more affluent community, and she recalled a time when she and her dad experienced racial profiling and racial microaggressions when they were shopping and sightseeing. Jenna shared more: "[T]here were people who, I don't remember but my dad said that, you know they kind of looked at us a certain way you know, when you walk into a store." In response, her dad helped to shield them from it, saying, "Don't mind them. Let's, let's just move on or go somewhere else." But Jenna explained that this episode confused her, and her dad helped her make sense of it. She explained: "[T]here are people who . . . will treat you differently because of the color of your skin. [T]here are people who are going to be like that, but we can't let that, you know get to us." Jenna shared how her dad, sister, and her would open a line of communication about racialized interactions, and her dad would warn them to "avoid areas where we would be a minority" and cautioned them from going places where they could be subjected to racial profiling. At the same time, her dad dismissed racial microaggressions and racist people: "Who cares what people think?"

Intimate Experiences with Education: Witnessing Parents and Extended Family Members Advance in College and Beyond

When parents pursued secondary or postsecondary educational opportunities, graduate students witnessed how central education was in the family and saw firsthand what it was like to go to school and be a student, particularly in college. Not just an academic achievement, parental experiences with higher education, in particular, helped see how mothers and fathers sacrificed by balancing home, work, and studies—adding to the awe that children felt in the ability to manage it all. Jaime reflected on how her mom's graduate school experiences impacted Jaime as a child. She described: "I thought that my mom also, not related, but I thought my mom also had, um, a huge impact on my education, because she's the one who has the master's degree and I thought that was pretty cool. Especially early on as, as a very impressionable elementary student, but also because, uh, she had a lot of academic achievement."

Hector knew members of his family had earned graduate degrees, and he understood how important these academic achievements were for his family. A lot of people in his family had followed educational journeys into advanced studies. For example, Hector noted that his great-grandfather, who migrated from the Philippines, got a doctorate at a public, very high-research activity, doctoral-granting university in the Midwest. As part of a special program, his great-grandfather earned his degree in the US, and returned to the Philippines to work in a specialized field. There were many opportunities for him, and Hector recognized how much it meant to them. He remembered more about his great-grandparents at that time in their lives. Referring to a photo taken at a gathering of a Filipino academic organization with his great-grandfather and great-grandmother together, he shared more: "[Y]ou see all these Filipino men and women, and my great grandmother. She like, she, she doesn't look, she you know, she looks Indian. She looks . . . Native, but, uh, I mean like you know dark-skinned and you know, you know it's just one of those things." Hector reflected: "I mention that because education is like a big, it was an important thing. I was something really revered."

When parents returned to school to finish a high school diploma program, there was a meaningful recognition in the effort to complete the academic work. For some, the costs to complete diploma or degree programs and desires to get ahead could be seen early in life. They saw the sacrifices, and they responded with a need to repay or support their parents in some way. Angela shared how her mom started and finished her undergraduate studies when Angela was in elementary school. Angela always remembered her mom in school, and she had a lot of respect for what her mom did. At the same time, the debt that Angela's mom accrued as an undergraduate student led Angela to find ways to fund her own undergraduate education—this seemed to be a way to pay her mom back and support her family for what they sacrificed to immigrate to the US and commit to a better life for Angela.

Kayla, a first-generation cisgender African American female who is married with two children, revealed her mom returned to school to finish her general education development (GED). About this time, Kayla remarked: "My mother didn't complete her, um, she didn't finish high school, but she got her GED. I think she might have been in her like thirties. But I know that she always wanted to continue her education, and, and maybe couldn't for different reasons. But, you know I think that part she definitely instilled in us." Similar to Kayla, Jenna's mom returned to school and started in college when Jenna was a child. Jenna remembered how her mom studied as an international student in the US, as they had recently immigrated. Jenna noted how her mom gave up a lot to go to school—spending long hours away from home, being "out of the house," and less time involved in care work.

Like Kayla's mother, both Karina's and Susan's fathers, respectively, went back to school as adults. Karina recalled how her father's experiences as a first-generation college student helped her learn how to not just work hard to get where she wanted to go but also overcome imposter syndrome as a student. Karina mentioned how her dad advised her that higher education can be competitive, and his repetitive messaging—and modeling—of hard work translated into a strategy for Karina to apply for scholarships, explore internships, and do much more in college. Here's more from Karina.

> [M]y father was like, yeah, you, you need to do whatever you need to do to, to get where you're at. And my father is also very much like, you need grit, um, because since he was first-generation he had to work really hard for the things that

he needed to do. Like, um, he, you know, he, he had to pay for college on his own, his textbooks. And so, you know he's, he kind of feels the same for me, that I need to work hard, I need to get all my experiences to catch up. And, um, especially 'cause higher, I know [applied humanities] is also, it can be a competitive field, um, and so he's like you need, you need to really work hard.

Similar to Karina, Jasmine's mom enrolled at a community college when she was younger. Jasmine, who identifies as a first-generation heterosexual Hispanic female, talked about what this meant for her when it was her turn to go to college: "[M]y mom was fond of it. Um, she went to like university in Mexico before she lost her vision, and she went to [a community college] here, so like. Um, but she was kind of like, you know, go with the flow. Like if I went I went, but if I didn't, but she was proud of me." Here, Jasmine knew her mom understood what it was like to be in college, and this made her mom's pride in her all the more meaningful.

Susan's father also had returned to do his undergraduate studies as an adult, and Susan recalled how hard he worked. She witnessed him as a college student and tagged along when he went to campus and athletic events—all of which inspired her to want to go to college. Of her dad at that time in his life, she said: "[H]e went to school full-time when I was young. So he got his undergrad from [a university in the West]." Susan detailed how hard college was for her father, in part due to his English language learning. She elaborated, further.

> I'm assuming it was hard for him. He did tell me a story one time that he basically went to school not knowing English, um, and I think it was the day Kennedy was shot, they must have had their radio on, or I don't know if they had televisions in the classroom at that time, I am guessing not, but, um, he said everybody around him was crying and he didn't know why. But, it was the day Kennedy was shot, 'cause he didn't know English, so he literally was just thrown into an English-speaking class and didn't know anything,

Later, Susan recalled her father as a college student and recounted of this time details here: "I remember going to his graduation when I was like probably five or six. Um, and he would take me to the campus, and take me to like basketball games and football games, and he just loved being a student."

Susan remembered how her dad worked hard as a student, and she wanted to be just like him—"so that really had a big impact on me growing up," Susan recalled fondly. So profound an impact did her father's educational journey have on her that she used it as motivation for her academic studies. Indeed, Susan wanted to please her mother and father, knowing how hard they worked for her. She shares more here: "I . . . always excelled in school I think because of that. Um, I always tried really hard 'cause I knew it was important to my parents. So I would try to please them. And seeing my dad get his degrees, I always wanted to do that."

The impact that Susan's father's college experiences had on her could be seen years later when Susan was ready to go to college. She linked his time at a university in the Western US with wanting to go there herself because it was his alma mater. But Susan's family had moved to the Southwestern US, so she focused on campuses in the region. Selecting a private, not-for-profit doctoral-granting, high research activity university in the Southwestern US, Susan felt connected to campus and felt her parents' pride in her. She shared more about this observation: "[Y]ou know my parents were superproud of me. Yeah, they were just superproud."

Chapter 5

Familial Contexts and Parenting Shape Self-Reliance, Independence, and Resilience as Students

From Elementary to Postsecondary Education

For most graduate students, early and ongoing experiences in families and schools seemed to contribute to a sense of personal autonomy and individual pathfinding to academic opportunities that supported enrollment, persistence, and completion in degree programs. In fact, a strong tendency toward independence undergirded a drive to succeed academically and achieve professionally. With some, this drive to work independently could be seen in cultural knowledge parents reproduced in the family, in which doing things on your own was rewarded. This message sometimes manifested in encouragement to play or socialize with peers or family friends outside the home, beliefs in the value of participating in a range of co-curricular and extracurricular activities at school, and a push to explore academic interests and resources to prepare for college. Even where first-generation graduate students had to do most of the work to prepare for college on their own, parents communicated the need to do so and offered strong emotional and financial support—mirroring cultural values that elevated education. Later, these experiences seemed to lead to more opportunities to advance interests in academic research, for some, and career preparation. Certainly, for most graduate students, a sense of agency shaped their ability to navigate complex systems to go to college and, later, graduate school.

But even while uniquely important to mothers and fathers alike, for many graduate students, independence seemed to relate to a sense of agency—and urgency—that transcended family value systems. As children, some had to learn to traverse multiple educational systems frequently without the direct involvement of parents, as first-generation college students. In some ways, self-reliance—and self-confidence—at a young age emerged in family contexts requiring children to navigate schools, college decision-making, and college campuses on their own or with help from older siblings, teachers, guidance counselors, and more. At times, anti-immigrant practices and few institutional resources in schools hastened a need to work independently and forced children into roles that called for more responsibility for their education early in life. Meanwhile, family income struggles sometimes required students to explore sources of undergraduate and graduate school funding on their own. Looking as far back as elementary school, several graduate students recalled having to navigate parent-teacher conferences or participate in school activities without their parents whose English language skills or work schedules had not been accommodated by teachers or administrators.

"I Feel Like I've Always Been Independent": Parental Values Pushing Students to Do Things Independently Early in Life

For some graduate students, parents seemed to push them at a young age to be as independent as possible, resolve problems on their own, explore potential solutions to challenges, and advocate for themselves. While the transition to emerging adulthood—the period in life from ages eighteen to twenty-five—tends to be characterized by increasing physical, emotional, and financial autonomy from parents (Arnett, 2000), a strong sense of agency and the ability to act on their own far earlier in life seems to be a unique characteristic for students who journey to graduate school and beyond. Tanya, who identifies as a first-generation heterosexual African American woman, illustrated what this was like for her. She talked about how her parents expected her to reach out to her teachers and discuss issues with them directly. Tanya explained more: "[I]f I had like any problems or anything then like, my parents already taught me, you know to talk to your teacher about it, advocate for yourself, at a young age."

Familial Contexts and Parenting Shape Self-Reliance | 183

At the same time, Tanya's mom intervened when needed and met with teachers and more if called for.

From their earliest recollections, independence could be seen as a family value reproduced in routine tasks or interactions with people at school and work for many graduate students. Jeremy recalled an incident as a child, where he was left to learn life lessons on his own to be as responsible as he could be, that illustrates how independence had been important to his family. He remembered how his parents let him learn things the hard way. Jeremy, a first-generation straight white and Italian cisgender male, narrated one of these lessons, from a parental perspective: "[H]ey, like you know don't touch the hot stove, and they'll tell me once, and if I go to touch the hot stove a second time, like they'll let me find out, like find out that it's hot, and I won't do it again."

Like Jeremy, Jessica recalled how her family focused on independence. Jessica, who identifies as a white female, shared more about this ethic and related it to what she's felt over the years.

> [P]retty much our family, um, we focus on being independent and not having to rely on someone else. So I've always had that like, when I grow up I need to be able to provide for myself. Even, like with or without a husband I need to be able to, to support myself just in case something does happen, to him or to me. Um, so I need to have that like education background, or that skilled background. So, that's pretty much been that, like my side of the family.

Jessica's mom insisted that she focus on providing for herself and demanded that she "be more like self-sufficient and independent mind-set," consistent with the family's value system.

For some, mothers had pushed them to be more independent, recognizing the need for women, in particular, to be less or not at all reliant on men and more focused on freely making decisions about career, relationships, and so on.

Over time, parents seemed to model and message independence to children, even as family events or contexts reinforced the idea. Brianna, a first-generation African American woman, commented on how she liked her independence—and reflected on how she got there as she described her parents' marriage and her mom's wisdom.

> I think sometimes the things, her marriage made me kind of feel like things I didn't want to go through. So I think it was kind of like, but she knows who she created, she created a monster, so. I think where she maybe heavily relied on, which it wasn't a bad thing, but I just think maybe I just didn't take it, you know, like relying so much on a husband or a man. You know, I've always wanted to make sure I could take care of myself.

But there seemed to be a limit on independence, for Brianna—she seemed to have grown too independent: "Sometimes I think I grown too independent, 'cause she's like, you can't always be so independent. You gotta ask for help sometime."

Zelma's mom had a similar message for her as Brianna's mom. Zelma, who identifies as a first-generation cis-hetero Indigenous Palestinian and Lebanese woman, talked about how her mom pushed her to be independent, free from men.

> [M]y mom in so many ways, even though she was raised in a very conservative traditional value and mind-set, she knew that the only way that any of us girls were gonna survive is to have an education so we could stand on our two feet in case your husband leaves, dies, and no one's there to take care of you. Right, so we were never raised with the mind-set that you needed a man to take care of you. And that's where I'm saying like that, that perspective of you're one husband away from poverty is, you know, education was a survival mechanism. And she didn't want us to be in that same.

Angela heard a similar message to Brianna and Zelma, respectively. With her mom as the breadwinner and college completer, Angela witnessed how her mom never really relied on men. Angela spoke to this point when she said: "I think for me growing up and seeing that, and even in pursuit of like relationships and partnership with folks, like I've kind of always had this mentality in the back of my head like, I can't rely on men. Or like, if I do, I also have to have that safety net behind me as a cushion just in case that doesn't work out."

Beyond parental values, independence seemed to always be a part of life from a young age. For some graduate students, early memories of making decisions "by myself" and always being an "independent kid" seemed to be a part of their personality. For example, Hua, who identifies as a Chinese female, felt like she had to tell her mom what she had decided about her studies or activities at school. Given that her "mom's actually the one like really involved what," her mom appeared to be bothered when Hua came to her late after making a decision. She reflected: "I think I truly feel independent about all the decision, and I am trying not to sharing everything to my mom because it's like getting to the parents, and you probably don't have time. I think educationally, I have more independen[ce]." In Sharon's case, learning had been a process independent of her parents from early in life. Reflecting on her love of education, Sharon, a first-generation heterosexual female, did a lot on her own that led to a growing sense of personal autonomy. Going to the library, playing tennis, climbing trees, and more allowed Sharon to blossom into her own person.

Parental Support for Early Life Turns Toward Independence for Graduate Students

Parents sometimes just followed the lead that kids set with patterns of doing things on their own at a young age. Gail, who identifies as a first-generation straight white female, reflected on how she was a "really independent kid." As she got older, she saw how her parents just let her play on her own. Even with cousins or friends, Gail would go on her way. She reflected more on this independent-leaning life: "I feel like I've always been independent. Like my mom said, I was a really good kid. Like as a baby even, like I didn't complain a lot, like cry for stuff but I wasn't like a really fussy kid." She continued: "And I remember just always being content like playing in my room alone. They, they'd come play with me, too, but I would just, like sometimes I would shut the door, like I want to play alone." Thinking about her dad's role in her independence, Gail said she was more stoic from his influence. Later, when it came time to transition to college, Gail knew she was on her own. While her parents talked about college with her, they never helped her apply or transition to college. "They let me do that all on my own, you know," Gail commented. Susan shared a similar independent streak as Sharon and Gail. Susan, a white and Latina cis-heterosexual female who identifies as Jewish and is married with children, reflected on her childhood and school experiences, seeing how she did a lot on her own. She said: "You know I always kind of did my homework and did well in school on my own, I never asked

186 | Shaping Students of Color from Preschool to Graduate School

Figure 5.1. Parental values, children's personalities, family circumstances, and institutional barriers shape early life independence for many graduate students. *Source:* By Vuemobi, CC BY-SA 4.0. https://commons.wikimedia.org/w/index.php?curid=89089707.

them for help. I never asked him for help, so he probably didn't think I needed help. He probably, you know, maybe he thought, oh, she's learning all that in school."

Jaime was also an independent kid and, like Gail, remembered a childhood where she was introspective. Jaime, a first-generation Vietnamese American female, spoke about how time alone at home led to her exploring her world and figuring things out on her own. She elaborated: "I had a lot of time alone in the house when I was very young. And there was like hours of nothing to do. And for some reason the thing that I wanted to do was kind of figure out my life at a really early age." Jaime connected her long stretches of time alone at home to disappointment with how parents—and family and friends—seemed to follow a separate set of expectations for how to behave from what they instructed Jaime to do. Jaime revealed more.

> I was kind of disappointed in the adults around me a little bit. Because they would tell me to follow these rules, and I would have these odd consequences, like go, go stand in the corner and think about what you've done. So okay, I'll go in the corner. I'll stand in the corner and think of what I've done. Um, but like I was getting these consequences for rules that adults didn't seem to be able to follow themselves. It's like, well what's, what's with that?

For Jaime, forgetting to do laundry on time or not finishing homework at a certain hour often resulted in punishment—and more time alone to think about things.

Independence Accompanies Transitions to Adulthood and College

College decision-making and transitions to college enhanced a sense of personal autonomy for many graduate students. For Susan, more independence seemed to follow college decision-making. Susan had done a lot on her own as a child, but now she associated her independence in the college admissions process to values she observed in her parents at a young age. She recalled what her parents used to say about school: "They're like, go to school, you'll learn everything you need for life and you'll be okay." She continued, reflecting on how her parents valued education but never really helped much with school.

> My parents, while they valued education, they told me do well, you know go to college, they never, they never really helped me with homework. Uh, they never guided me like on where to go to college, or even like what to do once I was in . . . like what major to do. So it was really, I, I felt kind of on my own doing all that stuff, um, and, and really had to figure it out on my own.

Susan's parents expected her to go to college—they just never did a lot to get her there. "SATs, all the applications, everything on my own," Susan remarked, "I guess that was another piece of it."

Frequently, a move toward more independence from parents emerged during college, as a natural transition to adulthood and campus life coincided with living on campus and apart from family or more time away from home. In Kaitlyn's case, starting college as a first-generation student meant greater decision-making on her own and freedom to choose the classes she wanted to take. Kaitlyn explained that she and her twin brother relied on each other a lot, including with schoolwork. In college, all that changed—and she did a lot more on her own. She elaborated as follows:

> I grew up going to every single class with my brother. And so college was really the first time where I wasn't with him. Um, and so I . . . grew independent, um, in terms of like choosing what I did, and, and, um, you know choosing the different classes 'cause, you know as a freshman you don't really know what to do. I, I found like a core group of friends who we would, um, kind of do everything with.

Kaitlyn turned toward these friends as she continued to grow on her own. She concluded: "So I grew independent from my family, but kind of dependent on those friends."

Like Kaitlyn, Jasmine, who identifies as a first-generation heterosexual Hispanic female, felt college was her opportunity to leave family and establish her own life. She spoke to this time in her life and what it meant for her growth: "I think I kind of saw college as a way to leave, like my family. Like I kind of wanted to be my own person and get out of like stressful situation." She summed up how she saw that time in her life: "I just, and I also wanted to be, become something better. Like better my life. Um, I think when you're at that level, it's kind of just like yourself at that point."

Similar to Jasmine, Juan moved out and lived on campus as an undergraduate. He had always been independent, he remarked, and was comfortable doing this on his own. Living on campus his first year of college made sense to him and validated his decision to move out and live on his own. Juan focused on "just figuring out how things were going to work out in terms of housing and stuff like that." Applying to jobs without consulting his parents, Juan referred to his parents as he continued: "I just always felt comfortable doing, um, doing things without having to, uh, you know get them involved. And I think it was, uh, likely because, uh, you know both my mom and dad would enforce this idea that they just trusted what I was going to do." This is all not to say that Juan did not have his parents' support—he did—he just felt like he could do it on his

Figure 5.2. Self-reliance and personal autonomy accompany many graduate students into adulthood and college. *Source:* By COD Newsroom, CC BY 2.0. https://www.flickr.com/photos/41431665@N07/12439109024.

own. He concluded: "[T]hey trusted that I was going to make decisions that I felt were right."

Now in graduate school, Natasha seemed to have been on her own for a while. Natasha, who identifies as a straight white female, talked about finding her own jobs, paying her own bills, and doing things on her own. Speaking about her father, she mentioned that he trusted her to take care of herself. She recalled a time last summer when she got COVID and how she relied on herself. Referring to her father, she said: "I can go to him if I'm having an emergency, but because we live so far apart, like there's, there's a limit to kind of what he can do. I still have to go and figure it out." She illustrated this idea with the story about when she got COVID. She said: "I got COVID over the summer I was like, well, you have to get yourself to the doctor, and you have to figure this out yourself. I can call him and he'll kind of like guide me or what not, but um, you know."

For a handful of graduate students, independence from parents in the college years seemed to be related to overcoming parental objections and challenging attempts to control major fields of study that had higher salaries and were more financially rewarding. Determined to challenge her dad's relentless drive for her to major in business, Karina pushed back on him. Karina, a heterosexual Latina woman who identifies as half Guatemalan and half Mexican, recalled how she had to tell her dad to back off and let her explore a major in education, which supported her career interest in teaching. Here's how Karina described it.

> And at first my father was very hesitant about my choice because he was like, you know, teachers don't make a lot of money, and you need to get a degree that's gonna benefit you in the future, so that you can start a family, and that you, you're not struggling. And, you know, at, at first that also made me kind of like angry because, um, because I wanted to do something that I thought I would be good at, and I didn't want to like do something that my father wanted me to do. And, um, he would always say like, you know, business is always the good option, just go for that if you don't know what to do. But I just didn't want to do that, so, um, so it was really hard for me. And, um, as time went on like around my first or second year, my father just didn't really say much about my option to become a teacher.

Karina had to resist her dad's expectations, which intensified her need to go it alone as an undergraduate student. "[O]bviously there were times where it was just kind of like I need to push back and I need to do this on my own," Karina said, "uh, make my own decisions." Eventually, the strategy Karina developed for interactions with her dad focused on avoidance and redirection. She explained more: "Yeah, I feel like it's always ongoing because he'll bring it up every now and then, but I just try to steer the conversation away because, um, I don't really like to hear when he's like, you know you gotta be making more money, you got to work hard."

Similar to Karina, Maria shared that she felt how her family reproduced cultural values that elevated higher-salary careers. She described how this dynamic played out when she was an undergraduate student. At times, she would have to answer questions from her parents about her major choice. She elaborated further.

> When I first like, the, the downside was that like, they want, in my culture they pretty much want you to study all those higher-paying jobs that are like, you know doctor, law, and all

these positions, but they were still open to me like exploring my own. Um, but they will always question, they're like oh, why are you, why are you doing, or like, they will still go back to that question of like oh, why are you doing this? But like, so they just don't know what I'm doing specifically.

In conversations with her dad about where to work and make her career, Maria revealed he had pushed her toward community colleges with the perception that salaries are higher in the sector.

Karina challenged her dad, arguing that she wanted to follow her passion of working on a university campus. She summarized these interactions: "But like, he tends to just go back to the idea of money. So money, money, money, because he struggled, you know, like, you know working and stuff, so he wants me to be successful. But unfortunately, like, my view is I don't look at my career as just making money, I'm looking at it as a passion." In the end, Karina and her dad avoided talking about career. She briefly spoke to this point: "So he tends to not really talk much about my education actually. Um, and when he does he just brings up that and, and he just doesn't get it, so."

Anti-Immigrant and Racist Experiences in Schools and Communities: Lack of Institutional Support Forced Students into Early Independence

For graduate students of color and graduate students whose parents immigrated to the US, family experiences with anti-immigrant and racist interactions could be readily recalled. Racialized and xenophobic workplaces, communities, schools, police forces, and more tended to mark fathers—given their gendered roles as providers that required them to work outside the home—and mothers—who worked outside the home and often interacted with school officials—with racial microaggressions and blatant discrimination that shaped families. More broadly, immigrant experiences with parents who faced harsh environments in their children's schools tended to be excluded from essential activities to support students' success—no language translation support, few accommodations for parents whose work prevented participation during or shortly after the school day, and more. In cases where parents experienced racism or xenophobia at school and beyond, graduate students tended to report that they had been forced or compelled into an advocate or liaison role for their parents or they just had to be more independent and take on more responsibility with academic work and rely less on their parents for support with school, and so on.

Sometimes graduate students voiced general concerns for how parents had been mistreated in a society that discounts the gravity of the effects of human migration, devalues life experiences of immigrants, and delays needs to legalize residency and citizenship status. This is what Stella characterized as part of her childhood, and she shared how "it is devastating to see how immigrants are treated." On a very personal level, Stella could see how her mom suffered from challenges that immigrants faced when they traverse the citizenship process in the federal bureaucracy and the local job market. Stella, a first-generation African American who uses gender pronouns she/her/hers, narrated her story here: "Um, my mom didn't get her green card until I was eighteen. And she's still trying to work in to getting an appointment for citizenship. I see more of what my mom went through because I was, you know I grew up . . . like visually seeing everything and all the barriers she had to go through, and all the hoops that she had to go through to even get a job." While witnessing her mom struggle with the US immigration system, a long process that profoundly impacted the entire family, Stella had to advocate for basic necessities and educational resources. She was uninsured from age sixteen to twenty-two and reported having to jump through hoops "because I had immigrant parents." These hoops included school, where she shared a pattern of "navigating school and doing signatures."

With children who experienced family immigration to the US, a fear of family separation tended to be a part of parental decisions to limit interaction at school or in the community. This fear focused on the threat of arrest, incarceration, and deportation. Zelma illustrated this concern that her parents consistently communicated. She said: "There was that, always that fear of you don't want to get deported. You don't want to get sent back. So, you know, they did grow up, we did grow up being instilled with a lot of fear, you know. Whether it was by him or just you know, you know you don't want to get in trouble." This seemed to lead to a "survival" mode for her dad, in particular, and a focus on fitting in, working hard, and a more "transactional" form of love for Zelma, where grades tended to be what mattered most to her dad. Good grades meant praise and attention, even if it was short-lived and hyperconditional. She elaborated: "[F]or better or worse, um, you know my dad, again, they, they say, they face, my parents faced more trauma. Now, as an adult I look at it, it's like, you know, the only way I can make my dad happy, you know, at least as a child, what I believed was, hey, I got to get good grades."

For graduate students whose parents immigrated to the US and had limited English language skills, elementary and secondary schools tended to not offer interpretive accommodations, which frequently forced students into an interpreter role. Josefina, a first-generation straight Chicana woman with children, illustrated this point bluntly: "But, but he never knew what was happening because everything was fully in English. So I was always the interpreter." While working and raising their family, Josefina's parents never learned to functionally speak English. She summarized her experiences here: "Well, first of all my parents never learned to speak English, so they're Spanish speakers, immigrants. Don't know the educational system, or just the, just the systems, institutional systems that we have in the United States."

Since the school didn't provide interpretive services, Josefina's parents were excluded from what was going in her life as a student. Josefina, who identifies as a first-generation straight Chicana woman with children, had to find the resources on her own and navigate the school system by herself. She illustrated what this was like when she shared the following story about her mother.

> I feel like my mother always, her limited English skills, really, to be honest, my mom didn't really speak any English more than my dad so I think for them it was, my mom it was really hard for her to be engaged. In meetings when it came to content, context on like what were they saying? I always had to play the translator role since I kept, since I was in grammar school. There were, it was rare to find someone that could speak Spanish or translate my parents. So I feel like my mom, her role has always been present, but not as involved

Josefina offered a final thought about institutional practices that excluded her mother from school-based participation given her limited English language skills: "My mother was just sort of like, why would I describe it? Like, it's almost like when you invite a guest to a house but they're just your guests in your, in your, in your journey, because they really don't know, and they can't really make a lot of decisions."

Both Winona and Kaitlyn shared similar experiences as Josefina. For Kaitlyn, her parents' limited language skills in English when Kaitlyn was younger led her to having to translate for them. All of this helped Kaitlyn understand how they worked tirelessly to support her as a student. She explained more.

> [M]y mom, she, she can't read in either language. And my dad, he can hold his own, you know reading in Spanish, but, uh, because he is a waiter he had to learn, you know English pretty fast. So he can read somewhat in English. Um, so with that like I think they always push like, we need to learn how to read, write. We kind of became translators for them, and we still do in a, in a way.

From these interactions, the message that Kaitlyn's parents repeated time and again was: "Um, so they always push like, get your education."

With Winona, a first-generation bisexual Asian American who identifies as Chinese and Vietnamese, she gained a feeling of independence from being largely on her own in school. For reasons related to her parents' limited language skills in English, Winona made her way through school work on her own. Early in life, she recalled how moving a lot required her to be as independent as possible. "So that means," she said, "that's where the independence kind of, kind of also came in was because I had to learn real quick with these curriculums and all this stuff, is that like, hey, like you can't just, you can't just slack off because then you're gonna be behind."

Later, Winona remembered what she did in high school to be independent. She said: "For the most part in the sense of independence, I've always had to learn by myself because my parents didn't understand what the language was or what was being taught in class. So either way I had to be independent." Frequent moves from one home to the next when Winona was a child contributed to her independence, as she had to learn quickly to adapt to new schools and classroom environments and learn to do homework assigned by new teachers. She explained what this was like: "So we moved quite a lot during my childhood. So that means, that's where the independence kind of, kind of also came in was because I had to learn real quick with these curriculums and all this stuff, is that like, hey, like you can't just, you can't just slack off because then you're gonna be behind." This dynamic led Winona to see how her personality pushed her to succeed academically: "And like I was also a kid that didn't want to be behind, so I like pushed it on myself."

Like Josefina, Kaitlyn, and Winona, Edith "would have to translate of what information the school needed" from her parents. Speaking about her mother and father, Edith continued: "If he didn't understand what, what they need, I needed to do that a lot, or the most for my mother." Edith, a first-generation Korean female, reflected on how she quickly learned to problem solve. As the oldest of three children, Edith had to figure things out, as she said, and felt good helping her parents. She concluded: "I needed to figure things out and figure things out quickly to do it."

With both parents migrating from Nigeria to the US when Angela was a baby, she remembered having to navigate the college admissions process largely on her own. While her mom had completed undergraduate and graduate degree programs, the application and financial aid process had changed so much that Angela's mom was "not well-versed at it." On top of the broad changes in the sector, Angela had to figure it out on her own as the oldest child in the family. Here's what she recalled about that time in her life.

> I was their first round in kind of understanding, okay, what is this all about? So like, for the most part, like, I really relied on my teachers. And I was also in a college prep class in high school, so I relied on them mostly for guidance, and just like applying to college. 'Cause again, my mom, when she got her bachelor's, was a nontraditional student. So the way that she got into college was just totally different than what I did. So I think, again, even with the area of like FAFSA, filling out the FAFSA for financial aid scholarships and more was just like, I had to kind of figure that out on my own.

While Angela worked in her college prep class and with her teachers, her mom supported her in critical ways in the admissions process. Angela, a first-generation African American female who identifies ethnically as Nigerian, reflected more on her mom's support: "I would say she was like sort of involved, yes, but also it was a point of just like I had other resources to lean into and tap into where I didn't need to really pull my mom unless it's for like a signature, or just for a second look at certain things, or to pick me up from school."

In Maria's early life, she had to learn do everything herself and work on her own to achieve academically. Maria recalled how her dad and mom couldn't support her academically as they went to school outside the US, and had moved here as adults. Maria spoke to this point when she said: "No, he wasn't involved because he just didn't know about the system here so I had to really do everything myself. I had to figure out myself what

I want to study. Like they weren't there to support me, but I understand why because they didn't have that educational background." Like Maria, Stella had to do a lot on her own as her parents had to learn to navigate a complex school system as immigrants. Stella referenced how this all changed her and she became more independent: "I was living with my family at the time, at sixteen I think, from there I was slowly changing." These changes emerged, in part, from having to access resources at school on her own. She described it this way: "And not having these resources, or jumping hoops because I had immigrant parents. And so, um, navigating school, and doing signatures, and the government was not easy either. So it was just a lot of, um, hoops and things that I went through that, um, made me have the awareness, and understanding, and wisdom that I, and the knowledge that I have now."

For Eugenio, a near-total lack of connections between school and home seemed to characterize his elementary education. Indeed, Eugenio seemed to struggle with the need to speak Spanish at home and English at school. Between few opportunities to invite his parents into his education and an absence of links between school staff and his parents, Eugenio revealed what it meant for him.

> I think, um, as an ESL learner, I think it's hard or difficult, especially for parents [who] didn't . . . teach us English because they didn't know. They, right now they understand it. They speak a little bit. My dad knows how to talk about it, talk, uh, at the same time one thing for sure about that is that, I think for us it was difficult because we couldn't ask for the help. Um, in elementary school or like, just thinking about it overall, when we knew we needed the help I guess we got quiet about it, and that's something for sure that, elementary school for sure he never told me to ask for stuff. And if I did I was very shy and timid, I'm not sure exactly. And I guess 'cause like, you're used to just being in your surroundings, you're speaking with Spanish speakers most of the time, you get used to speaking Spanish, and then when you're trying to speak in English it's just kind of more difficult.

Eugenio concluded: "But, um, yeah so I think it was very hard and difficult just learning the language."

Few Options for Parents Whose Work Limited School Participation

Beyond limited connections to US educational systems or limited or no language interpretation at their children's schools, immigrant parents who worked in manual labor or industrial jobs could not often make daytime events like parent-teacher conferences. This proved to be an obstacle to access educational services for some parents and narrowed opportunities to participate in school-based activities. Josefina explained how.

> I remember when I graduated from junior high . . . my dad didn't go. It was only my mom and my sisters. Because he just couldn't leave work cause if he left work, it meant losing hours of work, which meant money that he can provide for the family, pay bills, and so forth, send money to my siblings who were living in Mexico. So that was the thing that would prevent him from participating, engaging in school activities, if they were during the day. Um, there was a couple, just things that would happen during then and he wouldn't go. Like the parent-teacher conference was usually . . . I mean the, the accommodations were not late into like 5 p.m. or 6 p.m. So definitely my dad never went to those.

Similar to Josefina, Leonardo shared how his dad's work schedule—where he often labored for extended hours in the evening—often prevented him from doing much outside the home and surely not at Leonardo's school. About this situation, Leonardo said simply: "[A]s far as like graduations, and you know, Dad was always there, and he was always proud."

For graduate students who experienced racist environments at school and in the community, memories about racialized interactions shaped them at a young age and informed how they had to make sense of it all on their own. Brianna talked about experiences with residential segregation in their community and schools in the Midwest. Brianna recalled how racialized her experiences as a child were, as she never had been exposed to racial, ethnic or cultural experiences outside of the Black and white communities where she grew up. She reflected on these experiences, compared to her college experiences in the Southeast: "[I]t wasn't until like, my going to college, you know, being able to experience like different culture and food. Like, like wow. I think it, whereas my family were driving me and going to different places. Being in [the Southeast], you know, going with my friends; I remember my friends for, for Miami and they were like, yeah, this is, you know, Jamaican food. Well what's Jamaican food?" When Brianna returned home from college during breaks, she had to share with family just how important these experiences were for her.

Like Brianna's family, Josefina talked about people of color as the primary residents in her neighborhood in a community in the Western US, where you never saw white people. Of her neighborhood, when she was younger, she said: "[I]t was either Latinos or Black" people. Later, as she aged, she observed, "you see, more, more Latino," and her "high school . . . was predominantly Latino. Junior high, middle school . . . predominantly Latino. But you still see Black students, Asian students, some white students." While Josefina admitted her dad never really prepared her for racialized schools and college, she remembered how he faced anti-immigrant and anti-Latino discrimination. She shared: "I think he probably did, does recall experiences of like discrimination, specifically from white people." Despite these experiences, her dad embraced a broad peace and compassion toward all people.

Similar to both Brianna and Josefina, Andres remembered white flight from his urban neighborhood in the West. In the 1980s and 1990s, he knew economic depression had started to set into the area with businesses closing. Then, gangs and drugs started to take over the streets. Andres, a first-generation able-bodied cis-hetero male who identifies as Mexican, specifically Mexicah and Tepehuani, detailed more about what he remembered of that time and place: "My immediate neighbors were gang members. People across the street were gang members, too. Um, and I remember my dad scolding my brother not to hang out with those guys next door, you know, 'cause they were relatively the same age as my brother, and we're eight years apart so he's my oldest brother, which also kind of served as like a role model, father figure type of thing."

Navigating Complex College Admissions Processes
"On My Own" as a First-Generation College Student

With first-generation graduate students, the need to navigate an educational pipeline that often seemed more like a maze meant to challenge or exclude them supported their early steps to independence. With many or most high schools and college campuses not offering families of prospective students or first-gen families of prospective students any meaningful services, events, or opportunities to participate and learn more about programs, activities, and more, graduate students reported how they led the college decision-making and college-going processes largely on their own. Even with siblings who preceded them in college—with a trailblazing effect—they learned to rely on themselves in school settings. In family contexts where schools didn't readily accommodate or welcome nonnative English-speaking parents, kids had to frequently figure it out on their own and do things intended for parents. Between parent-teacher conferences, back-to-school nights, and open houses, many grad students reported how parents had to work and could not participate in these vital events in the school community.

In many cases, graduate students who shared stories with me identify as first-generation college students and/or from low-income households, racially segregated neighborhoods, high under-resourced schools, and communities systematically excluded from economic and business investment. For several, a turn toward independence seemed to follow the need to navigate precollege and college-going on their own, including looking into key requirements in the college decision-making process. For example, Maria described how her parents "didn't know how financial aid worked, but they were there providing all the information necessary." Maria's dad showed her where his income had to be reported on the application, and Maria ended up with support through financial aid awards. But getting through the process mostly on her own was tough. "When it came to like documents and stuff like," Maria revealed, her parents "have experience with that so they would just provide it every time I would ask for it."

Like Maria, Josefina illustrated how she had to "figure it out" largely without direct help of her parents. She said: "And you know he has no understanding what, what college life is like." She noted how he responded to her when they discussed applying to college: "[Y]ou know you figure it out because I can't help you. But all I can do is support you." She continued: "and every time he would say support, I didn't really understand what he meant by support. But as years have gone by, now I get what support means." For Josefina, support meant encouraging her "not to give up."

Even as parents of first-gen college students encouraged and expected children to go to pursue postsecondary educational opportunities, many had to navigate the college application and decision-making processes on their own. This was the case for Kayla, a first-generation cisgender

African American female, who remembered how her mom would insist she work with her high school guidance counselor on college admissions applications. "It was just more, you know you go to the guidance counselor and she'll help you," according to Kayla, "like she never went through that process herself." Kayla's mom's approach seemed to align with her parents' values that tied independence to achieving all your dreams and living to the highest standard in life—"for not just my drive to be independent and to be like, you know, have the highest, you know, outcomes in what I do." Kayla recalled how you cannot depend on "someone to do it," you have to do for yourself and ensure you get it done right.

Zelma admitted that her mom did so much for her as an elementary school student, but by the time she got to high school Zelma had the self-determination and habits of mind to succeed on her own. She confirmed: "I had enough like, um, structure and self-determination, and . . . to succeed at that point." With all her focus, Zelma developed an "ability to ask questions . . . to talk to counselors, to . . . talk to teachers, to ask those questions, because my parents had no clue what it meant to apply for a four-year college." Zelma, a first-generation cis-hetero Indigenous Palestinian and Lebanese woman, recalled her how family value systems reinforced a work-hard, carry-on, and hustle mentality and rewarded you to get where you need to go. She shared: [Y]ou know, the whole pulling yourself by bootstraps, right? Like, that's how we grew up. Like you have to do on your own because no one's gonna do it for you. And because my parents didn't have the education or understanding of the college system, we had to figure it out on our own."

Later, in high school, Zelma shared that, as her parents had no experience with college and university applications or federal financial aid applications, she'd have to do it on her own. She elaborated.

> [M]y parents not being college students . . . didn't know the process. By the time, I even decided, I'm gonna take my SATs just in case. I met with the counselors. I signed up for like pre, pre-early morning classes for SAT Prep at the high school. [I] tried to do a lot of things on my own; like applied for FAFSA on my own. My parents weren't gonna know what the hell they were doing. I asked them, well where are your, you know IRS papers. It really was us doing it on our own. All three of us, all three of us girls. They didn't know anything.

Zelma recalled how parental expectations to continue in school became a "need" for her. She remarked that at a point she knew she had to go to college, get a job, and live her life on her own. Like Zelma, Angela had to do a lot of her own work in college applications, financial aid, and more. Sometimes this led to conflict with her parents, who seemed to be frustrated that they could not be more directly involved. Angela explained as follows.

> Yeah, I think like, I want to say they didn't, like I don't want to say they didn't, but I feel like I did most of the navigation. Like I think they just didn't understand. Or like, like FAFSA was just like, we would get into so many arguments, 'cause like neither of us understood what was going on. I just don't like arguing with my parents. I feel like sometimes it never goes anywhere. So yeah. But for the most part, ehhh, they helped, but like, I think I had it down for the most part myself.

While Angela's parents had to rely on her to navigate the college-going process, they were in it to support and advocate for her. Describing a time when there was an issue with her state scholarship form, Angela recalled: "So that was like a point of time where I can vividly remember like them advocating for me." This experience reflected how Angela's parents had been central to her success as a student throughout her life. Primarily as home-based participation, Angela's parents supported her involvement in a host of activities, as she described: "[B]oth my parents were pretty involved in my educational career. Um, I was really involved in like extracurricular activities, especially throughout high school. My parents did a good job of like picking me up and supporting me."

Andres had to manage the college admissions process on his own, too. Like, Zelma, Andres's parents had limited to no experience with college, and his dad had only completed elementary school. They knew that Andres needed to go to college, and their message had been consistent since Andres was young: all the kids in the family had to go to college and family support would help them get to and through college and beyond. Beyond expectations and verbal support—*échale ganas* or give it your all—they helped financially with Andres living at home. But to get to college, Andres knew he had to find his way. He detailed more about how he felt supported by his parents and independent from them at the same time. Referring to his mom and dad, respectively, he said the following.

> I knew I had his support, by him saying like, you can do it. If you need anything, let me know. But in terms of like, hey, dad, can you help me with financial aid? Or hey, dad, what does this application mean right here? I couldn't go to him for that. My mom doesn't speak English, so her thing was just like, oh, good for you. I'm so happy for you, you know. Like still, to this day, you know, she still, you know, praises me and tells me, you know, good job. I knew that their love was unconditional, like their support, you know.

With his parents, Andres had set about to do what he had been expected to do all along: "Just because I think that foundation we built as kids in the house, I think was enough for me to know that I could come . . . [to] them with anything."

In middle school, Stella revealed how she "didn't know anything about college." Describing her parents' educational background, she explained: "Like I said my mom, she maybe did like her associate's for one year. Not even one year, but a few months. My dad didn't even finish middle school, so it's like they weren't really knowledgeable about the steps to get into college." For her parent's part, Stella said they knew about college more generally and associated college with campuses like "Harvard, Yale, UCLA, USC," but given that her dad hadn't complete middle school, her parents were not "really knowledgeable about the steps to get into college." Consequently, Stella had identified where she could go study after she graduated from high school.

Angela had a similar story to Stella. Angela discussed how her dad didn't know a lot about the educational system. Fortunately, Angela's mom had pursued a degree when Angela was younger and could support her in some ways. With her dad, though, Angela shared that she was on her own. She elaborated: "I think for the most part I had to navigate it. And luckily during my time in high school I took like college prep courses, so like that gave me the knowledge of just like navigating all these different like academic spaces, and jargon and everything." But where her dad could not guide Angela in college admissions, he did advocate for her. She recalled a time when he argued for a scholarship on her behalf:

"[T]here was this one time where I did, [the state] has like this system where it's kind of like a scholarship through the state, and my dad had to sign off some paperwork, but like they kept saying it was wrong, but he did the right thing." She continued: "I remember like he was on the phone like no, I did it. Check page eight. Like I did it, like I signed it, like I remember signing it."

In a story that involves her dad—like Angela—Jenna summarized how her mom left school-related activities to her dad, until she got to middle school—at which point she was on her own. Jenna mentioned that her mom's unfamiliarity with "American education," which reflected the school's lack of programs and resources for immigrant parents, forced her to study on her own with help from her dad in elementary school. Even though her mom was in college at the time when Jenna—who identifies as a first-generation Filipina heterosexual female—started to explore going to college, she shared what her mom revealed to her: "I don't understand all of this American education . . . and she was also studying herself." Given that her dad was a primary care-taker and not directly involved in her education as a high school student, Jenna was mostly on her own to navigate college application and decision-making processes. She spoke to this point: "I'm very, I'm very determined. And I'm very, okay, I'll apply to these colleges. I'll do this. I'll study for the SAT. I'm very career focused. And so he was really there to support me."

As the first in her family to go to college, Sharon counted on support from her parents, and she got it. Mainly as a commitment to support her financially and validate her decision to go to college, Sharon's parents "had no idea what to do or how to support" her college decision-making, so they left it to Sharon. In turn, she relied on the peer environment and institutional culture in high school, which formed a cohesive set of expectations to go to college and support network to facilitate the application process. She spoke more to this atmosphere here: "[My] high school years were, were really positive for me. I had a great experience in high school. [T]here was just, um, a sense of community that I really enjoyed. [I]t's a nationally renowned, um, college prep high school." She went on to describe the college-going expectations: "[T]he culture in the school was always about what you need to do to get into college. That was just the embedded expectation through, throughout. I credit that high school, and I credit kind of my own desire to, to go and continue."

Family Income Struggles in Emerging Adulthood and the Need for Financial Independence as Undergraduate Students

Sometimes a move toward independence and self-reliance emerged in the contexts of financial struggle in families. In fact, graduate students from households where money was tight and income had to be stretched to make it through each month tended to lead efforts to explore and secure financial aid, scholarships, and fellowships for both graduate and undergraduate studies. To these experiences, some reflected on how familial financial strain helped them to work hard on their own. In Stella's case, selling snacks to support her family at a young age undergirded her work ethic in graduate school. "When I was a kid in elementary school I used to sell candy's, chocolates, and chips so I could have food to eat. And that's what my mom taught me how to do. And so, because of that hustle mentality I've always had, it still carried on until me as an adult where she's so proud of how much I've achieved."

Whether to materially contribute to the family or witnessing parents who live paycheck to paycheck and putting food on the table, many graduate students recalled how experiences with financial stress taught them to hustle in life. Over time, parents who worked constantly to make ends meet offered grad students frequent opportunities to independently act on their own behalf and advocate for themselves in educational contexts and beyond. With Jenna, her "parents really like went from living paycheck to paycheck . . . now, they're, um, they're doing much better." But she remembered "as a kid seeing them struggle, like not being able to pay for ice cream or, or anything like that." She continued: "Um, they felt so bad because they couldn't buy my, my sister and I things. Um, they couldn't buy us things, and, and you know they thought oh, maybe you know, without that then we wouldn't be able to, to grow or learn." Reflecting on these experiences, Jenna connected them to a strong work ethic: "But, um, my sister and I turned out fine. And it's just not only seeing it, but also experiencing it, you know, experiencing all of the setbacks they've gone through. Like it really made me want to work harder for them too, you know." For Leonardo, the message was in the model. Between his six siblings and him, he remembered their daily routines: "So just making sure that, you know we had, you know breakfast, lunch, dinner, we had food on the table. He, you know, making sure we had clothes. You know he had seven children, you know, so, you know, working hard was, was kinda like, he had to."

Later in life, understanding that parents may not have had the financial resources or direct experience with college affordability and financial aid prompted graduate student efforts to finish classes in college and move on so as not to burden their families. This pattern seemed particularly acute when high school children started to explore college. Angela described how she secured assistantships, housing, and more in graduate school: "Even in grad school now like, I was like there's no way, like I have an assistantship. I'm working in housing right now, too. Like I have an assistantship that funds my apartment, that gives me a meal plan. I have a stipend, 'cause I just knew like, without this assistantship I'll be like 100K in debt. I'm gonna work my butt off to make sure that I make enough to do that." Behind her efforts to ensure she didn't pay out of pocket for graduate school, Angela shared how she did this work for herself and her parents: "So I knew, like I went into like these spaces knowing like, like for grad school I was like, I refuse. I refuse to pay. I know I'm not gonna pay, so. And like, I can't afford that. And I know my parents can't afford that."

Even before applying to college, Edith, a first-generation Korean female who uses she/her gender pronouns and is married with a child, talked about how she felt her dad couldn't afford to pay for college—which narrowed her choices of where to apply. Edith shared her thinking at the time: "[J]ust like, how do we pay for college? And I, I, and I purposely meant to go to the local community college first, because I was like, you know what? Because I, I know, like, you know, my dad [was] working really hard and still providing for us right, I knew that we also qualified." Beyond financial considerations, Edith described how she had less career—and college major—direction while still in high school, so going to a community college made sense to her. She revealed: "Go to a two-year. You don't even know what you want to do, what a two years, you know. Make it easier on your father, like help you pay for, and, and then like decide what you want to do in those two years to then transfer to the school that you want to." Gender played a role in Edith's college decision-making process, too, as her parents both agreed she'd "be a wife" someday and would need to prioritize her family and work in a field that would allow her to be a mother first—so teaching ended up as a leading career focus for her.

In addition to navigating the college admissions process on her own, Angela shared more about her parents, revealing why she had a strong need to take on work to ensure she funded her way through graduate school. She explained that "growing up it was always this notion of like, we are not rich." She knew that her parents could not "fund [her] way through school like other people can." Angela concluded that college decision-making came down to financial considerations: "I think when it came down to making decisions, I was just like, I need to have money to go to the school." She argued that "you have to work your booty off to like make, to get a scholarship. And luckily again like, I was [an] RA in college. Like I had to be an RA to pay for like meal plans, and to pay for housing. Like, I had to make a way." By her second year as an undergraduate at a public master's-granting university in the northeastern US, Angela noted that she was "gonna apply to be an RA [resident assistant] so that . . . you know, have to like burden your parents and everything like that. I was really considerate of like my family's involvement and contribution to just like my education." On her own, Angela worked with two friends from church to support her successful job offer and transition to an RA position on campus. Angela recalled what they said to her at the time: "[We will] help you through, like we will coach you through the interview."

More than financial considerations, while in high school graduate students had to manage classes, extracurricular activities, and student-teacher relationships on their own—all to prepare to go to college. "Basically," Ping declared, "I'm a very independent person and a self-motivated person." He had to be—from a very young age—as he left his home in a rural Chinese village to go to junior high school, then high school, and finally college. Only returning for breaks and talking with his parents on the phone for most of his time away at school in China, Ping learned to rely on himself and live independently. Ping confirmed: "I . . . went to good junior high and a very good high school in China. I, I thought, I, I left my village from, uh, I go the first year of, uh, junior high."

Diverse Family Structures, Major Life Changes, and Family Processes Lead to Finding Resources Independently

For graduate students who reported experiences with diverse family structures, a need to find their own way in educational institutions and navigate complex college admissions processes seemed to characterize their lives at an early age. For several graduate students, parental divorce and remarriage led to blended families, where new relationships had to be formed and norms negotiated. Zeke, who identifies as a first-generation married cisgender gay white male, shared how he struggled to come out while in high school, and he seemed to not find safety at home with either his mom and stepdad or his dad. The same high school guidance counselor who had helped him as a mentor connected him with an administrator who created a safe space. Zeke described what the counselor did for him: "I just remember him being supportive. You know, when I was starting to get bullied, um, he had me talk to another, um, administrator who like, she like indirectly came out to me. And was just like looking back, like, you know just this, oh it was such a cool, to me it was just like that's what I needed."

Zeke reflected on how he had developed a plan and identified with where he was going in his young life at the time: "I felt like I knew where I was going. I felt like I knew where I was going to go at every stage of my life. I had to find the right resource. There was always trying to figure out who I needed to talk to about something." But he admitted that he never really got what he needed at home to support his plans. Referring to his parents, he concluded: "They didn't get that, I just didn't get that at home I don't think." What's more, with his mom and stepdad, he witnessed excess partying and drinking—and physical abuse at the hands of his stepbrother. As a result, Zeke's grandparents raised him for part of his young life. About their roles, he said: "[M]y grandmother I remember being my primary caretaker [and] my grandmother and grandfather were there."

During high school, Zeke ended up living on the street, as he described, and couch surfing before moving into his dad's house, where he found some stability. After departing high school three months before graduation, he started to lose focus of his plans. After moving to the Southwest to live with his mom, he reflected about where his life went: "I looked at college a little bit. But everything else took precedent, you know. I mean, I started using drugs. Like you know, I was driving to [the West]. You know I was using a lot of meth. Like, I just like, I think maybe at some point I went too far and like lost my, myself in a way, you know through addiction and sexual [behavior]." Later in life, after having worked at a traumatic job, Zeke found himself ready to return to school. Again, he was on his own and relied on his sense of direction to get him to enroll in college classes.

Experiences with parents who divorced characterized early childhood for several graduate students. Jaime talked about how her relationship with her father changed throughout her life, starting with her parents' divorce when Jaime was two years old. With the loss of her father's mother around the same time as the divorce, her father "was going through a lot of things emotionally," and Jaime learned to do a lot on her own.

For both Jessica and Natasha, the breakup of the marriage of their parents, respectively, disrupted their lives at a young age and continued to follow them into adolescence and beyond. In Jessica's case, her parents started to divorce when she was in the first grade, and "was a lengthy drawn-out" process, according to Jessica. Concluding around the time Jessica was a junior in high school, it seemed to go on "forever" and brought her into the fight over child support. Here's what Jessica recalled about it: "[L]ike my dad, from what my mom told me when I was born, he wasn't involved. And then he didn't realize that he could get, um, what was, child support. So that's when he kind of came back into the picture when they were divorcing. Um, and he, I remember like being pulled out of middle school and like, um, talking to lawyers at the school, and all these things about the custody." Natasha remembered how her parents never really got along. "[L]ike the relationship that he had with my mom, um, wasn't exactly what I thought it was as a kid or anything," Natasha said in reference to her dad, "[s]o it's just kind of been hard for me." As a middle school student, her parents had shared custody until a judge allowed her to decide who'd she'd like to see and spend time with. From that point on, Natasha shared, she'd have a strained relationship with her dad. Here's how she described it in her own words: "So pretty much from that turning point, um, I haven't seen him. Um, so I haven't really had contact with him. Maybe like a sighting at school, like open house night I saw him in high school once, and we just, me and my mom just left after that." While her mom remarried when Natasha was in the seventh grade, Natasha still seemed to be on her own and, from what she shared, felt more connected to and comfortable with her now-fiancé's parents as she started to date him in high school. She elaborated: "[O]nce I started dating my fiancé, when we were in high school, so boyfriend-girlfriend at the time, his parents have been together, his grandparents have been together for as long as you can remember. They were, they helped me out a lot. Then my mother-in-law had a similar incident when she was a kid and went through." She concluded: "[W]e've been dating and together for almost ten years. So our, pretty much since I was fifteen, I grew up with him and his family, so I really do feel like a part of the family."

Family processes that did not function well, especially where parents fought and/or struggled to resolve conflict, shaped how graduate students experienced trauma as children at home. As a child, Stella described how she struggled in school due to a traumatic home environment, which led to a lack of interest in academic work and disengagement from learning in the classroom at the time. She elaborated: "I was trying to stop fights at home. I would be up till two in the morning, so like when I would go to school I was always tired. I was always the kid [who] would sleep in class." Then, in middle school, Stella struggled with substance abuse. But she always knew she had academic potential and reflected on what she needed to succeed as a student: "I just didn't have the right people to kind of just push me into those right places until college." Later, Stella revealed how she found the right people, but she also admitted she did a lot of research on her own. Referring to a program adviser and math teacher from high school, Stella told me more about what the mentors meant to college-going but also how she researched a lot of the information on her own.

> I've also met a female mentor. I developed a relationship with her where you know, with that she helped, also was another person that had me under her wing. And I was just that person that was just, once I'm into something I get superinvolved. I give 110 percent into something. So she saw that. [A]nd one math teacher. [T]hey both were like, you know, you should at least try. That was something that I personally researched on, on my own. And again, because I came from a low-income household, um, I didn't have no computers, so I would literally be after school . . . she had an after school running program for a week for seniors to be in the computer labs in the evenings to work on college apps.

Stella continued her story, focusing on how she "was there every day" with her college applications. Her mentors helped her navigate the college application process, but Stella would take after-school buses, stay on campus late, and sacrifice time to get it all done on time.

Chapter 6

Educational Connections in Precollege and College Years

Effects of Parents on College Choice, Transitions to College, and Experiences in College

While a range of parental involvement in education characterized early life and emerging adulthood for most graduate students, home-based involvement in education seemed to be the most frequent form. In this way, many parents generally served in a central support role for their children's education and built a family system guided by emotional and material educational support. Grounded in cultural beliefs about the value of education, parents tended to reproduce how important academic achievement and aspirations to go to college had been in the family in their home-based involvement in school. Through assistance with homework and assignments, consistent check-ins about school and general encouragement to persist and complete, and affirmations of academic self-image and identity as students, many parents focused on what they could do at home.

What prevented some parents from more school-based forms of participation was a feeling of exclusion, and perception of institutional barriers that did not allow for some to get close to teachers and school administrators. In fact, anti-immigrant environments at school, limited language accommodations, and lack of consideration for working-class job schedules that prevented daytime participation in school events led to some parents not directly participating in school. Instead, children had to go it alone—shaping more independence and agency at a young age, which tended to position them well to navigate more complex admissions systems and campus climates that sometimes made it difficult to persist in their studies.

While direct involvement in education by parents tended to be concentrated at home, parent participation spanned home and school for some graduate students. Indeed, for this small group, school-based parent involvement in parent-teacher conferences, participation in school events, and volunteering in the classroom supported children in their precollege educational journey.

Over the span of the educational pipeline, parents tended to have many touchpoints in the academic development and intellectual growth of their children. Parental involvement in education spanned precollege schooling to college decision-making, college transitions, and undergraduate studies. For most graduate students, a strong presence of parents along the educational pipeline shaped promotion through elementary school and graduation from high school. At school, parents volunteered and/or worked on campus, which strengthened student connections to learning. As an overarching role, parental encouragement and emotional support tended to directly impact and deeply root children in lives as students and help them to navigate all the way to college. Later, as graduate students, most parents continued to offer support through praise, which was still incredibly important to many graduate students.

Parental Relationship Effects on Precollege Experiences: Home-Based and School-Based Involvement in Education Spans Elementary and Secondary School Years

For some graduate students, both parents participated in home- and school-based activities with children. Edith had the fortune of her parents playing respective roles, particularly during her elementary school years. Edith, a first-generation Korean female who uses she/her gender pronouns and is married with a child, recalled how her mom was involved all the time. She said: "[M]y mom was there for the, the day to day, like homework, like, you know, make sure it gets done. Tools, materials you need for it, I'll make sure you have it." For her dad's part, he went to the school assemblies and parent-teacher conferences. Edith explained this unique split of her mom with more home-based participation and dad more school-based participation: "But my dad went to all the parent conferences. They both went to the assembly, you know the shows that, you know, and that . . . really like stay with me." She continued: "[A]t the conference the grades would be given and shared, and so he would, he would share that with my mom. But I, I remember my dad being a, a bit more gracious about my grades like, and then it's like, oh, my gosh, don't show off. But yeah, so I always, I didn't have anxiety ever about achievement . . . with my dad."

Beatrice's story seemed to start and end like Edith's. Beatrice felt supported by both her parents. With her dad, specifically, if she had questions, he'd help out—she remarked. She illustrated: "Like we were learning even just division, like I remember, like I have this memory of like division, he was like, oh, you do this, and then I was like, no, no, they're teaching us to do it this way. So he'd always take the time to like, try and familiarize, and learn the ways that they were teaching us." Beatrice had to ask her dad for help with math. While she had to learn to seek support and let her dad guide her in her math homework, she felt relieved to be supported by him. She spoke to this process at a time in her life when she was in high school. She said: I feel like the first thing that comes to mind is being able to ask for help. Whether it be my parents, my friends, an adviser, my mentor." She continued: "Um, that was one thing I really struggled with. I touched on it a little bit, taking Calc Three first semester. I just that remember that class, it was just not fun. So learning to ask for help. It took me a while to ask my dad for help." Recognizing her stubbornness, Beatrice understood why she had a hard time asking for help. She said: "Um, I was very stubborn. I was like, oh, I could do this. You know I was very stubborn 'cause I was used to succeeding easily at my high school."

Between praise for academic performance and help with homework, Hector remembers his dad's outsized role in his schooling. In high school, as Hector started to consider college, the conversations about his dad's own experiences in high school and college over the years seemed to come to the fore for Hector. More than just old stories, Hector felt his dad's support in the everyday issues of applying to college. Hector shared more.

> I think because he had been telling us from such . . . early days that, about these stories that he had experienced . . . was something I was looking forward to. [T]hat was already in my head, you know. So by the time you know, we were moving and getting ready to go from high school to college, um, he, he was very supportive of looking at different options. Like well,

you know, what are you . . . what are you thinking? Would you wanna do like four-year, you know kind of thing? Um, but also being realistic of like, you know what can we afford? What kind of things, what can, you know financial aid do? Can you fill it out? Help me, help me, you know get some of those things. Um, start to look at some of the FAFSA, you know forms.

Hector concluded about his dad: "just being really, really supportive of whatever, wherever I wanted to go, whatever I wanted to do."

In so many ways, Hector's mom had a uniquely central role in his success as a student, too. Thinking about his mom's impact on his education and, beyond school, his relationships in life, he reflected: "I feel like that was always a very prominent component of, of me growing up and thinking about my education, or thinking about the work that I would later do, or the relationships I have with friends and people." Focused on education, Hector talked about how his mom fueled his enthusiasm for school, encouraged him to do his best in his studies, unconditionally supported his academic work, and helped him to view himself as a student and value his role in the teaching and learning process. She created an environment where Hector felt safe at school and where he could focus on learning.

Beyond encouragement and identity development as a student, Hector talked about how his mom helped with homework and was always there for him. She helped with lower elementary schoolwork and later with writing skills development. Not just essential to home-based participation but integral to school-based participation, Hector's mom was involved on campus—which strengthened Hector's connections to learning and his life as a student. Referring to his mom's direct involvement in his education, here's what Hector recalled about this time in his life.

[E]arly on, like, you know, kindergarten, first grade, you know, I know there was helping me, you know, complete homework assignments. She was also really involved in, from k through eighth grade, really involved at my school. She, you know, showed up at all the, you know, anything that had involved with parents. And then, later, you know . . . did a lot of volunteer time there. And then later took a job at the school. We had, you know there was four of us, so she actually was a librarian at one point within our school. She taught, I

> think some art classes within our school. I never had her as a teacher, or really as a librarian. I think I was kind of past, a little bit past that age, but she was definitely involved. I think, having them there, you know, and knowing that they, that they advocated for things like that, and were very active within the, within, amongst other parents, it felt good. It felt like it, felt like, for me, like, you know, you had even more of a role, you had parent, people looking out, you know, for you as you're going through something.

His mom's support was so strong that Hector recalled she tended to fault others for issues or outcomes that perhaps Hector could have played a role in. "[Y]ou know you didn't do something really well," Hector recounted, "and your mom was still kind of like, yeah, but I'm sure it was, I'm sure it was somebody else."

Hector illustrated how his mom's unconditional love and support led to the following conversation.

> In some classes I was great, other classes I was like. And it was one particular class where, it was a Spanish like four class or something, you know, and I just, especially in the last semester I, I didn't put hardly any effort into it. And as a . . . of that I got like a really bad grade. It was probably like a D or an F, right. That's terrible. And, you know, I, I, I know I just didn't work hard, you know. I, I think, I feel like I earned that, that grade, you know. I could, I could say that. And so that's how I've always felt about it. And I was talking to somebody recently and they're like, yeah, no, but your mom was saying more it was like, you know, well, maybe that teacher was like, not fair to you.

In the end, Hector saw his mom as a center of love, where her optimism and outlook on life led her to protect, defend, and believe in Hector.

Centrally Important Roles for Mothers in Children's Educational Involvement

Perhaps related to gendered parental roles, mothers seemed to be central to home- and school-based involvement in precollege education, for many graduate students who reflected on early family life. Between her parents,

Sasha's mom was "really on top of it" with what was happening at school when she was younger. But her dad participated in a unique way, too. Using a dual approach when she was younger, Sasha's dad tended to check in about classes and help with math homework. Regulated by gender roles focused on men and technical fields like math and reinforced by his training in the military, Sasha's dad used to support her with math. She recalled: "I think mostly like math stuff is really what I remember like, him like sitting down with us at the dinner table and like us having our homework." Even though Sasha, who identifies as a pansexual white woman, was "superappreciative" of his support, it seemed to come at a price, as he "would be so like harsh, and like we would cry, it's mean." Outside of this limited scope of support, her dad was not very involved in her education.

Like Sasha, Hua's mom was an important part of her student life in elementary and secondary schools in China. Hua, a Chinese female, described how involved her mom was at school—even as her dad helped with homework. Once in high school, Hua's mom was still involved, but her focus turned to Hua's emotional and physical needs rather than scholastic. In China, Hua explained, an intense focus on academics and a tense schedule leaves high school students to study on their own. Speaking about her parents' role in her education as a high schooler, Hua said: "[T]hey don't need you like supervising you with a classwork or anything." But Hua's parents participated in the college decision-making process, as she explained: "I want to go to other cities. My parents more consider about my health. I was born with some problems, so they try to let me. Also, my dad explained to me. They try to let me study in the same city where they and I grew up. So if there is some emergency, [I can] count [on] my parents can get to school and picking me up. That's what they want."

With three girls at home, Zelma recalled how her parents pushed education as "the way out of everything and anything" and expected nothing less than a college degree. With only an eighth-grade education, Zelma's mom "would sit with us at the table after we had our lunch, came home from school, until we were done with our homework. Like my mom would not leave our side." When her mom could not help with math concepts, she resourcefully reached out to a neighbor to help. "She sat with us day in and day out until we were done," Zelma shared, "[a]nd once we started learning math that was more, you know, above her level of comprehension, we had neighbors next door." Her mom would work with neighbors to encourage and/or request their support. More than just homework help and coordination, her mom offered emotional support, too. When school challenged Zelma, her mom gently but firmly insisted she focus on college as the path to a better future. Here's what Zelma, a first-generation cisgender Indigenous Palestinian and Lebanese, Arab, and Middle Eastern woman who is married with children, recalled her mom telling her at the time: "[Y]ou are not quitting school. You're not not gonna go to college because you need to be able to stand on your own two feet, and your education is your path to that." Zelma emphasized: [Y]ou heard college from a very young age, like college, college, college, college." And the result? Three daughters with MA degrees or higher.

Angela's mom supported her a lot like Zelma's mom. "I do remember vivid times of like her sitting down with me, helping me to do my homework," Angela—a first-generation African American female who identifies ethnically as Nigerian—recalled. Beyond homework help, Angela's mom got her to where she needed to be on a daily basis and was there for her at ceremonies, competitions, performances, and events. While in high school, Angela remembered her mom getting her to and from band, sports, and National Honor Society—and her mom would check in to be sure she had everything to be successful. Sharon's mom was there for her, too—at all her school productions. Sometimes her dad could make it, but most of the time it was her mom who showed up.

Many more graduate students shared stories about mothers who had been directly involved in early education. Andres talked about how his mom embodied her value on education, modeling how to get ready for and get to school on time. Here's how Andres remembered it: "And she not only made it a point like verbally, but even the actions that she took. Waking us up in the morning, you know, making sure our clothes were clean and ready to go. Making sure that we were on, on the school bus in the morning." But his mom's focus on education seemed grounded as much in a desire for her children to get ahead in life as to avoid trouble. "I think her, her just drive to get us educated, or to make sure we're staying out of trouble was . . . her primary tool for like raising us," Andres revealed. He continued, speaking from his mom's perspective: "I'm gonna nurture them, but I'm gonna just push them to go to school and to be educated, you know."

What's more, Andres's mom's concern for her children could be seen in how she worried about their future, given early family experiences with carceral institutions. At a young age, Andres recalled visiting his cousins in prison. From his mom's perspective, education helped them all to stay away from prison systems and move toward bright futures. Here's more from Andres, a first-generation able-bodied cis-hetero male who identifies as Mexican, specifically Mexicah and Tepehuani: "I think, and again this is all in retrospect that my mom wanted us to go to school and be successful because she was witnessing what my cousins were going through with my *tia* [redacted], right. So I can only imagine that my mom's push for education was like driven by some of those things that she knew were possibilities in this country. If you fuck around, you're going to prison forever, right." Reflecting on his mom's experiences, Andres said: "I think that's what were one of the motivating factors that, you know, made my mom really press the importance of education on us."

Like Hua, Sasha, Zelma, Angela, and Andres, Liza remembered her mom's direct involvement in her life as a student in elementary and secondary school. Her mom helped with projects, got her the material and supplies she needed, and ensured assignments were turned in on time. "I think my mom lived through us in terms of . . . our projects and stuff," Liza, who identifies as a cisgender bisexual Latina woman, said as she described her mom's interest in their schoolwork. Liza illustrated what her mom did to support her.

> My mom was the parent that was going to Michael's at nine p.m. at night right before they closed to get, you know, the last few things that we needed to get for a school project kind of thing. Anytime we had a school project she always wanted to make sure that it was the best-looking project that we could turn in. And obviously was looked, by the time I brought it like to, to school it was very obvious that my parents helped me on it, you know. My mom had all the, the, glue guns, the superglue guns, all the little knickknacks.

About her mom at this time in her life, Liza concluded: "So if anything, my mom was the most involved in our school work with the projects and things like that."

As a student in elementary school, junior high school, and high school, Brianna's mom seemed to be involved everywhere. "[S]he's was PTA. A PTA parent," according to Brianna, "[s]o heavily involved." Her mom led school groups on field trips to the state capital, for example, and it was a gift to Brianna. She also worked in public schools, which fueled her involvement in Brianna's education. Here's what Brianna remembered about it, especially at a time when her family grieved her dad's passing.

> So that was like her gift of really kind of just being very much heavily involved. I would say also, like when we were in high school she was a aid. She, she worked for the public schools, and worked, you know, worked on, on, on campus you would say. So very much involved. We were, even though my dad, he passed away when we were sixteen, she's been just very much involved . . . very involved. They didn't have to worry about if we, if there was any issues, go downstairs to you mom.

Not just at school but at home, Brianna knew her mom was there for here. Brianna, who identifies first-generation African American woman, recalled what her mom used to say to her: "You know the, you can do this."

For some, mothers offered more encouragement and emotional support. With Kayla, her mom offered "leadership and guidance" that shaped Kayla's "drive to be successful." Kayla elaborated on her mom's support, which consistently pushed her to always do better in life. Kayla illustrated what her mom's messaging looked like in the context of her life as a student: "Like almost you have to, like that's like pushing that, that narrative for me. I, I remember that distinctly. Just, you know, like you know. And it's just like, okay, if you get an A, a B, why don't you get an A? What you could always do better, like that kind of narrative always remains as far as the leadership part of it." Another example of her mom's guidance could be seen in Kayla's story about when she shared with her parents that she didn't want to go to college. Instead, she wanted to go into the fashion industry. Here's how Kayla, who identities as a first-generation cisgender African American female who is married with two children, narrated the rest of the story.

> I really didn't want to go to college, but it was like, either you go to college, or you get a job. That was, that was the narrative in my house. Like you go to college, or you get a full-time job. So I didn't want to get a full-time job. Well, I didn't, I don't know, I just didn't feel like, I didn't really know what I wanted to be, so. And well, let me, let me back up. That's not true. I didn't know what I wanted to be then, but at the time what I wanted

to do, from my parents wasn't like a real career. So I wanted to go into fashion, and go into like modeling. And you know, at that time going into [the city] was a whole different thing than it is going to the city now. So that was like a non, that was a non-negotiable conversation, about fashion into fashion in [the city], at that time, for them. So that wasn't a real job.

Of course, Kayla's story ended with her going to college: "I'll just go to college."

Josefina's early years in elementary school saw her parents interested and involved in her education. With her mom's limited English skills, Josefina recalled the limitations of her mom's participation at school, given the lack of institutional resources and commitment to equitable and inclusive involvement of parents. But her mom did everything she could do to be involved at school. For example, she prepped cupcakes for baked goods sales with school fundraisers. Her mom's role, in particular, "was really about making sure there was, those basic needs were met," according to Josefina, who identifies as a first-generation straight Chicana woman with children. Making sandwiches, packing lunches, putting burritos or soup in a thermos to say warm on cold days, cooling drinks in a small ice chest to stay cool on hot days—this is how Josefina's mom took care of small details that added up to meaningful forms of support. Beyond basic needs and baked goods, Josefina looked back at an overarching image of her mom as someone who always encouraged her: "I would say her role was always, I think that's more of a verbal. So I guess you would say a little bit, it was more motivational support that my mother gave me through all my entire educational journey." This was all the more important, given how Josefina connected her elementary school to minoritized ethnic and cultural experiences. Her mom's motivational role had been critical at the time, as Josefina explained: "[B]ecause I grew up in a time where you know, I, I feel like the school district here in [the West] wasn't as diverse as it is today. I recall being probably one of the very few Brown kids in elementary."

Holly's mom offered the same kind of encouragement to go to college. Because her mom never felt accepted in the intellectual social circle that her dad hosted, she pushed Holly and her brother toward higher education so that they could feel a sense of belonging at home and more broadly in society. "I think because it was so painful for her," Holly shared, "she learned that education is, she wish, something she wish she had, but she never did." But education was something that Holly and her brother could do—and do well. Holly remembered: "[F]rom that point she always encouraged my brother and I. You know, like my, my father encouraged, that wasn't even a question. You know, but for her, for her it was she appreciated the importance."

"MY DAD WAS ALWAYS THE ONE": FATHER INVOLVEMENT IN EDUCATION

Like most mothers, many fathers supported elementary and secondary school student success, but their involvement tended to be more home-based and focused on encouragement. For Josefina's dad's part, he may not have been able to participate in all school events, but if he could not, "he made sure that my mom or my oldest, my sisters, who were old, much older than me, the one that I said that was ten years older than me, would attend . . . on his behalf." Zelma lamented how her father never really participated in school activities or events, deferring to her mom—in a traditional care-taking role—as the "one who went to the back-to-school nights, and went to teacher conferences because she was a stay-at-home mom." And her mom did homework with her late at night and hired a tutor to help her with math when needed. She told the story this way: "And my mom had the wherewithal when we were doing math, at the time we lived in n apartment complex, and next to us, next door to us was another Arab family. And next door to us there was some, you know, a family who had older men who were, one became a math professor, has a math PhD, Um, another one, again, an adult man who was working, running a business, and he, they would tutor us."

Zelma's mom did a lot more for her as a student, serving as a safe space when she needed a break. Zelma illustrated her mom's role in her education.

> I had just finished two years of community college and, you know that was terrifying to tell my dad I wanna take a semester off, you know. But of course I told my mom first, because I knew, you know. And for her it wasn't so much that she was angry or upset that I took a semester off, she was just like, I don't want you to lose track. I want you to keep going. I don't want you to give up. And just finding safety in that space, you know, at the time I just needed a break. But I think for her it's more,

it's always been more like I could tell her more of the issues I was having with school per se, or even other personal things.

At times, though, Zelma's mom took a more punitive approach, as when Zelma recounted this story from her precollege years: "We would be there, sitting there 'til sometimes nine, ten o'clock. We're like, I don't want to do my homework! No, you're gonna sit here and you're gonna do your homework. Whether it meant we got spanked or not."

While Zelma's mom helped her with math when she was younger, Karina's parents—particularly her dad—did the same. In fact, Zelma's story with her mom's punitive approach resembled Karina's description of her parents, who used similar measures with her academic work. Karina, a heterosexual Latina woman who identifies as half Guatemalan and half Mexican, described how, as a high school student, her parents expected her to get A's and B's in her classes, and her dad would be angry if she didn't meet those expectations: "[B]oth my parents honestly, but my dad was always the one who wanted us to get really good grades. Um, I wasn't really allowed to get like a C, I had to be a B or A. Um, and so when I would get a C, um, my, my dad would always be the one who was angry. Like no, you have to get good grades 'cause when you start applying for college they're gonna look back on all of this."

Beyond a focus on her academic performance, Karina's parents shaped her college major while she was still in high school. When Karina started to think about college majors and careers, her mom seemed to suggest teaching. "[I]n high school I was also not sure what I wanted to do," Karina revealed: "I knew I had to pick something because I needed to go to college right away. And so, um, one day my mom just told me, you know you'd make a really good elementary school teacher, and I was like, okay, I'm gonna go with that. Let's do that."

For a small group, fathers had a more prominent role in precollege education, being directly involved at home and school. Eileen's parents participated in her elementary school and checked in with her homework. "[T]hey would always know my class, my projects that I was working on, what, in my groups . . . they knew all my classmates, and knew who I was working with, and, um, they knew all my teachers." Eileen, a heterosexual married white female, elaborated on the extent of their school-based participation: "We had parent teacher conferences all the time at [the private school], and so they were very involved in, um, what was going on in the classroom, and asking questions about what I was learning, and kind of, um, encouraging me to think a little bit more about what I was learning, and kind of challenging that a little bit." What's more, Eileen's dad was helpful in her college search, admission, and selection process. Her dad helped to organized Eileen's application process and meet deadlines, along with exploring campus programs and institutions to consider applying to. But there was a bit of a judgment to his support—a sort of conditional approach where he advised her to apply to colleges with higher research activity "so, you can't, you can't go down for grad school. You can either stay horizontal or go up." This seemed to influence Eileen's decision making, at least on a subconscious level.

While her dad was as helpful as he could be in the college application process, given that college admissions looked different when her dad applied to college than now, Eileen felt her dad's support when she was ready to transition to and start her first year on campus. As a professor, her dad advised her on what undergraduate education meant for students and how to navigate college classrooms and instructors. She listed how he guided her: "I mean like, go to office hours, and scheduling classes, and how many classes you should be in, that kind of stuff, like really helpful and supportive." He helped her with class selection and enrollment, based on what classes interested her.

Above all, Eileen's dad's emotional support and investment meant a lot to her. In fact, her reflections about his presence can be seen here: "I think just that emotional, being interested and invested was really helpful in college. I think that like interest alone was really helpful and supportive." Eileen's dad helped financially, too, but in return her parents expected strong academic performance. Never as an "ultimatum," but more as a clear expectation.

Holly's dad seemed to be similarly ever-present in her early education. She recalled his influence from a young age, where he helped her learn an appreciation for education. In fact, her father's peers created an environment at home that reinforced the idea of education as key to career paths and a full life. "Not only from him, but also his friends . . . all of them were like highly educated." In the home, Holly experienced dinner parties and social events surrounded by intellectual discussions that piqued her interest in education.

"The Reason I'm in Education": Black and Latinx Parent Involvement and Family Support in School

Black parents participate at home, school, and in the community to support children's motivation and learning—and Black parents tend to rely on familial knowledge, family and friends, religious faith, and more to navigate educational system and overcome racialized stereotypes that have functioned as barriers (Threlfall, 2015). Parental involvement tends to relate to high self-esteem for children in Black families (Causey et al., 2015). For Black adolescent boys in junior high school and high school, father involvement supports school attendance and academic performance (Rodney & Mupier, 1999).

With Black graduate students, relationships with fathers, grandparents, and aunts and uncles functioned similarly, modeling what you need to succeed in education and life: presentation, punctuality, family support and unity, relationality and community engagement, "nothing in life is free" mind-set and hard work, and much more. Brianna, a first-generation African American woman, described how her grandfather, a father in her life, used to be at all the special occasions and important events in school, including graduation—with his tape recorder—and homecoming dances so that he could drive them around in a "limo because he had a funeral service so we just used, you know, that limo." Brianna's mother was involved in the school PTA, so Brianna felt connected to the school between her grandfather and mother.

Stella commented on how her parents did everything they could do when she was younger to support her learning at school. She shared the following:

> [M]y mom . . . made sure that if there's something that she didn't know that she'll make sure to have us have a tutor, you know, through other educational programs for low-income kids. She took the time to research . . . different tutors that can come into our home to like tutor us. Or there was a time where she bought in her sister . . . and she would help us like with our homework and stuff like that.

With her father, Stella remembered "his thing was English," and he would try to help her in this subject. Stella, a first-generation African American who uses the gender pronouns she/her/hers, elaborated: "Like he would try to like just sit down with us, like push us to finish our homework. Like he would try to support us and like, come on guys, like, try to finish your homework. Or, and if there was something he didn't know, he'll try his best to kind of help us figure it out, if that made sense." While in high school, Angela shared how both her parents participated in her school activities, which made her feel supported. She remembered: "My parents did a good job of like picking me up and supporting me. Like in high school I did band, I did some sports, I did some like leadership clubs, national honor society, all the different things."

For Latinx parents of high school students, involvement in children's education focused on factors that included support from extended family support, values that emphasized cultural expectations for involvement, financial and time resources, and internal motivation (Heredia, 2009). Further, family involvement—along with school-community partnerships—have been linked to Latinx high school student completion (Lopez, 2013). For Leonardo, a first-generation straight Mexican American male, parental and extended familial support reinforced his academic self-image. He remembered what happened when he was in high school: "And so bringing home the straight A, you know, showing it to my parents. You know, them being proud, putting it on the fridge. You know, other people coming over and seeing and then saying, wow, you know, good for you, you know. For me it was like, it was almost like common sense." Like Leonardo, Jasmine relied on extended family to support as a young student with strong academic interests. She turned to her aunt as a role model. As an immigrant from Mexico and an assistant principal, her aunt was well prepared to guide Jasmine through elementary and secondary school as she prepared for college and beyond. Here's how Jasmine put her aunt's role in her academic life in clear terms: "[S]he's the reason I'm in education."

Eugenio's parents offered him all the logistical support and coordination in school he needed, when he was younger. Eugenio, a first-generation heterosexual Latinx male who identifies as Oaxacan from an Indigenous Mexican background, illustrated: "Dropping me off and be like, oh, here's five bucks or five dollars for the food truck or something. Um, and then I had to go pretty much and that's it." His mom would walk his older brother and him to school, too, which was close to the house and easy for him to get to. In time, his older brother would lead them on the walk, and Eugenio's parents participated directly in these kinds of activities as they boys grew up. He recalled this change when he said: "But going to classes, going to events we had, my parents actually both of them didn't go."

Parental Involvement in Precollege Education for First-Generation College Students

For first-generation students, both parents seemed to shape precollege education. Andres, a first-generation able-bodied cis-hetero male who identifies as Mexican, specifically Mexicah and Tepehuani, understood

226 | Shaping Students of Color from Preschool to Graduate School

Figure 6.1. Many first-generation graduate students remember home- and school-based parent involvement in education. *Source:* By U.S. Army Combat Capabilities Development Command, CC BY 2.0. https://www.flickr.com/photos/34402227@N03/6883035090.

he had to do well in school and plan to go to college. In very real terms and on a practical level, he knew what his dad would do if didn't perform well academically. His dad reinforced his expectations in fear. In junior high school and high school, as a gang member running drugs and guns on the streets, Andres knew not to cross a line with his dad—he had to live up to high standards and work toward passing grades in his classes. Andres shared more.

> Because fails were not acceptable, right? I could not get any fails at, at all costs. Even if I was ditching, if I would miss school I would go talk to my teacher and be like, how can I make up all of that lost work? And I remember negotiating, because I'm a businessman, right? So, I'm talking to teachers like, hey, so I know I missed this assignment, but, you know, I'll make it up, and I'll do double the work, you know. And then they'll be like, uhhh, some of them would agree, some of

them wouldn't. Some of them would make me do like other stuff, like volunteer or do community service and they'll give me credit, and I did it.

Why did he do extra work and volunteer in the community? He knew he couldn't cross his dad. He put it this way: "I knew, I knew that if I got a fail my dad would, wouldn't like it. You know, and I remember, even though I know he wasn't going to hit me or beat me up or anything, I just didn't want to get him upset, you know."

Either on occasion or a regular basis, some parents volunteered or worked at school, so there was a direct connection between family and education. For Kayla, her mom worked at the school when Kayla was in kindergarten. There, she felt her mom was a part of her day. Jeremy remembered small elementary school celebrations in the form of a hosted breakfast in which he would be invited as an honor roll student. What was special about the breakfast was not just food or the fact that he got to skip class for a short time but that his parents were there—they made the trip to campus to sit with him at the table.

Academic ceremonies in middle school followed, and Jeremy's parents participated in those events, too. Often, his dad would go to school events in his work uniform, then leave immediately following the event to return to work. His dad missed many events at school, which tended to be in the morning, because he couldn't pull away from work. But an annual event at which both Jeremy's parents volunteered was Field Day. He explained in more detail.

> We also had this thing called Field Day. Um, it was like once a, once a year in December for elementary school, and [my dad] and my mom volunteered every single one of those um for the entire day. So I would always see them there. So, I did see [my dad] like a lot for like school events that like he, he would be at. Um, both my parents and him, like they were required to have 30 to 40 volunteer hours as parents, and they both had like a 100 plus total. So, um, they were both like very active.

While Jeremy, who identifies as a first-generation straight white and Italian cisgender male, remembered doing well academically in school—mostly on his own—his parents seemed to be present in everything else in his student life, including school drop off, pick up, and more. Jeremy's dad did

Figure 6.2. Black and Latinx graduate students connect parent involvement in education to their academic journey. *Source:* By USACE Europe District, CC BY 2.0. https://www.flickr.com/photos/34728058@N08/5664527584.

help him with math problems—until the problems were far too advanced for most parents to help. "I can't help you with this anymore, you're on your own buddy," Jeremy recalls his dad saying. "Like, so, um, then at that point I was like starting to figure things out of my own," Jeremy stated. But both his mom and dad would continue to check in and ensure he did his homework and he had what he needed in school.

Emotional Support Present in Parents Shaping College Decision-Making at Home

Jeremy's mom and dad never went to college. But his dad wanted to go and would've gone if not for his dad, who used to "put him down" and never seemed to support him. That left Jeremy largely on his own to get to college, even though he had his parents' full emotional and financial support. In fact, Jeremy described how central his dad's support was: "[He was] always on top of me with deadlines and making sure I got things submitted. And, um, if I needed like anything, especially like, if I was, if I needed to pay application fees like I'd go to him before I'd go to my mom." And it was, in part, because his mom "who was the one that asked other people the questions," including questions about college. When on campus visits, his mom would be out front with the tour guide asking questions.

But Jeremy still had to do a lot on his own, and these experiences led Jeremy to identify strongly as a first-gen student. He shared more.

> I think that like the, my first-generation status has always been very important to me. I think that like that's something that's been, that's very big, is like, I'm very well connected with the fact that like I am first-generation. And like I know like my first year in undergrad, like I felt, I felt a lot of pressure, like more so than sometimes I was willing to admit, um, for being first gen, cause I felt like if I didn't succeed, or if I didn't do well, or if I didn't get A's or B's, like that would sort of like be failing like my parents' mission, I guess.

He concluded: "[K]nowing like I'm the first in my family to do all this stuff. And like sometimes it's tough, like it's tough to like think about that. And it's tough to like, sometimes it's tough to move forward with that I guess."

In large part, Tanya made college decisions by herself and had to rely on her own judgment as resources and deadlines emerged and required attention. She commented on what she experienced in the process.

> [N]either one of my parents really had a say about like where I wanted to go to school at. It was just the part of like, I trust I know she's gonna go to a college that's best for her, and if she needs help she's gonna let us know. So they were just more like supportive of, we a hundred percent behind whatever decision you made. [J]ust being honestly like supportive and like, you know, being there for me so I know that, okay, y'all are not too far away.

Tanya noted how the college admissions process confused her parents and her, so she seemed to be on her own—but she had her parents' motivational and financial support. She spoke more directly about her dad, saying he supported her, encouraged her educational interests, and ensured that her financial needs were met, including meal plans and more. In discussing what she needed from him, Tanya would have to "walk through it slowly with him for him to understand just different things," because college was a "whole different language that he couldn't really understand," as she put it. She continued by saying "college was just a whole different language that he couldn't really understand. And so I would have to like walk through it slowly with him for him to understand just different things." She illustrated what this was like for her dad and her: "[G]etting him hip to like, okay dad, this is what this means, this is what this means, and he understands for the most part."

For Ping, who had to leave home for high school, given the remote rural community of his childhood in China, his father's assurances of support and financial assistance. Ping shared his memory of what his father used to say: "[E]very time I want to like, I want to study in the big city for high school, [and] my father say[s] if, if you can be admitted we, I will support you. Pay all the fees without uh hesitation." He continued: "That means the only thing I need to do is to study hard. I don't need to consider other factors. If I can be admitted by a very good high school and the . . . cost is higher than other, my peers in the village, he will support me, no matter."

With limited connections to US higher education, Zelma's parents didn't generally encourage her to do extracurricular activities in high school, but Zelma navigated curricular and co-curricular opportunities on her own. She elaborated: "You know I went through, I had AP English, I had AP this, AP that. Mind you my parents didn't know much about college and extra . . . curricular activities. We were never encouraged to go into sports. I wasn't encouraged to do any of that. I was just like, you go to school, you come home." But her parents directed Zelma to focus on school, laying a familial foundation for her to navigate high school on her own.

Even as she tried to continue working in a summer job before her junior year in high school, Zelma's father insisted she resign to focus on school. She described more: "By the time I started school, he said, you need to quit your job. You know I wanted a part-time job, I wanted to make some money." But her father reasoned with her: "[Y]ou need to focus on school."

Jenna described her dad's direct role in her early educational experiences. Primarily supporting her with homework help, Jenna likened her experiences to "these memes around where fathers get upset at math." But she admitted that it helped: "[N]ow that I look back, that he did help me a lot in math. But he was definitely more involved in terms of math. Now in terms of English, he would try to help with the essays, but around late middle school, early high school I started developing a different writing style." At that point, Jenna was on her own and largely did her homework by herself. But she never felt alone—Jenna's dad did a lot to support her as a student in middle and high school. She mentioned how he would do school drop off and pick up, but he also offered emotional support to Jenna. She reflected more: "[A]s a teenager, I didn't really understand, but I see it now . . . that . . . he really was there for me. If I had an exam coming up he'll say, okay, I'll take care of the dishes. You focus on that. And so that really helped me succeed." What her dad did, at the time, allowed Jenna to focus exclusively on school, including college admissions. She said: "And it really meant a lot, because . . . those were less obstacles that I had to deal with, you know? I didn't have to think about doing the dishes and studying for my finals. I just had to focus on one."

With a different dynamic but a similar effect as Jenna, Gail's parents guided her to where she felt more comfortable as a student—at an independent study school that helped her to explore academic interests. For the first year and a half of high school, Gail described how she was failing her classes at the "regular high school," until she transitioned to independent study, where she "did way better." Here's why independent study worked well for Gail.

> I could go at my own pace. I just did so much better 'cause like I was able to really pick the classes that I wanted, whereas at the regular high school I feel like, like I got to pick the language but I don't remember like really working with the counselor to like, pick my classes. [T]he independent school had some really cool teachers and cool classes. They had, um, a bunch of like field trips, too, which was weird for an independent study school. I even got like a scholarship trip to [the West], and I graduated seven months early. Like I just really excelled there.

Gail, who identifies as a first-generation straight white female, described how her mom drove her to and from school for in-person activities and events. Her mom was always there for her as a student, to which she recalled: "When it came to like studying for school I think that was more my mom, at least as a kid." Her dad helped her study, too, in a unique ritual, when he would walk with her in the evenings.

Later, Gail recalled how her dad would sometimes go for walks with her at night, allowing them to connect about her day at school and study for upcoming tests. Gail reflected more about this time in her life: "And a lot of times my, I would give my dad my flash cards and so he'd like . . . quiz me on my flash cards when we were walking." She continued: "And I think, also when we'd go for walks in the evening, he, he'd just like asked me about my classes. And so I'd try to like tell him about a concept I was learning until he was like acting like he understood it, you know. Sometimes he'd be like, I don't get it, but I would try to make him understand it." While her parents participated in her high school education, they seemed to give her space to decide about and apply to college, so I mean my parents did talk to me about how they both went to college—neither forcing her to go or helping her with applications. "They let me do that all on my own," Gail commented. After having graduated high school early, Gail knew she wanted to go to college and relied on her cousin to guide her to a community college, where Gail could be close to her as a sister figure in her life.

Like Jenna and Gail, Winona's dad and uncles—fictive fathers to her before her dad emigrated from Vietnam to the US when she was five years old—had direct roles in her early educational experiences. Winona, a first-gen bisexual Asian American who identifies as Chinese and Vietnamese, recalled how her uncles helped her learn to write in kindergarten. She shared: "But when it comes to like my uncles teaching me, it probably was like when you're like first starting to write and I would always mess up the letter *E*. Like kind of getting these workbooks and being like, okay, do these pages and then I'll check your work type of thing." Later in elementary school, with her mom always at work, her dad served in a care-taking role and got directly involved with her education. Revealing how she picked up school quickly, Winona described his approach in stark contrast to her uncles. She went into further detail.

> And I have to admit he was a very strict dude. He was not nice. He was not nice. 'Cause in some ways, I would say it's because of the education system in Vietnam, how they already had kids like learning multiplication, math was like priority. And let's just say my writing was really bad, so he was very like, you gotta redo it. Erase it, redo it. Um, or those cases of like, okay, you gotta get these multiplications in. So he, he took a, a strict route of like, hey, like now you gotta like start doing it properly, not messing around anymore.

Educational Connections in Precollege and College Years | 233

In middle school, Winona's dad remained involved, taking her to the library, checking out books, and monitoring her grades. She remembered her dad's focus on grades during this time in her academic life: "And then grade-wise it's always like, okay, why this not that type of thing. You know, like why is it not an A? You know, that kind of like strict mentality, but like it comes to an understanding after, after the end of it. Um, and then for middle-school-wise, he wasn't as on top of it, even though he did get the report cards and stuff."

Fast-forward, Winona's dad helped her in the college application process. He'd help her navigate the admissions process, making sense of complex procedures to apply to colleges and universities. These conversations helped Winona decide where to apply and go to college and, ultimately, what to major in. "I would talk to my dad about these, even career choices," Winona commented in her reflections on career directions to work in the private sector related to her applied science field. She detailed more about these conversations about career.

> [E]verything I do is like I tell my dad. Because when he's there, I also tell my mom but she's like, okay, whatever, whatever you do is like, you'll be successful in. So she was always at work, too. So, um, my dad would always be the person that would be of like, oh, in my opinion there's, there's this job or that job. And then how do you feel? And you should engage in these internships and things like that.

Back to support with college applications, Winona retold stories about her dad's guidance when she received admissions decisions. Between regional location, campus housing, financial aid packages, and major fields, Winona felt like she had a partner in the process.

As a sophomore in high school, Beatrice went to a college fair and learned more about a public, very-high research activity doctoral-granting university in the West, and her plans to go there and major in applied science intensified by a series of surgeries, where she got to know what it's like to be in the health-care field. After these experiences, Beatrice knew she needed to achieve a specific score on the SATs and focused on preparing for the exams. She had a lot of support from her mom, who helped her find scholarships and much more. "[M]y mom was very supportive with helping me find scholarships," Beatrice reported. She reflected on her mom's support at this time in her life: "And so, um, it was, it was stressful, but she helped, like we literally had like a stack of like Manila folders this high of just all these different scholarships she found." This helped Beatrice know she could go to the university, where she planned and major in applied science, keeping her on track to pursue her career goals.

With Sharon, whose dad seemed to support her interest in college but stopped short of expecting her to go to college and didn't participate centrally in the college decision-making process, friends filled in and prompted her to explore where to go. A business-like transaction of "that's great" when report cards came home and "[o]kay, go to school" characterized college decision-making time, her dad generally felt working hard, not going to school, is what paid off. Sharon remembered well his distant stance to her education when she was in high school. She explained more: "He only stepped foot in my high school when I graduated. [H]e would also come for theater performances. He and my mom would come to see those performances, and then they came for my graduation. And that, but that was it. They, they weren't engaged in, you know, parent-teacher meetings, anything like that." Only one other occasion did her dad come to campus, according to Sharon, and it was when she got into a bit of trouble. She smiled when she narrated the story, and she knew she had her dad's support throughout the incident, as she recounted.

> I did get into a tiny bit of trouble my senior year. It was one of those dumb things that you know, senior prank, a couple of friends thought it would be funny, and it just wasn't. And, and it was a Catholic school, so the principal was a priest, and . . . he was a pretty big, mean dude. He . . . struck fear in the students. [M]y parents got called to the office, and so that was the one other time that they were on campus with me. And . . . the priest was a smoker, and he lit a cigarette in his office, you know, and . . . he's having the cigarette and saying, you know, what was your involvement with this? And, you know . . . what do you kids think you're doing? You think you're funny, you're not funny. And . . . it wasn't so bad that I was going to get kicked out, but it, it was the conversation that was, you know, stern conversation with the principal. It's just like, oh, God! And . . . we walked out of there, and my dad said, was it just me, or did the smoke stand still in the room? You know, like everything stopped for this . . . priest, 'cause he was such . . . a formidable presence. But we actually kind of chuckled a little bit after that. [H]e didn't scold me. He just said, don't do stupid stuff like that, you know. Be respectful.

To Sharon, this story illustrated how her dad cared about who she was and loved her as his daughter—but he had only peripheral connections to her education.

COUNTERSTORIES ABOUT PARENTS AND FAMILIES WHO HINDERED COLLEGE DECISION-MAKING

While a broad range of parental involvement in precollege educational experiences and college-decision making seemed to be a part of graduate student lives in junior high school and high school, some parents and families either did not participate directly or actively undermined opportunities to participate or support children in school. In Susan's case, while her father had a college degree, both her parents seemed to offer little direction or guidance to Susan as she navigated her career path. Susan, a white and Latina cis-heterosexual woman married with children, described how she needed help "in terms of like picking classes, and finding orientation . . . [and] financial aid." She reported that she was on her own and learned a lot that she wished she had known from the start. Career planning seemed daunting to Susan, too, and she needed support from her parents, but with her mom a homemaker and dad an entrepreneur, she "only knew about a few careers, um, like the typical one, teacher, nurse, doctor." She shared more: "I had no idea all the things you could do with your life. So, you know, my dad was a [liberal arts] major so I'm like, well, I like [liberal arts], you know, I'll go learn about that. And then he went to law school, I was like, okay, I'll just, I was kinda just following his path. I, I really had no direction or guidance."

Like Susan, Sharon explained that family dynamics played a role in her feeling alone and on her own in the college decision-making process. In their blended family, the seven siblings tended to be divided on the value of education and college-going. In fact, Sharon explained that only two siblings—two of Sharon's sisters—earned master's degrees, which makes three of the seven siblings total with graduate-level education. Between the tension among her siblings who lined up on the other side of the higher education divide, Sharon felt their criticism about her advanced academic training. She shared what one sibling asked her: "[W]hat do you need all those degrees for? [S]he didn't value education, and she, she's passed that on to her children. [O]ne of her children went to college, but only one."

Not unlike Sharon, Jessica's family undermined her path to college—mostly in the form of critical remarks and negative feedback about her academic self-image and academic self-efficacy. Jessica detailed how her dad undermined her ability to engage in her classes as a student in middle school: "[H]e said that you're gonna fail all your classes and you're not gonna do anything. And I was like, what? Um, um, okay. I, pretty much from then I didn't really care about his opinion, or what he had Or, 'cause if he was like, you're gonna fail middle school, then like he probably doesn't care like that I'm in college or getting a second level degree." Later, in high school, Jessica used what her dad had said as motivation to achieve academically. "I pretty much just said I can do better than what he thinks," she revealed, "so I started pushing myself more. I guess in a way it turned out for the better, but I don't like to give him credit for that." Fortunately, Jessica's mom supported her, and her mom helped her in the college decision-making process. To this point, Jessica said: "But, um, my mom was really the one who like helped me like with applications, and, and looking at colleges, and doing the whole like high school college experience."

Jaime recalled a similar experience to Jessica with Jaime's father undermining who she was earlier in life. Jaime, who identifies as a first-generation Vietnamese American female, referenced a saying or phrase that her dad used to repeat that seemed punitive and threatened the loss of social and familial relationships. She elaborated: "I grew up, I couldn't tell if it's either because, um, one of the phrases that would be told to me if I was misbehaving, right, is like something along the lines of like, oh, no one's gonna like you anymore if you keep doing that. And it's like, oh, really? But it's, it's not word for word like that, but it gave off that impression to me."

Reflecting on her father's behavior when she was younger, Jaime observed a person who singularly focused on her sister's and her education. While Jaime admitted her dad never appeared to be angry, there seemed to be an emotional intensity that—at times—negatively impacted Jaime. Here's Jaime in her own words.

> I saw that he was a very angry person, but he was never, he, he was angry, but he put all that emotional energy towards my sister and my, uh, education. His main idea was that he, he wanted us to be educated, very much. Um, he would be angry whenever I didn't do my homework on time right before I didn't, uh, right before bedtime or something. And he, he was always checking our homework every night, um,

and making sure we had it a hundred percent correct, and if we didn't have it correct we would, he would teach us until we knew how to do it ourselves.

Jaime connected her dad's behavior to his hurt from her parents' divorce and his mother's death—"and possibly other things that happened along the way, too, that was never revealed."

Given her dad's intense interest in and control of her schoolwork, Jaime started to lie to him about her homework. In middle school, she shared how she would delay doing homework until her dad went to bed to avoid interacting with him about it. "I started lying about my homework a lot more often as I grew up," Jaime revealed. Here's more about her strategy: "[I]t would be like around the time that he would, like around six he would have to check my homework, and I would say, oh, I'm not done with it. So then it was just delayed until we had to go to sleep and I was still doing my homework." As she transitioned to middle school and high school, her dad's oversight of her homework tapered as Jaime continued to delay doing it until late at night as the subjects became more advanced.

Even as her dad's overbearing presence in her studies eased, Jaime shared how he helped her as she navigated the college decision-making process. In fact, as Jaime considered community colleges, her dad insisted she go to a four-year university. She connected her decision to go to a public master's-granting HSI university in the West to her dad's guidance, which she appreciated. "[H]e was a big, uh, part in my decision of going into [the university], Jaime shared, "he's like, um, no, you have to go to four-year."

Natasha's time in high school seemed to be as difficult as can be imagined. In her own words, Natasha, who identifies as a straight white female, described a "pretty messy high school experience." Under her mom's guidance, Natasha moved from one high school to another—she elaborated on what happened next in high school.

> My mom attempted to move me to a high school in [the West], but she didn't really research the, um, rhythmic gymnastics program that was there, 'cause that's what I was into at the time, and moved me in with a smoker, and I was like, I can't do this. And I, I bailed. And I ended up finishing high school through a correspondence program. Through, um, [a

> non-public high school] in [the Midwest] where you literally get shipped all of your books and your assignments, and you complete everything yourself and mail it into the teacher. Um, and I could have finished early. I didn't. I ended up basically finishing at the exact same time as I would have if I stayed at the [private school].

Given her experiences, Natasha never really applied to colleges, even though she wanted to go to NYU, for example. She ended up going to a private, not-for-profit baccalaureate college in the Northeast as a nursing major. Later, she moved out West and went to a private, not-for-profit special focus four-year school in the West, after which she decided to go to a community college, to finally transfer to the public master's granting HSI university in the West to finish her undergraduate studies.

Social and Fictive Parenting Roles and Roles for Life Partners in Precollege and College Years: How Bonds Formed with Educators Shaped Early Students Experiences

Before and during college, some graduate students relied on a widening circle of relationships for navigational, social, and emotional resources. Particularly critical for first-gen students, educators who crossed paths with graduate students before they got to college and while they were there offered a mix of advising mentoring, and/or care-taking support in the capacities in the classroom and on campus that complemented what parents did at the time in their lives. In essence, these figures tended to serve in fictive and social parenting roles for some graduate students. Beyond educators, a small group linked precollege and college-going directions to life partners—significant others—who extended the reach of parents and families as bonds of love and care formed.

Zeke's stories illustrate the central importance of connections to a caring educator in his adolescent life. Zeke, who identifies as a married cisgender gay white man and a first-generation student, revealed how this counselor made him feel safe but also supported him on a path to college.

> I would say in high school, after I got out of Catholic school, um, I remember I had this career counselor at [my] high school, uh, [counselor], and he was, um, I was very flamboyant

> in high school, and he kind of met my flamboyancy I think. He made me comfortable. And, uh, I could go into the office if I was having a bad day, and he was just the one there for me. Just still not having that parental unit, you know. Um, and that was that, like that year I met [counselor]. I think that was leading up into that. But there wasn't really that, he wasn't a parent, you know? Like my parents weren't parents. Like they were just kind of like, they're supposed to be, you know, like, but they're not. They, they just weren't. Like going to friends' houses and seeing family dinners, or seeing, you know, even like yelling at sisters or brother.

Zeke felt a special connection to this high school counselor and a safe space in his presence—all of which seemed to support his interest in going to college. Like Zeke, Jeremy connected with a high school teacher who transitioned to his guidance counselor and helped him in the tenth, eleventh, and twelfth grades. Over a three-year span, she supported his undergraduate admissions applications, exploring campuses and majors, and more. Jeremy remarked how she "really helped . . . a lot with . . . college application process," given that neither of "parents knew anything about it."

In college, Stella shared how mentoring relationships in college offered her opportunities to connect closely with fictive-family members who supported her work and development. She described in more detail.

> Definitely in college, my undergrad, I developed relationships with those that I kind of see as, not kind of, but they're my mentors, and more definitely like an uncle-type of relationship. [One] has been in my life and has supported me since I was seventeen, and encouraged me throughout navigating this whole college experience, and has pushed me to be where I'm at today. I work at the university now. And about two weeks ago I did a training, and I trained him. And it was a big, full-circle moment because he's like wow, like I remember, like I was seventeen, you were so lost, and now look, you've achieved so much. And I've always appreciated that, because again I didn't have that at all growing up. No one really like supported me, and just pretty much thought I was just gonna end up being pregnant, or doing drugs, or just not have a life for myself.

Later in college, Stella introduced another mentoring relationship with a professional colleague/supervisor. This time, Stella recalled how he helped her focus on next steps in her life, including graduate school. She elaborated: "[D]uring my sophomore year of my undergrad I joined [an academic support program], and so I would teach [math], and [another mentor] was, you know, the coordinator. [W]e realized we had so much in common. The way we kind of similarly grew up and, um, you know, chose college as our escape." Stella reflected on his role in her life: "And he just also was another person that had me under his wing. And, you know, you just had to be reminded of that, and just been pushed. And now look how much you've achieved. And . . . he's just another person that I still have established a relationship with him."

Gail also had a mentor in college—like Stella. A professor at the community college served as a mentor to Gail while she was a student there. Gail elaborated more on what his mentoring meant: "[H]e was like definitely a mentor for me at [the public, HSI, community college in the West]. Like I always sought his guidance because he, he was just an amazing professor. He got me in an internship at [the public, HSI, community college in the West], and then he was like, the [applied science] program at [the public master's-granting HSI university in the West] is like a really good program." Gail credited, in part, this mentoring relationship as a community college student to her academic achievement and academic identity. She concluded: "I've done really well in all my classes. In my whole college career, I've been like much more focused and dedicated to school."

Andres always felt the pride his parents had for his work in school, and he knew how much they supported him as a student—first by bussing him across town to go to elementary school, then by explaining they'd do whatever he needed to go to college, just like they had done for his siblings. Andres needed the support, after falling behind in his high school graduation credits, he needed help. His parents offered verbal, financial, and social support—and they told him he could live at home as long as he had wanted as long as he was in school. All of this helped Andres with his decision to go to college, but he got there with support from a high school counselor, community college instructors, and a chance encounter with a coworker.

First, a high school counselor suggested a dual-enrollment program with the local community college to make up credits to graduate on time. Offering classes on his high school campus, he felt like he could get a head start on college. Andres went beyond making up high school credits and had earned six college credits by the time he was done with dual enrollment. After he graduated high school, Andres had experienced carcerality and did time in jail related to his earlier gang activity, so he didn't go right to college. But the dual-enrollment classes stayed with him and introduced what it was like to be in college classes. After being released from prison, Andres did a lot of odd jobs, mostly in manual labor, but he was going nowhere. He explained further, as follows:

> [F]irst I started just looking for work. So college was not really a factor at the time, so I needed to work. So I started getting, uh, jobs working, um, construction, uh, working in factories, uh, working as a carpenter, working as a mechanic, um, just all these odd jobs that would hire me without doing background checks. [W]henever I did apply for jobs that required background checks, they, I would get that call that says, you know, unfortunately, you know, due to your, you know, felonious past we're not gonna be able to offer you this position. I was just working full-time. I was working full-time, you know, in construction, and carpentry, and, you know, auto mechanics, and things like that. Anything that, you know had to do with manual labor.

But one day while at work in a carpentry shop, Andres had a brief conversation with a coworker that changed the course of his life. He shared details of the interaction.

> [O]ne of the workers asked me, like hey, what are you doing here? And, and I was like, what do you mean? I'm doing the same thing that you're doing here, working. And he's like, no, no, no, but I mean, he's like, you're young. He's like, you speak English, you speak Spanish, you were born here, you have papers, *tienes papeles.* He's like, you shouldn't be working here, you should be working somewhere in a nice office, you know, with a nice view, you know. And then I was like, what the fuck is he talking about, you know? So he's like, he's like, you need to be in college, he told me. And I was like, and this is an older man, 'cause in the, in, in carpentry shops and in factories, things like that, you're working with older

gentlemen who, who are undocumented, you know, just trying to work. Um, so he told me like, you should be in college, getting . . . getting a career. You're wasting your time here with us. He's like, these types of jobs are for us. And at the time I was like, what does he mean, you know? But again in retrospect he meant like, undocumented folks who have no other choice, but you have a choice.

Andres remembered these words are what drove him back to college—community college where he had first experienced college teaching and learning. Initially, he didn't know what he wanted to do, but it was a turning point away from a life with "gang bangers, drug dealers, and gangsters." His world changed, and he started on his path.

Later in life, both Edith and Jessica shared similar stories about how life partners—Edith's husband and Jessica's fiancé—supported them in pursuit of their higher-education goals. Edith, a first-generation Korean female who uses she/her gender pronouns, described how her husband was honored and proud to help her in her credential program. As newlyweds, Edith and her husband agreed that he'd financially support her credential program studies and ensure that she prepared for her career. Long before she considered a master's degree program, she had her husband's support. She shared what he said: "[M]y husband who said to me, maybe even ten years ago, hey, you, you need to pursue this master's degree, and really and, and be in, in leadership in education because you, like he saw that in me." Jessica, a white female, referenced how her fiancé and his family were always there for her—so much so that their support "rubbed off" on her. Retelling how her fiancé's father's support for their housing, Jessica said that it "definitely helped a lot."

Navigational, Financial, Logistical, and Verbal Support in College: What Parents Did for Children as Undergraduate Students

For most graduate students, parental support contributed meaningfully to their success as undergraduates. The type of support from parents varied from navigational cues about college-going to financial help when tuition bills came due and textbooks or supplies needed to be purchased. But many reported parental motivational comments and positive feedback formed the focus of their identities about who they were and what they did on campus on their paths as college students. And this was especially important for first-gen students. Brianna, who identifies as a first-generation African American woman, shared a touching story about what her mom revealed to her brother and her about Brianna going to college after their dad passed away. Referring to what her dad said, Brianna recalled her mom's words: "I remember when my mom had said that, um, he said, he knew that [my brother] didn't want to go to school so he had told my mom, she's gonna want to go to school, so make sure that that happens."

Angela, a first-generation African American female who identifies ethnically as Nigerian, shared how verbal support from her parents helped her feel good about being an undergraduate student. She described how they responded to news of academic achievement and housing support associated with a resident assistantship. She told me: "If I made good grades, they were like woo! Good job. Or like when I became an RA, that was like a big, big deal. 'Cause like they knew, again, like my family's really, like our church community is really close so they just knew the gravity of what it meant to not pay for housing, and not to pay for a meal plan."

In a similar way, Maria's parents shared verbal feedback about her work as an undergraduate student. Maria, a first-generation LGBTQ-identified Armenian woman, described how her dad, specifically, would use body language to convey his happiness when she talked about her studies. "I would say just more of like the smiling," Maria said, "and you know, or, or just being, or just saying like, oh, good job." She continued: "Like, like just something quick, like not . . . much of expression really per se like words-wise, but more of like just wanting to listen and showing like a positive mood, if that makes sense. But like on my, in my end like education for me is a big thing so I continued, uh, and it really helped."

In many cases, parents tended to focus on primary concerns like how to pay for college and everyday issues like costs for textbooks, meals, and housing or commuting to campus as they offered strong emotional support to navigate life as a college student. Kayla's story illustrates how financial assistance is a critical component of family support for undergraduate studies. To this point, Kayla, a first-generation cisgender African American female, mentioned that her father paid for college and described what that meant for her. She said: "[Y]ou know going to college, like my father paid for, I don't know how he did it, 'cause we were all in school at the same time, but he paid for, he paid for my undergrad. He worked really hard. Like so, so that, like those quiet expressions of this is important for, for you. It's important to me. So I'm gonna make it happen." Similarly, Brianna described how her grandfather coordinated extended family support to fund her undergraduate student costs. She said: "[H]e said, you know, you need money to go to school. You need money to go to school. So, my aunts, they helped, you know, me go to school. Um, yeah. I wrote letters to go to school, get money to go to school."

Both Winona and Jaime had parents who focused on getting them to and from campus and ensuring that they were eating, sleeping, and resting enough—a focus on meeting their essential needs as college students. For example, Jaime's father drove her to and from school, Jaime recalled how she stayed on campus all day to accommodate her dad's work schedule that required her to be dropped off at 8 a.m. and picked up at 6 p.m. What's more, Jaime remarked, "living at home with my parents, I didn't really have to cook." She detailed this living arrangement: "I had all my meals there. There's Wi-Fi. I have a place to stay, of course." Winona had a similar experience as Jaime and described her commute to and from campus with her parents. Recounting how her mom would drop her off and dad pick her up from campus until she got her driver's permit, she shared.

> I was commuting, however[,] I didn't have my driver's license yet. So, my dad was also dropping me off. Well, my mom was dropping me off, my dad was picking me up. So for a good, like August, September, October month, until I got my permit basically, um, they were picking me up and dropping me off from school. So it was kind of a little rough on that edge of like of like, oh man, there's a lot of time, and have to make worth of my time and stuff like that.

Later, when Winona could drive to campus, things improved with her schedule, but her parents continued to focus on her basic needs. Winona recalled their questions turned to her eating, personal safety. Here are some of their standard questions, from Winona's perspective: "How long, um, like what your schedule is. How to get there and back. Are you bringing food along? [O]kay, you get home before dark or something."

For Andres, his parents had not known a lot about much about college, majors, degrees, and so on—but that didn't matter. What mattered was that they wanted all their kids to go to college. And they made it happen. Andres revealed how his dad's support came in many forms, but Andres recalls his dad just telling him, as the "saying goes *échale ganas*.

Figure 6.3. Parents reproduce navigational, financial, logistical, and verbal capital to support children in their undergraduate studies. *Source:* By Oregon State University, CC BY.SA 2.0. https://www.flickr.com/photos/33247428@N08/9067045597.

Échale ganas means like, just give it your all." Andres continued about his dad: "I knew I had his support, by him saying like, you can do it. If you need anything, let me know. [T]hey support me to the extent that they could, but if I know I need them, I know they're gonna be there, you know." What's more for Andres is that his father offered him financial support—which was huge. Not just his father, but his older brother gifted Andres his 1979 Mustang to get started in college.

Like Andres, financial support for college from Eugenio's dad was huge. Eugenio, a first-generation heterosexual married Latinx male who identifies as Oaxacan from an Indigenous Mexican background, recalled how his dad always encouraged him to go to college and both parents provided financial support, including a car to get to campus and home. His dad said how financially his parents would be there for him—they'd work for him. "Continue, I'll be here," Eugenio recalls his dad saying. Both parents used to comment: "We're supporting. [W]e're supporting to you." Given that his older brother stopped out of college, Eugenio surmised that his parents wanted to be sure he knew he had their backing: "I guess they were trying to tell me like, go for it. Go! We're there. They were always there, supportive in that way." As a first-gen student, Eugenio knew he'd be on his own, and his parents tended to not ask "process" questions about his studies but focused on the conversations that mattered to Eugenio, as he remembered: "[T]hey were talking to me a little bit sometimes like, how's it going? Just like here and there, just here just what I'm going through and stuff. I did tell them like, oh, this is difficult, this is what I'm going through. Or you know what, I'm, I'm working this on my résumé."

Similar to Andres and Eugenio, Kaitlyn's dad offered to support her financially in college. Kaitlyn shared how she did not receive financial aid her first two years of college. She had been working but not making ends meet. She detailed how her dad helped her: "I think for each semester it was like, I want to say what, three-thousand. And I think I was short like two grand, and you know he, he offered to, to pay for those two grand." Juan's dad financially helped him as a college student—but only after initially resisting to pay for Juan's education-related expenses. Eventually, his dad came around and strongly supported Juan—but it took some doing. Juan explained further.

> [W]hen I started going the, the college route um, you know my, my dad would say you know, okay, let's do what you have to do, but you know if you like it, uh, even though he, he wasn't happy with, with, uh, you know having to help out with tuition and all of that, um, sort of his mind-set was if, if you enjoy it and it's gonna lead to something that you love doing then, uh, you know, give it your all essentially. And I'd say trying your hardest, um for whatever you do was probably a major one as well.

As a first-year student, Juan didn't have to work—that's the level of financial support his dad gave him. Looking back at his dad's role in his experiences as an undergraduate student, Juan saw him as a "relentless force of encouragement" that "definitely kick-started" Juan's education. Juan illustrated how his dad motivates him in his own unique way: "[M]ake sure like you give it your all, and I'm like, okay."

Like Juan, Edith remembered her father as someone who ensured she had what she needed to succeed in college. Edith shared how her dad had a car, car insurance, and gas for her to commute to campus and back home. But her father did a lot more to support her—from conversations about FAFSA and financial aid to much more. Here's a glimpse at what Edith experienced with her father's support as a college student: "I'm gonna go. I'm gonna find out. Write all the dates, all the deadlines, everything that I need ask clarified questions, things like that. And then I would report it to my dad, and like he would, he would share his then income tax and things like that."

From what Natasha recalled, her dad had encouraged her to go to school and helped pay some of her bills when she left work to go back to school, but his verbal and financial support seemed to be limited and only go so far. Here's how Natasha, who identifies as a straight white female, recounted her dad's overall support for her to go to college: "I think definitely my dad was just like, more like just go to school." Even if he had been more disengaged from her college student experiences, "because he was just trying to work all the time," she felt like he had her best interests at heart. But her dad's verbal support didn't seem to translate to financial support. Natasha elaborated on why he couldn't help her when she needed him the most: "I think he's always worried about finances." As a college student, when she asked to borrow money, her dad tended to offer loans that had to be paid back. "So that part's been frustrating with him," Natasha revealed, "[c]ause you kind of think this is someone who would do anything for me." As a result, Natasha had to turn to family friends for support. In the end, Natasha remembered having to go it alone sometimes, as she mentioned here: "I've had to experience it to figure it out."

Needing logistical support from her parents, Jenna, a Filipina woman, knew her dad would offer her every possible way to help her just focus on her studies—and he was there in every way for her. She referenced her dad's everyday gestures when she was in college: "[H]e's the one who dropped me off at the train station and helped me when I didn't have a job. He helped me pay for the tickets to and from [campus]. Um, and then also I would have night classes, and you know the train doesn't continue into the evening so he would go and drive at like 7 or 9 p.m. at night to pick me up and then bring me back home." Jenna felt like she had what she needed to get her to and from campus and help her with costs associated with her commute, all of which relieved her and allowed her to focus on classes and more.

For Black college students, parental attachment is associated with peer attachment (Love et al., 2009), and both father involvement and nurturant fathering are associated with higher levels of college adjustment (Davis,

2012). Healthy college adjustment tends to promote feelings of belonging and a sense of community, and social adjustment includes development and use of social skills and social support network—which tends to enhance self-confidence and self-concept in social interactions (Davis). Beyond social adjustment, father involvement and nurturance tend to enhance psychosocial adjustment to college, in the form of psychological well-being, and academic attachment, further strengthening connections to campus and belongingness for Black college students (Davis).

When Angela went away for college, her parents visited her and surprised her with creature comforts—like a TV. Here's how Angela described the time they personally delivered a TV to her: "And also they bought me a TV, and I've been . . . begging for a TV. So it was just really, really sweet. Like moments like that, I'm just like, y'all came all the way here? Like, you didn't have to do that. You could have shipped it." These moments, Angela remarked, made all the difference in how she felt comforted and connected to them while away at school. Kayla's parents did the same for her, and she fondly recalled times when they would come to visit her in college. Kayla, a first-generation cisgender African American female, shared: "[T]hey would come up, you know on weekends when he was free, and just come to visit and have something to eat, and just, you know, see how I was doing and stuff like that. I remember eating at, at McDonald's." Her dad made special trips when he was available to "have something to eat" and see how Kayla was doing.

Tanya knew she had her dad's support as an undergraduate student—from check-ins and messages of pride, she felt connected to him and knew he'd be there for her in college. In fact, her dad loved that she was at a large public doctoral-granting, high-research activity university in the Southeast and identified with the school spirit, often commenting how proud he was of her. She described how he supported her "on the back end." Tanya, who identifies as a first-generation heterosexual African American woman, continued: "Like supporting me just like, okay, like, you know you got this, you know we got you." He also supported her financially with her first car, car insurance, and so on. He also connected Tanya to a job at his company so that she could earn extra income for personal expenses.

As a child in rural China, Ping remembers how his parents didn't understand "how the society works, how the university works, how the business works." But, he shared, they didn't need to, as they were "very diligent" and taught Ping—who identifies as a first-generation student—the skills so that he could overcome obstacles and navigate social and educational mazes. What's more, Ping's father helped him to understand that what he did in school was for himself, not his family. Here's Ping: "I feel one more thing my father told me is that, study for myself, not for them." Ping's father said to him: "[Y]ou study for yourself. You study hard you will get a bright future."

Leonardo had emotional support from his parents and family, too, while he was in college. He said simply: "I lived at home, and I worked. [L]iving at home I was, I was with my family . . . my younger siblings." And Leonardo needed his family's collective efforts to get him through a difficult first day of college. Recalling an event that changed his life forever, Leonardo revealed how his undergraduate student experiences started out with a car accident. He elaborated: "Long story short, on the first day driving out there, uh I got into an . . . it was like raining, I got into an accident. [T]he car that I was driving . . . my dad gave it to me, but he, he hadn't switched over the insurance to cover me. I hit someone and I ended up having to, to drop out." What happened after Leonardo left school? He explained he had to "get a job . . . in a warehouse driving a forklift." But he ended up enrolling in night classes at the community college and eventually transferred to the university to complete his baccalaureate degree.

In college, Sharon also had a job working for her dad in the family business. Sharon remembers how her dad supported her in college, saying that she would go home on the weekends, visit with her parents, and enjoy time together. But the more memorable experiences with her dad tended to be when she saw him in the office at his shop. "And so that . . . was my connection point," Sharon said. She continued: "If I ever needed to talk to my dad I could go into the office and have a conversation with him." Working for her dad made her feel supported as an undergraduate, and maybe the fact that his shop and her work there represented continuity in Sharon's life—she had started to work for him in high school—she seemed to feel connected to home and family in college.

As a first-gen student, Jeremy, who identifies as a straight white and Italian cisgender male, the message his parents repeated time and again is that they wanted a better life for him than what they could provide him. But the love and care his mom and dad showed to him far exceed any standard of living—and Jeremy always knew he could count on them for support. Jeremy illustrated how they demonstrated their care for him, recalling a time when his dad drove ten hours without stop to repair his mom's car while she was on her way to visit Jeremy on campus. After fixing the car, he managed to have lunch with Jeremy before he drove ten hours direct back home to avoid missing work. Jeremy knew he could go to his parents any time, even if they "don't fully understand what it is that" he'd been doing. For his mom's part, Jeremy remembered it this way: "That's always been something that like my mom has said, especially in the last like five or six years, I think with them it's like being able to support me if I need it now."

For continuing-generation college students of color, fathers' racialized and gendered experiences benefited children in nuanced and powerful ways. Close father-daughter relationships and intimate and informal conversations between fathers and daughters among Chicana/o families, generational and collective knowledge about college, experiences with discrimination and exclusion, and strategies to navigate the college choice and transition to college processes help to support daughters (Garcia & Mireles-Rios, 2020). The effects of these interactions and relationships between Chicana/o fathers and daughters are significant, improving well-being, college aspirations, and academic success (Garcia & Mireles-Rios, 2020).

For some graduate students, the contexts of close contact between fathers and daughters connected family members and meaningfully shaped the college-going process. While a first-generation college student, Josefina, a straight Chicana woman with children now, recalled how her dad offered support to her older brother when he revealed he wanted to go to medical school after his undergraduate studies. She remembered: "Because he finishes high school, he tells dad, 'hey dad, I want to go to Med school.' And he said, yeah! Go do it! But I can't help you. I don't know how to do that, but I will support you however I can."

But the father-daughter dynamic in continuing-generation college students of color could be seen in father-son relationships, too. In Hector's case, a close relationship with his dad influenced his decisions about college and next steps in his educational journey after high school. Hector mentioned how his dad was interested in what he was learning, no matter the school subject. They especially bonded over discussions about discrimination, exclusion, and systems of oppression discussed in social science classes. Hector talked about general topics and specific conversations that he had with his dad.

> [W]e could talk about those kind of things, yeah, and bond around those kind of things. That was a bonding point that we, him and I could talk about. About, you know the exclu-

sion of Native people, you know, and him giving me good information and good books to put in front of me, um, to encourage that, that thinking and to be like this, this is the history. He gave me this book from Russell Means called, um, *Where White Men Fear to Tread*. . . . And Russell Means was like a main, major, you know leader in the American Indian movement. Um, and just the title of that book made me feel like, yes, I want to read that book, and it empowers me, and it makes me feel like I'm connected to something. And so he gave me like this, this sense of readiness and preparedness to like, so when I go into the school, anywhere I go, I have this knowledge base here that I can, I can feel that I can challenge, and I can speak to. And I can speak to with some authority.

Between these literary resources his dad shared and discussions about social issues with his dad, Hector felt confident about interrogating claims made in school. After high school, Hector went to the same college as his dad—a public master's-granting HSI university in the West. As an undergraduate, Hector knew people his dad knew, and it helped him transition to and engage in academic work and student life. He felt his dad's presence when he was in class and on campus, and he continued to grow intellectually.

While in high school, Eileen, a heterosexual white female, accepted her dad's offers of support to proofread her papers. This helped her, she shared. But later, as an undergraduate, his help with the same type of tasks—writing, editing, and proofing class papers—got to be too much and seemed to be more intrusive. As a high-achieving student who exceeded his expectations for academic performance and worked hard to get into college, Eileen had had enough and admitted how frustrating the situation had become. In fact, Eileen talked about how she pushed back on her dad's insistent offers to help and intrusive questions about her academic work. She detailed more about this.

> In college, I definitely pushed back on it if he ever . . . once or twice he would want to read over something, but he, it, it wasn't necessarily helpful. If having him read over my . . . you know, APA format papers, he, it wasn't really useful. Um, so I pushed back, and we definitely like drew a line. There was a boundary set, at some point I was like, I'm in college, I don't

need you reading over my things, and it's not, it's not useful for me. And I, I'm pretty good about, um, I would say speaking up against, you know, pushing back to my dad.

Eileen's reflections extended to the impact of boundary setting with her dad. She referenced her self-efficacy but couldn't say exactly if or how she had been affected. In the end, though, Eileen knew she had to live her life for herself: "I think in college I was okay kind of separating and, and being on my own."

Like Eileen, Gail's dad tended to be involved in her work as an undergraduate, but in a bit different way: Her dad ended up in the applied science lab of one of her professors and mentors on campus. Yes, this was unusual and not typical of Gail's general experiences as an undergraduate—but Gail remembered her dad's connection to this professor. She discusses this further here.

> Yeah, so, um, my dad actually came to work with the, so I'm in the [applied science] lab with Dr. [redacted] and he's my adviser. And I'm in the [other applied science] lab, which is under Dr. [redacted]. And in the [applied science] lab we had a time when we made tie-dye shirts and screen-printed them for the lab. And my dad and mom are like pro tie-dye people, and my dad does like amateur screen-printing. So he came into the lab and helped us with the tie-dye and the screen-printing. And so my dad knew Dr. [redacted], and I think my dad, you know he would also always called him like [redacted] or [redacted], like he'd never call him the right letters, 'cause it's just [his initials]. And, so I think my dad . . . liked him more 'cause he knew him.

Outside of this anomaly in Gail's life as a college student, her dad's interest in her academic work followed a similar pattern as when she was a high school student—he inquired about her day on campus and more, encouraging conversation about what was important to Gail. They'd go on walks in the evening, like when Gail was in high school, to help her prepare for an exam. "Mostly about the material of classes, or like an exam coming up, or how I did on an exam," she described as she illustrated how he would express his interest in her academic work. Gail's strongest impression of how her parents helped her could be seen in her use of "support system," which she said "has helped a lot, because I, I do still live at home so I don't have to pay for rent or food half the time. And so my both of my parents really have played a big role in that, because I couldn't do it if I didn't have a place to stay, and feel safe, and study in."

Like Eileen's and Gail's fathers, respectively, Beatrice's dad got involved directly in her academic work as an undergraduate student. When she was taking a calculus series in college, her dad stepped in and helped to tutor her. Beatrice, a heterosexual female who identifies as white and Mexican, recalled: "I probably would have tried to get a tutor but he was able to help me a lot then. But I would say, yeah, it was, it was very helpful because that was a stressful semester. But he, um, same thing with that, too, he had to like relearn it but he did his best to help me." More broadly, Beatrice recalled how her parents supported her in college. She illustrated how they both had been there for her. When she had several banquets for graduation, they were there. Here's what she said about it.

> I had all these banquets and stuff for college, and one of them was, um, a banquet that I wasn't, like I wasn't, there was no awards. It was just like, um, recognizing all the students, and I was like, oh, you guys don't need to come 'cause that, my college is two hours away from our hometown. And I was like, you guys don't need to drive, because then they'd drive there, drive back, and then two days later drive back up again for my graduation. And I said, you don't need to come, but they said family is appreciated. And of course they came. Like my mom was superhappy the entire time, and I was just kind of bored. It was kind of a boring ceremony, but my mom was so excited, and so was my dad.

At moments like these and more, Beatrice felt their "unrelenting support" with "a positive feedback loop" in what they said and did—even for the little things in her life as a college student.

Sharon remembered living at home and working in her dad's store when she was in college—and this structure seemed to support her work as an undergraduate student. She felt close to her dad and spent a lot of time with him at the store. Starting in high school and continuing in college, Sharon did inventory, light cleaning, and more. Later, in college, her role evolved into more of an office manager, especially after a second and third store opened. Before the stores closed—due to employee theft—Sharon enjoyed working at the shop and felt connected to her dad. For Sasha she felt her family supported her in college, even if her dad initially pushed her to go to vocational school. She mentioned: "[T]he ways like, my family like most supported me with the whole college thing." She continued: "I think they like really supported me in terms of like helping me like, move and making sure like I was supported like, and just like helping me with like the logistics of that." Later, her dad would visit her on campus and helped financially, too. Both parents, Sasha shared, showed up for important events, which meant a lot to her.

Chapter 7

Parenting Relationships While in Graduate School

Changing Roles, Conflicting Demands, and Remaining Connected Later in Life

In emerging adulthood and later as adults, direct contact with parents took place less frequently, even if consistently, than when graduate students were undergraduates or in high school. In very few cases, parental relationships or educational involvement directly factored into decisions to pursue degrees beyond the baccalaureate or supported transitions and adjustments to graduate education. As more complex decisions about advanced study with major career implications emerged, most graduate students tended to redefine who they were in relation to their families and continued to naturally separate from them, a process started long ago as personal autonomy and individual agency developed earlier in life. Still, the strong bonds that many parents and children formed earlier in life and the cultural knowledge and values in education, hard work, and more reproduced at home generally followed students into graduate school—seeming to serving as a driving force in their studies.

Leading up to and in graduate school, many talked about finding their own way and navigating academic programs and career opportunities with fewer conversations with parents and more consultations with partners, peers, faculty, and mentors. More frequently, parental relationships offered support and comfort and seemed to ground them in their purpose to persist and complete program milestones and entry requirements in the discipline. Over time, increasingly distant but emotionally stable relationships with mothers and fathers—jointly and respectively—meant a dependable voice and steady presence was accessible to them when they needed it. Through praise, affirmation, and brief discussions, parental contributions to graduate school success for their children connected parents to students, which seemed to reinforce family value systems and needs to give back and continue to honor parents for their sacrifices.

New Relational Ties and Close Bonds to Parents and Families Later in Life

Once in graduate school, most students in this project described distant interactions but generally close emotional links to parents. Commonly, parental contact happened less frequently, even if consistently, than when they were undergrads or in high school. And this pattern seems to make sense, given that emerging adulthood tends to be defined by personal responsibility, independent decision-making, and financial independence (Arnett, 2000). While only a few grad students lived at home with family, most generally maintained regular, if less frequent, contact with parental figures and continued to rely on them for motivational support. In a few cases, parents still played an outsized role in supporting adult children in grad school—mostly though career advice or guidance on navigating academic fields.

Over the life course, parent relationships with adult children can shape graduate school experiences—in some cases more directly. For example, while independence follows transitions to emerging adulthood and beyond, nurturant fathering has been associated with higher levels of graduate school adjustment (Davis, 2012). But while direct parental involvement in graduate student lives may have been genuine on the part of parents, adult children sometimes felt a bit overwhelmed, overly scrutinized, or just annoyed by the comments or feedback. More frequently, the consistent "go to school, go to school" and "échale ganas" talks helped graduate students feel connected to something outside of the academy and uplifted by someone whom they feel loves and cares for them.

For a small group of graduate students, close relational ties *and* frequent direct contact with parents remained later in life. Consistent with current patterns in relationships between adult children and parents—parents are involved (Fingerman et al., 2012), provide financial and emotional support (Fingerman, et al.), and both parents and children are fine with more involvement (Miller, 2024), relationship quality with mothers and fathers tended to vary, with a few patterns in how graduate students continue to maintain bonds with one or the other parent. For example, Hector illustrated just how close his dad and he have remained today. Characterized by an overall loving warmth, Hector listed several ways he bonds with his dad today. Even as their sense of humor had changed over the years, they still connected on humor, including "one-liners from different movies . . . or you know from TV shows, or actors, all these kind of things." And jazz music still brings them together. "[W]e listen to a lot of jazz," Hector recounted.

While close ties to parents remained for some graduate students, others described narrower bonds to parents shaped by specific connections to support them as adults and students in graduate school. Zelma, a first-gen cis-hetero Indigenous Palestinian and Lebanese woman, said her dad was happy when she shared her admission into a master's degree program with him and offered to pay her tuition, books, and more. He said to her: "I'll support you whatever you need financially. You need books, whatever the case might be." Later, when Zelma learned about her admission into a doctoral program in applied humanities at a public master's-granting HSI in the Western US, her dad disclosed how he had longed for her to achieve her academic credentials. She said: "I'm older, older, and you know, like at one point we had a conversation not long ago about like, you know, what he had hoped. And he was like, you know I had dreamed that all of you guys would have doctor in your name, you know. I was already in the doctorate program at that point."

When the master's degree in social sciences program at a public, doctoral-granting institution in the Southeast denied admission to Tanya, she opted for a gap year, then another gap year to explore the next move on her educational journey. She remained committed to graduate school but needed time off. All of this happened at an opportune time—just as the COVID-19 pandemic emerged. Tanya knew she was in the right place at home, and her dad took care of her and ensured that she felt the care and love of family. While working as a restaurant trainer for the two gap years during the pandemic, her dad offered her to live at home rent-free—all she needed to do was take care of her personal care items, and such. Tanya shared more about this time: "I'm just gonna take a break after, um, graduating, and they were very supportive. They were happy for me to just come back home, so they were, they were supportive with that. I told them about my plan, like hey, I eventually want to go to graduate school. So my gap year was originally supposed to be one year." Tanya continued, describing how she felt at home and what it meant to be there: "I got to kind of like, just live life a little bit and be kind of like simple, stay at home, I didn't have to pay rent. My only agreement with my daddy was, okay, you don't have to pay rent or anything, just make sure you take care of all of your, your items." She concluded: "[Y]ou know, my daddy made sure, I didn't have to pay anything honestly until, honestly until like, four months until I was about to move out and go to grad school." Things were similar for Andres, who always felt his parents' support with his education. With his older siblings and him, when they graduated from high school, his parents always said they could live at home as long as they wanted and as long as they were working or in school. "And that was it," Andres said, summing up how they all needed this source of love and care in their young lives at the time.

Changing Relationship Quality with Parents Moving Further into Adulthood

For many graduate students, relationship quality tended to decrease as children matured and transitioned to adulthood—characterized by less frequent and lower-quality interactions. Within the context of emerging adulthood, a movement toward more individualism is consistent with being responsible and making decisions independently (Arnett, 2000). But, in many cases, parental support still meant a lot to students. For example, Stella, a first-generation straight African American who is questioning her gender identity, talked about how she reconnected with her dad in graduate school. After separating from her dad as a child, due to a restraining order against him by her mom, and only third-party visitations with him at home, Stella reconnected with him as an adult. After several attempts, she experienced a better relationship with him, even if there was a sadness to their interactions. Referring to her dad, she described it this way: "He doesn't know the adult version of me. So it's like when we try to navigate conversations he will always be like, do you remember like, when you were at this age and this? And I'm like, well, I'm about to be [in my mid-twenties]. I can't even barely remember what I did when I was that age." She concluded: "And you know that's the only things that he's only held on to because that was a time where he was really like in my life."

But Stella knew her relationship, contextualized by traumatic experiences with her dad as a child at home, would be more focused on her needs and tempered by her personal growth as an undergraduate and now graduate student. More measured in her relationship with her dad at this time in her life, Stella shared how he offered his praise and pride for her.

> [W]hen I was applying for graduate school, he was like what? You're applying for graduate school? And that was another thing he was surprised about. But, you know what? It was really nice, um, calling him and like telling him that I got accepted to graduate school, because again he was never there for all the other stuff. So he was crying because, he was just like, you know, I'm honored that you called me to like let me know you got into school because I missed that whole phase that you did when you [were] undergrad. So for him to actually . . . hear that I got accepted, and he was superhappy for me, and proud of me and stuff. And he said whatever decision you make with whichever school you want to go to like, I'm just overall proud of you with like, you know, he said that I inspire him every day.

This was an emotional moment for Stella, but one that she tried to understand from a less personal lens, too.

Tanya shared how her dad needed to "just grow up." Describing how their relationship had been strained as of late, she tended to limit their interaction at times. While she knew how much he loved her, she still needed to move into a more meaningful relationship with him. She shared more: "I was talking to my daddy . . . like two, three times a week. [H]e worked my nerves, we got into it probably like two, three weeks ago, so I'm not talking to him as frequently right now." Tanya reflected on how their respective personalities probably got in the way: "[T]he older I get, just me and my daddy, like . . . our character, the makings of us it's just, bumps head. Um, we're both strong-willed, so you know. I just tell my daddy, you just need to work on like your communication skills and taking accountability."

Many more stories about strained or tense relationships emerged in adulthood. Sometimes physical distance brought parents and graduate students closer. Jeremy's relationship with his dad seemed to grow closer as he transitioned into graduate school and moved farther away from home. Jeremy talked about how they engaged in more conversation and interacted more when he visited on the weekends and holidays, bonding over their love of sports. Growing up as local college sports fans, they planned to get together and go to a home game one day in November. Jeremy explained further.

> Like, so I, what I did was I ended up flying in like 5:30 a.m. on a Saturday, and I left at 5:30 a.m. on Sunday just, just so I could go to the game and spend time with my dad. Um, so yeah. And so like, I think at this point that's the sort of relationship that we have, is like it, sometimes it's like a, I'll see you when I see you kind of thing, um, and like we don't always talk as much.

But Jeremy had reservations about connecting with his dad intermittently, feeling guilty that he tended to reach out when he needed something. Still, Jeremy felt like he had a close relationship overall with his father and mother. He knew he could call home and they'd be there, ready to help him. When he spoke about his dad, he knew how much he was loved. He shared more: "I could tell, and also, um, he loves me to, loves me to the fullest. [T]here are times, even like now in our relationship where . . . there are things that like he says that are . . . that still make me feel emotional, and I know that he is still attached." Today, Jeremy felt like his relationship with his parents had moved "more towards like the friendship side of things in a way." He elaborated: "[T]hey are my parents, too, right, and we do have that sort of relationship. But like conversations will move more into stuff that like maybe they wouldn't have discussed like four or five years ago . . . about relationships that they have with their friends."

Like Jeremy, Maria reflected on how her relationship with her parents evolved since she moved out of their house as a graduate student. When Maria, a first-gen LGBTQ-identified Armenian woman, started her program two years ago, she said her move to her own place seemed to help her parents value her more and, in turn, contributed to healthier boundaries between them and her. As an example of her relationship with her parents today, she talked about how they express their love for her in a traditional cultural way of sharing gifts and food. She elaborated: "I would say, um, just by giving. So like they love giving gifts. They love giving, um, like when I go over to their place, giving food, and fruits, and coffee, like it's a big thing for us. Giving is a way of showing love for them. Um, also nurturing side does come in." Speaking specifically about her dad, he "tends to show a little bit more expression now." Maria elaborated: "Like I've seen him cry when I wasn't around because he would

Figure 7.1. Changing relationships with parents characterize emerging adult children's lives. *Source:* By alcoholica182, CC BY 2.0. https://www.flickr.com/photos/59607188@N04/15689561380.

miss me. Um, or, like just get emotional like, you know, and sometimes to the point where they would think that I forgot them or something, but the reality is not that." Still, her dad does not generally text her, so she has to see him in person. But overall, Maria said, they now know "when to communicate and stuff."

More than improved communication and healthier boundaries, Maria's parents seemed to give more to her and affectionately embrace her. She remarked how she sees their "nurturing side" now. Hugging, touching, and kissing as a way of showing love, too, meant a lot to Maria, and her dad had been doing a lot more of it lately. She described it this way: "I, so my form of language is like, uh, physical touch because of that. So like I tend to hug people a lot, or like hold, hold hands, so he tends to hold my hand, or kiss my forehead. Um, so like just little things like that, like, um, as a . . . way of showing love."

For Karina, a heterosexual Latina who identifies as half Guatemalan and half Mexican, tension seemed to follow her relationship with her dad now. Karina cited both her dad's hyperfocus on careers that pay high salaries and conservative political beliefs for the wedge that had been driven between them later in life. As a human resource manager, Karina's dad tended to ask a lot of questions about what she had been thinking as her ideas about a career evolved in graduate school. Here's how Karina described it: "[H]e also goes in the process of like interviewing individuals and looking at résumés, so he's always telling me like what I need to do and so that can be very stressful in myself."

Even though his efforts may have seemed supportive, Karina shared that her dad tried to "steer" her in a career direction she didn't want to go, resulting in stressful interactions with him. When her dad talked politics, it also could be stressful for Karina. She spoke to this dynamic in detail: "[T]here's also some tension as well because our political beliefs are very, very different. [M]y dad is very conservative." In her academic discipline, Karina noted, there tended to be a stronger identification with progressivism. As a result, Karina felt she couldn't share much about her work in graduate school for fear her dad would be upset. She said: "I don't tell him of what I'm learning about, um, or the experiences that I'm listening to, like students and the diversity of students. And so it's very, it's very hard to talk about that with him, so I, I always avoid those conversations."

Winona, a first-gen bisexual Asian American who identifies as Chinese and Vietnamese, still lives at home with her parents while in graduate school. When we spoke about her relationship with her dad now, she mentioned how they communicated "as much as possible." It wasn't always that way, though, and Winona shared a time when their relationship was under a lot of strain. She elaborated as follows:

> [W]e had one situation where he was also . . . he was concerned about whether I was eating or sleeping enough. So, he kind of blew up on me, kind of snapped. And we kind of took our time to be like separate for a moment. And at that time I was also mad. So I wrote him a four-page essay saying like, this is what's going on. This is how it's gonna happen. I am eating, I am sleeping. It's just you're not seeing it. And, um, I printed that out, and I, I translated it to Vietnamese and proofread it, and then I handed it to him. So, um, it, after that incident we kind of sat down the next day. Like he texted me like, oh,

I got your letter. Like thank you, right. We kind of sat down and talked again, figuring out that why are you stressed, and why are you blowing up on me, and in addition, what is going on with me.

Winona and her dad connected better now. She helped out around the house with chores and the like. She detailed more: "I still help him with his chores outside the yard. And then I help around the kitchen and stuff like that, so I'm, instead of me standing there watching him cook, now it's me preparing the food so that he can cook."

Time together in the kitchen was a way to keep the lines of communication open, but Winona took nothing for granted when it came to her relationship with her dad—they exchanged updates about each other's lives to avoid any relational issues. They avoided assumptions about what each other was doing, which tended to stress them out, respectively. Winona shared more: "So whenever, let's say like, um, at least for me and my dad, we do have a closer relationship than me and my mom. Um, so in that aspect my dad and I understand each other pretty well, and know that we can't come home all mad and then blow up on each other just because. Um, so the current relationship is pretty well."

More and more graduate students framed relationships with parents as friendship. Just like friendly relationships with peers, there had been ups and downs—but overall they described friendships with parental figures in their live. Sasha, who identifies as a pansexual white woman, talked about how her relationship with her dad evolved to a point where they get along well and have more meaningful interactions. While her relationship with her dad was strained when she was younger—due to his emotional instability—she described how they got along now: "Later, he like things have like really calmed down. He's like superchill. Really like . . . philosophical guy, um, which is just like totally different than I, like what I remembered of him growing up. But it's nice. Like I love the hanging out with him now. It's great. You know we have a lot in common."

In a similar way to Sasha, Gail described her relationship with her dad now as a friendship. "Currently it's really good," Gail said. She continued: "I consider my dad like a friend. Um, he's a funny guy. I think he's gotten better at like being more emotionally supportive, like for me and my mom. And, um, I, I consider him a friend. I, I get along with him well, and we joke around with each other a lot." Earlier in life, though, Gail knew that her dad was never all that involved but cited her rebellious teenage years for this distance. Those years seemed to pass, and she and her dad have grown closer—to the point where he expressed his love to her when she left the house for the day. Living at home as a graduate student now, Gail explained how her dad was always home and expressed his love to her in ways she appreciated. Gail, who identifies as a first-generation straight white female, mentioned more: "Like I'll be like, bye, I'm heading to school, love you, and he'll say, love you. Or he'll like give more hugs now, too, when I'm like leaving for a trip, or he's leaving for a trip." Gail felt like this was the way she had remembered her dad when she was younger—holding hands with her and being around for her.

Feeling as though she could tell her dad anything, Beatrice communicated well with him. Beatrice, a heterosexual female who identifies as white and Mexican, still talked with her mom more than her dad and shared more intimately with her mom. With her mom, Beatrice shared, "I oftentimes talk to my mom more about stuff, like if I have issues like in college I'll most likely call my mom. But I know that she always keeps my dad in the loop." She described her relationship with her mom as closer—"it's just kind of a different relationship"—where they spoke more and opened up more with each other. In reality, she admitted, she approached each of them about different things. She shared an example about how she recently contacted her dad about a problem she had with a roommate. She shared more: "But just today I was venting to him about roommate issues, 'cause I'm trying to find roommates, and I found roommates but they're, like we're just trying to find like a location. It's been hard. But, um, so he's always there to listen." She knew that her dad would always be there for her, even as strict as he was when she was younger. As her softball coach, he tended to be hard on her. But that rigidness seemed to soften and evolve into an openness in the relationship Beatrice appreciated and needed more now. Even though they had not been physically expressive in their relationship—neither one liked to hug a lot but they did fist bumps and hug occasionally—they have been there for each other when needed and communicated regularly and on the important issues.

As an adult, Eugenio saw his dad as more involved now. Eugenio, a first-generation heterosexual Latinx male who identifies as Oaxacan from an Indigenous background from Mexico, talked about how his dad would sit with him at home—while watching TV, for example—and connect with Eugenio. They talked about projects around the house and about what was happening in their lives. While his dad is still not emotionally expressive, he responds to events or experiences that impact him. Eugenio feels connected to him at this time and shared more: "Um, just talking about it as well him. His emotions, he don't really share to be honest, I guess, unless he sees something that really happened. I know he'll share if I go with him, like that will happen and stuff, he will just, he broke down before. Um, and he'll say what he's going through."

While many graduate students seemed to move closer their parents as relationships evolved to meet the needs of adult children, a small group felt a lack of closeness to parents—and, in some cases, specifically to fathers—later in the life course. For some, distance between them remained to this day, while a mix of closeness and distance seemed to characterize this time in their lives. More recently Kaitlyn felt like her father and her cared for each other but knew that there was no close connection between them. There had been a recognition that her dad was just not capable of close relational ties. Here's what Kaitlyn, a first-generation cisgender straight Latina, said about it: "I think in terms of like, like a huge emotional connection, we don't share that. Um, but again, like we, we recognize that's, you know our dad."

Juan had similar experiences to Kaitlyn, with a lack of closeness with his dad—and he cited his dad's work schedule as a barrier to time to develop a close, loving relationship over the years. Juan, who shared that his dad is from Mexico, framed it this way: "[I]n terms of expressing love, my, my dad's never, my dad's always been, and I guess . . . it's because he, he would work so much, but he'd be the kind to just come home and as soon as he'd come home, you know, eat, and get ready to go to sleep, and then redo it the next day. So there wasn't a lot of time to bond with him." Juan reported that, at one time when he was younger, he felt much closer to his dad, but then his dad seemed to turn away. Later, he felt like some of the closeness had returned. He shared how his dad, now working just one job, had more time to spend with Juan. When Juan and his dad have spent time together, they tended to sometimes have "an hour-long conversation and it feels like time flew by," for example. Juan's dad has inquired about school and Juan's hobbies, like weightlifting. Juan summed it up this way: "I definitely think our, our bond is stronger maybe than it, than it ever has been, as far as I could remember. Maybe it was when I was a baby and I was, I was this new thing. Yeah, it's definitely stronger than it has been in a long while."

Jessica had experiences with her stepfather similar to Kaitlyn's and Juan's experiences with their fathers, respectively. With Jessica, who identifies as a white female, her relationship with her stepfather was "rocky" until she moved out with roommates and fiancé. After many "rocky nights," Jessica shared that things have improved with her father, but it all seemed to start when she was in high school. At the time, her stepfather tended to equate a messy room that typifies teenage years with drug addiction and personal problems for Jessica. While Jessica conceded that her stepfather had been affected by his daughter's experiences with substance abuse, Jessica in no way resembled her and "never was really into the substances, and, um, illegal contraband or whatever." Referring to her stepfather, she concluded, "It was just him trying to be overbearing, and me rebelling and trying to rebel. Just like at him, not like in grades or school or anything." Now in graduate school, Jessica reported that she hadn't talked with him lately, but she knew that he saw how well she'd been doing. "[H]e hasn't said sorry, or hasn't like acknowledged it, but which is okay, but as long as he is like talking," said Jessica—it was all good. And for Jessica, the close relationship she'd had with her fiancé's father made all the difference in support for her studies and more.

Like Jessica, Natasha left the home in which she grew up when she moved out West to go to college. Natasha, a straight white female, said that while she had only seen her father a few times in the last decade, she remained distantly connected to him and primarily communicated with him via phone calls and email messages. "I mean usually it's just me calling to vent," she mentioned. "And like he'll tell me what he's up to. Um, but it's pretty chill," she summarized. With her father an early riser—given the difference between time zones, Natasha could call him in the middle of the night and he'd be awake. These long-distance conversations helped Natasha to work through issues in her life, and she'd been grateful for their role in resolving problems that she'd faced. She elaborated further.

> [W]e actually do a lot of email communication. Um, which is kinda nice, and, and he'll share like, oh, this is a remodel that I did on the house and he'll send me like a little photo. So it's like we still have that connection, but I think it's, um, he's okay with it being email-based. It doesn't have to be phone-based, or Zoom-based. We'll just, um, it's just like a hey, I watched this cute movie with a cat in it. I think you'd like it, go check it out, you know. I guess he's like, he's always the one that I can pick up the phone and call, anytime, um, day or night, which is really great. He doesn't own a cell phone so it's kind

of like, if you call him it's the house phone that's ringing. It'll, it'll wake him up and like, yeah. Um, you know I think he, I think he's very supportive.

Even with this communication, Natasha questioned how close she could be to her father, as they rarely saw one another. There seemed to be a limit to the connection, from her point of view: "I don't know, like I don't know that I would consider us that close."

For Jasmine, who identifies as a first-generation heterosexual Hispanic female, closeness with her parents seemed out of reach as she transitioned into emerging adulthood and graduate school. When her mom and dad divorced when Jasmine was in the fifth grade, the distance grew greater between her dad and her. He "started making a different family," while Jasmine, her brother, and her mom moved on. For a time, before losing contact with her dad, Jasmine reported that he would visit her brother and her on the weekends, but then it sort of got to the point where he stopped coming over altogether. Fast-forward to when Jasmine went to college as an undergraduate, she and her dad had reconnected and saw each other. She recalled when she moved into the dorms, and he was there for her. Of that time, she said: "Not until that day did he like cry and hug me, and he just, you know, I'm proud of you." Today, Jasmine felt like both parents "have her back" and that she could talk with them. What's more was that her dad more frequently said how proud he was of her.

Residual Effects of Gender-Regulating Relationships in Families: Continuing to Move away from Parents in Graduate School

At the graduate level, complex work manifest in tasks as diverse as identifying and applying to scholarships and fellowships, negotiating housing and assistantship packages, recruiting participants and collecting data related to dissertation and sponsored research, managing professional networks, and transitioning to early career roles. Beyond the complexity of the work, navigating program requirements, degree requirements, and campus environments alone is challenging enough. To have to contend with gendered expectations and patriarchal restrictions in daily life, family relationships, and parental interactions is far too much for most graduate students.

For women who face gender-regulating behavior from parents, especially father figures, it was enough to put a wedge in their relationships with parents. For Angela, whose mom completed her undergraduate studies when Angela was a child and served as the family breadwinner, independence as a graduate student related to her mother's advice when Angela was younger. She explained more.

> [I]n my graduate school career, I'm kind of in this mind-set of like, I don't know. I think growing up too, my mom always taught us like, necessarily like, you don't need a man. Like you, like to be able to provide for yourself, like. And I've had long talks with my mom of just like, her struggle with just provide, 'cause again she's the sole breadwinner for the household so she's like the main one providing and bringing in money. And just talking with her she's just like, well, you know you're getting older. You're gonna get married, and make sure that you have a man who, basically isn't like your dad. Make sure you have a man who is able to provide for you, who's able to take care of your household. Who's able to bring home money and income. Um, so I think growing up I've always been in this mind-set of like, I have to take care of myself first, 'cause I can't be always just taking care of a man 'cause he should be able to provide himself and for our kids too one day.

Beyond what her mother advised, Angela tied early family income struggles, underemployment for her father, and lack of financial freedom for her mother with the need to plan for graduate school study on her own: "I went straight into my graduate program. Um, and I think it's different too, 'cause now I knew, I had more knowledge about like assistantships and everything like that." The result for Angela? She felt confident in which admissions offers to accept: "Um, and then of course when I got like my financial aid packages and assistantship offers they're just like, okay like, this is real. Like, you choose whatever the best package is for you." When the primary consideration is affordability, Angela shared, she knew "the options to pay for it, 'cause that's kind of the biggest thing, like just paying and affording it."

Similarly, Sasha shared how her mom's struggle with financial freedom, due to traditional gender roles in her family, and advice that her mom gave her about being independent, led Sasha to focus on her own agency.

> I think seeing like my mom specifically, like not having a lot of like financial freedom, and just like, not a lot of, I think she like had a lot of regrets about like settling down. Like she got, like they got married when they were like nineteen, which I think is a little young. So I mean, I mean they're still together, so I mean I guess it's worked out. But like I, and then my mom was like always sort of like encouraging me not to do, not to do that. Like to go and like get an education, and like, um, like build a life for myself so I wouldn't be in that situation, um, you know.

Sasha said that this "isn't bad," but she concluded: "I think it's, you know, like having, especially like the financial freedom aspect, I think, for women is more difficult."

Zelma returned to a familiar theme for many women who shared their stories: gender expectations that circumscribe what they could do and not do. For Zelma, she felt a force to marry and leave home as a narrow way to move on in her life. In fact, what she recalled is how her older sister resisted these expectations and went away to school, never returning home. Zelma reported: "As a woman, I need to get married. This is the only way I can get out of the house. But it's funny because, here's my sister who left the house to go, left home to go get a college degree who never returned."

Fathers tended to be central to the reproduction of gender norms, just as earlier in life for many women who shared stories. Tanya, a first-generation heterosexual African American woman, revealed how her dad tended to not understand what she was doing in school but always supported her. It wasn't until later in life, though, that Tanya recalled how her dad started to realize what she had made of herself. She remembered well: "I don't think my dad really realized like, everything until he'd actually seen like my apartment here in [the Southeast]." At that point, Tanya mentioned, "[H]e's like, oh, okay, I get it. Like okay, this is what you, okay, okay, okay. And so now he kind of understands a little bit, like a more, a little more than he did before." She repeated about his support: "But, again, kind of that same theme of like supporting me, not really knowing what's going on but trusting my judgment, and just being there for me, you know every step of the way. And being a good like financial support for me as well."

Jenna, a first-generation Filipina heterosexual female, talked about how, at times, she struggled with her dad to do what she needed and wanted to do in graduate school. With her dad's expectations for her to be at home and spend more time with the family, she had to push back. She explained: "I just wanted to say that it's been a struggle, but one, a few wins is I was able to go to the [redacted] conference for one night. And then, so yay! My first night traveling somewhere without my family. So that was, that was crazy, but it was, it happened." Speaking to boundaries she's setting with her dad, Jenna concluded: "I'm kind of pushing those boundaries and advocating for myself as well. I mean I still have an ideal semester, but I'm kind of at a happy, like a good median point."

While in graduate school, values and role conflicts arose when, for example, family connectedness and gendered expectations mediated conversations about academics. This was the case for Jenna, who described a recent fight she had with her dad "because he was upset about how I've overcommitted to a lot of my . . . academics and extracurriculars." Jenna continued: "And it's mainly because he, he told me that he wanted me to make sure I rest and spend time with the family." But she contended: "I'm very, like I said earlier, I'm very career focused. So a lot, I tend to overcome it, and do a lot on my plate throughout the week." Jenna summarized it this way: "I'll have to say, hey, I'm not gonna be home. And again the tension is like . . . I don't want you coming home late. Or, why don't you come at home, you know chores or spending time with family."

As adults, women who participated in this project described how they had to set boundaries with parents and, more often, father figures. Across women in the project, negotiating new normative limits could be challenging but necessary to maintain a healthy bonds. While renegotiated relationships with fathers tended to characterize the status for most women, a few reported strains in their connections with fathers—partly due to boundary setting. Perhaps related to how gender circumscribed behavior in social settings outside the home or how fathers felt a need to monitor or police them more closely, a few students talked about the need to negotiate relational boundaries where fathering relationships still included intrusive questions about careers or unwanted advice about professors or peers, for example.

Tension developed in current relationships with fathers where fathers tended to overstep relationship boundaries with overly intrusive questions about school or oversharing of personal issues. Jenna spoke directly to the need to set boundaries with her dad. She prefaced, "[I]t's a little bit different, but you know my family is very family based, and, and I, I admire that value. I like it." But Jenna continued: "I think I've kind of, um, changed. [H]ow do I say it? Like not as much family based as how I'm growing up, but . . . continuing, you know the importance of family in the future when I'm going to have my own family." She concluded, "So still that, but also setting those boundaries of you know, being able to grow in other aspects of my life."

When Values Conflict: Fathers' Focus on Family Unity Collides with Emerging Adult Children's Work in Graduate School

Jenna reflected more on values that elevated family unity for her father. She surmised that gender regulated her father in his push to keep family together and protect women in the family. Jenna spoke to this dynamic: "[Y]ou know the generational and cultural thing. And so my parents, especially my dad you know with two daughters, he, he wanted to shelter us, you know protect us" from danger he perceived in their community. But later in life—now in graduate school—the same pattern persisted, and Jenna interpreted it a bit differently now.

> And that's gone on, and since I'm the elder child, you know I'm the one who's pushing those boundaries of, can I do this? Can I do that? Can I do, I want to do research, but this requires this commitment. Or I want to go to this um, this convention, and that requires me to go to [a city in the West] and stay over the night. So it's, there is that tension of you know, why are you doing this? You should stay safe at home. And then other things too where I want to go out with friends, or do extracurriculars like research, like I'm part of research, so doing that, part of a club. And so it's more of, you should, you know you should stay at home, spend this much time with our family. Um, you know and, and sometimes he says, I wish I spent more time with you guys as kids. You know he feels like there wasn't enough time. So there's a little bit of tension there. Whereas my sister, my sister, she's more of an at-home person. They kind of have similar personalities. So it's like, okay, I'll stay home, no matter what. My mom and I are more, can we go out? Like let's go explore the day, you know.

Jenna concluded that there continued to be tension with her dad that led to periods of silence and distance between them. Had it been resolved more recently? Not really, Jenna reported: "That's something that I'm still trying to figure out, because I'll try to share my point of view . . . I don't think I'm truly being heard from my perspective. I kind of lose hope and give up at a point where it's like, okay, I can only say so much." She lamented that there's no "connecting and talking about okay, what can we do next time?"

Tension, at times, seemed to characterize Eileen's relationship with her dad while she explored program options for graduate school. After she settled on a major in the social sciences, she knew she had to finish an MA degree for her career. But when she shared evolving plans about where to go and what programs interested her, she discovered her dad's contempt for programs he deemed to be beneath him as an academic. She shared more.

> [F]or a long time I'd wanted to do a particular area of applied humanities, and, um, my dad was not supersupportive of that. Um, and I, I'm glad he wasn't 'cause I, I don't think that would

Figure 7.2. Peers serve as support networks in precollege and college education. *Source:* By University of Essex, CC BY 2.0. https://www.flickr.com/photos/46452859@N03/10871201174.

have been the right profession for me, but it . . . was like a little moment of conflict. [M]y dad is, can be, he can be a little, um, elitist I would say, a little bit judgmental. I think [it]'s a little hypocritical of his background and his upbringing.

Later, Eileen revealed how she explored going into nursing or dental hygiene, but her dad swiftly denounced her plans, arguing that he could not tell his friends his daughter would be a dental hygienist.

Once in graduate school, Eileen talked about how there were "little areas of conflict" with her dad that centered on his insistence on helping her with her academic work, even as she described their relationship as positive. She shared more: "And even still in grad school he's been, if you want me to, if you want a second set of eyes on your papers, like, I do not send him anything now. But, um, yeah, he always wanted to, he would always proofread and edit them for me."

"And Both of Them Supported Me": A More Limited but Meaningful Role for Parents in Graduate School Decision-Making

Even as parenting relationships had little to no direct effects on decisions to go to graduate school, emotional and motivational support from mothers and/or fathers seemed to be central for many graduate students. For Gail, proximity to home served as a strong factor in where to apply to graduate school, as she felt being physically close to her parents would help her remain emotionally close. And her mom needed more support, too. Gail spoke more about it: "I definitely want to try to stay in state so I can be close to my parents. Especially since my mom's like not necessarily the healthiest, so I don't want to move very far from them." Kaitlyn also felt a need to stay close to home for graduate school. She explained how her parents—and her mom, in particular—had anxiety about her not being at home. She explained more: "I think my mom especially, like they both have like this anxiety of like what's gonna happen if they're not home type of deal. And it, I think it really pushed on me specifically of like, okay, maybe I do have to stay home, um, for them, you know. But that was, so that, that's one of the biggest reasons why I did stay at [the public master's-granting HSI university in the West]." Gravitating toward research as an undergraduate student, Kaitlyn didn't know exactly in which direction she wanted to go—but her sister did. Kaitlyn narrated further: "And my sister, because she's a, she's a teacher for kids with special needs, she mentioned how, oh, I should become a physical therapist. Because, you know, they help people, and they're able to do inpatient care like in, uh, hospitals."

Coupled with Kaitlyn's interest as a sports fan, she explored physical therapy as a career and knew graduate school study would be where she went next. Her parents—like her sister—served in a "guiding role" but never really emotionally supported her. Referring to her parents, she explained: "I think in terms of like them communicating their hardships in college, there wasn't really huge communication. Um, because I think similar to my relationship with my dad, with my siblings it's kind of that same thing of, like a guiding role, but there's not a huge emotional type of attachment."

Sometimes, all it took was a parent to say they'd be there for a graduate student to feel supported. As Josefina put it, her father's supportive comments about her decision to further her education meant a lot. Josefina, who identifies as a first-generation straight Chicana woman with children, remarked: "Like, you know when he knew that I decided to go back to school and get the doctorate, he said, oh, he was so, he was so proud, and he was just . . . so full of joy." When Jenna, who identifies as a first-generation Filipina heterosexual female, revealed her decision to go to graduate school and pursue a master's degree at the same university where she just did her undergraduate work, a public master's-granting HSI in the West, her parents supported her. After graduating with her baccalaureate degree, she discovered that she needed higher credentialing to enter her applied science field. She shared the rest of the story: "And then I find out no, you have to go through a program and pay for it. I told my parents the pathway. I did all of my research and they both supported me, and we're saying . . . yes, go for the assistant program. And both of them supported me." As Jenna contemplated taking a year off to save tuition money for her program, her dad expressed his concern. She revealed: "My dad was only worried that if I take a year off I'm going to lose my motivation and all of that. But he still supported me because I had this pathway. So as well he . . . just wanted me to make sure that I had a pathway and I was still determined, and that was fine. But he fully supported me going back to grad school." Ultimately, Jenna's family's support meant a lot to her work in graduate school.

Parental excitement about graduate school seemed to matter to several graduate students. Hector's dad expressed elation about Hector's decision to go to graduate school. Being deeply embedded in the "culture and mystique" of campus, his dad was all about Hector getting his MA degree at a private, not-for-profit, very high-research activity, doctoral-granting university in the West. "He's a huge fan," Hector said about his dad's close emotional connection to the campus. Later, when he planned to get his doctorate after eighteen years away from school, Hector's dad was equally excited, as Hector, a cisgender heterosexual married male who identifies as a person of color with multiracial and multiethnic identities of Mexican, Filipino, Italian, and Native American, would be continuing the family tradition of terminal degree attainment after his great-grandpa earned a doctorate. For Maria, both parents were excited about her decision to apply to graduate school. She said: "I just applied one day and I was like, hey, I'm going into master's. They're like, oh, cool. Like that's exciting, like, that's it. But they were like happy about it."

While Jeremy's parents knew less about differences between undergraduate and graduate degree programs, they could tell what he was doing was at a more advanced level, based on his more intense engagement in the material. "They can tell a difference, they can tell a difference in my personality between like maturity and level of understanding, and like, I know what I'm doing now, and like I can see where I'm going in my career path, and they're very comfortable in that regard," Jeremy explained. They backed him and gave him their full support for graduate school. They wanted a better life for him than what they could provide, according to Jeremy, and he could feel this in what they said to him.

Black doctoral students—especially from middle- and upper-income families where at least one parent has a graduate degree—report how early messaging from parents about graduate education supports their academic work and program completion (McCallum, 2016). Black graduate students who shared stories here talked about how they had felt supported by their parents to go to and succeed in graduate school. Even when plans to apply to graduate school evolved, Black graduate students felt supported at home. Angela, a first-generation African American female who identifies ethnically as Nigerian, revealed how involved family had been in her life as a graduate student. She shared: "[P]retty involved and pretty supportive. Sometimes they don't know what I'm doing even now in [applied humanities], but they're just like, okay, she's just doing something. She's getting her master's. So that's pretty good." Angela repeated how her parents reinforced her decision, in part, based on the institutional support for her studies. She said: "And my parents were like, they were like, as long as it's paid for you can go to Alaska and we'll be fine. Like we'll support you."

Figure 7.3. Many graduate students frame faculty mentoring and advising relationships with faculty as key to their success in graduate school. *Source:* By MDGovpics, CC BY 2.0. https://www.flickr.com/photos/64018555@N03/8904617226.

For Black women, in particular, father involvement shaped their interest in and movement toward doctoral studies and careers in mathematics (Borum & Walker, 2011). In fact, exposure to math at a young age via practical applications, homework help, and games played with their fathers and/or grandfathers contributed to their preparation for the doctorate. In addition to family, high school teachers, college professors, peers, and enrichment programs all seemed to serve as sources of support for Black women mathematicians in doctoral programs (Borum & Walker). More generally, extended and fictive family members—communities of caregivers—tend to form networks of support for Black doctoral students (McCallum, 2016) and Black women in their professional careers, where extended family networks shape self-efficacy and self-confidence to for career success (Pearson & Bieschke, 2001).

Kayla, a first-generation cisgender African American female who is married with two children, shared how her extended family helped her go to college and formed her support network when she was an undergraduate student. She explained: "My father's brothers and my mother's brothers as well. Just like, not a whole lot of conversation about it, but you know, yeah, if this is what you need, this is gonna help you be a good person and achieve your goals, I'm gonna help support you, right."

With Tanya, extended family—her dad's dad and dad's brothers, in particular—helped her get through school. Tanya recalled how her grandpa and uncles were the "big push" in education and helped to financially support her educational expenses, too. But her extended family included her dad's friends, and their care, along with her uncles and grandpa, always made her feel supported. She shared how they would praise her about how she'd always take care of herself well. Here's what this meant to Tanya: "Kind of instilling that and help build my self-esteem, you know or making sure my self-esteem was really good before coming into the world. I had, when it came to building my self-esteem, really good role models coming from my uncles, my daddy, and my [grandpa]." Tanya's mom connected her to women in the family, too, and Tanya felt their support. She said: "And my mom did an amazing job with that, and the women in my family [whom] I had [around me]."

Uncles played a prominent role in Tanya's educational journey. In fact, her grandpa, dad, and dad's brothers were all big into supporting Tanya as a student. Her uncles, in particular, and her dad's friends pushed her to see herself as smart, talented, and academically gifted. But they helped financially, too, and ensured that Tanya had what she needed materially to finish her degree. Tanya elaborated on how her extended family supported her: "[L]ike all of the males around me, even my, my daddy's friends, um, my uncle was my, my older uncle's cousins and things of that nature, and my brothers as well like, just instilling like, you know you're smart, you know make sure you, you take care of yourself, and things of that nature." Similarly, Tanya's mom and the "women in the family" reinforced Tanya's academic self-confidence and supported her in everything she did. In the end, Tanya felt her family relied on her judgment in terms of what she did at that time in her life. While her parents had little say in where she went to graduate school, they trusted her. She remembered their overall approach: "I know she's gonna go to a college that's best for her, and if she needs help she's gonna let us know."

Even with all the support from family and friends, Tanya needed time off after finishing her BA degree. She shared how her parents understood: "I was just tired, and I just needed a break. And so, I talked to my mom and my dad about, you know, hey, I think I'm gonna come home.

I don't think I want to work, like I'm just gonna take a break after, um, graduating, and they were very supportive." With Stella, a first-generation African American who uses gender pronouns she/her/hers, her undergraduate and graduate work "has been a big culture shock within my family that they definitely had to get used to." Given that Stella's the first in her family to go to college and graduate school and transition to a career in an institution of higher education, her family has been "intimidated" and "surprised," but it's "something they're getting used to."

With several students whose parents migrated to the US or who were the first in their family to go to college, the process to explain their decisions to go to graduate school ensured they had parental support that helped them to transition to graduate student roles. Leonardo, a first-generation straight Mexican American male, recalled just how important his parents—and his father, in particular, were to his success and what his accomplishments in graduate school meant for his parents. Leonardo elaborated about what he shared with them: "I set out to do something, and . . . I got it done. You know, with my dad, and you know, being proud of, of raising us the way he did . . . encouraging us." Leonardo continued, describing how he showed his dad his gratitude: "I was grateful for the opportunities that he, he provided to us because of his sacrifices coming to this country . . . and going through the struggles that he went through. "I wanted to let him know that this . . . is me showing you how . . . I appreciate what you did."

Not just one conversation but a series of discussions about his career plans and how a master's degree aligned with his steps to promote in his role as a school psychologist and help him serve families in education, Leonardo described how he was encouraged by his parents. Leonardo explained that his parents were proud of him, as he shared here.

> I think they were proud. But taking on this new, you know, I guess challenge, and explaining to them the same thing I just explained now, you know that I want to help, you know, I want to, I want to do what, what needs to be done for the people who don't know, you know, don't have that person to go to, I think it was, it was big for them. And I think they, they saw that I was capable of doing that, you know, because they saw me with my siblings and how I was with them, always encouraging and supporting them. And so, and they, you know they were definitely supportive.

Leonardo said his dad "always would say, yeah, but you're working towards something and that's important. And you're helping others, that's important. And so, he would always just let me know that I was on the right path." Leonardo's dad would check in with him and share his pride about what Leonardo was doing, which was important to Leonardo. Later, when Leonardo decided to apply to a doctoral program, the pattern persisted. He reported how he explained to his parents what the degree meant to his career and what he would endure as a doctoral student. Leonardo recounted what his dad said: "And so I, you know, told him about the doctorate, and you know, he was very proud. He said, you know, that's good, you know. I'm proud of you. Keep doing it, you're doing great." Leonardo concluded, he knew his dad was proud of him, primarily through bragging to family and friends.

While her father had passed away years prior to her pursuit of a doctoral degree, Holly recalled her mother's pride in her admission to the doctoral program. But between the time she interviewed for doctoral program admission and enrollment in fall term, her first term in the program, her mother passed away. Struggling with the loss and in incredible grief, Holly—a cisgender heterosexual white woman who identifies ethnically as Russian—still felt anchored by her parents, while just trying to survive in the moment and get through that period of her life.

Sasha seemed to say her family split in terms of support for her to go to and complete graduate school. Her dad, ever focused on a "real job" and immediate employability, didn't appear to help Sasha as she transitioned to and completed her master's degree before starting doctoral studies. Her mom, by contrast, was there for her. Sasha explained that with her parents, they "don't really talk about it that much other than like," instead focusing on "the whole like if I'm gonna get a job or not." With her mom, though, Sasha felt well supported: "But my mom is like, my mom is like definitely, I notice it about my dad, but I don't think, in terms of like staying in school and getting education, I, like my mom has always been like, I think much more supportive of that. Like, like when I finished my master's my mom was like, really like happy."

For graduate students who self-identify as being raised in poverty, a parent, family member, and teacher form support networks to succeed academically (Turner & Juntune, 2018). Stella talked many times about her network as a critical source of support from high school to graduate school. Speaking to her upbringing, she mentioned how she was on her own: "[T]he way I grew up it was so frugal, so poor that it's why I was able to survive at such a young age to just move out of my own and kind of navigate everything on my own." But Stella's academic network, in particular, supported her in applying to college as an undergraduate student and later as a graduate student. When she referred to her intern supervisor from her undergraduate degree program, Stella described her passion for the work and support from her to follow a career that interested her and go to graduate school to advance in her career. She elaborated as follows:

> So with that I was so passionate about the [applied science and applied humanities] stuff, and so my intern supervisor, her name is [redacted], which is another mentor of mine, um, I was telling her about how I'm kind of stressed. Like I don't know if I should do master's right now, and I know what I want to achieve like, I need my master's for. Um, but she was telling me, you know with graduate school it's not a race.

When she was ready to apply to graduate school, she reached out to her intern supervisor and another mentor to support her. She spoke to their roles: "And they're like you know, if you're ready, you know I'll support you. I'll encourage you. You need a letter of rec, you need anything like, you know you could always like email me. And so that's what I did. They did letter of recs for me. They supported me throughout this whole process."

At the same time, first-gen doctoral students report high expectations related to program completion from family and a divide between family and academic life (Holley & Gardner, 2012). For first-gen grad students who spoke with me, stories about being on their own and navigating both the graduate school admissions process and graduate school studies on their own—many with support from parents and involvement from peers and mentors—emerged from experiences with adversity, tenacity, and resilience as undergraduate students determined to continue their educational journey. Talking about the need to take a gap year between undergraduate and graduate education, Stella described how she was on her own—with the stress of it all taking a toll and needing to take a break in studies. She elaborated: "Of course you gotta establish a full-time job. Keep in mind, since I'm doing everything on my own right, like I need to financially take care of myself." Referring to her initial graduate school application and the advice of her undergraduate intern supervisor, she concluded: "So dealing with all of that, um, I just ended up pulling my application out and taking her advice, um, and taking a gap year." "You know, figure out the application, get that submitted, things like that," is what Winona remembered about her parents when she shared her plans to apply to graduate school. She recalled being on her own in the application process, but it all went well. She reported: "So it turned out well. And they're kind of like, after that point it was kind of like based on my decision, but still talking to my dad like, hey, like I'm considering this and I don't know what to do, kind of conversations again." Winona, a first-generation bisexual Asian American who identifies as Chinese and Vietnamese, said her parents supported her and she knew she could count on them as the navigated the admissions process. Reflecting in the cultural value of education, Winona talked about how her parents encouraged her to continue her studies at the graduate level.

> I mean they, both my parents encouraged it anyway, because not only that, it was just 'cause, they just want to see . . . I don't know if it's like a, a Vietnamese thing or so, too, but like the more degrees you have the more respected you are in a sense, in that aspect. So, it could be in that perspective that they were having it, but in addition it was like as long as it helps with your career path of what you want to do.

She said her parents would support her all along the way, noting what they said to her: "[T]hey, they were like, okay, yeah, it's totally fine."

When Andres, a first-generation able-bodied cis-hetero male who identifies as Mexican, specifically Mexicah and Tepehuani, shared his plans for graduate school, his dad immediately responded in a familiar way: "*echale ganas*." Andres knew he had his dad's unshakable support to go to graduate school. His dad would check in and asked Andres if he needed help with applications, financial aid, and more. His mom supported him, too. She would share her pride and praise, letting him know how well he was doing—and his parents were there when he needed it. But his parents could only do so much, as Andres navigated more complex institutional and program processes for admissions to graduate school. Instead, Andres started to explore graduate programs on his own and consulted folks in the department. He shared more: "I just figured it out on my own. You know, doing research, you know, and just researching and figuring stuff out, I started talking to folks in . . . the department and they were kind of guiding me on how to apply for graduate programs."

When she was an undergraduate student, Beatrice shared that she didn't know a lot about graduate school. Like Andres, she knew she had to advance in her studies and continue doing research, but she had to first figure out what it was she needed to do to start the application process. She revealed more: "I had no idea what graduate school was going into undergrad. I don't know why. I don't know why I didn't understand, but I remember I was applying for a job and they were like, oh, are you a graduate or undergrad here at [the public, very-high research activity doctoral-granting university in the West]? And I was like, graduate. And, and then they were like, really? And I was like, wait, what's that again?" Focused on staying at the public, very high-research activity, doctoral-granting university in the Mountain West where she was an undergraduate, Beatrice wanted to work in orthopedics—"just being a bridge between, um, engineers and the surgeons, and kind of helping improve surgical practices, procedures."

When Beatrice got word that she had been admitted and received a stipend and institutional support to cover tuition, her parents were excited. She shared how "they were very supportive." Later, she revealed more: "But I think it hit all of us after graduation. I was like, wow, this is, like that whole chapter is done and now I'm actually like going to grad school." As she prepared to transition to her program, Beatrice anticipated needing to connect with her dad, in particular. Here's how she put it: "He hasn't given me any advice about grad school per se, but I'm sure I'll be calling him up asking for help once I start."

Early in the graduate-school decision-making process, there seemed to be a common response from parents: go for it. This general endorsement often translated into a sense of support and confirmation that it was a good decision to continue work toward a graduate degree. For example, Jessica, who identifies as a white female, recalled telling her mom about how—with a bachelor's degree in her field—she "couldn't really do anything like, like high-paying wise" and probably needed to get a master's degree. Jessica concluded that she needed an "extra credential and possibly research" before entering a doctoral program in physical therapy. Similarly, when Natasha was exploring teaching dance and physical education (PE) or going into the physical therapy field, she reported that her dad offered general encouragement. "[J]ust go to school," he said to Natasha, "get your work done."

Hua, who identifies as a Chinese female, had a similar experience to Jessica and Natasha, but the details diverge from their stories and follow what Hua identifies as a family expectation for advanced study. Hua recalled how she shared news of her interest in a PhD program with her parents, who reacted with little excitement but strong support. Hua surmised that their initial response had been largely devoid of emotion because there may have been a general expectation for her to do the same as her dad and uncle did: get a PhD. She recounted: "And then PhD is also a really normal thing in this family. I, my, my major professor, I'm not the first PhD in this family. So my parents isn't like. Okay, did you did it? Okay, fine. It's like not a big celebration like oh, you are the first . . . generation of PhD. In your, your dad and uncle already [have one]." As the time to make a final decision approached, Hua knew she would have her parents' unwavering support. Hua spoke to this point, when she recalled how her dad told her to go to the US to study, regardless of whether she received institutional support—he would underwrite her terminal degree studies, if needed. Hua recalled: "I actually told my parents if I apply to a graduate school in America and I got the scholarship, then I'll get to the graduate school, if I'm not getting the scholarship and I'm not going to graduate school, and you just go to work." But her dad responded: "[I]f you still want to get to graduate school . . . we can support you."

Chapter 8

Where Parents, Families, and More Fit into Academic Life and Student Outcomes

Spanning elementary, secondary, and postsecondary educational sectors, this project expands on what we know about how families and parents impact graduate students of color and first-generation graduate students on their educational paths. Focusing on how children relate to parents over time, graduate student stories emphasize both interdependent and agentive patterns in their life journeys and academic trajectories. Over time, the ebbs and flows of children's relationships with parents illustrate how families form essential assets among many that graduate students possess and how families are integral, if invisible, members of educational communities with key support and foundational resources for academic success.

Leveraging a family socialization lens that centers familial roles in children's development (Kalmuss & Seltzer, 1989), focusing on significant moments over time with a life course perspective (Roy & Settersten, 2022), and using a community cultural wealth framework that embraces the strengths of families of color and first-generation families, this project frames what students learn from their upbringing as assets that they take with them into graduate school. All of this affirms the positive roles of families in the long-term success of first-generation graduate students and graduate students of color.

Taking it all in, it's clear that unique patterns in families shape children on their routes to graduate school. In this project, familial contexts generally impacted the trajectory of children who navigated elementary, secondary, and postsecondary educational systems toward graduate school and prepared graduate students of color and first-generation graduate students for academic study at advanced levels. Through cultural knowledge reproduction and value transmission, parents contributed to how graduate students negotiated academic spaces, programmatic and institutional environments, demanding schedules, and degree requirements.

Considering specific contributions of families and parents, in particular, you can see that they seem to lay foundational values that center education, advance interests in giving back to family members, circumscribe agency to act early in life, enhance beliefs about serving a greater good and broader humanity, affirm curiosity to explore important questions about society, structure material and emotional support to persist in educational institutions, and offer care and love that help to navigate academic and career experiences. To be sure, parent relationships and involvement in education do a lot to support children in their pursuit of advanced studies, but they appear to have their unique place among many dimensions of graduate student lives. Throughout stages of development from a young age to emerging adulthood, parents tend to socialize children to live by a set of values that drive career and academic aspirations and support a work ethic that leads to strong academic performance.

As primary agents of socialization, most parents tended to use a mix of direct messaging, discussing, modeling, and encouraging to reproduce cultural knowledge as integral to raising children into a family system that reinforced a constellation of important beliefs that supported children's educational journeys into and beyond graduate school. These values seemed to connect children to broader forces in the family and community and facilitated engagement with people in the family, at school, and in society. Indeed, families tended to teach children to value education and simultaneously reify a set of beliefs that supported navigating schools and colleges. Indeed, parents built a family unit that developed values to promote family unity and spirituality. Early and ongoing recognition of familial and ancestral sacrifices encouraged children to give back to parents and remember where they came from. For some, this idea led to more empathetic and compassionate needs to give to others or contribute to broader community well-being. Further, resisting gendered roles and challenging racialized structures contributed to a sense of social justice. Even if some values didn't seem directly related to education, what parents communicated as important beliefs in the family tended to be translated into a support system for children to navigate educational sectors and persist in their academic pursuits throughout graduate school.

Early in childhood, a turn toward independence—sometimes forced on children by factors external to families but also encouraged by parents in family value systems—followed most graduate students later in life. This personal autonomy seemed to be associated with a sense of agency and self-efficacy, often taking the form of doing things on their own and figuring out what next steps needed to be taken to achieve their academic goals. Sometimes family values molded children's identities as independent, while at other times familial circumstances required children to navigate entrenched institutional barriers to full parent participation where limited English language fluency needed to be accommodated at school.

In a family system that elevated education to a position of central importance, many parents participated in their children's schooling. For most graduate students, parents consistently delivered emotional encouragement and financial or material support during elementary and secondary school years. Through homework and assignment help, regular check-ins and consistent affirmations about academic abilities and identities, parents created environments at home for children to pursue educational goals and achieve academically. For some, precollege, school-based parental involvement in conferences, classrooms, and school events further reinforced family values on education and offered a unique form of academic support to children. For a small group, anti-immigrant institutional barriers to language accommodations and limited opportunities to be on campus with job schedules that prevented daytime participation in school events obstructed direct participation in school—so children had to lean into more independence and agency to navigate schools and classrooms alone. In college and graduate school, most parents supported students through encouragement and praise.

Looking back over the life course, parents and families formed part of a complex system that supported graduate students to successfully navigate and complete postbaccalaureate degree programs. At transition points from high school to college and undergraduate to graduate school, parents served in critical support roles, offering a mix of material, financial, and emotional help to their children. In graduate school, encouragement and emotionally close but often physically distant parent-child relationships continued to support students. Beyond parents, peers, faculty, and professional colleagues seem to contribute to graduate student experiences. At this point in their lives, families and parents complimented a broader system of direct academic and career support from graduate student peers and faculty mentors and advisers. At the center of all of it are the

288 | Shaping Students of Color from Preschool to Graduate School

Figure 8.1. Parental and familial relationships shape children on their path to graduate school. *Source:* By University of Essex, CC BY 2.0. https://www.flickr.com/photos/46452859@N03/10871193694.

personal characteristics and personality traits of graduate students themselves—grit, resilience, and strength to overcome challenges and see it to the end.

Implications of Understanding How Families Shape Children Over the Life Course: Connections for Graduate School Educators and Researchers

With graduate school enrollment expected to continue to rise and racial and gender equity gaps in graduate school enrollment and completion, there is a strong need to consider ways to recruit and retain students of color and women students. Historically, predictors of graduate student outcomes have been tied to academic and programmatic characteristics, but while these factors remain central to student success in graduate school, they're not sufficient to expand opportunities for groups who continue to be underrepresented in postbaccalaureate degree programs.

Beyond GPA, GRE scores, early graduate-level academic and research experiences, disciplinary affiliation, institutional and program culture, academic employment, financial support, and mentorship, what matters to graduate student success happens off campus—in families who shape and support children in graduate school.

What we learn from this work can support campus and program communities to continue to co-create climates that, at their core, value the unique experiences and personal strengths of students of color. With institutional foci on closing gaps in outcomes of undergraduate and graduate students of color and first-generation students, learning about the students' family lives may help shift approaches to supporting students. In fact, findings from this work can more closely integrate parents, families, and lived experiences of students into the curricular and co-curricular features of graduate degree programs. Doing so means that faculty, staff, and administrators communicate to students that partners, parents, and families are central to their success and center program mission, vision, and values reflected in courses, centers, and events and activities.

As a starting point, understanding what led students to graduate school can include programming that honors familial experiences, parental relationships, and cultural values. For example, programs can include a question in supplemental material in admissions applications that asks prospective students to discuss how their family shaped who they are today and/or how their families and friends have impacted their personal and professional lives. At the program's start, orientations can welcome partners, parents, and family members to campus or a virtual gathering and ensure that family and community events are multilingual where applicable. In this way, commencement and hooding ceremonies are not the first time people important to students set foot on campus.

In programs, promoting a community culture grounded in a holistic approach to welcoming students and affirming who they are advances inclusive and equitable institutional and programmatic environments that validate connections between personal and familial backgrounds of students of color and first-generation students and academic work on campus. Hosting scholarly events—like talks, lectures, panel discussions, film screening, and so on—can include invitations to loved ones, especially if topics may be of broad interest to the community. Social events are also opportunities for partners and families to enjoy time together in spaces where students study and work. In my own EdD in Educational Leadership Program at California State University, Northridge (CSUN), we host a fall family picnic outside on a shaded lawn on campus—and event complete with a food, games, and opportunities to socialize and network among students, staff, faculty, administrators, alumni, and their loved ones.

In classrooms, faculty can extend an inclusive environment by shaping culturally relevant pedagogical practices that accounts for personal experiences of students. Here, selecting supplemental readings, case studies, assignments, discussions, and/or activities can incorporate cultural and familial dimensions of research, theory, and concepts in the discipline. For example, in my advanced applied qualitative methods class, I can include sample research questions, dissertation studies, and data analysis exercises that focus on family influences or impacts in education. Outside the classroom, in dissertation or thesis advising and faculty mentoring, simple changes to how a meeting or session starts can make a meaningful difference in how students feel connected to campus. For instance, inquiring about loved ones may signal to students that who they are matters and their whole person is valued.

Undermining Graduate Student Development: Racialized and Gendered Programs and Institutions as Barriers to Meaningful Experiences and Successful Outcomes

For several students of color who spoke with me, racialized graduate program culture seemed to be normative and shaped how they socialized with peers and faculty. These experiences led to feelings of being unwelcome or an outsider in the department or on campus and impacted how they interacted with colleagues. While racial and/or gender microaggressions and campus or program racial climate never kept students in this project from persisting or completing graduate programs of study, they made life more than difficult and had reverberating and residual effects.

For Jenna, who identifies as a first-generation Filipina heterosexual female, she always felt like a part of a larger campus community, which she described here: "I feel like I'm part of you know more of the, like in quotations, majority where you know it's always been supporting my point of view. So I, I'm not sure about, about others and other populations." But when Jenna discussed her racial identity, she revealed more complexity in her experiences. Referring to the larger campus, she felt a community, particularly with Filipino students at the university and nearby Filipino restaurants and more: "I think that's one of the reasons why I came back for my master's program is . . . the fact that there is a big Filipino population, a big Filipino community there, and Filipino food nearby, I feel like the people there are just diverse. And, and they have all these different experiences. And so it's been great." But describing racial climate in her graduate program, Jenna noted that she felt less welcome and tended to gravitate toward students and faculty of color, given the majority white faculty and student groups. She said: "[M]y program tends to be like . . . yeah . . . but . . . the majority of my program in grad school is mainly white, predominantly white. And then the faculty is also actually majority white. And then we have one professor, my research professor, who I'm the closest to, and . . . she is Chinese." Jenna talked about how the racial climate in her program led to her socializing with students who looked like her.

> I think in grad school, we're in a cohort group, but I tend to kind of move towards people who are, who are either of a different, of a similar culture, or you know who come from a minority background. Those are the people that I tend to move towards, because there are clicks as well in the grad program. You know people who knew each other from undergrad or whatnot. And, and I feel like it's not exactly noninclusive, but they kind of have their own thing, and we don't really understand each other.

Jenna concluded: "I think I tend to move towards people who have a similar identity or, or background, or experience." Similarly, Kaitlyn, a first-generation cisgender straight Latina, observed how her department—in the applied sciences—"wasn't as diverse" as when she started in her first year. What's more, she felt like you had to learn a specific skill set to succeed in higher education, and—dating back to high school—she experienced educational environments that didn't prepare her well for graduate school, including skills related to academic writing, conducting a literature review, designing and implementing a research study, managing time and projects, developing and maintaining professional networks, and more. As a first-gen student, this seemed to be particularly vexing as Kaitlyn shared more: "[W]e aren't really taught that. We're taught how to memorize, and how to kind of spill out anything that we do memorize, and to test. Um, so it was, it was really hard trying to adjust to that."

Kaitlyn shared that she had what she described as an identity crisis "because everyone in my department at least is white." Indeed, she felt like she didn't fit in and was never really a part of peer groups that formed in her master's program in applied sciences at a public master's-granting Hispanic-serving institution (HSI) in the Western US. Having been raised in a tight-knit community where many residents shared experiences as immigrants, Kaitlyn revealed how she gravitated "towards like immigrant students, or people whose like families are immigrants. Um, because again, we, we understand that shared experience." With people who do not share immigrant experiences, Kaitlyn admitted she had less in common and fewer attachments. She elaborated: "And with other people that don't have that same experience, like I, I can't, I don't have that emotional attachment to really understand where they come from. Um, because it's completely different to either my morals or my values. Um, but I again, like I'm, I'm obviously friendly with them, like I can talk to them, but it's not that same emotional attachment or emotional connection." Back on campus, Kaitlyn felt that her department was not racialized or gendered—but the broader discipline was. Kaitlyn described the field in stark terms.

> I think it's really just the field itself. Um, because [applied science] really, or I think a lot of research, but [applied science] in like specific, it's very black and white. It's either your female or your male. They don't, they look at sex and not gender. And in the literature they actually kind of confuse it at times. But, you know if we were to understand different types of like sexual orientations in research, there's a very huge lack of evidence with research. And there, um, so like if, if you were to look at, for example, um, transgender athletes in, in sports. They don't really have, um, a lot of research out there that supports it. Um, so there's a huge . . . disconnect just within the field.

Fortunately, Kaitlyn was close to her parents, who generally had an open mind and support for people from diverse backgrounds and experiences, and connected with her family as she navigated work with peers and faculty in the department.

At the program level, Angela felt a community that supported her—sharing how her seven Black student colleagues in the cohort formed a community. Angela, who identifies as a first-generation African American female who identifies ethnically as Nigerian, described how her college sponsored identity-based groups for graduate students, but she preferred to maintain close contact and connect with her Black colleagues in the cohort. She explained how she had the broader identity student group experiences as an undergraduate and now needed more intimate and personal relationships with close professional colleagues. However, Angela felt a strong racialized experience was at the campus level, where she observed a need to maintain an institutional reputation at all costs. Speaking to the effects on Black members of the campus community, she shared: "I don't think [the university] really affirms Black people at large. Like, I want to say Black people only make up four, like this is a school that has like [thousands of] people, and I want to say five to seven percent of the population." At the public, doctoral-granting, high-research activity university in the Southeast where Angela went to graduate school, she felt "siloed" in her program, but she knew there was a larger racialized campus climate. She shared a story of a recent campus renaming movement, to illustrate her point: "[F]or example there was a building, [an old building], and like they were trying to remodel it. Come to find out it had [an abhorrent history], and the university didn't, um, didn't deal with that very well. Or even right now, the residence hall that I'm living at like, it's on [disputed land]. Um, so it's just like, these little [messages]" Angela went further and shared more observations about the campus racial climate for Black students: "Black people make up three to five percent. But on the football roster they make up majority of the team yet are graduating at lower rates. [T]he parallels to the recruitment process versus slavery and how that looks like, um, is something of interest to me. In the end, Angela felt "affirmed, yes, but also affirmed, no."

As a graduate student at a public, doctoral-granting, high-research activity university in the Southeast, Tanya, a first-generation heterosexual African American woman, personally had not experienced or witnessed racial microaggressions on campus, but she conceded that "a lot of things" go on. And Tanya strategically navigated spaces where few Black women occupied. She described more: "But I also honestly don't put myself in spaces that I don't see a lot of Black women that don't look like me. Like I just a hundred percent don't, I don't put myself in those spaces. [N]ot saying that I . . . isolate myself, I'm just very big on, why even deal with the headache if I don't have to, you know?" At the program level, however, Tanya felt supported and felt confident challenging or resisting racialized structures, including with her internship.

More broadly, Winona described her experiences with race and racism early in life. Winona, a first-generation bisexual Asian American who uses she/her gender pronouns and identifies as Chinese and Vietnamese, talked about how she learned at a young age that Americans tend to be racist or discriminatory. Exploring her Vietnamese cultural experiences, she described how she first encountered her dad using words like *racist* and *discriminatory* in reference to Americans. Winona elaborated: "Like I've asked him, like oh, 'cause I was learning Vietnamese at the same time, like, oh, what does that word mean? Or how do I use it in a sentence? Type of thing. So he would try to explain it. And then he did, like he, he still says it now, too, is that, like Americans are considered racist and discriminatory." Describing her dad, Winona commented: "[H]e himself was, was kind of, he never really sat down and said, hey, this is what you're gonna deal with as a woman of color and stuff like that." Rather, her dad would caution that Winona may have to challenge or argue against them. Winona illustrated with memories from elementary school. She recalled times when she was exotified or made to feel different because of what she ate for lunch. She shared: "I remember like bringing food from home and people would kind of be like, what's that food? But they never said like, *eww*, it smells bad or anything."

Personal Characteristics as Foundational Footing for Graduate School Success

Offering insight into what moved them into advanced studies, several factors seemed to come to the fore for graduate students: connections to emerging and evolving questions in the social, behavioral, applied physical or biomedical sciences; curiosity to follow new leads; drive to complete projects; resilience to overcome obstacles and achieve a goal; a sense of agency to make decisions and act on their intuitive feelings; interest in improving the world around them; and responsibility to a collective greater good. Beyond their own characters, a mix of peers and colleagues, faculty, and family members emerged as important to grad school achievements—with parental relationships described as still central and relevant to several individuals.

Across multiple dimensions of their lives, most cited their inner qualities as the source that best supported their work as grad students. While parenting relationships and family socialization helped them in their early development—specifically value reproduction and expectations within families and direct involvement in education by parents with support for financial and emotional needs—their own personalities and personal characteristics seemed to carry them through the rigors of coursework, thesis, or dissertation work, and the challenges of entering and navigating academic fields.

Hector returned to his commitment to his education and a strong, ever-present, seemingly endless push to do what he needed to do as a student. He connected all this to his parents, who pushed him "too hard on that," but which helped when he went to the community college and later to graduate school. He elaborated: "I always really, and my parents didn't have to push me too hard on that. I only feel like, they would never even know me, like do your homework. Like I was, whatever they did early on it, it made it stick 'cause I was, I was very committed as a student." He shared more about his time in the MA program in applied social sciences: "I could explore. I was open to everything. So I, I tried to learn everything, learn about things. I was really, really committed. I spent a lot of time, I'm not a fast learner, I'm not a great test taker." But Hector—a cisgender heterosexual married male who identifies as a person of color with multiracial and multiethnic identities of Mexican, Filipino, Italian, and Native American—persisted and continued on his journey to a doctorate.

Like Hector, Jessica pushed herself to keep going as a graduate student. Feeling burnt out, Jessica, who identifies as a white female, told herself to keep going. She elaborated: "I feel like at every, like end of the semester, everyone just kind of feels burnt out, and like I would definitely feel burnt out. And I'm like, oh, like, I can't do this anymore, there's just so many assignments, and big assignments. But, I kept like pushing myself to like finish the semester. Okay, let's do the next semester."

Jaime also pushed herself and kept going, in the face of adversity, to persist in graduate school. Jaime, who identifies as a first-generation Vietnamese American female, talked about identifying more and more with the profession. "But, um, my identity with the, it's developing," Jaime commented. She talked about patience in this process, and that helped a lot. So did the pride she had in herself. She elaborated on this.

> [T]he first thing I thought of was myself, giving myself the patience. But then, um, and kind of like just letting, there were a lot of times where I, I thought I wanted to drop out of the program but then I thought, you know, just go for a little bit longer. You never know. Um, there's that. I am so freaking proud of [the public master's-granting HSI university in the West's] [applied humanities] program. I am so proud of it. I

can't, for me when I first enroll it was just a me soon, and like get your degree, and, and so go be the leader. You're supposed to be, wasn't really expecting much.

What's more, Jaime connected "the hard work, the diligence, the showing up, the preparation" to her success in graduate school.

Having done so much on her own—including financially taking care of herself as an undergraduate—Stella felt like she could take on a lot more in life. But this early autonomy came at a price, including high and prolonged levels of stress and a toll on mental health. As an emerging adult, Stella reflected on how her lead role in her education gave her "the awareness, and understanding, and wisdom" that she had now. She shared: "[I was] able to survive at such a young age to just move out on my own and kind of navigate everything on my own." Stella shared that she learned to strategize independently about what she needed in life and career, having had to navigate early life on her own. She talked about what she did: "[J]ust to change my life, reevaluate my life, and change it for me and no one else, and him to see that and see the woman that I became on my own, you know it was just a reminder of how, regardless of whatever anyone put on me, my family, men, anyone, like I'm not gonna let that, you know affect me, or you know I'm gonna build a career for myself."

Independence, personal autonomy, and self-reliance seemed to cluster as a central theme for many graduate students. Sharon cited her independent work style, time management skills, and ability to multitask or manage multiple projects at once as reasons for her success as a student in the MA program she was in. Natasha, who identifies as a straight white female, framed her work in graduate school as a journey she had to do alone. She remarked how, even though she feels like she's alone in her journey, it was a good choice. She said: "I'm just doing it alone, but everyone's like, it's a good choice that you decided to go there given the current job market."

For Sasha, a who identifies as a pansexual white woman, graduate school adjustment seemed to come later, given COVID-era lockdown measures and related transitions to virtual instruction in her doctoral program at a public, very high-research activity, doctoral-granting university in the western US. Moving from her family home in the Southeast out West, she initially struggled with connections to the program and campus. She elaborated: "And like, but I think like actually now that I'm starting to like learn the history of the institution, I feel more connected to it, and . . . it's something I would want to like invest my time in." Previously, she observed her "department being bad, and funding being bad," but things changed and she summarized how she felt more recently: "I definitely feel more attached to it now."

Like Sasha, Juan felt connected to campus—like he belonged at the public master's-granting HSI university in the Western US. He illustrated what he feels when he's there: "I enter the, the sort of building and, and get into the lab I feel like I'm in, I'm in my environment where I'm comfortable. Um, you know comfortable to, to sort of be myself, you know casually as a person, and even academically, and, and sit down and, and be able to, um, feel in the mood to, you know work hard." As a student in a master's program, Juan wished that the department offered a PhD program so that he could remain there and complete a terminal degree. "I've just really fallen in love with the, with the program and the associate professors involved, um, and the type of research um definitely," Juan said, "you know resonates to me." Juan shared how two forces motivated him to pursue an advanced degree: (1) exploring a career that supports him financially and (2) being happy to do it every day. "That's always sort of been the thing," Juan concluded as he connected his motivation to an enjoyment of learning—which sustained his interest in education and propelled him to graduate school.

Karina shared that she had been motivated by financial security, like Juan, in her pursuit of a graduate degree. Karina's father had messaged money, salary, and income security as top priorities in a career, and Karina internalized these messages as motivation, in part, for her advanced studies. Guided by an interest in a career that paid well and she enjoyed, she reported how she balanced her needs with what would satisfy her father. Karina, a heterosexual Latina woman who identifies as half Guatemalan and half Mexican, revealed more about how she had planned to tell her parents about career directions as a graduate student.

> I was excited to tell them, but I didn't tell them how much I was going to be paid, because I knew that that would kind of lower the excitement. I was always looking at, uh, positions that would make the most money. And I still do, because I'd be able to tell my dad like, I'm gonna be making this much money, because I feel like he'll be most proud . . . the highest paying job. But I, I really do, I try like saying like, oh, this is a really great opportunity for me, and I can work in this place,

I can work this place, I'd be learning a lot. And so he's like, but how much are you gonna make, so. But at the same time, I, I'm just happy that I'm pursuing something that I love to do, which is [applied humanities] and working with students.

Beyond considerations about salary enjoyment in work, Karina focused on giving back to the community as a motivation for pursuing a graduate degree. "I'll be doing something that I love, and also giving back to the community in a way," she shared, "supporting students who are usually underrepresented in college."

Edith talked about giving back to the community, too, like Karina. Edith, a first-generation Korean female, framed her graduate school focus on advocacy in her career: "And now that I'm in that graduate [program] and I'm learning that your, you need to be in people's corner, especially those who, who need, you know who . . . are like, you know, who are experiencing hardship in any way." Edith connected this stance to her dad's values and "what he stood for."

For a small group, lifelong learning and love of learning had sustained interests in and work to navigate graduate school. Susan, a white and Latina cis-heterosexual female who identifies as Jewish, talked about she "loved the coursework" in her program. She elaborated: "I . . . would call myself a lifelong learner. I mean if I could always be in school I feel like I would. I find this work fascinating, too. Just all the intricacies of education as a whole." Over her lifetime, learning has pulled Holly closer to her intellectual interests and kept her on her educational journey. Holly loved being in school and was fascinated by an immersive experience in the classroom. "Like I couldn't get enough," Holly remarked about her time in school. "You know leaving at ten o'clock was not, was not late enough for me. And I remember somebody from class said, oh, I can't wait till it's over, and I was like, what? Like I wish this would never end," she shared.

Jeremy remarked how—beyond peers in the program and staff in the office where he completed his first-year internship—his internal drive and motivation have helped him to persist. Referring to his colleagues, he shared more: "I can't say that like if I didn't have them, I wouldn't be where I am, because part of me still feels like even if I didn't have that support I would still be where I'm at, um, because of myself, my, my self-motivation and drive." Jeremy, who identifies as first-generation straight white and Italian cisgender male, relied on these internal resources and his colleagues to navigate the transition to graduate school. Jeremy described what it was like for him: "[T]o me, again, like coming to grad school like I just felt like I was in college still. [F]iguring out the difference between being, figuring out the difference between being an undergrad and a grad student was something that I only was able to figure out with the help of like staff members. That's not something like my family could have ever like, shown me how to be, or, um, something that like my, um, friends."

Peers as Colleagues Who Care and Support Each Other in Graduate School

For most graduate students, peers played a prominent role in their experiences in graduate school. As professional relationships with colleagues developed over the course of several years in programs, these connections proved vital to navigate a range of academic and career challenges and became much more personal as connections strengthened through it all. From enhancing a sense of belonging and creating community to overcoming imposter syndrome and developing career interests, peers tended to form a network of support. What Jessica shared seemed to illustrate this feeling. Jessica, a white female, indicated that she "really connected well with . . . fellow students." She summed it up here: [W]e're all pretty close as far as like graduate students and stuff."

Several graduate students described a sense of community. For example, Tanya felt a sense of belonging in her program at a public, doctoral-granting, high-research activity university in the Southeast. She cited a cohort model and closeness of colleagues in the program. Compared to her undergraduate experiences, Tanya felt a part of a community in graduate school, which contributed to her perception of support in the program. Peers were a major influence in shaping Hector's experiences in his doctoral program in applied humanities at a public master's-granting Hispanic-serving institution in the Western US. Hector described how a feeling of community and interpersonal connections created an "imprint" on him. Here's what he said: "I think, um, you know, having, having a connection to community. So it's not just, you know not just relationships with other academics, and teachers, and colleagues here, and students, but in, in the community. You know, can you, can you also do that? And, um, so that's been a really big part, and I think that's, that's definitely his imprint . . . all that." Hector's experiences connected him to communities on and beyond campus, and learning from members in these communities linked him to resources that guided him on his journey. "[B]eing open to, to a lot of different perspectives and, and points . . . of view," Hector said, "are things that like I, I find it valuable." He concluded: "And it definitely guided me throughout all this"

Like Hector, Sasha felt that the people in her doctoral program in a liberal arts field at a public, very high-research activity, doctoral-granting university in the Western US made all the difference in her experiences. To illustrate this point, Sasha recalled how her sister who'd been living with her while she was in her doctoral program out West—far from their home in the South—had meant a lot to her and probably helped to keep her from leaving the program. Having started in the program during the COVID-19 pandemic and experiencing virtual learning away from campus, she explained how her peers in the program and her sister had helped her stay connected to what she was doing: "But I think that like the people, I think also, also I didn't mention that I live with my sister. Like my sister moved out here with me, and she's like really supportive."

Figure 8.2. Once in graduate school, parents and families tend to be in the background of children's lives but remain a foundational source of support. *Source:* By MIKI Yoshihito (#mikiyoshihito), CC BY 2.0. https://www.flickr.com/photos/7940758@N07/9529061293.

In his doctoral program in applied humanities at a public doctoral-granting, high-research activity university in the southeastern US, Ping mentioned how a student peer who studied abroad in the life sciences in a university outside mainland China inspired him to do the same. As undergraduates, he recalled how she helped him see the benefits of studying abroad. Ping, who identifies as a first-generation straight Chinese man, intimated that they seemed to make an informal pact to study abroad, together or separately, and push themselves outside their comfort zones at home in China. Similarly, Jeremy had close friends whom he felt supported him. In his master's degree in applied humanities at a public doctoral-granting, high-research activity university in the Southeast, Jeremy felt that the people who surrounded him were what kept him on track in graduate school. Referring to colleagues in the office where he did an internship his first year in the master's program, he said: "I guess if I had to like say like . . . a lot of my support just comes from like staff that I've worked with . . . yeah I think like staff, and maybe like a couple close friends."

With a strong attachment to her MA degree program in applied humanities at a public doctoral-granting, high-research activity university in the Southeast, Eileen appreciated the different experience of being a graduate versus an undergraduate student. Between staff members in her internship on campus and student members of her cohort, she felt a closeness to colleagues across her roles. Speaking about her cohort, she shared more: "We're all, I think, um, very close. I mean it's, I think it's been kind of unusual. [W]e all get along remarkably well. I mean we all have our own little smaller groups where we do other things, but when we're all in the classroom together we all get along really, really well." Focusing on program features that created spaces for students to form relationships, she concluded: "I feel very connected to my classmates and peers," who had helped each other complete group projects and collectively collaborate well. Jenna described her experience with peers in similar terms as Eileen, a heterosexual white female. Speaking about the master's degree program in applied sciences at a public master's-granting HSI in the Western US, Jenna referenced peers who had supported her, especially with test prep. Beyond her immediate friends, she's connected well with peers in the cohort. She commented: "And a good chunk of the cohort, even though I'm not close to them, we still help each other out, and that's been really helpful."

In some cases, peers served as the resources needed to overcome imposter syndrome in graduate school. Karina illustrated how she leaned into the cohort model in her master's program at a public master's-granting HSI in the Western US, and how a peer helped her see that she belonged there. Karina explained what the cohort model meant to her as a student: "[W]ell one of the aspects that mainly attracted me to the program was the cohort model, so I stay with my peers all throughout the program. And my peers are definitely one of those things that, those aspects that is like a support system for me." Later, Karina described how she met a peer in the program who had similar experiences with imposter syndrome.

> And of course there's always imposter syndrome that I'm facing within my program itself because there's so many individuals that already have experience, or are already in those positions, and so, um, I think that's one thing that's really holding me back. Like, uh, for example one of my peers was already a professor and he was teaching biology, and when I first met him I was like, oh, I don't belong here, I don't have enough experience. But after I got to know him, he was feeling . . . in a similar way. He's like, oh, everyone here is so much younger than me, and everyone has more experience in [applied humanities] and I only had teach, teaching experience.

Karina narrated how her colleague helped her see herself as a graduate student: "And that was very eye opening to me, that I wasn't the only one that was feeling that way." Karina connected her experiences with imposter syndrome to the first-gen students she's working with now: "I currently work with first-generation students in their career development, uh, one of our main topics in our sessions is imposter syndrome. And so, I tell them the same things like, you know, everyone around you is feeling similar ways." She summed it up well: "Like it's okay."

While most graduate students cast peer relationships as constructive, several described the peer environments in their programs as less supportive and/or less connected. But even when a cohort model didn't serve students as well as they had hoped, there was something still valuable about peer interaction. For example, Edith, a first-generation Korean female who uses she/her gender pronouns and is married with a child, described how she recognized how important relationships with graduate student peers were. At the same time, she felt distance from her colleagues in the program, given their divergent career paths. She reflected: "I feel a little apart from my cohort only because, as of now, I'm the only one who aspires to be a principal in the very near future. There's our like assistant principal."

Like Edith, Maria, a first-generation LGBTQ-identified Armenian woman who immigrated from Iran and identifies culturally as Middle Eastern and Armenian, talked about how differences in ages among peers in her master's program in applied humanities at a public master's-granting HSI in the Western US seemed to create a sense that students were all going in different directions. Maria shed light in this experience: "[W]e just wish that the program, like connected, the core was more connected to each other so where everyone can talk together, and go out, or study together." Instead, Maria lamented: "I feel like it was more like separated. Or, or there were people but they just tend to be with their own people in the cohort." Still, Maria found that when everyone participated in class and engaged in class assignments or in-class activities, it was helpful. She elaborated: "[W]hen it came to the presentations that we had . . . I would tend to focus more on them to learn more um, cause we, each team would have like different topics. I enjoyed learning about those, or just discussions I think helped a lot. Just knowing about like, what . . . goes around in [applied humanities], the issues happening."

Similarly, Jaime revealed how she had been stressed as she navigated the program. Jaime, who identifies as a Vietnamese American female, talked about how she never really built strong relationships with peers in her program. Even though she felt that they didn't know her well, they seemed "to accept me as I am," Jaime remarked. But peer-peer interaction ended there, as Jaime revealed.

> I've never really felt the, felt free to kind of build on those relationships. Like all of my peers, I can tell that in a way we're still acquaintances because we really only reach out to each other for studying purposes. And if we, and it's kind of odd to reach out for each other for other things, too, because it's kind of like, there's a lot of energy in that. It's like, oh, you're here to talk to me about something, but I'm gonna see you on Monday.

Given the more limited connections to her peers, Jaime seemed to think that there was a decline in a professional network that would endure far beyond the program.

For Natasha, given the enrollment patterns in her classes—where some classes had undergraduate and graduate students—she "struggled really hard to relate to anybody in the class." But Natasha, a straight white female, found community in a dance studio and nonprofit dance company. With connections between dance and her master's program in applied sciences at a public master's-granting HSI in the Western US, she connected with instructors—one of whom was a professor in a difference department at the university—helped Natasha get through her studies. She elaborated on what it all meant for her: "Like take a break, take a mental break from my studies, or from work and get a little stress relief, 'cause I'm not really getting it anywhere else. And I meet a lot of other women there, mostly who, they're, they're single mothers, or they're running straight from work to class and then back to their families."

Faculty Mentoring and Support Connect Students to Academic and Early Career Interests

Discussed as frequently as peers, faculty interaction, advising, and mentoring is another dimension of graduate school that students connected to their development. From pre-admissions advising and admissions interviewing to interacting in instructional or research contexts to partnering with an adviser and mentor for thesis or dissertation projects, many talked about how faculty made a meaningful difference in their work in the program and helped them navigate coursework, campus, career, and more. Illustrating the value in student relationships with faculty, Karina described how faculty linked her to campus resources as a student in a master's program at a public master's-granting Hispanic-serving institution (HSI) university in the Western US. She detailed: "[F]aculty and staff are very open, luckily, and helping me, you know, make more connections and figure out next steps I need to do for my career is. Um, and then other resources on campus, um, luckily those are available to me."

Beyond campus resources, faculty advisers created networks for students to develop peer and professional relationships. Jessica illustrated what relationships with faculty mean to graduate students when she talked about how connected she felt to her adviser and program faculty: "I feel really connected with, uh, like my adviser, and the fellow students and with the same adviser, and other teachers. And so I feel like in the [applied science] department we're all pretty close as far as like graduate students and stuff." Jessica's relationship with her adviser extended beyond faculty mentoring to facilitating peer networking and co-creating a social peer environment. She continued: "I am mostly with my adviser, and then I go across the hall and like, like hang out with those kids 'cause we, our two labs kind of like intermix. So there's a good, um, friendship, social

Where Parents, Families, and More Fit into Academic Life | 305

dynamic. There's a good teacher and student dynamic. So I really do feel connected in our department." Edith talked about how faculty in her master's program in applied humanities had helped her develop professionally. Referring to faculty members, she elaborated on what these relationships meant for her leadership skills.

> They're really setting me up, setting up to be, hmm, the leader. Not if this isn't just like, hey, run a school. This is leadership. This is you. These are the types of leadership. You need to be this type of leader, and [it's] just really laying the foundation. And for them to then say, hey, here's my like office hours. Isn't really a thing I don't, I don't know if you agree with this, but like office hours is this like we have access to them email, they get back. And so there's culture, climate of, of like, I'm here for you, like I'm available to you.

Edith concluded: "I definitely feel like I belong among the professors."

Figure 8.3. Graduate program communities can co-create climates that value the lived experiences and personal strengths of students of color and first-generation students whose families play a key role in their educational trajectory. *Source:* By Zeete, CC BY-SA 4.0. https://commons.wikimedia.org/w/index.php?curid=135655772.

As a primary program requirement, coursework seemed to be central to some graduate students' descriptions of connections to faculty. In fact, several framed faculty as supportive course instructors. Tanya reported that faculty in the master's degree program in applied humanities at a public doctoral-granting, high-research activity university in the Southeast had supported her. She said: "They were amazing . . . and they try care about you, you now, our well-being . . . they preach that we advocate for ourselves." Tanya went on to describe how accommodating faculty had been, granting assignment submission extensions and more.

Similarly, Sharon reported positive experiences with faculty in her MA program in humanities at a private, not-for-profit, master's-granting college in the West. She loved what she was doing in the program and felt she had a lot of control over the coursework she had to complete for the degree. Like Sharon, Natasha focused on faculty who taught in the program and described her favorite class—a "qualitative research design class" with a "professor [who] is phenomenal."

Outside the classroom, Ping benefited from faculty advisers and a research center coordinator. He said: "I mainly talk with my advisers on research projects and the classes. But I, at the [public doctoral-granting, high-research activity university in the Midwest where I earned my master's degree] I benefited a lot from the the, the, the coordinator [of the research center where I worked]." Similarly, Jenna described her faculty adviser as central to her success: "Now, in terms of my program, my, my research professor has been really supportive. And so that really helped as well."

While most graduate students formed close relationships with faculty, a few reflected on how they could have built stronger links. For example, Eileen mentioned that she could have done more to strengthen ties to program faculty. She spoke to how she developed strong relationships with faculty but needed to do more to maximize opportunities. She spoke to this point: "I don't feel like I participated as much as I probably should have. And I think because of that, I don't feel like my relationships with faculty have been as strong as I maybe would have liked. So I think because of that I don't know if I feel like I have a very strong relationship with, um, necessarily with people and faculty." Similarly, Maria never connected to faculty in her master's program in applied humanities at a public master's-granting Hispanic-serving institution (HSI) university in the Western US. She described how she had learned a lot and experienced growth in the program, but the curricular focus—"mainly focused on community college"—never resonated with her professional interests. She revealed more: "[P]rofessors, not all of them were effective, um, because they were just thrown out of nowhere, like oh, you need to teach this, and most of them didn't have that background needed to, um, teach about, for example, human resource, because they've only had experience with mainly community college."

Even though Beatrice experienced "phenomenal" faculty mentoring, she also illustrated how a faculty mentor's lab linked her to lab research opportunities driven by industry, and this is not what she had expected or preferred to do in her doctoral program in applied sciences at a public, very high-research activity, doctoral-granting university in the Mountain West. Beatrice, a heterosexual female who identifies as white and Mexican, described her experience with a faculty mentor in the program whose lab she felt did not allow her to pursue her career interests.

> I went into that lab and it was just not what I had expected. It was kind of more, very, um, what's the word? Um, it was influenced a lot by business and partnerships that they had with companies. It, it felt more like working in the industry and that's kind of not what I wanted to do. I wanted to steer clear from all that, and it felt like they didn't have much say in the research they'd be conducting. And it was all like, oh, we have to meet these quotas and, and make this cool new prosthesis for this company, even though it might not fit all the criteria for the people using it. That's the kind of feeling I got from it.

Beatrice connected her feelings to experiences she had as a child: "I had physical therapy for all my knee surgeries, and, um, there was this one guy that had physical therapy around the same time that I did every week, and he had a prosthesis and so I would talk to him about all this stuff and that was like one of my long-term goals." But she concluded that her current faculty mentor and university-industry lab research did not get her to where she planned to go in a career: "I knew that I wanted to either help improve surgeries, or I've also loved robotics, and prosthesis, and prosthetics, so. But I steered clear from that 'cause I just got a feeling that it wasn't the best."

Both Jaime and Eugenio seemed to not connect well with faculty in their programs, respectively. In her master's program in applied sciences, Jaime talked about how both student peers and professors didn't seem to want to build a community. Overall, she had mixed feelings about her experiences with faculty: "I'm not really sure. Uh, I do know that my professors, um, they, I think they're open to building, I'm never sure, but I think they're open to building a, a kind of like a mentor-mentee relationship. But then with my professors, they're also doing other things, and we're, both the students and the professors are like quick to leave because they have something else to do." Similarly, Eugenio talked about how he worked for the program director and helped to promote events for students, but it was still not enough to feel like he belonged. He revealed more: "I was working like with my director, and I was working my supervisor. I was the one making phone calls with my cohort, inviting them to events, professional development day. I was able to work, um, like zoom. I was doing admissions and records and which is, as in like presentations for new incoming graduate students. I was reaching out to, I love my students, and that's where everything for me started, as in the connection network." While he felt connected to peers, Eugenio—a first-generation heterosexual married Latinx male who identifies as Oaxacan from an Indigenous Mexican background—seemed to feel the same way about the general program culture. Looking deeper into how he came to feel like he didn't fit in, Eugenio cited a sense that never he never felt accepted with his own cultural identity: "They always were welcoming, everyone, sure, but I personally didn't feel like that. So I felt like I had to try to do my best to fit in. As in now, let's say, for example, if I ever see anyone I'll be like, hey, how's it going? Or, *como estás*? Just be myself. That's really who I am. But before I'd be like, good afternoon, how's it going? And I understand the professional of course, but I feel like now, where, where I'm at, I try to embrace more my culture and try to see it."

Framing Parents and Families as a Factor in Graduate School Success: Life Histories and Current Relationships Intersect to Form Sources of Support

While student peer and faculty relationships appeared to be central to meaningful graduate student experiences and outcomes, most graduate students tied their advanced academic and career work to familial foundations and parental relationships that formed significant parts of their life histories and current identities. Between intermittent motivational messages of *échale ganas*—give it your all—and general check-ins for emotional support, parents connected with adult children in graduate school in a number of ways. First, current relational links to parents, grandparents, and ancestors seemed to continue to serve as a resource to anchor adult children to a secondary system of support outside of partners, friends, colleagues, mentors, student peers, and faculty. This is the "background character" that Angela talked about when she described her parents. Second, specific and unique effects that parents had on children—over the life course—could be seen in what drove students to graduate school. Third—and maybe this is more important with adult children enrolled in graduate school—values learned in families and personality traits developed at home tended to prepare graduate students for what they had to do in their programs.

When Andres talked about his success as a graduate student, he referenced his ancestors, whom he centered as guides in his life. The connections to generations of family members remained ever-present in his life. He elaborated: "So all of my success is due to my people, you know my family, my, my grandfathers, and my grandmothers, my, my ancestors. Um, until this day they, they guide my work. So, so that, in short, is why I'm so successful, is because I allow my ancestors to guide me." Further, Andres connected his success in life to new perspectives from his travels to Mexico City, Chiapas, and Guatemala—where he started to see links between these ancient cities and the natural world. Honoring his physical surroundings changed his life, and he treated people differently after returning from his trip to Mexico and Central America.

Parental Support as General Encouragement in Graduate School

For most graduate students, parental support at this point in life tended to be in the form of general encouragement—and this is exactly what was needed to get through the demanding schedule of classes, internships, teaching and research assistantships, and career planning. Eugenio knew his parents supported him and—in fact—felt like he owed them a lot for all their care in his life as a graduate student. His parents were there for him and looked forward to his graduation from his MA degree program in applied humanities at a private, not-for-profit, doctoral-granting, high-research activity, HSI university in the West. But their focus on his well-being and their concern for his health was where he felt their love the most. Speaking about his parents, Eugenio shared the following story that illustrated their care for him.

> They see me really busy and stressed, 'cause I . . . got really stressed. I was working two jobs, um, through two colleges. I was working, and I'm still currently working at two colleges. But I was working like fifty hours, I was doing full-time. That was last semester. And I was working sometimes Saturdays and Sundays. So doing all that has caused me, and I learned so many things, I got Bell's palsy on the, on December. Uh, my parents saw that, how much I've been putting in the work, has been dedicated to my education.

Eugenio reflected on how his parents saw his drive to complete his degree more clearly now, asking him questions and wanting to know more about what he'd been doing. Beyond a parental focus on his well-being, Eugenio's dad spent more time with him and bonded with him later in life. He described it this way: "Just spend that bonding time, and, or just be like, let's go to [another state]. Let's go there. But my parents and everyone else as a family cherish those good moments. . . . So I really appreciate that from him a lot. I know he did his best, and he's always doing his best he can."

Like Eugenio, Jasmine's family had been there for her when she was in graduate school, too. Jasmine, a first-generation heterosexual Hispanic female, talked about how her family was a major source of support, even as they experienced a lot of setbacks at the time, including housing instability and mental health issues for her brother. Between her internal motivation to finish her degree program and her aunt, who worked as an assistant principal, Jasmine felt like she had what she needed to finish. Speaking about her aunt and family, she said: "And she emigrated here also from Mexico, and she's the reason I'm in education I think. So my aunt probably. But I guess like my family, and like the fact that I wanted to finish what I started." Jasmine, a first-generation heterosexual Hispanic female, went on to talk about how her family always seemed to be there for her and described the unique contributions of several members. In addition to the central role of her aunt, the assistant principal, Jasmine talked about what her uncle, dad, and mom meant to her as a graduate student. For her uncle's part, she said: "My uncle that I mentioned, the one who gave me a hug, um, he came to my house and like, he couldn't go to my graduation, but he texted me that he wanted to do something small for me. So him and his wife came here with food to celebrate like my graduation." With her dad, Jasmine talked about how he had been there through car breakdowns and more. "I'd call him, and like he'd come," she said, "[a]nd like when I text him, like I'll send him pictures of how I'm doing and he says he's proud." Finally, Jasmine's mom had gone to university when she was in Mexico and a community college in the US, and she seemed to know how to best support Jasmine as a graduate student.

Between dramatic changes in family structure and vast distances from Russia to the US, where Holly emigrated as a young adult, she felt her parents supported her. Holly reflected on more recent experiences with her mom and stepdad's presence in her life as a doctoral student. Referencing her stepdad, she described how he was the only parental figure alive for her, after her mom passed away six years ago and her father long ago. She elaborated as follows:

> [W]hen I went into the doctoral program it was just four months after I lost my mom. And, um, I, um felt responsible for my stepdad, you know, who was actually more frail than my mom, you know. But, uh, and so, but they lived across the street from me. . . . I felt responsible like for taking care of him. So, um, it was pretty tough, you know to be like first semester, maybe it was okay, but then it just got really busy, and, um, I just couldn't give him the attention, um, that he needed.

This time together, with Holly caring for him, helped her see how proud he was of her. She commented: "I think, so he definitely was very proud of me, and very encouraging, you know, for me going into the program." Holly connected the pride he had for her with how her mom felt. She recalled: "[F]rom my mom and, and from him as well. And I feel like my mom, although she didn't have a high, like that, she didn't have higher education, but she . . . was so proud of me that I kept going, you know. And, and not only, not only I went to school, I went to school in America, which was like a whole, another level of going to school. They were, they were very, very proud of me, definitely. They may not kind of fully understand what that entailed, but they were very proud of me."

When graduate students described parental support later in life, there seemed to be general patterns of encouragement, but many talked about the unique effects of specific parental or familial figures. For example, Sasha tied advanced study in a doctoral program to her dad's curiosity. Later in life, Sasha recalled how her dad's more philosophical approach shaped her interest in learning and how she felt supported by her dad in grad school.

> And like, I think I mentioned he is becoming more philosophical, but like he has a lot of different interests. And even though like, yeah. He has different things he likes to do, and like, he likes doing research on his own time, um, like into those things. And he likes learning new stuff, and like I, I think that like that is how I've sort of like approached grad school. And I think that like, um, like when I think about like specifically like my dad being supportive like these days, it's like we can connect over like, I guess just like a love for like learning and like curiosity, even though like maybe that doesn't translate into like, necessarily like, um, I mean for me it's grad school, but for him it's like something different. But I think, I think overall like, the fact that there is someone who has been in my life so like consistently like, sharing things that interest him, and then I can share things that interest me, um, I think that's like really important to have, even though like our trajectories are very different. So, I don't know if that makes, did that make sense at all?

Sasha seemed to feel like her dad was someone with whom she could share and who was interested in what she was doing in graduate school.

"As Long as You're Happy": Unique Effects of Support from Fathers While in Graduate School

Liza's parents had always been there for her and supported her work in graduate school, but her dad had a special place in her life as a student. Liza, who identifies as a cisgender bisexual Latina woman, recalled how they had told her that whatever she wanted to do, they'd support her. "That's all that matters," Liza remembered them telling her, "[a]s long as you're happy, and you feel that you're making that right decision, who are we to tell you what to do with your life. Especially when it looks like you have goals and ambitions, you know. They just said, go for it." But Liza's dad did something different to encourage her as a graduate student—he invested his physical appearance in her persistence. Here's the story Liza tells about it: "[M]y dad always had a mustache. My mom, even when they met the mustache was there. She's never known him without a mustache. He's had one, he'd had one all the way through high school. And so he made a pact, he says, you go to grad school and finish, I'll shave my mustache. So I was like, okay! So that was kind of like this deal that we, that we made, you know, when I started the program." Her dad followed through on the promise and, as Liza put it, "sure enough, like as I was getting ready for graduation, he shaved it off. And he kept it shaved the whole rest of the time of his life. Yeah, he shaved it. And people were complimenting him at work, and saying how young he looked, and . . . he loved it."

Eileen's dad seemed to be a similar presence in her life as a graduate student as Sasha's and Gail's dads, respectively. Eileen engaged him in conversations about conceptual or theoretical topics from classes—"that's interesting to him," Eileen remarked. Both Eileen's parents seemed interested in her work on campus. She spoke to this pattern when she said: "[B]oth my parents still kind of ask about my, my projects I'm working on, and what's going on in class. Um, but I wouldn't say, and it's maybe a little bit more now that I'm working too, they're more interested in what I do in the [office]." More than inquiries about class and work, Eileen's parents offered emotional support to her when she needed to talk about what's going on in her life as a graduate student. She described how she could "vent" and talk about things that she "maybe can't talk to about with" classmates. To this point, she said: "I think that's been really useful. I, I don't know if they're advice is necessarily like, I don't want to say I don't need it, 'cause I think I do."

Like Sasha and Eileen, Gail characterized her dad as someone to whom she could go when she needed advice. To this point, she said: "[H]e allows that space for me to like bounce my ideas off of him and what I'm learning. And I feel like when he didn't get it, that encouraged me to explain it in more ways and think about it in more ways so that I could get him to get it, you know. Um, that really helped. Like I was really appreciative of walks with him where we would talk about like my studies." Gail concluded: "Mostly like the material and not really what was going on in the class, but he, cause like he likes to learn, too, and I feel like I like to learn maybe because of him, but mostly because of myself I think."

Hua shared similar experiences with her dad as Gail, Sasha, and Eileen. Specifically, Hua, who identifies as a Chinese female, mentioned how her dad had been supportive, but his more meaningful role seemed to be to model what it's like to be in graduate school. Describing her dad during that time, she elaborated: "He's like, oh, if you didn't read enough keep reading. You didn't you keep reading. He the only thing he said, and that's also the same thing my professor said to me just like I have read already." Hua connected her dad's work as a Chinese doctor to his concern about her mental health. She recalled how he could look at her face and know what was going on in her life and how she was feeling: "How like symptoms from your face. And you're talking. It's like that. So every time we talk to him it's kind of nervous, because I'm so afraid he noticed something from it." Ultimately, Hua felt her dad was an academic role model—as a "researcher, and professor, and scholar," he had inspired her to continue her education. "[K]eep learning," she remembered him telling her.

Hua, Gail, Sasha, Eileen, and Winona all shared stories about their fathers, respectively, who had been a strong presence in their lives. In sometimes gendered forms, fathers tended to be associated with characteristics traditionally associated with men. In Winona's case, her dad impressed on her the need to be "organized and efficient" in school and manage time well. Winona reflected on what his message meant for her in graduate school: "[M]y dad pushed that a lot as a young age. So, but even currently now being organized and efficient, that's like literally what makes up most of it. Is because of that then I can be able to manage my time. I can manage, you know, being able to sleep, and eat, and do my academics and stuff like that. But because of that, of being organized . . . it just helps with the flow of every day. Kind of creating that routine."

Knowing that her dad would be there for her is what Beatrice needed as she adjusted to graduate school. Beatrice said her dad was "what a father should be." She elaborated: "He's very driven, very motivated. I appreciate his tenacity, and just, he's gone through a lot. And just, I see him and he is definitely a role model. That is, you know. And he's a phenomenal role model." When she looked ahead at the ups and downs of her studies, she was comforted at the thought of her dad's support. She said: "It's gonna be tough and I don't even know how tough yet, but I know it'll be another adjustment and I know that he'll be there to support me throughout it all." In a similar way, Stella reflected on what she associated with her dad and mom. Stella, a first-generation African American who uses the gender pronouns she/her/hers, tied the empathy from her dad and hustle mentality from her mom to her life achievements, saying "putting those things together is what made me who I am today. And I, I take the positive things I get from my parents, and I've developed my own identity with the things that I, you know, gained the wisdom of as an adult throughout my journey too."

Like Stella and Beatrice, Josefina focused on her dad when she contemplated her success in graduate school. Looking back, she reflected on her dad's wisdom: "Now that I'm older and he's older, I see how wise, I mean, for a man who never had any formal education. He has these amazing, um, amazing words of, of wisdom. And I think that's where, where it comes from." Josefina, who identifies as a first-generation straight Chicana woman with children, tied his life knowledge to her focus on a terminal degree: "It's the desire that education is the tool of betterment. So that was always instilled in us." More recently, Josefina's father's support has meant just as much as it did when she was younger. She shared what her father said to her when she revealed she was going to graduate school: "I'm proud of you. Keep going, you know. I'm here to support you. These words, Josefina said, "meant enough for me to feel like, okay, I gotta get this done."

Jaime and Edith's fathers, respectively, offered their unconditional support. In Jaime's case, her dad focused on her continuing her graduate education from a master's to a doctoral program. She shared how he approached her studies: "He definitely wants me to one, graduate. Um, complete it. He's even looking forward to me possibly doing a PhD. He brings it up sometimes. He's like, oh, you know, a doctorate right afterwards." Edith remembered her dad as someone who worked hard to ensure she could go to school. But his advice to her always seemed to focus on balance—taking care of yourself while pursuing your educational goals. Referring to her dad, Edith put it this way: "So while he values hard work, he's saying to me, just make sure you take, don't overwork yourself. He still says that to me to this day, even as I pursue all these certifications, all . . . these degrees. He's like, just don't overdo it, where, where he, your wellness overall, wellness is compromise. He's just like, that's great, just don't overdo it. I think not just education, but it again all endeavors." In the end, Edith's dad supported her but cautioned her to not overdo it. "He supports us, like he, he's like yes," she recalled, "do it, do it well, but just not, don't sacrifice yourself."

Maternal Relationship Effects Continue in Graduate School as Central Support

As with fathers, many graduate students described what their mothers meant to them in graduate school. In unique and shared ways with fathers, mothers tended to offer emotional encouragement, motivational energy, and role modeling. From general appreciation to specific words of encouragement, mothers tended to be a key sources of support graduate studies. Angela elaborated on what her mom's role meant to her.

> Like, you know, for example, like I just recently watched like a Broadway show, for example, and I was thinking about like how you have all the actors on the front line, but like that wouldn't be possible without the people who are making the setups, and making the lights and everything like that. So I feel like my mom is like, almost like, I'd say a background character, but I don't want, I feel like background characters get like this, there's this connotation that they're not as important or as needed.

Angela emphasized how central her mom had been to her as a graduate student. In fact, for a small group, her mother's own academic achievement seemed to serve as motivation to do the same.

Angela, a first-generation African American female who identifies ethnically as Nigerian, talked about how her mom "instilled in me that motivation to pursue higher education and to not settle." With a MA degree in health-care administration earned while Angela was younger, Angela witnessed how hard her mom worked and what it meant to the family. Indeed, Angela's mom insisted she not stop until she earned a terminal degree. Here's what Angela said about it: "But I think like, she just always instilled in me like pursuing a degree. Even right now she's giving me talks about, okay, PhD, when are you gonna get it? I'm like, it'll come. So yeah, I, I will say definitely she's a go-getter." Her mom continued, as Angela recalled when she completed her MA degree. Her mom expressed pride but turned to the next degree that she wanted to see Angela earn: a PhD. Angela shared more: "I mean super, she was superproud that I got my master's. I think like now she's just, you know, the conversation of just like, okay, when's your PhD? We want, 'cause if I do get my PhD I'll be the first doctor in my family . . . she's really just like, okay, I really want you to do that."

Figure 8.4. During graduate school, parents offer general encouragement with unique effects from relationships with mothers and fathers, respectively. *Source:* By Jack Duval, CC BY 2.0. https://www.flickr.com/photos/92978364@N00/173605130.

Similarly, Jaime remembered how her mom's own academic achievement encouraged her to continue her education, saying: "I thought that my mom also, not related, but I thought my mom also had, um, a huge impact on my education, because she's the one who has the master's degree and I thought that was pretty cool. Especially early on as, as a very impressionable elementary student, but also because, uh, she had a lot of academic achievement." In this way, Jaime felt her mom understood and appreciated how hard it was to earn a master's degree—and this connected Jaime to her.

Many more mothers meaningfully encouraged and, in some cases, materially supported children while in graduate school. This was the case for Josefina, whose mom washed clothes for her on the weekend. Josefina remembered how her mom would ask what she could do for her. "[W]hat can, what can I, if I, if I could wash clothes for this weekend so you could focus, or whatever that might have been." More than washing clothes, Josefina recalled her mom's emotional support, too. To this point, she said, "So I think her words of encouragement were just, for me it was just more powerful even though I knew she could do anything else."

As a mother herself while in graduate school, Holly remembered how her mother cared for her daughter. Holly, a cisgender heterosexual white woman who identifies ethnically as Russian and who is married with a daughter, asked her mom for help before she even applied to a program. Without hesitation, her mom offered it to her—which made all the difference in Holly's decision to apply. At the time, Holly's mom lived with her, so it made care-taking logistically feasible. Here's what it meant for Holly's graduate school work to have her mom there for her.

> I basically told her I would need your help. Because I had a teenage daughter and, and yeah. So she said, she absolutely, she encouraged me to do that, and she said, any, any, if there is any way we can help, we will. I will help. What I can, what can I do? And I said, what I, I would need from you is to help me with my daughter. Because otherwise, you know, it wouldn't be possible for me to have a full-time job, have a, have a teenage child.

Beyond childcare, Holly's mom motivated her to achieve. Sharing pride in Holly, even as higher education had been expected in their family, her mom could not contain her excitement when Holly was admitted to her doctoral program. Through pain during end-of-life care, her mom expressed her joy at Holly's doctoral degree plans. Here's how Holly recalled those moments: "I called, I, I told her, say, I'm going for an [admissions] interview. She was very proud. I called her after the interview, I said, I think it went well. I hope, you know I'll be accepted, all that. So she was very, she was very, very, very excited. And, yeah. And she was, it was, 'cause she was in pain, something, anyway, she was in pain." When Holly's mom shared that she could not go on with the pain, Holly insisted she continue to live to see her graduate: "I said, no, no, no, no, no. I said, don't, don't say that, because you need to come to my graduation."

In the end, mothers could be recalled as sharing their joy, appreciation, and encouragement for the dreams of graduate school studies of their children. This is how Andres, a first-generation able-bodied cis-hetero male who identifies as Mexican, specifically Mexicah and Tepehuani, framed his mother's influence late in his educational journey. For Andres, his mom appreciated "how far all of us were able to get education, education-wise, right, as far as education." Andres elaborated: "That's why I dedicated all my diplomas to her. Like she has all of my original degrees for that reason. You know, 'cause it was 'cause of her, for that, that infrastructure that she built in order for us to grow, like sturdy, you know. And, and like, and like you said those roots, they have to be strong, you know." Like Andres, Sharon's mom encouraged her to finish her MA and doctoral degrees. Sharon talked about how her mom would comment on Sharon's strong academic work ethic in her MA program. "You're always working so hard," her mom would say." Sharon, who identifies as a first-generation heterosexual female, reflected on what her mom used to say: "You know, and as, kind of as an admiration, but I think there was always, also kind of a, a caution in there for me, where she's just like, you don't have to work that hard, you know." Later, for her final doctoral dissertation defense, Sharon felt her mom's presence via Zoom, where her mom joined to watch Sharon's public presentation. Sharon shared: "[S]he was actually in, she sat in the office space with [my husband] while I was in another room in the house, defending, and she watched me defend. And so I think, you know, she, because she wanted to see it. And she told me, she said, when I told her it was possible for her to see it, and she was like, I'll be there, you know." This was all the more meaningful for Sharon because her mom was terminal at the time. Sharon recalled the following:

> And at that point, and even, because this, this was now late November, she was spending ninety-five percent of her time in bed because she was just not mobile, not very mobile. But I said, there's a way for you to see this if you, you know, it's just, it's gonna be on the computer, on camera, you'll be able to see and watch. And she said, how do I do that? You know, how, how can you help me?

Sharon asked her to join on Zoom, and she did. Sharon concluded: "[W]hen I was done, you know, came in and she was, gave me a big hug, and she was just so happy."

References

Adams, M., & Coltrane, S. (2005). Boys and men in families. In M. S. Kimmel, J. Hearn, & R. Connell (Eds.), *Handbook of studies on men & masculinities*. Sage.

Adams, T., & McBrayer, J. (2020). The lived experiences of first-generation college students of color integrating into the institutional culture of a predominantly white institution. *Qualitative Report, 25*(3), 733–756.

Aguirre-Covarrubias, S., Arellano, E., & Espinoza, P. (2015). "A pesar de todo" (despite everything): The persistence of Latina graduate engineering students at a Hispanic-serving institution. *New Directions for Higher Education, 2015*(172), 49–57.

Alexander, Q. R., & Bodenhorn, N. (2015). My rock: Black women attending graduate school at a Southern predominantly white university. *Journal of College Counseling, 18*(3), 259–274.

Almeida, D. M., & Galambos, N. L. (1991). Examining father involvement and the quality of father-adolescent relations. *Journal of Research on Adolescence, 1*(2), 155–172. https://doi.org/10.1207/s15327795jra0102_3

Altschul, I. (2012). Linking socioeconomic status to the academic achievement of Mexican American youth through parent involvement in education. *Journal of the Society for Social Work and Research, 3*(1), 13–30.

Amato, P. R. (1987). Family processes in one-parent, stepparent, and intact families: The child's point of view. *Journal of Marriage and Family, 49*(2), 327–337.

Amato, P. R. (2010). Research on divorce: Continuing trends and new developments. *Journal of Marriage and Family, 72*, 650–666.

Amato, P. R., & Gilbreth, J. G. (1999). Nonresident fathers and children's well-being: A meta-analysis. *Journal of Marriage & Family, 61*(3), 557–573. https://doi.org/10.2307/353560

Arnett, J. J. (2000). Emerging adulthood: A theory of development from the late teens through the twenties. *American Psychologist, 55*(5), 469–480.

Attiyeh, G. M. (1999). Determinant of Persistence of Graduate Students in Ph.D. Programs. *ETS Research Report Series, 1999*(1), i–43. https://doi.org/10.1002/j.2333-8504.1999.tb01802.x

Baker, J. G. (1998). Gender, race and Ph.D. completion in natural science and engineering. *Economics of Education Review, 17*(2), 179–188. https://doi.org/10.1016/S0272-7757(97)00014-9

Barger, M. M., Kim, E. M., Kuncel, N. R., & Pomerantz, E. M. (2019). *The relation between parents' involvement in children's schooling and children's adjustment: A meta-analysis* [Unpublished manuscript]. American Psychological Association.

Barker, M. J. (2016). The doctorate in black and white: Exploring the engagement of Black doctoral students in cross race advising relationships with white faculty. *Western Journal of Black Studies, 40*(2), 26–140.

Barker, G., Hayes, C, Vlahovicova, K., & Gupta, T. (2023). *The state of America's fathers: Mobilizing men for a better care ecosystem.* Equimundo.

Barnett, R. C., Kibria, N., & Baruch, G. K. (1991). Adult daughter-parent relationships and their associations with daughters' subjective well-being and psychological distress. *Journal of Marriage & Family, 53,* 29–42. https://doi.org/10.2307/353131

Baruch, G. K., & Barnett, R. C. (1986). Consequences of fathers' participation in family work: Parents' role strain and well-being. *Journal of Personality & Social Psychology, 51,* 983–992. https://doi.org/10.1037/0022-3514.51.5.983

Black, M. M., Dubowitz, H., & Starr, Jr., R. H. (1999). African American fathers in low income, urban families: Development, behavior, and home environment of their three-year-old children. *Child Development, 70*(4), 967–978.

Blair, B. L., Perry, N. B., O'Brien, M., Calkins, S. D., Keane, S. P., & Shanahan, L. (2014). The indirect effects of maternal emotion socialization on friendship quality in middle childhood. *Developmental Psychology, 50*(2), 566–576.

Benzon, B., Vukojevic, K., Filipovic, N., Tomić, S., & Glavina Durdov, M. (2020). Factors That Determine Completion Rates of Biomedical Students in a PhD Programme. *Education sciences, 10*(11), 336. https://doi.org/10.3390/educsci10110336

Bermúdez, J. M., Zak-Hunter, L. M., Stinson, M. A., & Abrams, B. A. (2014). "I am not going to lose my kids to the streets": Meanings and experiences of motherhood among Mexican-origin women. *Journal of Family Issues, 35*(1), 3–27.

Birks, M., & Mills, J. (2011). *Grounded theory: A practical guide.* Sage.

Bornstein, M. H., & Putnick, D. L. (2021). Dyadic development in the family: Stability in mother-child relationship quality from infancy to adolescence. *Journal of Family Psychology, 35*(4), 445–456.

Borum, V., & Walker, E. (2011). Why didn't I know? Black women mathematicians and their avenues of exposure to the doctorate. *Journal of Women and Minorities in Science and Engineering, 17*(4), 357–369.

Borum, V., & Walker, E. (2012). What makes the difference? Black women's undergraduate and graduate experiences in mathematics. *Journal of Negro Education, 81*(4), 366.

Bray, G. B., Pascarella, E. T., & Pierson, C. T. (2004). Postsecondary education and some dimensions of literacy development: An exploration of longitudinal evidence. *Reading Research Quarterly, 39*(3), 306–330.

Brunsma, D. L., Embrick, D. G., & Shin, J. H. (2016). Graduate students of color. *Sociology of Race and Ethnicity, 3*(1), 1–13.

Bui, K., & Rush, R. A. (2016). Parental involvement in middle school predicting college attendance for first-generation students. *Education (Chula Vista), 136*(4), 473–489.

Burt, B., Knight, A., and Roberson, J. J. (2017). *Racializing experiences of foreign-born and ethnically diverse Black male engineering graduate students: Implications for student affairs practice, policy, and research.* Journal of International Students, 7(4), 925–943.

Burt, B., McKen, A. S., Burkhart, J., Hormell, J., & Knight, A. (2020). Black men in engineering graduate education: Experiencing racial microaggressions within the advisor–advisee relationship. *Journal of Negro Education, 88*(4), 493.

Burt, B. A., Williams, K. L., & Palmer, G. J. M. (2018). It takes a village: The role of emic and etic adaptive strengths in the persistence of Black men in engineering graduate programs. *American Educational Research Journal, 56*(1), 39–74.

Burt, B. A., Williams, K. L., & Smith, W. A. (2018). Into the storm: Ecological and sociological impediments to Black males' persistence in engineering graduate programs. *American Educational Research Journal, 55*(5), 965–1006.

Cabrera, N. J., Tamis-LeMonda, C. S., Bradley, R. H., Hofferth, S., & Lamb, M. E. (2000). Fatherhood in the twenty-first century. *Child Development, 71*(1), 127–136.

Camacho-Thompson, D. E., Gonzales, N. A., & Tein, J. (2019). Parental academic involvement across adolescence contextualized by gender and parenting practices. *American Psychological Association, 34*(4), 386–397.

Capannola, A. L., & Johnson, E. I. (2022). On being the first: The role of family in the experiences of first-generation college students. *Journal of Adolescent Research, 37*(1), 29–58. https://doi-org.libproxy.csun.edu/10.1177/0743558420979144

Caron, C. (2022, June 16). Navigating fatherhood as a Black man. *New York Times.* https://www.nytimes.com/2022/06/16/well/mind/black-fathers-mental-health.html

Carone, N., Lingiardi, V., Baiocco, R., & Barone, L. (2021). Sensitivity and rough-and-tumble play in gay and heterosexual single-father families through surrogacy: The role of microaggressions and fathers' rumination. *Psychology of Men & Masculinities, 22*(3), 476–487.

Cataldi, E. F., Bennett, C. T., & Chen, X. (2018). *First-generation students: College access, persistence, and postbachelor's outcomes* Institute of Education Sciences. US Department of Education.

Causey, S. T., Livingston, J., & High, B. (2015). Family structure, racial socialization, perceived parental involvement, and social support as predictors of self-esteem in African American college students. *Journal of Black Studies, 46*(7), 655–677. https://doi.org/10.1177/0021934715592601

Cavanagh, S. E., Schiller, K. S., & Rielge-Crumb, C. (2006). Marital transitions, parenting, and schooling: Exploring the linkage between family structure history and adolescents' academic success. *Sociology of Education, 79*, 329–354.

Charmaz, K. (2006). *Constructing grounded theory: A practical guide through qualitative analysis.* Sage.

Chen, Z., & Kaplan, H. B. (2001). Intergenerational transmission of constructive parenting. *Journal of Marriage and Family, 63*, 17–31.

Christopher, K. (2012). Extensive mothering: Employed mothers' constructions of the good mother. *Gender & Society, 26*(1), 73–96.

Cohn, D. A. (1990). Child-mother attachment of six-year-olds and social competence at school. *Child Development, 61*(1), 152–162.

Coles, D. C., & Cage, J. (2022). Mothers and their children: An exploration of the relationship between maternal health and child well-being. *Maternal and Child Health Journal, 26*, 1015–1021.

Coley, R. L. (2003). Daughter-father relationships and adolescent psychosocial functioning in low-income African American families. *Journal of Marriage and Family, 65*, 867–875.

Coltrane, S. (1998). *Gender and families.* Pine Forge Press.

Coltrane, S., & Adams, M. (1997). Children and gender. In T. Arendell (Ed.), *Contemporary parenting: Challenges and issues* (pp. 219–253). Sage.

Connell, R. W. (1987). *Gender and power: Society, the person, and sexual politics.* Stanford University Press.

Cox, G. W., Hughes, W. E., Etzkorn, L. H., & Weisskopf, M. E. (2009). Predicting computer science Ph.D. completion: A case study. *IEEE Transactions on Education, 52*(1), 137–143. https://doi.org/10.1109/TE.2008.921458

Cuellar, M.G., & Gonzalez, A.M. (2019). Beyond the baccalaureate: Factors shaping Latina/o graduate degree aspirations. *Journal of Hispanic Higher Education, 20*(1), 59–74.

Cutrona, C. E., Cole, V., Colangelo, N., Assouline, S. G., & Russell, D. W. (1994). Perceived parental social support and academic achievement: An attachment theory perspective. *Journal of Personality and Social Psychology, 66*(2), 369–378. https://doi.org/10.1037/0022-3514.66.2.369

Dad arranges for special graduation ceremony for his daughter. (2020, May 19). *NPR.* https://www.npr.org/2020/05/19/858499071/dad-arranges-for-special-graduation-ceremony-for-his-daughter

Davis, D. J. (2007). Access to academe: The importance of mentoring to Black students. *Negro Educational Review, 58*(3–4), 217–231, 279.

Davis, A.N., Carlo, G., Streit, C., Schwartz, S. J., Unger, J. B., Baezconde-Garbanati, L., & Szapocznik, J. (2018). Longitudinal associations between maternal involvement, cultural orientations, and prosocial behaviors among recent immigrant Latino adolescents. *Journal of Youth and Adolescence, 47*(2), 460–472.

Davis, G. R. (2012). *Exploring the relationship between African American father involvement and the academic success of their college-age children* (Publication No. 3517357) [Doctoral dissertation, Alliant International University]. ProQuest Dissertations and Theses.

DeAngelo, L. (2010). Preparing for the PhD at a comprehensive institution: Perceptions of the "barriers." *Journal of the Professoriate, 3*(2), 17–49.

Doucet, A. (2012). Gender roles and fathering. In Cabrera, N. J., & Tamis-LeMonda, C. S. (Eds.), *Handbook of father involvement: Multidisciplinary perspectives*, 2nd ed. (pp. 297–319). Taylor & Francis Group.

Felder, P. (2010). On doctoral student development: Exploring faculty mentoring in the shaping of African American doctoral student success. *Qualitative Report, 15*(2), 455–474.

Figueroa T. (2015). *Underrepresented racial/ethnic minority graduate students in science, technology, engineering, and math (STEM) disciplines: A cross institutional analysis of their experiences* (Publication No. 3706144) [Doctoral dissertation, University of California, Los Angeles]. ProQuest Dissertations and Theses.

Fingerman, K. L., Cheng, Y. P., Tighe, L., Birditt, K. S., & Zarit, S. (2012). Relationships between young adults and their parents. In A. Booth, S. Brown, N. Landale, W. Manning, & S. McHale (Eds.), *Early adulthood in a family context* (pp. 59–85). Springer.

Fingerman, K. L., Cheng, Y. P., Wesselmann, E. D., Zarit, S., Furstenberg, F., & Birditt, K. S. (2012). Helicopter parents and landing pad kids: Intense parental support of grown children. *Journal of Marriage and Family, 74*(4), 880–896.

Forbes, L. K., Donovan, C., & Lamar, M.R. (2020). Differences in intensive parenting attitudes and gender norms among US mothers. *Family Journal, 28*(1), 63–71.

Franklin, J. D. (2019). Coping with racial battle fatigue: Differences and similarities for African American and Mexican American college students. *Race, Ethnicity and Education, 22*(5), 589–609.

Franklin, J. D., Smith, W. A., & Hung, M. (2014). Racial battle fatigue for Latina/o students. *Journal of Hispanic Higher Education, 13*(4), 303–322.

Frome, P. M., & Eccles, J. S. (1998). Parents' influence on children's achievement-related perceptions. *Journal of Personality and Social Psychology, 74*(2), 435–452.

Gair, M., & Mullins, G. (2001). Hiding in plain sight. In E. Margolis (Ed.), *The hidden curriculum in higher education* (pp. 21–43). Routledge.

García, I. O., & Henderson, S. J. (2014). Mentoring experiences of Latina graduate students. *Multicultural learning and teaching, 10*(1), 91–109.

Garcia, N. M., & Mireles-Rios, R. (2020). "You were going to go to college": The role of Chicano fathers' involvement in Chicana daughters' college choice.

American Educational Research Journal, 57(5), 2059–2088. https://doi.org/10.3102/0002831219892004

Garner, P. W., Dunsmore, J. C., & Southam-Gerrow, M. (2008). Mother-child conversations about emotions: Linkages to child aggression and prosocial behavior. *Social Development, 17*(2), 259–277.

Gildersleeve, R. E., Croom, N. N., & Vasquez, P. L. (2011). "Am I going crazy?!": A critical race analysis of doctoral education. *Equity & Excellence in Education, 44*(1), 93–114.

Ginsburg, G. S., & Bronstein, P. (1993). Family factors related to children's intrinsic/extrinsic motivational orientation and academic performance. *Child Development, 64*, 1461–1474.

Glaser, B. G., & Strauss, A. L. (1967). *The discovery of grounded theory: Strategies for qualitative research.* Aldine de Gruyter.

Gordon, M. S. (2017). Self-perception and relationship quality as mediators of father's school-specific involvement and adolescent's academic achievement. *Children and Youth Services Review, 77*, 94–100. https://doi.org/10.1016/j.childyouth.2017.04.001

Gorski, P. C. (2018). Racial battle fatigue and activist burnout in racial justice activists of color at predominately white colleges and universities. *Race Ethnicity and Education, 22*(1), 1–20.

Grolnick, W. S., Slowiaczek, M. L. (1994). Parents' involvement in children's schooling: A multidimensional conceptualization and motivational model. *Child Development, 65(1)*, 237–252.

Grusec, J. E. (2011). Socialization processes in the family: Social and emotional development. *Annual Review of Psychology, 62*, 243–269.

Harwood, R. L., Schoelmerich, A., Ventura-Cook, E., Schulze, P. A., & Wilson, S. P. (1996). Culture and class influences on Anglo and Puerto Rican mothers' beliefs regarding long-term socialization goals and child behavior. *Child Development, 67*, 2446–2461.

Hearn, J. (1992). *Men in the public eye: The construction and deconstruction of public men and public patriarchies.* Routledge.

Heredia, R. C. (2009). *Latino parents' perceptions of their involvement in their children's secondary education and the college preparation process* (Publication No. 3352203) [Doctoral dissertation, Pepperdine University]. ProQuest Dissertations and Theses.

Herndon, M. K., and J. B. Hirt. (2004). "Black students and their families: What leads to success in college." *Journal of Black Studies, 34*(4): 489–513.

Holley, K. A., & Gardner, S. (2012). Navigating the Pipeline: How Socio-Cultural Influences Impact First-Generation Doctoral Students. *Journal of diversity in higher education, 5*(2), 112–121.

Holmes, E. K., Wikle, J., Thomas, C. R., Hectornsen, M. A., & Egginton, B. R. (2021). Social contact, time alone, and parental subjective well-being: A focus on stay-at-home fathers using the American time use survey. *Psychology of Men & Masculinities, 22*(3), 488–499.

Hong, S., Hardi, F., & Maguire-Jack, K. (2023) The moderating role of neighborhood social cohesion on the relationship between early mother-child attachment security and adolescent social skills: Brief report. *Journal of Social and Personal Relationships, 40*(1), 277–287.

Hsu, A. (2020, November 11). 'I'm a much better cook': For fathers, being forced to stay at home is eye-opening. *NPR.* https://www.npr.org/2020/11/11/931650888/for-dads-in-the-pandemic-lows-highs-and-constant-uncertainty

Hughes, D. (2003). Correlates of African American and Latino parents' messages to children about ethnicity and race: A comparative study of racial socialization. *American Journal of Community and Psychology, 31*(1/2), 15–33.

Jacobs, C. (2023). Parental educational support to adolescents: Exploring the role of emotional capital in low-income single-mother families in South Africa. *South African Journal of Education, 43*(2), 1–9.

Jason, K., Richardson, S., & Dennis, K. N. (2023). Relieving the burden of self-reliance: Centering the experiences of Black women graduate students in predominantly white institutions. *Journal of African American Women and Girls in Education, 2*(3), 8–33.

Jeffe, D. B., Andriole, D. A., Wathington, H. D., & Tai, R. H. (2014). Educational outcomes for students enrolled in MD–PhD programs at medical school matriculation, 1995–2000: A National Cohort Study. *Academic Medicine, 89*(1), 84–93. https://doi.org/10.1097/ACM.0000000000000071

Johnson-Bailey, J., Valentine, T., Cervero R., & Bowles, T. A. (2008). Lean on me: The support experiences of Black graduate students. *Journal of Negro Education, 77*(4), 365–381.

Johnson-Bailey, J., Valentine, T., Cervero R., & Bowles, T. A. (2009). Rooted in the soil: The social experiences of Black graduate students at a Southern research university. *Journal of Higher Education, 80*(2), 178–203.

Johnson-Motoyama, M., Petr, C. G., & Mitchell, F. M. (2014). Factors associated with success in doctoral social work education. *Journal of Social Work Education, 50*(3), 548–558. https://doi.org/10.1080/10437797.2014.916955

Kalmuss, D., & Seltzer, J. A. (1989). A framework for studying family socialization over the life cycle: The case of family violence. *Journal of Family Issues, 10*(3), 339–358.

Kapaona, A., & Ono, M. (2016, June). Re-envisioning parental involvement in higher education: Shifting the paradigm of the helicopter parent. *Academic Advising Today, 39*(2). https://nacada.ksu.edu/Resources/Academic-Advising-Today/View-Articles/Re-envisioning-Parental-Involvement-in-Higher-Education-Shifting-the-Paradigm-of-the-Helicopter-Parent.aspx

Kerns, K. A. (1996). Peer relationships and preadolescents' perceptions of security in the child-mother relationship. *Developmental Psychology, 32*, 457–466.

King, M. F. (2008). *Ph.D. completion and attrition: Analysis of baseline demographic data from the Ph.D. completion project.* Council of Graduate Education.

King, V., Pragg, B., & Lindstrom, R. (2020). Family relationships during adolescence and stepchilden's educational attainment in young adulthood. *Journal of Marriage and Family, 82*(2), 622–638. https://doi.org/10.1111/jomf.12642

Kramer, S. K. (2020, June 3). When your dad owns a pizzeria, the pandemic means learning to make the perfect pie. *NPR.* https://www.npr.org/sections/coronavirus-live-updates/2020/07/03/886033575/when-your-dad-owns-a-pizzeria-the-pandemic-means-learning-to-make-the-perfect-pi

Kuncel, N. R., & Hezlett, S. A. (2007). Standardized tests predict graduate students' success. *Science (American Association for the Advancement of Science), 315*(5815), 1080–1081. https://doi.org/10.1126/science.1136618

Lamb, M. E. (1977). Father-infant and mother-infant interaction in the first year of life. *Child Development, 48*, 167–181.

Lamb, M. E. (2010). How do fathers influence children's development? Let me count the ways. In Lamb, M. E. (Ed.), *The role of the father in child development* (3rd ed.). John Wiley.

Lamb, J. H., Pleck, J. H., & Levine, J. A. (1985). Effects of paternal involvement on fathers and mothers. *Marriage & Family Review, 9*(3–4), 67–83.

Lamb, M. E., & Lewis, C. (2010). The development and significance of father-child relationships in two-parent families. In M. E. Lamb (Ed.), *The role of the father in child development.* John Wiley.

Lamb, M. E., & Lewis, C. (2012). Father-child relationships. In N. J. Cabrera & C. S. Tamis-LeMonda (Eds.), *Handbook of father involvement: Multidisciplinary perspectives.* Taylor & Francis.

Lansford, J. E., Ceballo, R., Abbey, A., & Stewart, A. J. (2001). Does family structure matter? A comparison of adoptive, two-parent biological, single-mother, stepfather, and stepmother Households. *Journal of Marriage and Family, 63*(3), 840–851. https://doi.org/10.1111/j.1741-3737.2001.00840.x

LeBouef, S., & Dworkin, J. (2021). First-generation college students and family support: A critical review of empirical research literature. *Education Sciences, 11*(6), 294. https://doi.org/10.3390/educsci11060294

Leidy, M. S., Schofield, T. J., & Parke, R. D. (2012). Fathers' contributions to children's social development. In N. J. Cabrera & C. S. Tamis-LeMonda (Eds.), *Handbook of father involvement: Multidisciplinary perspectives.* Taylor & Francis.

Levin, J. S., Jaeger, A. J., & Haley, K. J. (2013). Graduate student dissonance: Graduate students of color in a U.S. research university. *Journal of Diversity in Higher Education, 6*(4), 231–244.

Livingston, G., & Parker, K. (2019, June 12). *8 facts about American fathers.* Pew Research Center. https://www.pewresearch.org/fact-tank/2019/06/12/fathers-day-facts/

Lopez, R. I. (2013). *A study of prevention and retention strategies for successful urban secondary high school Hispanic students* (Publication No. 3572158) [Doctoral dissertation, Texas A&M University]. ProQuest Dissertations and Theses.

Louque, A. (1999). Factors influencing academic attainment for African-American women Ph.D. recipients: An ethnographic study of their persistence. *Negro Educational Review 50*(3–4): 101–108.

Love, B. H. (2017). *More than a silhouette: African American women's graduate student experience* (Publication No. 10745602) [Doctoral dissertation, University of San Francisco]. ProQuest Dissertations and Theses.

Love, K., Tyler, K., Thomas, D., Garriott, P., Brown, C., & Roan-Belle, C. (2009). Influence of multiple attachments on well-being: A model from African Americans attending historically Black colleges and universities. *Journal of Diversity in Higher Education, 2*(1), 35–45.

Lovitts, B. E., & Nelson, C. (2000). The hidden crisis in graduate education: Attrition from Ph.D. programs. *Academe, 86*(6), 44–50.

Luengo Kanacri, B. P., Pastorelli, C., Thartori, E., Lunetti, C., Di Giunta, L., Bacchini, D., & Lansford, J. E. (2021). Longitudinal relations among maternal self-efficacy, maternal warmth, and early adolescents' prosocial behavior. *Parenting: Science & Practice, 21*(1), 24–46.

Lunneborg, C. E., & Lunneborg, P. W. (1973). Doctoral study attrition in psychology. *Research in Higher Education, 1*(4), 379–387. https://doi.org/10.1007/BF00991671

Lytton, H., & Romney, D. M. (1991). Parents' differential socialization of boys and girls: A meta-analysis. *Psychological Bulletin, 109*(2), 267. https://doi.org/10.1037/0033-2909.109.2.267

Malone, B. G., Nelson, J. S., & Van Nelson, C. (2004). Academic and affective factors contributing to degree completion of doctoral students in educational administration. *Teacher Educator, 40*(1), 33–55. https://doi.org/10.1080/08878730409555350

Marsiglio, W. (2005). *Stepfathers: Stories of love, hope, and repair*. Rowan & Littlefield.

Marshall, S. L., Barnett, III, C., Hinton Q., & Morris, C. B. (2023). Factors for success: Supporting Black doctoral students. *Language Arts Journal of Michigan, 38*(2).

Martinez, A. (2018). Pathways to the professoriate: The experiences of first-generation Latino undergraduate students at Hispanic Serving Institutions. *Applying to Doctoral Programs Education Sciences, 8*(1), 32.

McBride, B. A., & Mills, G. (1993). A comparison of mother and father involvement with their preschool age children. *Early Childhood Research Quarterly, 8*, 457–477.

McCallum, C. M. (2016). "Mom made me do it": The role of family in African Americans' decisions to enroll in doctoral education. *Journal of Diversity in Higher Education, 9*(1), 50–63. https://doi.org/10.1037/a0039158

McCoy, D. L., and R. Winkle-Wagner (2022). Cultivating 'generational blessings': Graduate school aspirations and intergenerational uplift among women of color. *Journal of College Student Development 63*(5): 491–507.

McGee, E. O., Griffith, D. M., & Houston, II, S. L. (2019). "I know I have to work twice as hard and hope that makes me good enough": Exploring the stress and strain of Black doctoral students in engineering and computing. *Teachers College Record: The Voice of Scholarship in Education, 121*(4), 1–38.

Mendoza-Denton, R., Patt, C., Fisher, A., Eppig, A., Young, I., Smith, A., & Richards, M. A. (2017). Differences in STEM doctoral publication by ethnicity, gender and academic field at a large public research university. *PloS one, 12*(4), e0174296-e0174296. https://doi.org/10.1371/journal.pone.0174296

Mendoza-Sanchez, I., deGruyter, J. N., Savage, N. T., & Polymenis, M. (2022). Undergraduate GPA predicts biochemistry PhD completion and is associated with time to degree. *CBE Life Sciences Education, 21*(2), ar19–ar31. https://doi.org/10.1187/cbe.21-07-0189

Miller, C. C. (2024, February 9). Parents are highly involved in their adult children's lives, and fine with it. *New York Times.* https://www.nytimes.com/2024/02/09/upshot/parenting-young-adults-relationships.html

Milne, A., & Plourde, L. A. (2006). Factors of a low-SES household: What aids academic achievement? *Journal of Instructional Psychology, 33*(3), 183–193.

Min, J., Silverstein, M., & Lendon, J. P. (2012). Intergenerational transmission of values over the family life course. *Advances in Life Course Research, 17*(3), 112–120.

Mireles-Rios, R., & Garcia, N. M. (2018). What would your ideal graduate mentoring program look like? Latina/o student success in higher education. *Journal of Latinos and Education, 18*(4), 376–386.

Monarrez, A., Frederick, A., Morales, D. X., Echegoyen, L. E., & Wagler, A. (2022). Hispanic/Latinx STEM majors applying to graduate school: The role of family, peers, and undergraduate research programs in facilitating community cultural wealth. *Journal of Latinos and Education*, ahead-of-print (ahead-of-print), 1–15. https://doi.org/10.1080/15348431.2022.2122973

Nelson, J. A., Leerkes, E. M., Perry, N. B., O'Brien, M., Calkins, S. D., & Marcovitch, S. (2013). European-American and African-American mothers' emotion socialization practices relate differently to their children's academic and social-emotional competence. *Social Development, 22*(3), 485–498.

Nock, S. L., & Kingston, P. W. (1988). Time with children: The impact of couples' work-time commitments. *Social Forces, 67*(1), 59–85.

Ohio dad figures out socially distant trick or treating. (2020, September 21). *NPR.* https://www.npr.org/2020/09/21/915171232/ohio-dad-figures-out-socially-distant-trick-or-treating

Owens, D., Lockhart, S., Matthews, D. Y., & Middleton, T. J. (2019). Racial battle fatigue and mental health in Black men. In Jennifer T. Butcher, Johnny

R. O'Connor Jr., Freddie Titus (Eds.), *Research Anthology on Empowering Marginalized Communities and Mitigating Racism and Discrimination*. IGI Global Scientific Publishing.

Özyürek, A., & Çetin, A. (2022). The investigation of the effect of secure attachment to mother on self-perception in middle childhood. *International Journal of Contemporary Educational Research, 9*(2), 272–282.

Palkovitz, R. (1997). Reconstructing "involvement": Expanding conceptualizations of men's caring in contemporary families. In A. J. Hawkins & D. C. Dollahite (Eds.), *Generative fathering: Beyond deficit perspectives*. Sage.

Patterson-Stephens, S. M., Lane, T. B., & Vital, L. M. (2017). Black doctoral women: Exploring barriers and facilitators of success in graduate education. *Higher Education Politics & Economics, 3*(1), 157–180.

Patton, L. D. (2009). My sister's keeper: A qualitative examination of mentoring experiences among African American women in graduate and professional schools. *Journal of Higher Education, 80*(5), 510–537.

Pearson, S. M., & Bieschke, K. J. (2001). Succeeding against the odds: An examination of familial influences on the career development of professional African American women. *Journal of Counseling Psychology, 48*(3), 301–309. https://doi.org/10.1037/0022-0167.48.3.301

Perna, L. W. (2004). Understanding the decision to enroll in graduate school: Sex and racial/ethnic group differences. *Journal of Higher Education, 75*, 487–487.

Perry, N. B., Dollar, J. M., Calkins, S. D., Keane, S. P., & Shanahan, L. (2020). Maternal socialization of child emotion and adolescent adjustment: Indirect effects through emotion regulation. *Developmental psychology, 56*(3), 541–552.

Petersen, C. C. (2007). *Father involvement, nurturant fathering, and the psychological well-being of young adult daughters* (Publication No. 1445069) [Doctoral dissertation, Utah State University]. ProQuest Dissertations and Theses.

Pew Research Center. (2013). *Modern parenthood: Roles of moms and dads converge as they balance work and family*. Washington, DC: Pew Research Center.

Phinney, J. S., Dennis, J., & Osorio, S. (2006). Reasons to attend college among ethnically diverse college students. *Cultural Diversity and Ethnic Minority Psychology 12*(2): 347–366.

Pleck, J. H. (1997). Paternal involvement: Levels, sources, and consequences. In M. E. Lamb (Ed.), *The role of the father in child development* (3rd ed.). Wiley.

Pollack, C. (2019, June). Tracing the expanding definition of fatherhood. *NPR*. https://www.npr.org/sections/pictureshow/2019/06/14/674585374/tracing-the-expanding-definition-of-fatherhood

Pomerantz, E. M., Moorman, E. A., & Litwack, S. D. (2007). The how, whom, and why of parents' involvement in children's academic lives: More is not always better. *Review of Education Research, 77*(3), 373–410.

Pruett, K. D. (1985). Fathers as 'mothers': how are their children doing? *Consultant, 25*(6), 152–160.

Putney, N. M., & Bengtson, V. L. (2002). Socialization and the family revisited. *Advances in Life Course Research, 7,* 165–194.

Qu, D., Huang, J., Yu, N. X., Hui, L. L., & Kouros, C. D. (2021). Association between mother-adolescent relationship quality and subjective well-being: Resilience resources as a mediating factor among Hong Kong Chinese adolescents. *Journal of Child and Family Studies, 30,* 1990–2002.

Quaye, S. J., Karikari, S. N., Carter, K. D., Okello, W. K., & Allen, C. (2020). "Why Can't I Just Chill?": The visceral nature of racial battle fatigue. *Journal of College Student Development, 61*(5), 609–623.

Radin, N. (1994). Primary-caregiving fathers in intact families. In A. E. Gottfried & A. W. Gottfried (Eds.), *Redefining families: Implications for children's development* (pp. 11–54). Plenum Press.

Ramirez, E. (2014). "¿Qué estoy haciendo aquí? (What am I doing here?)": Chicanos/Latinos(as) navigating challenges and inequalities during their first year of graduate school. *Equity & Excellence in Education, 47*(2), 167–186.

Ramirez, E. (2011). "No one taught me the steps": Latinos' experiences applying to graduate school. *Journal of Latinos and Education, 10*(3), 204–222.

Ricks, J. R., & Warren, J. M. (2021). Transitioning to college: Experiences of successful first-generation college students. *Journal of educational research and practice, 11*(1), 1. https://doi.org/10.5590/JERAP.2021.11.1.01

Robinson, S. J. (2013). Spoketokenism: Black women talking back about graduate school experiences. *Race Ethnicity and Education, 16*(2), 155–181.

Rodney, H. E., & Mupier, R. (1999). Behavioral differences between African American male adolescents with biological fathers and those without biological fathers in the home. *Journal of Black Studies, 30*(1), 45–61. https://doi.org/10.1177/002193479903000103

Rohner, R. P. (1998). Father love and child development: History and current evidence. *Current Directions in Psychological Science, 7*(5), 157–161.

Rohner. R. P., & Veneziano, R. A. (2001). The importance of father love: History and contemporary evidence. *Review of General Psychology, 5*(4), 382–405.

Roy, K. M., & Settersten, R. A., Jr. (2022). The family life course framework: Perspectives on interdependent lives and inequality. In K. Adamsons, A. L. Few-Demo, C. Proulx, and K. Roy (Eds.), *Sourcebook of family theories and methodologies.* Springer. https://doi.org/10.1007/978-3-030-92002-9_20

Schwartz, R. A., Bower, B. L., Rice, D. C., & Washington, C. M. (2003). "Ain't I a woman, too?": Tracing the experiences of African American women in graduate school. *Journal of Negro Education, 72*(3), 252–268.

Schwartz, S. J., & Finley, G. E. (2006). Father involvement, nurturant fathering, and young adult psychosocial functioning differences among adoptive, adoptive stepfather, and nonadoptive stepfamilies. *Journal of Family Issues, 27*(5), 712–731.

Schwartz, S. J., Zamboanga, B. L., Ravert, R. D., Kim, W. Y., Weisskirch, R. S., Williams, M. K., Bersamin, M., & Finley, G. E. (2009). Perceived parental relationships and health-risk behaviors in college-attending emerging adults. *Journal of Marriage and Family, 71*, 717–740.

Seagram, B. C., Gould, J., & Pyke, S. W. (1998). An Investigation of Gender and Other Variables on Time to Completion of Doctoral Degrees. *Research in higher education, 39*(3), 319–335. https://doi.org/10.1023/A:1018781118312

Sheridan, P. M., & Pyke, S. W. (1994). Predictors of time to completion of graduate degrees. *Canadian Journal of Higher Education (1975), 24*(2), 68. https://doi.org/10.47678/cjhe.v24i2.188439

Silverstein, L. B., & Auerbach, C. F. (1999). Deconstructing the essential father. *American Psychologist, 54*(6), 397–407. https://doi.org/10.1037/0003-066X.54.6.397

National Center for Education Statistics. (2022a). Graduate Degree Fields. Condition of education. U.S. Department of Education, Institute of Education Sciences. Retrieved January 9, 2023 from https://nces.ed.gov/programs/coe/indicator/ctb/graduate-degree-fields

National Center for Education Statistics. (2022b). Postbaccalaureate enrollment. *Condition of Education*. U.S. Department of Education, Institute of Education Sciences. Retrieved January 9, 2023 from https://nces.ed.gov/programs/coe/indicator/chb/postbaccalaureate-enrollment

Tefteller, D. H. (2014). *The influence of father involvement and family structure variables on young adult-father relationship quality* [Doctoral dissertation, University of Akron]. ProQuest Dissertations and Theses.

Threlfall, J. (2015). *Parent involvement in education and college planning for African American high school students* (Publication No. 3718122) [Doctoral dissertation, Washington University]. ProQuest Dissertations and Theses.

Thomas, P. A., Krampe, E. M., & Newton, R. R. (2008). Father presence, family structure, and feelings of closeness to the father among adult African American children. *Journal of Black Studies, 38*(4), 529–546.

Turner, J. S., & Juntune, J. (2018). Perceptions of the home environments of graduate students raised in poverty. *Journal of Advanced Academics, 29*(2), 91–115. https://doi.org/10.1177/1932202X18758259

Updegraff, K. A., McHale, S. M., Crouter, A. C., & Kupanoff, K. (2001). Parents' involvement in adolescents' peer relationships: A comparison of mothers' and fathers' roles. *Journal of Marriage and Family, 63*(3), 655–668. https://doi.org/10.1111/j.1741-3737.2001.00655.x

U.S. Bureau of Labor Statistics. (2021). Education pays. Office of Occupational Statistics and employment projections. U.S. Bureau of Labor Statistics. https://www.bls.gov/emp/chart-unemployment-earnings-education.htm

van de Schoot, R., Yerkes, M. A., Mouw, J. M., & Sonneveld H. (2013). "What took them so long? Explaining PhD delays among doctoral candidates." *PloS One 8*(7): e68839–e68839.

van der Gaag, N., Gupta, T., Heilman, B., Barker, G., & van den Berg, W. (2023). *State of the world's fathers: Centering care in a world in crisis*. Equimundo.

Velazquez, M. (2017). Primero madres: Love and mothering in the educational lives of Latina/os. *Gender and Education, 29*(4), 508–524.

Vergara-Lopez, C., Sokol, N. A., Bublitz, M. H., Gaffey, A. E., Gomez, A., Mercado, N., Silk, J. S., Stroud, L. R. (2024). Exploring the impact of maternal and paternal acceptance on adolescent girls' emotion regulation. *Child psychiatry and human development, 55*(2), 320–326.

Volling, B. L., & Palkovitz, R. (2021). Fathering: New perspectives, paradigms, and possibilities. *Psychology of Men & Masculinities, 22*(3), 427–432.

Walkington, L. (2017). How far have we really come? Black women faculty and graduate students' experiences in higher education. *Humboldt Journal of Social Relations, 1*(39), 51–65.

Walsh, B. A., Mitchell, S., Batz, R., Lee, A., Aguirre, M., Lucero, J., Edwards, A, Hambrick, K., & Zeh, D.W. (2023). Familial roles and support of doctoral students. *Family relations, 72*(5), 2444–2464. DOI: 10.1111/fare.12848

Wang, M., Hill, N. E., & Hofkens, T. (2014). Parental involvement and African American and European American adolescents' academic, behavioral, and emotional development in secondary school. *Child Development, 85*(6), 2151–2168.

Wao, H. O., & Onwuegbuzie, A. J. (2011). A mixed research investigation of factors related to time to the doctorate in education. *International Journal of Doctoral Studies, 6*, 115–134. https://doi.org/10.28945/1505

Wen, W., Chen, S., Kim, S. Y., & Hou, Y. (2022). Mother-adolescent perceived parenting profiles and Mexican-origin adolescents' academic performance. *Journal of Youth and Adolescence, 52*, 344–358.

Wigfield, A., Eccles, J. S., Fredricks, J. A., Simpkins, S., Roeser, R. W., & Schiefele, U. (2015). Development of achievement motivation and engagement. In M. E. Lamb & R. M. Lerner (Eds.), *Handbook of child psychology and developmental science: Socioemotional processes, Vol. 3*, 7th ed. (pp. 657–700). John Wiley.

Williams, M. R., Brewley, D. N., Reed, R. J., White, D. Y., & Davis-Haley, R. T. (2005). Learning to read each other: Black female graduate students share their experiences at a White research I institution. *Urban Review, 37*(3), 181–199.

Wright, T., & Cochrane, R. (2000). Factors influencing successful submission of PhD theses. *Studies in Higher Education (Dorchester-on-Thames), 25*(2), 181–195. https://doi.org/10.1080/713696139

Ye, Z., & Rudolph, K. D. (2024). Talk it out or tuck it away: The contribution of maternal socialization of coping to depression in youth with early pubertal maturation. *Developmental Psychology, 60*(2), 322–334.

Yosso, T. J. (2005). Whose culture has capital? A critical race theory discussion of community cultural wealth. *Race Ethnicity and Education, 8*(1), 69–91. https://doi.org/10.1080/1361332052000341006

Zagame, A. C. (2022). *Understanding fathering and adolescents' wellbeing: Father figures and transition to young adulthood* (Publication No. 29704239) [Doctoral dissertation, Brown University]. ProQuest Dissertations and Theses.

Zarate, M. E. (2023). A nanny's daughter in the academy. In T. L. Buenavista, T. L., D. Jain, & M. C. Ledesma (Eds.), *First-generation faculty of color: Reflections on research, teaching, and service* (pp. 41–53). Rutgers University Press. https://doi.org/10.36019/9781978823488

Zimmerman, M. A., Salem, D. A., & Maton, K. I. (1995). Family structure and psychosocial correlates among urban African-American adolescent males. *Child Development, 66,* 1598–1613.

Zwick, R., & Braun, H. I. (1988). Methods for analyzing the attainment of graduate school milestone: A case study. *ETS research report series, 1988(1),* i–79. https://doi.org/10.1002/j.2330-8516.1988.tb00286.xer

Index

Andres (interviewee)
  on applying to college, 201–2
  on applying to graduate school, 281–82
  on education, 112
  on gangs, 198, 226, 241, 242
  on gender norms, 37–38
  and high school counselor, 240
  on his ancestors, 309
  on his brother, 115–17, 245
  on his cousins, 217–18
  on his father, 46, 123, 226–27, 244–45
  on his mother, 85, 124, 137, 217–18, 318–19
  and his parents, 76–77, 159, 240, 258
  and his travels, 309
  on letter, 115–16
  and prison, 241
  on segregation, 170–71
  on white flight, 198
  on working, 241–42
Angela (interviewee)
  on applying to college, 195, 201, 202–3
  on background character, 309
  on care, 133, 162–63
  on community, 292–93
  on education, 101–2
  on financial issues, 205, 206
  on her elders, 135
  on her father, 87
  on her mother, 62–64, 84, 122, 177, 316
  on her parents, 124, 248, 275
  on her sisters, 120
  on independence, 184, 268
  on Nigerian cultural pride, 166
  on parental involvement in education, 217, 224–25
  on religion, 144–45, 147, 161–62
anti-immigrant issues, 19, 153, 182, 191, 211, 287
ATLAS.ti, 24–25

background character, 309
Beatrice (interviewee)
  on applying to college, 233–34
  on applying to graduate school, 282
  on faculty, 307
  on family gatherings, 128
  on fathers, 58
  on gender norms, 50–51, 68–69
  on her father, 88–89, 114–15, 213, 314
  on her parents, 127, 264
  on independence, 69
  on parental involvement in education, 253

Beatrice (interviewee) *(continued)*
  on physical therapy, 307
  on religion, 149
  on sports, 69
Brianna (interviewee)
  on care, 134
  on her aunts & uncles, 119
  on her father, 46, 81, 126
  on her grandfather, 53, 81, 224, 244
  on her grandparents, 72–73, 99, 126–27
  on her mother, 42, 62, 83, 119
  on independence, 66, 183–84, 184
  on letters, 134
  on parental involvement in education, 99, 218–19
  on religion, 143–44, 147
  on segregation, 197
burnout, 3, 295
Burson, Torrence, 9

care, 128–29, 162
code-switching, 167–68, 174
coming out, 92, 207
confidentiality, 23
COVID-19, 8–9, 35, 189, 257, 296, 300

"Dad arranges for special graduation ceremony for his daughter" (NPR), 9
discrimination, 191
dissertations, 15, 319
divorce, 71, 150, 206
double guessing, 174
double thinking, 174

échale ganas, 201, 244–45, 256, 281, 309
Edith (interviewee)
  on education, 102
  on faculty, 305
  on financial issues, 205
  on gender norms, 38–39, 205
  on giving back to the community, 298
  on her father, 58–59, 78–79, 315
  on her husband, 242
  on her parents, 126
  on immigration, 102
  on Korean connections, 167
  on language issues, 194–95
  on parental involvement in education, 212–13, 246–47
  on peers, 302
  on religion, 146
  on social justice, 139
Eileen (interviewee)
  on applying to college, 223
  on colleagues, 301
  on education, 109
  on faculty, 306
  on family unity, 131
  on gender norms, 39
  on her parents, 313
  on parental involvement in education, 77, 222–23, 251–52, 272–73
Eugenio (interviewee)
  on community, 139
  on family gatherings, 94–95, 130
  on his father, 46, 94, 127, 264–65
  on his mother, 54
  on his parents, 157–58, 245–46, 309–10
  on not fitting in, 308
  on parental involvement in education, 196, 225
  on religion, 142–43

family processes, 70, 208–9
family structures, 70, 72
fear of family separation, 192
fictive family members, 10, 17, 232, 238, 239, 276

Field Day, 227
Floyd, George, 137

Gail (interviewee)
  on education, 114
  on gender norms, 46
  on her cousin, 119, 232
  on her father, 93, 94, 263–64, 313
  on high school, 231
  on independence, 185
  on mentors, 240
  on parental involvement in
    education, 231–32, 232, 252–53
  on proximity to home, 273
  on religion, 151
gangs, 198, 226, 241, 242
gap years, 257–58, 280–81
gender norms
  discussed, 6, 35, 36–37, 58, 70, 122
  resistance to, 36, 48–50, 52–53,
    62–64, 74
grounded theory, 21–22, 24, 25

Hannon, Michael, 11
Hector (interviewee)
  on applying to college, 213
  on care, 135–36
  and code-switching, 174
  on community, 299–300
  on cultural and ethnic pride, 167
  on discrimination, 171–72
  and double guessing, 174
  and double thinking, 174
  on education, 98–99
  on family gatherings, 132
  on gender norms, 55, 61
  on high school, 173
  on his father, 55, 250–51, 257,
    274–75
  on his great-grandparents, 176
  on his mother, 42, 61, 80, 214–15
  on his siblings, 120
  on parental involvement in
    education, 214–15
  on pushing himself, 295
  and racism, 174
  on religion, 142
  on social justice, 136–37
  on sports, 55, 79
Holly (interviewee)
  on education, 108–9, 223
  on family unity, 129
  on gender norms, 53–54
  on her father, 160–61
  on her mother, 83–84, 220–21, 318
  on her parents⊠ deaths, 279, 311
  on her stepfather, 311
  on love of learning, 298
  on respect, 138
Hua (interviewee)
  on applying to graduate school, 283
  on education, 98
  on family support, 134
  on fathers, 45
  on her father, 314
  on her parents, 64
  on independence, 185
  on parental involvement in
    education, 216
  on religion, 150

immigration, 91, 104, 154, 162–63
imposter syndrome, 177, 299, 301–2,
  302
independence, 181–82, 192, 198, 199,
  204, 212, 287
interviewees, 23
interviews, 22–23, 24, 25

Jaime (interviewee)
  on divorce, 89, 207–8, 237
  on education, 102
  on faculty, 308
  on fathers, 59

Jaime (interviewee) *(continued)*
  on gender norms, 50, 67–68
  on her aunts, 89
  on her father, 125–26, 236–37, 315
  on her mother, 54–55, 176, 317
  on independence, 186
  on parental involvement in education, 236–37, 237, 244
  on peers, 303
  on pushing herself, 296
  on racism, 174
  on religion, 146
  on speaking Vietnamese, 167
Jasmine (interviewee)
  on divorce, 73, 267
  on family gatherings, 130
  on family support, 310–11
  on her aunt, 225
  on her brother, 74
  on her father, 73, 267
  on her mother, 178
  on her uncles, 74
  on independence, 188
Jenna (interviewee)
  on community, 290–91
  on faculty adviser, 306
  on financial issues, 204
  on gender norms, 49–50, 271
  on giving back to immigrant communities, 164
  on her father, 70–71, 166, 247, 269–72
  on her grandparents, 72
  on her mother, 177
  on her parents, 78
  on honoring her parents' sacrifices, 164
  on independence, 50
  on parental involvement in education, 203, 230–31
  on parental support, 274
  on peers, 301
  on racial climate, 291
  on racism, 175–76
  on religion, 141–42
Jeremy (interviewee)
  on applying to college, 239
  on fathers, 45
  on Field Day, 227
  on friends and colleagues, 301
  on gender norms, 41
  on his brother, 120–21
  on his father, 259–60
  on his mother, 43, 124
  on his parents, 125, 249–50
  on independence, 183
  on motivation, 298
  on parental involvement in education, 102–3, 227–29
  on parental support, 275
  on sports, 259–60
Jessica (interviewee)
  on applying to college, 235–36
  on applying to graduate school, 282
  on burnout, 295
  on divorce, 74, 208
  on faculty advisers, 304–5
  on fathers, 45
  on gender norms, 65, 74
  and her fiancé, 266
  on her fiancé and his family, 74, 89–90, 242
  on her stepfather, 265–66
  on independence, 183
  on peers, 299
  on physical therapy, 137
  on pushing herself, 295
  on religion, 148
Josefina (interviewee)
  on applying to college, 199
  on discrimination, 198
  on education, 103–4
  on family gatherings, 130
  on family unity, 129

on gender norms, 41–42, 45–46,
  60–61, 66–67
on her brother, 118
on her father, 41, 51, 90, 124–25,
  158, 250, 315
on her mother, 84, 137–38, 138–39,
  317–18
on her parents, 77–78, 103–4
on language issues, 193, 220
on parental involvement in
  education, 221
on religion, 145–46
on schedule issues, 90, 197
Juan (interviewee)
  on gender norms, 64
  on his brother, 117
  on his father, 89, 127, 246, 265
  on his parents, 56
  on independence, 188–89
  on motivation, 297
  on religion, 151
  on sports, 117

Kaitlyn (interviewee)
  on community, 139
  on education, 156–57
  on family gatherings, 141
  on fathers, 45
  on gender norms, 40, 68
  on her brother, 188
  on her father, 125, 246, 265
  on her parents, 274
  on her sister, 273–74
  on independence, 188
  on language issues, 193–94
  on not fitting in, 291–92
  on physical therapy, 274
  on preparing for graduate school,
    291
  on proximity to home, 273
  on religion, 141
  on her siblings, 117

Karina (interviewee)
  on applying to college, 117–18
  on education, 112–13
  on faculty, 304
  on family support, 132–33
  on gender norms, 46–47, 59–60, 68
  on giving back to the community,
    298
  on her brother, 117–18
  on her father, 88, 114, 124, 177–78,
    262
  on imposter syndrome, 301–2
  on independence, 190, 191
  on machismo, 60, 88
  on making her parents proud, 165
  on motivation, 297–98
  on parental involvement in
    education, 113–14, 222
  on peers, 302
  on politics, 262
  on religion, 46–47, 140–41
Katonah Pizza & Pasta, 9
Kayla (interviewee)
  on applying to college, 200
  on care, 133–34
  on education, 99–100, 101, 106
  on family gatherings, 131, 134–35
  on her cousins, 44, 134
  on her family, 276–77
  on her father, 47, 81, 99–100, 125,
    243
  on her mother, 59, 61–62, 66, 86,
    177, 219–20
  on her parents, 248
  on her sisters, 117
  on independence, 66, 200
  on parental involvement in
    education, 227
  on racism, 168–70
  on religion, 145
  on sports, 82
  on working, 106

Kramer, Sarah Kate
  "When your dad owns a pizzeria, the pandemic means learning to make the perfect pie," 9

Leonardo (interviewee)
  on car accident, 249
  on care, 133
  on education, 104–5
  on family support, 135
  on family unity, 131
  on gender norms, 48–49, 93–94
  on his father, 104–5, 110, 122–23, 164, 171
  on his mother, 44
  on his parents, 225, 249, 278–79
  on his siblings, 120, 204
  on immigration, 105
  on machismo, 47
  on religion, 142
  on schedule issues, 197
  on sports, 94
  visits Guadalajara, 159
Liza (interviewee)
  on family gatherings, 130–31
  on gender norms, 43, 57
  on her definition of parents, 35–36
  on her father, 312–13
  on her grandmother, 86
  on her mother, 175
  on her parents, 138
  on living in a white neighborhood, 174–75
  on parental involvement in education, 218
  on religion, 151

machismo, 47, 60, 88
manual labor, 126
Maria (interviewee)
  on applying to college, 199
  on coming out, 92
  on education, 156, 195–96
  on faculty, 306–7
  on family unity, 129
  on fathers, 58
  on gender norms, 38
  on her father, 94, 125
  on her parents, 91–92, 190–91, 260–61, 275
  and parental involvement in education, 38
  on peers, 303
  on religion, 141
Means, Russell
  Where White Men Fear to Tread, 251
microaggressions, 3, 70, 172, 191, 290
Montanaro, Francesca, 9
Montanaro, Paul, 9

Natasha (interviewee)
  on applying to graduate school, 282
  and college, 238
  on community, 303–4
  on COVID-19, 189
  on divorce, 208
  on faculty, 306
  on her father, 247, 266–67
  on high school, 237–38
  on independence, 189, 296
networks, 279
NPR
  "Dad arranges for special graduation ceremony for his daughter," 9
  "Ohio dad figures out socially distant trick or treating," 9
nurturant fathering, 78

"Ohio dad figures out socially distant trick or treating" (NPR), 9

parental involvement in education, 12–13, 18–19

Pierce, Gabrielle, 9
Ping (interviewee)
   on education, 107
   on faculty advisers, 306
   on gender norms, 40
   on high school, 230
   on his father, 41, 90, 107, 123
   on his mother, 64
   on his parents, 158–59, 248–49
   on his sisters, 118, 119
   on his students, 163
   on independence, 206
   on peers, 301
   on suicidal ideation, 40–41

questions, 24, 25

racial battle fatigue, 3

Sasha (interviewee)
   and COVID-19, 296, 300
   on education, 107–8
   on family unity, 129
   on gender norms, 268–69
   on her father, 49, 87, 107–8, 216, 263, 312
   on her parents, 279
   on her sister, 300
   on manual labor, 126
   on parental involvement in education, 216, 254
   on peers, 300
schedule issues, 19, 182, 199, 211, 287
Sharon (interviewee)
   on care, 140
   on faculty, 306
   on firearms, 56
   on gender norms, 111–12
   on her father, 47, 56, 87–88, 110–11, 123
   on her mother, 43–44, 84–85, 319
   on her parents, 57–58, 203
   on high school, 111, 112, 203
   on independence, 185, 296
   on parental involvement in education, 217, 234–35
   on religion, 148–49
   on working, 249, 253–54
social justice, 136–37, 139
socialization, 5, 165–66, 286
Stella (interviewee)
   on code-switching, 167–68
   on colleague/supervisor, 240
   on education, 110
   on fictive family members, 239
   on gap years, 280–81
   on gender norms, 42, 53, 64–65
   on her family, 119–20, 278
   on her father, 72, 86–87, 258–59
   on her mother, 66, 123–24, 161, 163
   on her parents, 44, 202, 314–15
   on immigration, 192
   on independence, 66, 196, 296
   on mentors, 209
   on networks, 279–80
   on parental involvement in education, 110, 224
   on racism, 168
   on religion, 144, 147–48
   on substance abuse, 209
   on working, 204
stepfamilies, 71
stereotype threat, 3
substance abuse, 207, 209
suicidal ideation, 40–41
Susan (interviewee)
   on being a good person, 139
   on career planning, 235
   on education, 160
   on family gatherings, 128–29
   on fathers, 58
   on gender norms, 40
   on her father, 115, 178–79, 179

Susan (interviewee) *(continued)*
  on her siblings, 235
  on immigration, 128
  on independence, 185–86, 187
  on love of learning, 298
  on parental involvement in education, 82–83
  on religion, 149

Tanya (interviewee)
  on applying to college, 229–30
  on community, 299
  and COVID-19, 257
  on education, 100–1
  on faculty, 306
  on family gatherings, 130, 145
  on fathers, 45
  on gap years, 257–58
  on gender norms, 269
  on her family, 277–78
  on her father, 56, 67, 81–82, 248, 259
  on her grandfather, 81–82
  on her grandparents, 174
  on independence, 182
  on racism, 174
  on religion, 145, 147
trailblazers, 115, 199
two spaces, 165–66

"When your dad owns a pizzeria, the pandemic means learning to make the perfect pie" (Kramer), 9
Where White Men Fear to Tread (Means), 251
Winona (interviewee)
  on applying to college, 233
  on applying to graduate school, 281
  on family orientation, 133, 135
  on fathers, 45
  on gender norms, 73
  on her elders, 135
  on her father, 73, 93, 262–63, 314
  on her parents, 92, 244
  on her uncles, 73, 92, 232
  on independence, 194
  on language issues, 194
  on parental involvement in education, 233
  on racism, 293–94
  on religion, 149–50

Zeke (interviewee)
  and career counselor, 238–39
  on coming out, 207
  on his family, 71, 207
  and parental involvement in education, 110
  on religion, 150–51
  on substance abuse, 207
Zelma (interviewee)
  on applying to college, 200
  on fear of family separation, 192
  on gender norms, 51–53, 154, 269
  on her father, 80, 93, 110, 123, 166, 257
  on her mother, 59, 83
  on her parents, 90–91
  on immigrant child guilt, 154
  on independence, 107, 184
  on parental involvement in education, 106–7, 216–17, 221–22
  on religion, 53, 141, 148
  on two spaces, 165–66
  on working, 230
Zoom, 24, 25

www.ingramcontent.com/pod-product-compliance
Ingram Content Group UK Ltd.
Pitfield, Milton Keynes, MK11 3LW, UK
UKHW041937210426
5322IPUK00016B/227